D0497648

Twentieth Century Voices
Selected Readings in World History

Revised Edition

Edited by Michael G. Vann

California State University, Sacramento

Bassim Hamadeh, CEO and Publisher
Kristina Stolte, Senior Field Acquisitions Editor
Kaela Martin, Project Editor
Abbey Hastings, Associate Production Editor
Jess Estrella, Senior Graphic Designer
Michael Skinner, Senior Licensing Specialist
Natalie Piccotti, Director of Marketing
Kassie Graves, Vice President of Editorial
Jamie Giganti, Director of Academic Publishing

ISBN: 978-1-5165-4033-4 (pbk) / 978-1-5165-4034-1 (br)

Contents

CHAPTER 3: THE FIRST WORLD WAR   81

CHAPTER 5: ANTI-COLONIALISM AND NATIONALISM   205

CHAPTER 6: WORLD WAR II   271

CHAPTER 7: HOT RHETORIC OF THE COLD WAR   331

Dedication

This study of the twentieth century is dedicated to Maa Ngala, even though she will only ever know the twenty-first century.

Acknowledgments

In a very practical sense, this book would not be possible without the support of the Department of History at Sacramento State University. In particular, my Chair, Aaron Cohen, provided monetary assistance during a "photocopying emergency." My colleagues Jeff Dym, Katerina Lagos, and Jeffery Wilson suggested a number of sources. Kevin Hoffman and Briana Ely provided much needed editing help with my ongoing struggle with the English language. In a larger sense, this book would be impossible without what Tyler Stovall and Edmund "Terry" Burke, III, taught me about the Twentieth Century, the field of World History, and the art of making history all those years ago at the University of California, Santa Cruz. Speaking of all those years ago, I owe a great moral debt to Carl Ackerman and Peter Armstrong, two of Iolani's finest teachers when I was a rather lost high school student in their history classes. They never gave up on me and I will never forget the enthusiasm they showed for the study of the recent past.

Michael G. Vann
Santa Cruz, June 2011

Introduction

To be perfectly frank, this collection of readings is gloomy and perhaps even depressing. However, these selections serve as a fair representation of the twentieth century, arguably the worst century in human history, one which the historian Eric Weitz dubbed a "century of genocide." We could also make the argument for the twentieth century as one of war, revolution, and dictatorship, or even a century of over-population, environmental degradation, and species extinction. This is a century that saw the introduction of machine guns, poison gas, and atomic weapons to the battlefield and in civilian centers. Humans wreaked massive destruction throughout the world, from the capital cities of Asia and Europe to the villages of Southeast Asia and Central America. Considering that this century's cast of characters includes Hitler, Stalin, and Pol Pot, this fact should not be surprising. Indeed, historical events in this one-hundred year span were so horrifying that humanity had to coin new terms such as "world war," "genocide," "ethnic cleansing," and "crimes against humanity" to describe the indescribable. These horrific events even compelled the global community to establish an international court to try those who acted beyond what was deemed acceptable behavior in this violent setting. Yet in many ways this was also a century of hope and optimism. Gandhi, Dr. Martin Luther King, and the 14th Dalai Lama stand as examples of those who rejected hatred, anger, and vengeance, and who instead embraced *ahimsā*, the principle of non-violent action, in their struggles for national liberation and social justice. Dozens of nations in Africa and Asia won their independence from repressive colonial regimes. From North America to South Africa, activists worked tirelessly to topple regimes of white supremacy, such as Jim Crow and Apartheid. In the final decades of the twentieth century, popular revolutions, called "people power," overthrew dictators such as Marcos in the Philippines and Suharto in Indonesia, and toppled the repressive Communist regime of the Soviet Bloc. The century saw the sustained effort, first with the League of Nations and then with the United Nations, to establish a means other than warfare to settle international disputes. Science, technology, and medicine conquered diseases and reduced infant mortality rates. The century ended with what might seem to be a rejection of repressive political systems and the spread of democratic values and respect for the individual.

If the final verdict on these one hundred years remains open to debate, no one can deny their global historical significance. Politically, the planet went from an age of empires to the triumph of the nation-state. A plethora of ideologies produced revolutions from extreme left to extreme right, each seeking to create their own utopia. Various economic experiments, new forms of mass production, and expanding markets created a standard of living for many that was simply unimaginable in previous generations. First imperialism, and then decolonization, created much of the world's current political map and far too many of the world's current crises. Post-colonial immigrations saw huge shifts in populations and the formation of new multi-cultural societies. Today, cultural diversity is a central characteristic of cities from London to Rio de Janeiro, Singapore to Toronto, and Sacramento to Jakarta. Technological advances, from steam ships and trans-oceanic cables to jetliners and the Internet, linked humanity in an increasingly tight web of communication, exchange, and interdependence. Humans even managed to break free of Earth's gravity for brief visits to the moon, and set satellites into the stratosphere to map and photograph every inch of our planet. Of course, countering this progress, the century also witnessed wars, revolutions, and famines whose death toll can be measured in the millions. Humans began to speak of "world wars" and "world revolutions," conflagrations that impacted not just Tokyo, Paris, and Moscow but Guadalcanal, the Aleutian Islands, and outposts in the vast Sahara Desert. For good or bad, for better or worse, the twentieth century made the world one community.

This reader offers a selection of primary source readings from key historical phases in this century. While no single volume could claim to offer a complete collection, here we find most of the key moments represented. This collection is specifically designed for students who will be teaching courses guided by the *History–Social Science Content Standards for California Public Schools* as adopted by the California State Board of Education. As the tenth-grade history curriculum explores the history, culture, and geography of the modern world, these readings fit with standards 10.3 through 10.11. That said, all students of the twentieth-century world will find this book to be a valuable resource. While keeping the primary goals of the standards in mind, this collection was also designed along the lines of recent developments in the historiography of World History. In particular, the readings de-center Europe. Rejecting the Eurocentrism once dominant in the Western Civilization curriculum, various selections give voice to traditionally under-represented or marginalized groups and historical figures. Rejecting the "Great Man in History" approach, attention is paid to relatively unknown individuals caught up in the larger forces of history. The selections also take oppositional forces, even those who may have failed, seriously. Thus, prominent revolutionaries killed by their enemies such as Rosa Luxembourg and Che Guevara have a place here. So do figures seemingly at odds with each other such as Churchill and Gandhi, Dr. Martin Luther King and Enoch Powell, and Hitler and the 14th Dalai Lama. To make sense of the immense diversity of the human experience, we, as historians, must listen to all sides in any given historical moment.

Students should think of this book as an archive. It is their own personal archive that will allow them to do the work of historians: reading primary sources, evaluating them for relevance and credibility, and constructing a persuasive historical argument with the sources as evidence. This is what professional historians do in archives, libraries, and ivory towers (or dilapidated public university campuses with asbestos issues, as the case may be) around the world. Historians are not merely bards or chroniclers who recount what happened, despite what Rush Limbaugh has said about our discipline. We analyze evidence and give meaning to past events. This is also the task of students in a university classroom. This book, this archive, will allow students to conduct historical research, come to their own conclusions, and then present their history in term papers or on exams.

Chapter 1

The World in 1900

Introduction

The dawn of the twentieth century marked the zenith of European power. For much of human history, Europe had been a provincial and war-torn backwater. After the collapse of the Roman Empire, political disunity, intellectual stagnation, and economic isolation characterized the region. Compared with the glories of the Islamic world at its height, India's cultural dynamism, and China's economic might and longevity, Europe had little to offer. When the continent did overcome its isolation with the Iberian voyages of the 1490s, it did so from a position of relative weakness and desperation. With little to offer the outside world, Europeans used violence to force their way into the global economic order, be it in the slave trade and plantation systems of the Atlantic world or the seizure of trade routes and ports in the Indian Ocean Basin. Yet over the course of the one hundred and fifty years from 1750 to 1900 a remarkable change occurred. Thanks to the convergence of surplus capital from the spice, sugar, and slave trades, the technological innovations of the industrial revolution, and the increased efficiency of modern states' fiscal and military systems, Europeans were able to establish hegemony around the globe. Perhaps the most dramatic demonstration of this was the British Empire's ability to send the coal- and steam-powered battleship the *Nemesis* (named for the Greek goddess of retribution and vengeance) into the interior of China during the first Opium War (1839–1842). British industrial might was also displayed in its ability to destroy India's millennia-old cotton manufacturing sector by flooding the market with cheap mass-produced imports from factories in cities such as Manchester. Europe's rapid economic rise meant the collapse of India and China's economies. Material power coincided with the rise of Social Darwinism (a "scientific" racism) as an ideology used to justify the spread of European imperialism. At the dawn of the century, Europeans controlled most of Africa and Asia, as well as the world's new transportation, communications, and commercial infrastructure. The documents in this section highlight Europe's power and self-confidence, yet they also reveal the frustrations felt by some toward European dominance.

This chapter relates to section 10.3 of the History-Social Science Content Standards for California Public Schools.

The World of Security

By Stefan Zweig

Stefan Zweig (1881–1942) was an Austrian writer, considered by some to have been one of the most famous writers of the inter-war era. Of Austrian Jewish heritage, Zweig was a non-observant Jew who did not gravitate towards Zionism. He was also a pacifist who refused to fight in the First World War. After the rise of Hitler, Zweig fled Austria and eventually wound up in Brazil where he and his wife committed suicide out of despair for Europe's future. He mailed his posthumously published autobiography the day before his death. In this work he recalls the calm and confidence of Europe before World War One, a period known as la belle époque (the beautiful time).

When I attempt to find a simple formula for the period in which I grew up, prior to the First World War, I hope that I convey its fullness by calling it the Golden Age of Security. Everything in our almost thousand-year-old Austrian monarchy seemed based on permanency, and the State itself was the chief guarantor of this stability. The rights which it granted to its citizens were duly confirmed by parliament, the freely elected representative of the people, and every duty was exactly prescribed. Our currency, the Austrian crown, circulated in bright gold pieces, an assurance of its immutability. Everyone knew how much he possessed or what he was entitled to, what was permitted and what forbidden. Everything had its norm, its definite measure and weight. He who had a fortune could accurately compute his annual interest. An official or an officer, for example, could confidently look up in the calendar the year when he would be advanced in grade, or when he would be pensioned. Each family had its fixed budget, and knew how much could be spent for rent and food, for vacations and entertainment; and what is more, invariably a small sum was carefully laid aside for sickness and the doctor's bills, for the unexpected. Whoever owned a house looked upon it as a secure domicile for his children and grandchildren; estates and businesses were handed down from generation to generation. When the babe was still in its cradle, its first mite was put in its little bank,

Stefan Zweig, "World of Security" *The World of Yesterday: An Autobiography*, translated by Helmut Ripperger pp. 1-5. Copyright © 1943 by Viking Press. Reprinted with permission.

or deposited in the savings bank, as a "reserve" for the future. In this vast empire everything stood firmly and immovably in its appointed place, and at its head was the aged emperor; and were he to die, one knew (or believed) another would come to take his place, and nothing would change in the well-regulated order. No one thought of wars, of revolutions, or revolts. All that was radical, all violence, seemed impossible in an age of reason.

This feeling of security was the most eagerly sought-after possession of millions, the common ideal of life. Only the possession of this security made life seem worthwhile, and constantly widening circles desired their share of this costly treasure. At first it was only the prosperous who enjoyed this advantage, but gradually the great masses forced their way toward it. The century of security became the golden age of insurance. One's house was insured against fire and theft, one's field against hail and storm, one's person against accident and sickness. Annuities were purchased for one's old age, and a policy was laid in a girl's cradle for her future dowry. Finally even the workers organized, and won standard wages and workmen's compensation. Servants saved up for old-age insurance and paid in advance into a burial fund for their own interment. Only the man who could look into the future without worry could thoroughly enjoy the present.

Despite the propriety and the modesty of this view of life, there was a grave and dangerous arrogance in this touching confidence that we had barricaded ourselves to the last loophole against any possible invasion of fate. In its liberal idealism, the nineteenth century was honestly convinced that it was on the straight and unfailing path toward being the best of all worlds. Earlier eras, with their wars, famines, and revolts, were deprecated as times when mankind was still immature and unenlightened. But now it was merely a matter of decades until the last vestige of evil and violence would finally be conquered, and this faith in an uninterrupted and irresistible "progress" truly had the force of a religion for that generation. One began to believe more in this "progress" than in the Bible, and its gospel appeared ultimate because of the daily new wonders of science and technology. In fact, at the end of this peaceful century, a general advance became more marked, more rapid, more varied. At night the dim street lights of former times were replaced by electric lights, the shops spread their tempting glow from the main streets out to the city limits. Thanks to the telephone one could talk at a distance from person to person. People moved about in horseless carriages with a new rapidity; they soared aloft, and the dream of Icarus was fulfilled. Comfort made its way from the houses of the fashionable to those of the middle class. It was no longer necessary to fetch water from the pump or the hallway, or to take the trouble to build a fire in the fireplace. Hygiene spread and filth disappeared. People became handsomer, stronger, healthier, as sport steeled their bodies. Fewer cripples and maimed and persons with goiters were seen on the streets, and all of these miracles were accomplished by science, the archangel of progress. Progress was also made in social matters; year after year new rights were accorded to the individual, justice was administered more benignly and humanely, and even the problem of problems, the poverty of the great masses, no longer seemed insurmountable. The right to vote was being accorded to wider circles, and with it the possibility of legally protecting their interests. Sociologists and professors competed with one another to create healthier and happier living conditions for the proletariat. Small wonder then that this century sunned itself in its own accomplishments and looked upon each completed decade as the prelude to a better one. There was as little belief in the possibility of such barbaric declines as wars between the peoples of Europe as there was in witches and ghosts. Our fathers were comfortably saturated with confidence in the unfailing and binding power of tolerance and conciliation. They honestly believed that the divergencies and the boundaries between nations and sects would gradually melt away into a common humanity and that peace and security, the highest of treasures, would be shared by all mankind.

It is reasonable that we, who have long since struck the word "security" from our vocabulary as a myth, should smile at the optimistic delusion of that idealistically blinded generation, that the technical progress of mankind must connote an unquali-fied and equally rapid moral ascent. We of the new generation who have learned not to be surprised by any outbreak of bestiality, we who each new day expect things worse than the day before, are markedly more skeptical about a possible moral improvement of mankind. We must agree with Freud, to whom our culture and civilization were merely a thin layer liable at any moment to be pierced by the destructive forces of the "underworld." We have had to accustom ourselves gradually to living without the ground beneath our feet, without justice, without freedom, without security. Long since, as far as our existence is concerned, we have denied the religion of our fathers, their faith in a rapid and continuous rise of humanity. To us, gruesomely taught, wit-nesses of a catastrophe which, at a swoop, hurled us back a thousand years of humane endeavor, that rash optimism seems banal. But even though it was a delusion our fathers served, it was a wonderful and noble delusion, more humane and more fruitful than our watchwords of today; and in spite of my later knowledge and disillusionment, there is still something in me which inwardly prevents me from abandoning it entirely. That which, in his childhood, a man has drawn into his blood out of the air of time cannot be taken from him. And in spite of all that is daily blasted into my ears, and all that I myself and countless other sharers of my destiny have experienced in trials and tribulations, I cannot completely deny the faith of my youth, that some day things will rise again—in spite of all. Even in the abyss of despair in which today, half-blinded, we grope about with distorted and broken souls, I look up again and again to those old star-patterns that shone over my childhood, and comfort myself with the inherited confidence that this collapse will appear, in days to come, as a mere interval in the eternal rhythm of the onward and onward.

Today, now that the great storm has long since smashed it, we finally know that that world of security was naught but a castle of dreams; my parents lived in it as if it had been a house of stone. Not once did a storm, or even a sharp wind, break in upon their warm, comfortable existence. True, they had a special protection against the winds of time: they were wealthy people, who had become rich gradually, even very rich, and that filled the crevices of wall and window in those times. Their way of life seems to me to be so typical of the so-called "good Jewish bourgeoisie," which gave such marked value to Viennese culture, and which was requited by being completely uprooted.

The British Rule in India

By Karl Marx

Karl Marx (1818–1883) was many things; philosopher, journalist, economist, sociologist, historian, political theorist, and, of course, a revolutionary socialist who dreamed of the day when industrial capitalism would collapse in a revolution stemming from its internal contradictions. While Marxism became the dominant revolutionary theory of the twentieth century, he was surprisingly unknown in his lifetime. Also surprising are Marx's writings on imperialism. Despite Marxism's becoming central to many anti-colonial struggles from Vietnam to Angola, Marx himself saw imperialism as a progressive force in history, creating modernity in Asia. For example, while Marx saw British rule in India as obviously self-serving and hypocritical, he praised its assault on the power of tradition.

June 25, 1853

Hindostan is an Italy of Asiatic dimensions, the Himalayas for the Alps, the Plains of Bengal for the Plains of Lombardy, the Deccan for the Appenines, and the Isle of Ceylon for the Island of Sicily. The same rich variety in the products of the soil, and the same dismemberment in the political configuration. Just as Italy has, from time to time, been compressed by the conqueror's sword into different national masses, so do we find Hindostan, when not under the pressure of the Mohammedan, or the Mogul, or the Briton, dissolved into as many independent and conflicting States as it numbered towns, or even villages. Yet, in a social point of view, Hindostan is not the Italy, but the Ireland of the East. And this strange combination of Italy and of Ireland, of a world of voluptuousness and of a world of woes, is anticipated in the ancient traditions of the religion of Hindostan. That religion is at once a religion of sensualist exuberance, and a religion of self-torturing asceticism; a religion of the Lingam and of the Juggernaut; the religion of the Monk, and of the Bayadere.

I share not the opinion of those who believe in a golden age of Hindostan, without recurring, however, like Sir Charles Wood, for the confirmation of my view, to the

Karl Marx, Selections from *The Marx-Engels Reader*, pp. 653–664.

authority of Khuli-Khan. But take, for example, the times of Aurung-Zebe; or the epoch, when the Mogul appeared in the North, and the Portuguese in the South; or the age of Mohammedan invasion, and of the Heptarchy* in Southern India; or, if you will, go still more back to antiquity, take the mythological chronology of the Brahmin himself, who places the commencement of Indian misery in an epoch even more remote than the Christian creation of the world.

There cannot, however, remain any doubt but that the misery inflicted by the British on Hindostan is of an essential different and infinitely more intensive kind than all Hindostan had to suffer before. I do not allude to European despotism, planted upon Asiatic despotism, by the British East India Company,† forming a more monstrous combination than any of the divine monsters startling us in the temple of Salsette.‡ This is no distinctive feature of British colonial rule, but only an imitation of the Dutch, and so much so that in order to characterise the working of the British East India Company, it is sufficient to literally repeat what Sir Stamford Raffles, the *English* Governor of Java, said of the old Dutch East India Company:

> The Dutch Company, actuated solely by the spirit of gain, and viewing their subjects with less regard or consideration than a West India planter formerly viewed a gang upon his estate, because the latter had paid the purchase money of human property, which the other had not, employed all the existing machinery of despotism to squeeze from the people their utmost mite of contribution, the last dregs of their labour, and thus aggravated the evils of a capricious and semi-barbarous Government, by working it with all the practised ingenuity of politicians, and all the monopolising selfishness of traders.

All the civil wars, invasions, revolutions, conquests, famines, strangely complex, rapid and destructive as the successive action in Hindostan may appear, did not go deeper than its surface. England has broken-down the entire framework of Indian society, without any symptoms of reconstitution yet appearing. This loss of his old

---

* The conventional designation in English history of the seven Saxon Kingdoms (sixth to eighth century). Marx by analogy uses this term here to denote the feudal dismemberment of the Deccan before its conquest by the Moslems.

† The British East India Company was organised in 1600 for the purpose of carrying on a monopoly trade with India. Under cover of the Company's "trading" operations the English capitalists conquered the country and governed it for decades. During the Indian uprising of 1857–1859 the Company was dissolved and the British Government began to rule India directly.

‡ A cave temple situated on the island of that name near the city of Bombay. It contains a huge number of stone carvings.

world, with no gain of a new one, imparts a particular kind of melancholy to the present misery of the Hindoo, and separates Hindostan, ruled by Britain, from all its ancient traditions, and from the whole of its past history.

There have been in Asia, generally, from immemorial times, but three departments of Government: that of Finance, or the plunder of the interior; that of War, or the plunder of the exterior; and, finally, the department of Public Works. Climate and territorial conditions, especially the vast tracts of desert, extending from the Sahara, through Arabia, Persia, India and Tartary, to the most elevated Asiatic highlands, constituted artificial irrigation by canals and waterworks the basis of Oriental agriculture. As in Egypt and India, inundations are used for fertilising the soil of Mesopotamia, Persia, etc.; advantage is taken of a high level for feeding irrigative canals. This prime necessity of an economical and common use of water, which, in the Occident, drove private enterprise to voluntary association, as in Flanders and Italy, necessitated, in the Orient where civilisation was too low and the territorial extent too vast to call into life voluntary association, the interference of the centralising power of Government. Hence an economical function devolved upon all Asiatic Governments the function of providing public works. This artificial fertilisation of the soil, dependent on a Central Government, and immediately decaying with the neglect of irrigation and drainage, explains the otherwise strange fact that we now find whole territories barren and desert that were once brilliantly cultivated, as Palmyra, Petra, the ruins in Yemen, and large provinces of Egypt, Persia and Hindostan; it also explains how a single war of devastation has been able to depopulate a country for centuries, and to strip it of all its civilisation.

Now, the British in East India accepted from their predecessors the department of finance and of war, but they have neglected entirely that of public works. Hence the deterioration of an agriculture which is not capable of being conducted on the British principle of free competition, of *laissez-faire* and *laissez-aller*. But in Asiatic empires we are quite accustomed to see agriculture deteriorating under one government and reviving again under some other government. There the harvests correspond to good or bad government, as they change in Europe with good or bad seasons. Thus the oppression and neglect of agriculture, bad as it is, could not be looked upon as the final blow dealt to Indian society by the British intruder, had it not been attended by a circumstance of quite different importance, a novelty in the annals of the whole Asiatic world. However changing the political aspect of India's past must appear, its social condition has remained unaltered since its remotest antiquity, until the first decennium of the 19th century. The hand-loom and the spinning-wheel, producing their regular myriads of spinners and weavers, were the pivots of the structure of that society. From immemorial times, Europe received the admirable textures of Indian labour, sending in return for them her precious metals, and furnishing thereby his material to the gold-smith, that indispensable member of Indian society, whose love of finery is so great that even the lowest class, those who go about nearly naked, have commonly a pair of golden ear-rings and a gold ornament of some kind hung round their necks. Rings on the fingers and toes have also been common. Women as well as children frequently wore massive bracelets and anklets of gold or silver, and statuettes of divinities in gold and silver were met with in the households. It was the British intruder who broke up the Indian hand-loom and destroyed the spinning wheel. England began with driving the Indian cottons from the European market; it then introduced twist into Hindostan and in the end inundated the very mother country of cotton with cottons. From 1818 to 1836 the export of twist from Great Britain to India rose in the proportion of 1 to 5,200. In 1824 the export of British muslins to India hardly amounted to 1,000,000 yards while in 1837 it surpassed 64,000,000 yards. But at the same time the population of Dacca decreased from 150,000 inhabitants to 20,000. This decline of Indian towns celebrated for their fabrics was by no means the worst consequence. British steam and science uprooted, over the whole surface of Hindostan, the union between agricultural and manufacturing industry.

These two circumstances—the Hindoo, on the one hand, leaving, like all Oriental peoples, to the central government the care of the great public works, the prime condition of his agriculture and commerce, dispersed, on the other hand over the surface of the country, and agglomerated in small centres by the domestic union of agricultural and manufacturing pursuits—these two circumstances had brought about, since the remotest times, a social system of particular features—the so-called *village system*, which gave to each of these small unions their independent organisation and distinct life. The peculiar character of this system may be judged from the following description, contained in an old official report of the British House of Commons on Indian affairs:

> A village, geographically considered, is a tract of country comprising some hundred or thousand acres of arable and waste lands; politically viewed it resembles a corporation or township. Its proper establishment of officers and servants consists of the following descriptions: the *potail*, or head inhabitant, who has generally the superintendence of the affairs of the village, settles the disputes of the inhabitants, attends to the police, and performs the duty of collecting the revenue within his village, a duty which his personal influence and minute acquaintance with the situation and concerns of the people render him the best qualified for this charge. The *kurnum* keeps the accounts of cultivation, and registers everything connected with it. The *Tallier* and the *totie*, the duty of the former of which consists in gaining information of crimes and offences, and in escorting and protecting persons travelling from one village to another; the province of the latter appearing to be more immediately confined to the village, consisting, among other duties, in guarding the crops and assisting in measuring them. The *boundary man*,

who preserves the limits of the village, or gives evidence respecting them in cases of dispute. The Superintendent of Tanks and Watercourses distributes the water for the purposes of agriculture. The Brahmin, who performs the village worship. The schoolmaster, who is seen teaching the children in a village to read and write in the sand. The calendar-Brahmin, or astrologer, etc. These officers and servants generally constitute the establishment of a village; but in some parts of the country it is of less extent; some of the duties and functions above described being united in the same person; in others it exceeds the above-named number of individuals. Under this simple form of municipal government, the inhabitants of the country have lived from time immemorial. The boundaries of the villages have been but seldom altered; and though the villages themselves have been sometimes injured, and even desolated by war, famine or disease, the same name, the same limits, the same interests, and even the same families, have continued for ages. The inhabitants gave themselves no trouble about the breaking up and divisions of kingdoms; while the village remains entire, they care not to what power it is transferred, or to what sovereign it devolves; its internal economy remains unchanged. The *potail* is still the head inhabitant, and still acts as the petty judge or magistrate, and collector or rentor of the village.

These small stereotype forms of social organism have been to the greater part dissolved, and are disappearing, not so much through the brutal interference of the British tax-gatherer and the British soldier, as to the working of English steam and English free trade. Those family-communities were based on domestic industry, in that peculiar combination of hand-weaving, hand-spinning and hand-tilling agriculture which gave them self-supporting power. English interference having placed the spinner in Lancashire and the weaver in Bengal, or sweeping away both Hindoo spinner and weaver, dissolved these small semi-barbarian, semi-civilised communities, by blowing up their economical basis, and thus produced the greatest, and, to speak the truth, the only *social* revolution ever heard of in Asia.

Now, sickening as it must be to human feeling to witness those myriads of industrious patriarchal and inoffensive social organisations disorganised and dissolved into their units, thrown into a sea of woes, and their individual members losing at the same time their ancient form of civilisation, and their hereditary means of subsistence, we must not forget that these idyllic village communities, inoffensive though they may appear, had always been the solid foundation of Oriental despotism, that they restrained the human mind within the smallest possible compass, making it the unresisting tool of superstition, enslaving it beneath traditional rules, depriving it of all grandeur and historical energies. We must not forget the barbarian egotism which, concentrating on some miserable patch of land, had quietly witnessed the ruin of empires, the perpetration of unspeakable cruelties, the massacre of the population of large towns, with no other consideration bestowed upon them than on natural events, itself the helpless prey of any aggressor who deigned to notice it at all. We must not forget that this undignifed, stagnatory, and vegetative life, that this passive sort of existence evoked on the other part, in contradistinction, wild, aimless, unbounded forces of destruction and rendered murder itself a religious rite in Hindostan. We must not forget that these little communities were contaminated by distinctions of caste and by slavery, that they subjugated man to external circumstances instead of elevating man to be the sovereign of circumstances, that they transformed a self-developing social state into never changing natural destiny, and thus brought about a brutalising worship of nature, exhibiting its degradation in the fact that man, the sovereign of nature, fell down on his knees in adoration of *Hanuman*, the monkey, and *Sabbala*, the cow.

England, it is true, in causing a social revolution in Hindostan, was actuated only by the vilest interests, and was stupid in her manner of enforcing them. But that is not the question. The question is, can mankind fulfill its destiny without a fundamental revolution in the social state of Asia? If not, whatever may have been[§] the crimes of England she was the unconscious tool of history in bringing about that revolution.

Then, whatever bitterness the spectacle of the crumbling of an ancient world may have for our personal feelings, we have the right, in point of history, to exclaim with Goethe:

> Sollte diese Qual uns quälen,
> Da sie unsre Lust vermehrt,
> Hat nicht Myriaden Seelen
> Timur's Heerschaft aufgezehrt?[§]

The future Results of British Rule in India

London, Friday, July 22, 1853

How came it that English supremacy was established in India? The paramount power of the Great Mogul was broken by the Mogul Viceroys. The power of the Viceroys was broken by the Mahrattas.[¶] The power of the Mahrattas was broken by the Afghans, and while all were struggling against all, the Briton rushed in and was enabled to

---

§   Should this torture then torment us since it brings us greater pleasure? Were not through the rule of Timur Souls devoured without measure? (Goethe, *Westöstitcher Diwan.An Suleika*)

¶   A group of people in Central India who rose against the Mohammedans and, in the beginning of the eighteenth century, formed a confederation of feudal princedoms.

subdue them all. A country not only divided between Mohammedan and Hindoo, but between tribe and tribe, between caste and caste; a society whose framework was based on a sort of equilibrium, resulting from a general repulsion and constitutional exclusiveness between all its members. Such a country and such a society, where they not the predestined prey of conquest? If we knew nothing of the past history of Hindostan, would there not be the one great and incontestable fact, that even at this moment India is held in English thraldom by an Indian army maintained at the cost of India? India, then, could not escape the fate of being conquered, and the whole of her past history, if it be anything, is the history of the successive conquests she has undergone. Indian society has no history at all, at least no known history. What we call its history, is but the history of the successive intruders who founded their empires on the passive basis of that unresisting and unchanging society. The question, therefore, is not whether the English had a right to conquer India, but whether we are to prefer India conquered by the Turk, by the Persian, by the Russian, to India conquered by the Briton.

England has to fulfil a double mission in India: one destructive, the other regenerating—the annihilation of old Asiatic society, and the laying of the material foundations of Western society in Asia.

Arabs, Turks, Tartars, Moguls, who had successively overrun India, soon became *Hindooised*, the barbarian conquerors being, by, an eternal law of history, conquered themselves by the superior civilisation of their subjects. The British were the first conquerors superior, and therefore, inaccessible to Hindoo civilisation. They destroyed it by breaking up the native communities, by uprooting the native industry, and by levelling all that was great and elevated in the native society. The historic pages of their rule in India report hardly anything beyond that destruction. The work of regeneration hardly transpires through a heap of ruins. Nevertheless it has begun.

The political unity of India, more consolidated, and extending farther than it ever did under the Great Moguls, was the first condition of its regeneration. That unity, imposed by the British sword, will now be strengthened and perpetuated by the electric telegraph. The native army, organised and trained by the British drill-sergeant, was the *sine qua non* of Indian self-emancipation, and of India ceasing to be the prey of the first foreign intruder. The free press, introduced for the first time into Asiatic society, and managed principally by the common offspring of Hindoo and Europeans, is a new and powerful agent of reconstruction. The *Zemindars* and *Ryotwar*** themselves, abominable as they are, involve two distinct forms of private property in land—the

---

**Zemindars*: New big landowners who were established by the British from among former tax collectors and merchant-usurers through the expropriation of the Indian peasantry. The zemindar system was widespread in Northeast India. *Ryotwar*: A system of renting land to peasants for an unlimited period of time. Introduced by the British in the South of India, it permitted them to let land to peasants on extremely onerous terms.

great *desideratum* of Asiatic society. From the Indian natives, reluctantly and sparingly educated at Calcutta, under English superintendence, a fresh class is springing up, endowed with the requirements for government and imbued with European science. Steam has brought India into regular and rapid communication with Europe, has connected its chief ports with those of the whole south-eastern ocean, and has revindicated it from the isolated position which was the prime law of its stagnation. The day is not far distant when, by a combination of railways and steam vessels, the distance between England and India, measured by time, will be shortened to eight days, and when that once fabulous country will thus be actually annexed to the Western world.

The ruling classes of Great Britain have had, till now, but an accidental, transitory and exceptional interest in the progress of India. The aristocracy wanted to conquer it, the moneyocracy to plunder it, and the millocracy to undersell it. But now the tables are turned. The millocracy have discovered that the transformation of India into a reproductive country has become of vital importance to them, and that, to that end, it is necessary, above all, to gift her with means of irrigation and of internal communication. They intend now drawing a net of railways over India. And they will do it. The results must be inappreciable.

It is notorious that the productive powers of India are paralysed by the utter want of means for conveying and exchanging its various produce. Nowhere, more than in India, do we meet with social destitution in the midst of natural plenty, for want of the means of exchange. It was proved before a Committee of the British House of Commons, which sat in 1848, that "when grain was selling from 6s. to 8s. a quarter at Kandeish, it was sold at 64s. to 70s. at Poonah, where the people were dying in the streets of famine, without the possibility of gaining supplies from Kandeish, because the clay-roads were impracticable."

The introduction of railways may be easily made to subserve agricultural purposes by the formation of tanks, where ground is required for embankment, and by the conveyance of water along the different lines. Thus irrigation, the *sine qua non* of farming in the East, might be greatly extended, and the frequently recurring local famines, arising from the want of water, would be averted. The general importance of railways, viewed under this head, must become evident, when we remember that irrigated lands, even in the district near Ghauts, pay three times as much in taxes, afford ten or twelve times as much employment, and yield twelve or fifteen times as much profit, as the same area without irrigation.

Railways will afford the means of diminishing the amount and the cost of the military establishments. Col. Warren, Town Major of the Fort St. William, stated before a Select Committee of the House of Commons:

The practicability of receiving intelligence from distant parts of the country in as many hours as at present it requires days and even weeks, and of sending instructions with troops and stores, in the more brief period, are considerations which cannot be too highly estimated. Troops could be kept at more distant and healthier stations than at present, and much loss of life from sickness would by this means be spared. Stores could not to the same extent be required at the various dépôts, and the loss by decay, and the destruction incidental to the climate, would also be avoided. The number of troops might be diminished in direct proportion to their effectiveness.

We know that the municipal organisation and the economical basis of the village communities has been broken up, but their worst feature, the dissolution of society into stereotyped and disconnected atoms, has survived their vitality. The village isolation produced the absence of roads in India, and the absence of roads perpetuated the village isolation. On this plan a community existed with a given scale of low conveniences, almost without intercourse with other villages, without the desires and efforts indispensable to social advance. The British having broken up this self-sufficient *inertia* of the villages, railways will provide the new want of communication and intercourse. Besides, "one of the effects of the railway system will be to bring into every village affected by it such knowledge of the contrivances and appliances of other countries, and such means of obtaining them, as will first put the hereditary and stipendiary village artisanship of India to full proof of its capabilities, and then supply its defects." (Chapman, *The Cotton and Commerce of India.*)

I know that the English millocracy intend to endow India with railways with the exclusive view of extracting at diminished expenses the cotton and other raw materials for their manufactures. But when you have once introduced machinery into the locomotion of a country, which possesses iron and coals, you are unable to withhold it from its fabrication. You cannot maintain a net of railways over an immense country without introducing all those industrial processes necessary to meet the immediate and current wants of railway locomotion, and out of which there must grow the application of machinery to those branches of industry not immediately connected with railways. The railway-system will therefore become, in India, truly the forerunner of modern Industry. This is the more certain as the Hindoos are allowed by British authorities themselves to possess particular aptitude for accommodating themselves to entirely new labour, and acquiring the requisite knowledge of machinery. Ample proof of this fact is afforded by the capacities and expertness of the native engineers in the Calcutta mint, where they have been for years employed in working the steam machinery, by the natives attached to the several steam engines in the Hurdwar coal districts and by other instances. Mr. Campbell himself, greatly influenced as he is by the prejudices of the East India Company, is obliged to avow "that the great mass of the Indian people possesses a great *industrial energy*, is well fitted to accumulate capital, and remarkable for a mathematical clearness of head, and talent for figures and exact sciences." "Their intellects," he says, "are excellent." Modern industry, resulting from the railway-system, will dissolve the hereditary divisions of labour, upon which rest the Indian castes, those decisive impediments to Indian progress and Indian power.

All the English bourgeoisie may be forced to do will neither emancipate nor materially mend the social condition of the mass of the people, depending not only on the development of the productive powers, but on their appropriation by the people. But what they will not fail to do is to lay down the material premises for both. Has the bourgeoisie ever done more? Has it ever affected a progress without dragging individuals and peoples through blood and dirt, through misery and degradation?

The Indians will not reap the fruits of the new elements of society scattered among them by the British bourgeoisie, till in Great Britain itself the now ruling classes shall have been supplanted by the industrial proletariat, or till the Hindoos themselves shall have grown strong enough to throw off the English yoke altogether. At all events, we may safely expect to see, at a more or less remote period, the regeneration of that great and interesting country, whose gentle natives are, to use the expression of Prince Soltykov, even in the most inferior classes, "*plus fins et plus adroits que les Italiens*,"[††] whose submission even is counterbalanced by a certain calm nobility, who, notwithstanding their natural languor, have astonished the British officers by their bravery, whose country has been the source of our languages, our religions, and who represent the type of the ancient German in the *Jat* and the type of the ancient Greek in the Brahmin.[‡‡]

I cannot part with the subject of India without some concluding remarks.

The profound hypocrisy and inherent barbarism of bourgeois civilisation lies unveiled before our eyes, turning from its home, where it assumes respectable forms, to the colonies, where it goes naked. They are the defenders of property, but did any revolutionary party ever originate agrarian revolutions like those in Bengal, in Madras, and in Bombay? Did they not, in India, to borrow an expression of that great robber, Lord Clive himself, resort to atrocious extortion, when simple corruption could not keep pace with their rapacity? While they prated in Europe about the inviolable sanctity of the national debt, did they not confiscate in India the dividends of the *rajahs*, who had invested their private savings in the Company's own funds? While they combatted the French revolution under the pretext of defending "our holy religion," did they not forbid, at the same time, Christianity to be propagated in India, and did they not, in order to make money out of the pilgrims streaming to the temples of

---

[††] Marx quotes from A. D. Soltykov's book *Lettres sur l'Inde*, Paris, 1848.

[‡‡] *Jat:* A member of an agricultural caste in Northwest India. *Brahmin*: A member of the highest Hindu caste.

Orissa and Bengal, take up the trade in the murder and prostitution perpetrated in the temple of Juggernaut? These are the men of "Property, Order, Family, and Religion."

The devastating effects of English industry, when contemplated with regard to India, a country as vast as Europe, and containing 150 millions of acres, are palpable and confounding. But we must not forget that they are only the organic results of the whole system of production as it is now constituted. That production rests on the supreme rule of capital. The centralization of capital is essential to the existence of capital as an independent power. The destructive influence of that centralisation upon the markets of the world does but reveal, in the most gigantic dimensions, the inherent organic laws of political economy now at work in every civilised town. The bourgeois period of history has to create the material basis of the new world—on the one hand the universal intercourse founded upon the mutual dependency of mankind, and the means of that intercourse; on the other hand the development of the productive power of man and the transformation of material into a scientific domination of natural agencies. Bourgeois industry and commerce create these material conditions of a new world in the same way as geological revolutions have created the surface of the earth. When a great social revolution shall have mastered the results of the bourgeois epoch, the market of the world and the modern powers of production, and subjected them to the common control of the most advanced peoples, then only will human progress cease to resemble that hideous pagan idol, who would not drink the nectar but from the skulls of the slain.

Boxer Rebellion Proclamation

The Gods assist the Boxers.
The Patriotic Harmonious corps,
It is because the "Foreign Devils" disturb the "Middle Kingdom."
Urging the people to join their religion,
To turn their backs on Heaven,
Venerate not the Gods and forget the ancestors.
Men violate the human obligations,
Women commit adultery,
"Foreign Devils" are not produced by mankind,
If you do not believe,
Look at them carefully.
The eyes of all the "Foreign Devils" are bluish,
No rain falls,
The earth is getting dry,
This is because the churches stop Heaven,
The Gods are angry;
The Genii[*1] are vexed;
Both come down from the mountain to deliver the doctrine.
This is no hearsay,
The practices of boxing will not be in vain;
Reciting incantations and pronouncing magic words,
Burn up yellow written prayers,

[*1] Minor spirits.

"Boxer Rebellion Proclamation," *Sources of Twentieth-Century Global History*, p. 23.

Light incense sticks
To invite the Gods and Genii of all the grottoes.
The Gods come out from grottoes,
The Genii come down from mountains,
Support the human bodies to practice the boxing.
When all the military accomplishments or tactics
Are fully learned,
It will not be difficult to exterminate the "Foreign Devils" then.
Push aside the railway tracks,
Pull out the telegraph poles,
Immediately after this destroy the steamers.
The great France
Will grow cold and downhearted.
The English and Russians will certainly disperse.
Let the various "Foreign Devils" all be killed.
May the whole Elegant Empire of the Great Qing Dynasty be ever prosperous!

On the Way to Pretoria (1893)

By Mohandas Karamchand Gandhi

Mohandas Karamchand Gandhi (1869–1948) is one of the most famous figures of the twentieth century. Born near Bombay and educated as a lawyer in England, Gandhi's political awakening occurred in South Africa in the 1890s. Here, the young barrister learned that the racial hierarchies of colonialism trumped his social status and education. Seeing that colonial racism made a mockery of the values he had learned in England, he launched a civil rights campaign.

On the seventh or eighth day after my arrival, I left Durban. A first class seat was booked for me. It was usual there to pay five shillings extra, if one needed a bedding. Abdulla Sheth insisted that I should book one bedding but, out of obstinacy and pride and with a view to saving five shillings, I declined. Abdulla Sheth warned me. "Look, now," said he, "this is a different country from India. Thank God, we have enough and to spare. Please do not stint yourself in anything that you may need."

I thanked him and asked him not to be anxious.

The train reached Maritzburg, the capital of Natal, at about 9 P.M. Beddings used to be provided at this station. A railway servant came and asked me if I wanted one. "No," said I. "I have one with me." He went away. But a passenger came next, and looked me up and down. He saw that I was a "colored" man. This disturbed him. Out he went and came in again with one or two officials. They all kept quiet, when another official came to me and said, "Come along, you must go to the van compartment."

"But I have a first class ticket," said I.

"That doesn't matter," rejoined the other. "I tell you, you must go to the van compartment."

"I tell you, I was permitted to travel in this compartment at Durban, and I insist on going on in it."

"No, you won't," said the official. "You must leave this compartment, or else I shall have to call a police constable to push you out."

Gandhi, "On the Way to Pretoria," *Gandhi's Autobiography*, pp. 140–146. Copyright © 1948 by Perseus Books. Reprinted with permission.

"Yes, you may. I refuse to get out voluntarily."

The constable came. He took me by the hand and pushed me out. My luggage was also taken out. I refused to go to the other compartment and the train steamed away. I went and sat in the waiting room, keeping my hand-bag with me, and leaving the other luggage where it was. The railway authorities had taken charge of it.

It was winter, and winter in the higher regions of South Africa is severely cold. Maritzburg being at a high altitude, the cold was extremely bitter. My overcoat was in my luggage, but I did not dare to ask for it lest I should be insulted again, so I sat and shivered. There was no light in the room. A passenger came in at about midnight and possibly wanted to talk to me. But I was in no mood to talk.

I began to think of my duty. Should I fight for my rights or go back to India, or should I go on to Pretoria without minding the insults, and return to India after finishing the case? It would be cowardice to run back to India without fulfilling my obligation. The hardship to which I was subjected was superficial—only a symptom of the deep disease of color prejudice. I should try, if possible, to root out the disease and suffer hardships in the process.

Redress for wrongs I should seek only to the extent that would be necessary for the removal of the color prejudice.

So I decided to take the next available train to Pretoria.

The following morning I sent a long telegram to the General Manager of the Railway and also informed Abdulla Sheth, who immediately met the General Manager. The Manager justified the conduct of the railway authorities, but informed him that he had already instructed the Station Master to see that I reached my destination safely. Abdulla Sheth wired to the Indian merchants in Maritzburg and to friends in other places to meet me and look after me. The merchants came to see me at the station and tried to comfort me by narrating their own hardships and explaining that what had happened to me was nothing unusual. They also said that Indians traveling first or second class had to expect trouble from railway officials and white passengers. The day was thus spent in listening to these tales of woe. The evening train arrived. There was a reserved berth for me. I now purchased at Maritzburg the bedding ticket I had refused to book at Durban.

The train reached Charlestown in the morning. There was no railway, in those days, between Charlestown and Johannesburg, but only a stage-coach, which halted at Standerton for the night en route. I possessed a ticket for the coach, which was not cancelled by the break of the journey at Maritzburg for a day; besides, Abdulla Sheth had sent a wire to the coach agent at Charlestown.

But the agent only needed a pretext for putting me off, and so, when he discovered me to be a stranger, he said, "Your ticket is cancelled." I gave him the proper reply. The reason at the back of his mind was not want of accommodation, but quite another. Passengers had to be accommodated inside the coach, but as I was regarded as a "coolie" and looked a stranger, it would be proper, thought the "leader," as the white man in charge of the coach was called, not to seat me with the white passengers. There were seats on either side of the coachbox. The leader sat on one of these as a rule. Today he sat inside and gave me his seat. I knew it was sheer injustice and an insult, but I thought it better to pocket it. I could not have forced myself inside, and if I had raised a protest, the coach would have gone off without me. This would have meant the loss of another day, and Heaven only knows what would have happened the next day. So, much as I fretted within myself, I prudently sat next the coachman.

At about three o'clock the coach reached Pardekoph. Now the leader desired to sit where I was seated, as he wanted to smoke and possibly to have some fresh air. So he took a piece of dirty sack-cloth from the driver, spread it on the footboard and, addressing me said, "Sami, you sit on this, I want to sit near the driver." The insult was more than I could bear. In fear and trembling I said to him, "It was you who seated me here, though I should have been accommodated inside. I put up with the insult. Now that you want to sit outside and smoke, you would have me sit at your feet. I will not do so, but I am prepared to sit inside."

As I was struggling through these sentences, the man came down upon me and began heavily to box my ears. He seized me by the arm and tried to drag me down. I clung to the brass rails of the coachbox and was determined to keep my hold even at the risk of breaking my wristbones. The passengers were witnessing the scene—the man swearing at me, dragging and belaboring me, and I remaining still. He was strong and I was weak. Some of the passengers were moved to pity and exclaimed: "Man, let him alone. Don't beat him. He is not to blame. He is right. If he can't stay there, let him come and sit with us." "No fear," cried the man, but he seemed somewhat crestfallen and stopped beating me. He let go my arm, swore at me a little more, and asking the Hottentot servant who was sitting on the other side of the coachbox to sit on the footboard, took the seat so vacated.

The passengers took their seats and, the whistle given, the coach rattled away. My heart was beating fast within my breast, and I was wondering whether I should ever reach my destination alive. The man cast an angry look at me now and then and, pointing his finger at me, growled: "Take care, let me once get to Standerton and I shall show you what I do." I sat speechless and prayed to God to help me.

After dark we reached Standerton and I heaved a sigh of relief on seeing some Indian faces. As soon as I got down, these friends said: "We are here to receive you and take you to Isa Sheth's shop. We have had a telegram from Dada Abdulla." I was very glad, and we went to Sheth Isa Haji Sumar s shop. The Sheth and his clerks gathered around me. I told them all that I had gone through. They were very sorry to hear it and comforted me by relating to me their own bitter experiences.

I wanted to inform the agent of the Coach Company of the whole affair. So I wrote him a letter, narrating everything that had happened, and drawing his attention to the threat his man had held out. I also asked for an assurance that he would accommodate me with the other passengers inside the coach when we started the next morning. To which the agent replied to this effect: "From Standerton we have a bigger coach with different men in charge. The man complained of will not be there tomorrow, and you will have a seat with the other passengers." This somewhat relieved me. I had, of course, no intention of proceeding against the man who had assaulted me, and so the chapter of the assault closed there.

In the morning Isa Sheth's man took me to the coach. I got a good seat and reached Johannesburg quite safely that night.

Standerton is a small village and Johannesburg a big city. Abdulla Sheth had wired to Johannesburg also, and given me the name and address of Muhammad Kasam Kamruddin's firm there. Their man had come to receive me at the stage, but neither did I see him nor did he recognize me. So I decided to go to a hotel. I knew the names of several. Taking a cab I asked to be driven to the Grand National Hotel. I saw the Manager and asked for a room. He eyed me for a moment, and politely saying, "I am very sorry, we are full up," bade me good-bye. So I asked the cabman to drive to Muhammad Kasam Kamruddin's shop. Here I found Abdul Gani Sheth expecting me, and he gave me a cordial greeting. He had a hearty laugh over the story of my experience at the hotel. "How ever did you expect to be admitted to a hotel?" he said.

"Why not?" I asked.

"You will come to know after you have stayed here a few days," said he. "Only we can live in a land like this, because, for making money, we do not mind pocketing insults, and here we are." With this he narrated to me the story of the hardships of Indians in South Africa.

The Souls of Black Folk (excerpts)

By W.E.B. Du Bois

W.E.B. Du Bois (1868–1963) lived a long life, born during Andrew Johnson's presidency and dying during Lyndon Johnson's administration. A scholar and an activist, he was the first African-American to earn a Ph.D. in history from Harvard and frequently challenged the assumptions and strategies of other African-American leaders such as Booker T. Washington and Walter White. His 1903 The Souls of Black Folk *argued that African-Americans were not yet free. In this selection he predicts that "the problem of the Twentieth Century is the problem of the color line" and asks the famous question, "How does it feel to be a problem?"*

Herein lie buried many things which if read with patience may show the strange meaning of being black here at the dawning of the Twentieth Century. This meaning is not without interest to you, Gentle Reader; for the problem of the Twentieth Century is the problem of the color line. I pray you, then, receive my little book in all charity, studying my words with me, forgiving mistake and foible for sake of the faith and passion that is in me, and seeking the grain of truth hidden there.

I have sought here to sketch, in vague, uncertain outline, the spiritual world in which ten thousand thousand Americans live and strive. First, in two chapters I have tried to show what Emancipation meant to them, and what was its aftermath. In a third chapter I have pointed out the slow rise of personal leadership, and criticized candidly the leader who bears the chief burden of his race to-day. Then, in two other chapters I have sketched in swift outline the two worlds within and without the Veil, and thus have come to the central problem of training men for life. Venturing now into deeper detail, I have in two chapters studied the struggles of the massed millions of the black peasantry, and in another have sought to make clear the present relations of the sons of master and man. Leaving, then, the white world, I have stepped within the Veil, raising it that you may view faintly its deeper recesses,—the meaning of its religion, the passion of its human sorrow, and the struggle of its greater souls. All this I have ended with a tale twice told but seldom written, and a chapter of song.

Some of these thoughts of mine have seen the light before in other guise. For kindly consenting to their republication here, in altered and extended form, I must thank the publishers of the Atlantic Monthly, The World's Work, The Dial, The New World, and the Annals of the American Academy of Political and Social Science. Before each chapter, as now printed, stands a bar of the Sorrow Songs,—some echo of haunting melody from the only American music which welled up from black souls in the dark past. And, finally, need I add that I who speak here am bone of the bone and flesh of the flesh of them that live within the Veil?

> O water, voice of my heart, crying in the sand,
> All night long crying with a mournful cry,
> As I lie and listen, and cannot understand
> The voice of my heart in my side or the voice of the sea,
> O water, crying for rest, is it I, is it I?
> All night long the water is crying to me.
> Unresting water, there shall never be rest
> Till the last moon droop and the last tide fail,
> And the fire of the end begin to burn in the west;
> And the heart shall be weary and wonder and cry like the sea,
> All life long crying without avail,
> As the water all night long is crying to me.
> ARTHUR SYMONS.

Between me and the other world there is ever an unasked question: unasked by some through feelings of delicacy; by others through the difficulty of rightly framing it. All, nevertheless, flutter round it. They approach me in a half-hesitant sort of way, eye me curiously or compassionately, and then, instead of saying directly, How does it feel to be a problem? they say, I know an excellent colored man in my town; or, I fought at Mechanicsville; or, Do not these Southern outrages make your blood boil? At these I smile, or am interested, or reduce the boiling to a simmer, as the occasion may require. To the real question, How does it feel to be a problem? I answer seldom a word.

And yet, being a problem is a strange experience,—peculiar even for one who has never been anything else, save perhaps in babyhood and in Europe. It is in the early days of rollicking boyhood that the revelation first bursts upon one, all in a day, as it were. I remember well when the shadow swept across me. I was a little thing, away up in the hills of New England, where the dark Housatonic winds between Hoosac and Taghkanic to the sea. In a wee wooden schoolhouse, something put it into the boys' and girls' heads to buy gorgeous visiting-cards—ten cents a package—and exchange.

The exchange was merry, till one girl, a tall newcomer, refused my card,—refused it peremptorily, with a glance. Then it dawned upon me with a certain suddenness that I was different from the others; or like, mayhap, in heart and life and longing, but shut out from their world by a vast veil. I had thereafter no desire to tear down that veil, to creep through; I held all beyond it in common contempt, and lived above it in a region of blue sky and great wandering shadows. That sky was bluest when I could beat my mates at examination-time, or beat them at a foot-race, or even beat their stringy heads. Alas, with the years all this fine contempt began to fade; for the words I longed for, and all their dazzling opportunities, were theirs, not mine. But they should not keep these prizes, I said; some, all, I would wrest from them. Just how I would do it I could never decide: by reading law, by healing the sick, by telling the wonderful tales that swam in my head,—some way. With other black boys the strife was not so fiercely sunny: their youth shrunk into tasteless sycophancy, or into silent hatred of the pale world about them and mocking distrust of everything white; or wasted itself in a bitter cry, Why did God make me an outcast and a stranger in mine own house? The shades of the prison-house closed round about us all: walls strait and stubborn to the whitest, but relentlessly narrow, tall, and unscalable to sons of night who must plod darkly on in resignation, or beat unavailing palms against the stone, or steadily, half hopelessly, watch the streak of blue above.

After the Egyptian and Indian, the Greek and Roman, the Teuton and Mongolian, the Negro is a sort of seventh son, born with a veil, and gifted with second-sight in this American world,—a world which yields him no true self-consciousness, but only lets him see himself through the revelation of the other world. It is a peculiar sensation, this double-consciousness, this sense of always looking at one's self through the eyes of others, of measuring one's soul by the tape of a world that looks on in amused contempt and pity. One ever feels his twoness,—an American, a Negro; two souls, two thoughts, two unreconciled strivings; two warring ideals in one dark body, whose dogged strength alone keeps it from being torn asunder.

The history of the American Negro is the history of this strife,—this longing to attain self-conscious manhood, to merge his double self into a better and truer self. In this merging he wishes neither of the older selves to be lost. He would not Africanize America, for America has too much to teach the world and Africa. He would not bleach his Negro soul in a flood of white Americanism, for he knows that Negro blood has a message for the world. He simply wishes to make it possible for a man to be both a Negro and an American, without being cursed and spit upon by his fellows, without having the doors of Opportunity closed roughly in his face.

This, then, is the end of his striving: to be a co-worker in the kingdom of culture, to escape both death and isolation, to husband and use his best powers and his latent genius. These powers of body and mind have in the past been strangely wasted, dispersed, or forgotten. The shadow of a mighty Negro past flits through the tale of Ethiopia the Shadowy and of Egypt the Sphinx. Through history, the powers of single black men flash here and there like falling stars, and die sometimes before the world has rightly gauged their brightness. Here in America, in the few days since Emancipation, the black man's turning hither and thither in hesitant and doubtful striving has often made his very strength to lose effectiveness, to seem like absence of power, like weakness. And yet it is not weakness,—it is the contradiction of double aims. The double-aimed struggle of the black artisan—on the one hand to escape white contempt for a nation of mere hewers of wood and drawers of water, and on the other hand to plough and nail and dig for a poverty-stricken horde—could only result in making him a poor craftsman, for he had but half a heart in either cause. By the poverty and ignorance of his people, the Negro minister or doctor was tempted toward quackery and demagogy; and by the criticism of the other world, toward ideals that made him ashamed of his lowly tasks. The would-be black savant was confronted by the paradox that the knowledge his people needed was a twice-told tale to his white neighbors, while the knowledge which would teach the white world was Greek to his own flesh and blood. The innate love of harmony and beauty that set the ruder souls of his people a-dancing and a-singing raised but confusion and doubt in the soul of the black artist; for the beauty revealed to him was the soul-beauty of a race which his larger audience despised, and he could not articulate the message of another people. This waste of double aims, this seeking to satisfy two unreconciled ideals, has wrought sad havoc with the courage and faith and deeds of ten thousand thousand people,—has sent them often wooing false gods and invoking false means of salvation, and at times has even seemed about to make them ashamed of themselves.

Away back in the days of bondage they thought to see in one divine event the end of all doubt and disappointment; few men ever worshipped Freedom with half such unquestioning faith as did the American Negro for two centuries. To him, so far as he thought and dreamed, slavery was indeed the sum of all villainies, the cause of all sorrow, the root of all prejudice; Emancipation was the key to a promised land of sweeter beauty than ever stretched before the eyes of wearied Israelites. In song and exhortation swelled one refrain—Liberty; in his tears and curses the God he implored had Freedom in his right hand. At last it came,—suddenly, fearfully, like a dream. With one wild carnival of blood and passion came the message in his own plaintive cadences:—

"Shout, O children!
Shout, you're free!
For God has bought your liberty!"

Years have passed away since then,—ten, twenty, forty; forty years of national life, forty years of renewal and development, and yet the swarthy spectre sits in its accustomed seat at the Nation's feast. In vain do we cry to this our vastest social problem:—

"Take any shape but that, and my firm nerves

Shall never tremble!"

The Nation has not yet found peace from its sins; the freedman has not yet found in freedom his promised land. Whatever of good may have come in these years of change, the shadow of a deep disappointment rests upon the Negro people,—a disappointment all the more bitter because the unattained ideal was unbounded save by the simple ignorance of a lowly people.

The first decade was merely a prolongation of the vain search for freedom, the boon that seemed ever barely to elude their grasp,—like a tantalizing will-o'-the-wisp, maddening and misleading the headless host. The holocaust of war, the terrors of the Ku-Klux Klan, the lies of carpet-baggers, the disorganization of industry, and the contradictory advice of friends and foes, left the bewildered serf with no new watchword beyond the old cry for freedom. As the time flew, however, he began to grasp a new idea. The ideal of liberty demanded for its attainment powerful means, and these the Fifteenth Amendment gave him. The ballot, which before he had looked upon as a visible sign of freedom, he now regarded as the chief means of gaining and perfecting the liberty with which war had partially endowed him. And why not? Had not votes made war and emancipated millions? Had not votes enfranchised the freedmen? Was anything impossible to a power that had done all this? A million black men started with renewed zeal to vote themselves into the kingdom. So the decade flew away, the revolution of 1876 came, and left the half-free serf weary, wondering, but still inspired. Slowly but steadily, in the following years, a new vision began gradually to replace the dream of political power,—a powerful movement, the rise of another ideal to guide the unguided, another pillar of fire by night after a clouded day. It was the ideal of "book-learning"; the curiosity, born of compulsory ignorance, to know and test the power of the cabalistic letters of the white man, the longing to know. Here at last seemed to have been discovered the mountain path to Canaan; longer than the highway of Emancipation and law, steep and rugged, but straight, leading to heights high enough to overlook life.

Up the new path the advance guard toiled, slowly, heavily, doggedly; only those who have watched and guided the faltering feet, the misty minds, the dull understandings, of the dark pupils of these schools know how faithfully, how piteously, this people strove to learn. It was weary work. The cold statistician wrote down the inches of progress here and there, noted also where here and there a foot had slipped or some one had fallen. To the tired climbers, the horizon was ever dark, the mists were often cold, the Canaan was always dim and far away. If, however, the vistas disclosed as yet no goal, no resting-place, little but flattery and criticism, the journey at least gave leisure for reflection and self-examination; it changed the child of Emancipation to the youth with dawning self-consciousness, self-realization, self-respect. In those sombre forests of his striving his own soul rose before him, and he saw himself,—darkly as through a veil; and yet he saw in himself some faint revelation of his power, of his mission. He began to have a dim feeling that, to attain his place in the world, he must be himself, and not another. For the first time he sought to analyze the burden he bore upon his back, that dead-weight of social degradation partially masked behind a half-named Negro problem. He felt his poverty; without a cent, without a home, without land, tools, or savings, he had entered into competition with rich, landed, skilled neighbors. To be a poor man is hard, but to be a poor race in a land of dollars is the very bottom of hardships. He felt the weight of his ignorance,—not simply of letters, but of life, of business, of the humanities; the accumulated sloth and shirking and awkwardness of decades and centuries shackled his hands and feet. Nor was his burden all poverty and ignorance. The red stain of bastardy, which two centuries of systematic legal defilement of Negro women had stamped upon his race, meant not only the loss of ancient African chastity, but also the hereditary weight of a mass of corruption from white adulterers, threatening almost the obliteration of the Negro home.

A people thus handicapped ought not to be asked to race with the world, but rather allowed to give all its time and thought to its own social problems. But alas! while sociologists gleefully count his bastards and his prostitutes, the very soul of the toiling, sweating black man is darkened by the shadow of a vast despair. Men call the shadow prejudice, and learnedly explain it as the natural defence of culture against barbarism, learning against ignorance, purity against crime, the "higher" against the "lower" races. To which the Negro cries Amen! and swears that to so much of this strange prejudice as is founded on just homage to civilization, culture, righteousness, and progress, he humbly bows and meekly does obeisance. But before that nameless prejudice that leaps beyond all this he stands helpless, dismayed, and well-nigh speechless; before that personal disrespect and mockery, the ridicule and systematic humiliation, the distortion of fact and wanton license of fancy, the cynical ignoring of the better and the boisterous welcoming of the worse, the all-pervading desire to inculcate disdain for everything black, from Toussaint to the devil,—before this there rises a sickening despair that would disarm and discourage any nation save that black host to whom "discouragement" is an unwritten word.

But the facing of so vast a prejudice could not but bring the inevitable self-questioning, self-disparagement, and lowering of ideals which ever accompany repression and breed in an atmosphere of contempt and hate. Whisperings and portents came home upon the four winds: Lo! we are diseased and dying, cried the dark hosts; we cannot write, our voting is vain; what need of education, since we must always cook and serve? And the Nation echoed and enforced this self-criticism, saying: Be content to be servants, and nothing more; what need of higher culture for half-men? Away with the black man's ballot, by force or fraud,—and behold the suicide of a race! Nevertheless, out of the evil came something of good,—the more careful adjustment of education to real life, the clearer perception of the Negroes' social responsibilities, and the sobering realization of the meaning of progress.

So dawned the time of Sturm und Drang: storm and stress to-day rocks our little boat on the mad waters of the world-sea; there is within and without the sound of conflict, the burning of body and rending of soul; inspiration strives with doubt, and faith with vain questionings. The bright ideals of the past,—physical freedom, political power, the training of brains and the training of hands,—all these in turn have waxed and waned, until even the last grows dim and overcast. Are they all wrong,—all false? No, not that, but each alone was over-simple and incomplete,—the dreams of a credulous race-childhood, or the fond imaginings of the other world which does not know and does not want to know our power. To be really true, all these ideals must be melted and welded into one. The training of the schools we need to-day more than ever,—the training of deft hands, quick eyes and ears, and above all the broader, deeper, higher culture of gifted minds and pure hearts. The power of the ballot we need in sheer self-defence,—else what shall save us from a second slavery? Freedom, too, the long-sought, we still seek,—the freedom of life and limb, the freedom to work and think, the freedom to love and aspire. Work, culture, liberty,—all these we need, not singly but together, not successively but together, each growing and aiding each, and all striving toward that vaster ideal that swims before the Negro people, the ideal of human brotherhood, gained through the unifying ideal of Race; the ideal of fostering and developing the traits and talents of the Negro, not in opposition to or contempt for other races, but rather in large conformity to the greater ideals of the American Republic, in order that some day on American soil two world-races may give each to each those characteristics both so sadly lack. We the darker ones come even now not altogether empty-handed: there are to-day no truer exponents of the pure human spirit of the Declaration of Independence than the American Negroes; there is no true American music but the wild sweet melodies of the Negro slave; the American fairy tales and folklore are Indian and African; and, all in all, we black men seem the sole oasis of simple faith and reverence in a dusty desert of dollars and smartness. Will America be poorer if she replace her brutal dyspeptic blundering with light-hearted but determined Negro humility? or her coarse and cruel wit with loving jovial good-humor? or her vulgar music with the soul of the Sorrow Songs?

Merely a concrete test of the underlying principles of the great republic is the Negro Problem, and the spiritual striving of the freedmen's sons is the travail of souls whose burden is almost beyond the measure of their strength, but who bear it in the name of an historic race, in the name of this the land of their fathers' fathers, and in the name of human opportunity.

And now what I have briefly sketched in large outline let me on coming pages tell again in many ways, with loving emphasis and deeper detail, that men may listen to the striving in the souls of black folk.

Illusions of the White Race (1921)

By Okuma Shigenobu

Okuma Shigenobu (1838–1922) was a Japanese politician who was twice prime minister of Japan (1898 and 1914–16). He was of a generation of Japanese statesmen who transformed Japan from the isolated and traditional Tokugawa Shogunate to the Meiji Restoration's modern constitutional state and industrialized economy. Okuma founded Waseda University in 1882. During his second tenure as prime minister he oversaw Japan's increasingly aggressive pressure on China. In this piece he critiques the West's imperialist ambitions and argues for Japan's right to be a great power.

The Renaissance during the Middle Ages stimulated the progress of the material civilization in Europe and helped the Europeans to grow richer and stronger than the Asiatic races who kept on slumbering in their old civilization. Being seized by an insatiable, aggressive desire, the Europeans took full advantage of their lethargy and swooped down on India and other parts of Asia. They either conquered the Asiatic people by force, or dominated them by dint of superior economic organization, or cheated them out of their territories. The ascendance of the white races is due to the fact that they came into the possession of material civilization a little earlier than their non-white brothers.

The white are obsessed with the mistaken theory that they are superior to all other races. This is the most serious obstacle in the way of the realization of racial equality.

Now the Japanese, the Chinese, the Mongolian, the Turks, the Indians, the Afghans, the Persians, the Arabs, the Malayans, the American aborigines, and the African peoples are all non-white. They are all held in contempt by the whites. And it is the common belief among the whites that the darker the skin, the more inferior is the race. It is based neither upon science, nor upon any positive experience. It is mere superstition backed by historical prejudices.

Okuma Shigenobu, Excerpts from *What Japan Thinks*, pp. 160–170.

The whites are of the conviction that they are too superior a people to be governed by their non-white fellows. Therefore, they demand the privilege of extraterritoriality in the countries of the Asiatic races. They establish their own courts and trample under foot the laws and courts of Asiatic countries....

Of all the non-white countries, Japan had taken the lead in adopting the best parts of European civilization—including its military side. She codified her laws, and reformed her police and judicial systems, her military and naval forces, thus placing herself almost on an equal footing with that of the European countries. Therefore, the Europeans were compelled to withdraw their extraterritorial rights from Japan....

Some whites regard the development of Japan as an unjustifiable encroachment upon their own rights. They either instigate a non-white race against Japan or plan to organize a league of the white nations to perpetuate a white supremacy in the world. Be it remembered, however, that no unjust and unreasonable agitation against this country will ever succeed, as God never sides with an unjust cause.

It is, of course, true that there are still peoples in this world who are so backward in civilization that they cannot at once be admitted into the international family on an equal footing. But it will never do to give discriminatory treatment to them. What is needed by them is proper guidance and direction. And when they have reached a certain stage of civilization, they should be given an equal place and rank in the comity of the nations. Although most Asiatic nations are fully peers of European nations, yet they are discriminated against because of the color of the skin. The root of it lies in the perverted feeling of racial superiority entertained by the whites. If things are allowed to proceed in the present way, there is every likelihood that the peace of the world will be endangered. It, therefore, behooves all well-wishers of mankind to exert their utmost to remove this gross injustice immediately.

Confucius, the ancient sage of China, taught that all peoples of the earth were brethren; Shakya Muni, the founder of Buddhism, preached that all human beings were equal, while Christ emphasized the necessity of philanthropy. They were the founders of the three leading religions. They came into the world at different times and in different places; yet their teachings unquestionably centered upon the truth and the necessity of human equality. God makes no discrimination against any race or any man. Men are created equal and have equal rights.

With the steadily increasing propagation of mankind the struggle for existence has been growing keener and keener, tending toward the dominance of the stronger over the weaker, who is groaning pitiably under inhuman oppression. The strong having step by step come to occupy an advantageous position in society, the class system has gradually been established; and it is through such processes that nobles, commons, and slaves have come to exist....

We may read with pride the pages of our Japanese history, in which slaves do not figure. There are circumstances which make us doubt whether our ancestors, in their conquest of the Korean Peninsula, did not bring the vanquished warriors of the Ye and Myaku tribes to Japan and force them into the occupations which were held in contempt by the natives, such as footgear makers, butchers, and janitors, but the authenticity of this fact remains to be proved. The history of Europe is black with its barbarous record of reducing the vanquished warriors to slaves....

Even modern Europe did not develop a conscience strong enough to bring about the abolition of this baneful system; and not until the slave system became a fitting tool to force a civil war in America, did we see its end even there....

The negroes in America, now numbering more than 11 millions, are not yet emancipated in the true sense of the word. The American law prohibits all invidious discrimination against the negroes; yet they are subjected to constant persecutions by the Americans whose prejudices against them are too deep-rooted to be removed by the mere promulgation of laws. Worst of all, the negroes in America are frequently lynched, a vindictive method the parallel of which cannot be found in the history of even the barbarians of the world....

The example set by Japan has convinced the other Asiatic races of the possibility on their part to be on equal footing with the white races, if only they reform their political system and adopt the needed portion of European civilization. In other words, the rise of Japan and the consequent abolition of extraterritoriality have exploded the superstition that the world is to be ruled by the whites.

In this connection, the whites at first believed that Japan's civilization was a mere imitation or a mere veneer, and that it was only fine in appearance, but entirely hollow in reality and void of sustaining qualities. The result of the Sino-Japanese War, however, was a great surprise to the Europeans. Again the Europeans were taken aback by the outcome of the Russo-Japanese War, in which Russia, one of the strongest white nations, with a most powerful army, was beaten by a non-white nation of the Far East....

But what happened after the Russo-Japanese War came as a miserable disappointment to the whites. Since the war with Russia, Japan's industry witnessed a phenomenal development. Hitherto, she was entirely dependent upon other countries for the supply of machinery and industrial products, but after the war she began to export her industrial products and machines to the outside world, thus changing her status from that of an importer to that of an exporter....

Just as Japan's successes in warfare testified to her military strength, development of her industry, shipping, and commerce accounts for the growing national wealth. In consequence, the white peoples have been obliged to give up their mistaken idea about Japan....

Thus Japan has demonstrated the possibility on the part of non-white races to take rank with the white peoples if only they exert themselves.

Chapter 2

The New Imperialism

Introduction

The three decades that preceded the twentieth century saw a mad race for colonies. With the exception of Thailand, all of South and Southeast Asia came under British, French, Dutch, or American control. White men sitting around tables in Berlin, Brussels, Paris, Rome, and London claimed thousands upon thousands of square miles of the vast continent of Africa, often in places few, if any, of their troops had actually visited. China, while escaping formal annexation, was divided into spheres of influence; carved up like a melon, as the saying went. While the colonizers often spoke of such things as the French "Civilizing Mission" or President McKinley's "Benevolent Assimilation," the reality of empire was one of brutality, exploitation, and injustice, more often than not rationalized by racism. As Joseph Conrad wrote in *The Heart of Darkness*: "The conquest of the earth, which mostly means the taking it away from those who have a different complexion or slightly flatter noses than ourselves, is not a pretty thing when you look into it." European invaders overpowered indigenous populations by using the weapons and techniques of industrialized warfare in attacks on places as diverse as the deserts of the Sudan, the island of Bali, and Burmese royal cities along the Irrawaddy River. While we lack specific statistics, millions certainly died. That said, colonial regimes did lay the basis for the territorial, legal, and linguistic framework of many societies when they achieved independence. For example, judges in Malaysia wear the robes and wigs of their English counterparts, sandwiches made from French baguettes can be found in Laos, and French is by far the most useful language for travelers in West and North Africa. The colonizers also introduced modern medicine, urban sanitation, and other reforms that helped to lower infant mortality and fight a variety of childhood diseases. These documents reveal some of the ironies and paradoxes of the era of the New Imperialism.

This chapter relates to section 10.4 of the History-Social Science Content Standards for California Public Schools.

Mandalay (1892)

By Rudyard Kipling

Joseph Rudyard Kipling (1865–1936) was one of the most prominent writers in the era of the New Imperialism. He was born in Bombay as Queen Victoria was tightening her grip on British ruled India, known as "the Raj," after the widespread rebellion of 1857. Kipling wrote novels, poems, and short-stories primarily about life in the British colonial world. His legacy is complex with some seeing him as celebrating empire and others claiming a more nuanced and critical stance. He dedicated his most famous poem, "The White Man's Burden," to the United States of America after its seizure of the Philippines from Spain. The verses describe a Sisyphean struggle to modernize a conquered population who do not seem to be particularly happy about their loss of independence. "Mandalay" presents a white man's vision of life in the colonies. While it romanticizes the attractive women, spicy food, and sunshine of the colonies, it also speaks rather condescendingly of Buddhism and presents Burma as a site of pleasures for the white troops of the conquering army.

By THE old Moulmein Pagoda, lookin' lazy at the sea,
There's a Burma girl a-settin', and I know she thinks o' me;
For the wind is in the palm-trees, and the temple-bells they say:
"Come you back, you British soldier; come you back to Mandalay!"
    Come you back to Mandalay,
    Where the old Flotilla lay:
    Can't you 'ear their paddles chunkin' from Rangoon to Mandalay?
    On the road to Mandalay,
    Where the flyin'-fishes play,
    An' the dawn comes up like thunder outer China 'crost the Bay!
'Er petticoat was yaller an' 'er little cap was green,
An' 'er name was Supi-yaw-lat—jes' the same as Theebaw's Queen,
An' I seed her first a-smokin' of a whackin' white cheroot,

Rudyard Kipling, "Mandalay," *Barrack-Room Ballads, and Other Verses*, pp. 418-420.

An' a-wastin' Christian kisses on an 'eathen idol's foot:
Bloomin' idol made o' mud—
Wot they called the Great Gawd Budd—
Plucky lot she cared for idols when I kissed 'er where she stud!
On the road to Mandalay...
When the mist was on the rice-fields an' the sun was droppin' slow,
She'd git 'er little banjo an' she'd sing "*Kulla-lo-lo!*"
With 'er arm upon my shoulder an' 'er cheek agin my cheek
We useter watch the steamers an' the *hathis* pilin' teak.

    Elephints a-pilin' teak
    In the sludgy, squdgy creek,
    Where the silence 'ung that 'eavy you was 'arf afraid to speak!
    On the road to Mandalay...

But that's all shove be'ind me—long ago an' fur away,
An' there ain't no 'buses runnin' from the Bank to Mandalay;
An' I'm learnin' 'ere in London what the ten-year soldier tells:
"If you've 'eard the East a-callin', you won't never 'eed naught else."

    No! you won't 'eed nothin' else
    But them spicy garlic smells,
    An' the sunshine an' the palm-trees an' the tinkly temple-bells;
    On the road to Mandalay...

I am sick o' wastin' leather on these gritty pavin'-stones,
An' the blasted English drizzle wakes the fever in my bones;
Tho' I walks with lifty 'ousemaids outer Chelsea to the Strand,
An' they talks a lot o' lovin', but wot do they understand?

    Beefy face an' grubby 'and—
    Law! wot do they understand?
    I've a neater, sweeter maiden in a cleaner, greener land!
    On the road to Mandalay...

Ship me somewheres east of Suez, where the best is like the worst,
Where there aren't no Ten Commandments an' a man can raise a thirst;
For the temple-bells are callin', an' it's there that I would be—
By the old Moulmeiri Pagoda, looking lazy at the sea;

    On the road to Mandalay,
    Where the old Flotilla lay,
    With our sick beneath the awnings when we went to Mandalay!
    O the road to Mandalay,
    Where the flyin'-fishes play,
    An' the dawn comes up like thunder outer China 'crost the Bay!

La Petite Tonkinoise

By Henri Christiné

Henri Christiné (1867–1941) wrote the lyrics to this popular pre–World War One dance hall song. Like Kipling's "Mandalay," the lyrics present the colonies as a place where the average white man can find an exotic and devoted woman. Also as in Kipling's poem, the white man uses her for his pleasure and then leaves her. Both the song and the poem illustrate that white power in the colonies extended beyond merely political, economic, and military control to dominating the very bodies of the colonized. French colonial rule broke the united kingdom of Vietnam into three colonies: Tonkin, Annam, and Cochinchina. With the term "Vietnam" banned to prevent nationalist agitation, the French used the condescending Chinese term Annam ("Pacified South"). Many Vietnamese viewed the term Annamite as derogatory and humiliating. The song contains several obvious and vulgar double entendres.

At the end of my deployment
I am leaving Tonkin.
Oh! What a pretty land of ladies!
It's a paradise of little women.
They are beautiful and loyal
And I became the lover
Of a little lady of this land
Who is named Mélaoli.

(refrain)
I fell for a little lady
Its Anna, its Anna, an Annamite.
She is lively, she is charming
Like a singing bird.

Henri Christiné; Michael Vann, trans., "La Petite Tonkinoise," Copyright © 2011. Reprinted with permission.

I called her my little bourgeoise,
My Tonkiki, my Tonkiki, my Tonkinoise.
There are others who catch my eye
But its her that I love the best.

The evening brings a lot of things
Before we hit the sack
I learn the geography
Of China and Manchuria,
The frontiers, the rivers,
The Yellow River, the Blue River,
And curiously there is also love
That gets the Middle Kingdom wet.

(Refrain)
Very sweet, she is the daughter
Of a famous mandarin.
That's why on her chest
There are two mandarins.
Not a big eater, when we eat together
She only wants some banana
Since they are so cheap
I give her all she wants.

But everything must pass and break.
To France I must return.
With sadness hurt my heart
I said good bye to my mistress.
With a painful soul, my little queen
Accompanied me as I left
But before we separated
I told her in a kiss:

"Don't cry when I leave you
Little Anna, little Anna, little Annamite.
You gave me your youth,
Your love, and your caresses.
You were my little housewife
My Tonkiki, my Tonkiki, my Tonkinoise.
In my heart I will always keep
The memory of our love.

Racial Hatred (1922)

By Ho Chi Minh

Ho Chi Minh (1890–1969) was born Nguyen Sinh Cung but would change his name to Paul Tat Tanh and Nguyen Ai Quoc (Nguyen the Patriot) and eventually become the president of the Democratic Republic of Vietnam (North Vietnam). Son of a Confucian scholar who hated the French colonial rule, this Vietnamese patriot devoted his life to liberating and uniting his homeland. He left Vietnam before the First World War, living and working in New York, Boston, London, and finally Paris. He joined the French Socialist Party and sided with the radical faction that left to found the French Communist Party in 1921. In the early 1920s he published the radical newspaper Le Paria. His passionate articles condemned imperialism, racism, and capitalist exploitation.

For having spoken of the class struggle and of equality among men, and on the charge of having preached racial hatred, our comrade Louzon has been sentenced. Let us see how the love between peoples has been understood and applied in Indo-China of late. We will not speak for the time being of the poisoning and degradation of the masses by alcohol and opium of which the colonial government is guilty; our comrades in the parliamentary group will have to deal with this matter one day.

Everybody knows the deeds of derring-do of the assassin-administrator Darles. However, he is far from having the monopoly of savagery against the natives.

A certain Pourcignon furiously rushed upon an Annamese who was so curious and bold as to look at this European's house for a few seconds. He beat him and finally shot him down with a bullet in the head.

A railway official beat a Tonkinese village mayor with a cane.

M. Beck broke his car driver's skull with a blow from his fist.

M. Bres, building contractor, kicked an Annamese to death after binding his arms and letting him be bitten by his dog.

M. Deffis, receiver, killed his Annamese servant with a powerful kick in the kidneys.

Ho Chi Minh, "Racial Hatred," *Selected Works of Ho Chi Minh* Vol. 1.

M. Henry, a mechanic at Haiphong, heard a noise in the street; the door of his house opened, an Annamese woman came in, pursued by a man. Henry, thinking that it was a native chasing after a 'con-gai' snatched up his hunting rifle and shot him. The man fell, stone dead: it was a European. Questioned, Henry replied, 'I thought it was a native.'

A Frenchman lodged his horse in a stable in which there was a mare belonging to a native. The horse pranced, throwing the Frenchman into a furious rage. He beat the native, who began to bleed from the mouth and ears; after which he bound his hands and hung him from them under his staircase.

A missionary (oh yes, a gentle apostle!), suspecting a native seminarist of having stolen 1,000 piastres from him,, suspended him from a beam and beat him. The poor fellow lost consciousness. He was taken down. When he came to it began again. He was dying, and is perhaps dead already… etc.

Has justice punished these individuals, these civilizers? Some have been acquitted and others were not troubled by the law at all. That's that. And now.

Accused Louzon, it's your turn to speak!

Equality! (1922)

By Ho Chi Minh

To hide the ugliness of its regime of criminal exploitation, colonial capitalism always decorates its evil banner with the idealistic motto: Fraternity, Equality, etc....

Here is how these champions of equality put their slogan into practice.

In the same workshop and for the same work, a white workman is several times better paid than his coloured brother.

In administrative offices, despite length of service and recognized ability, a native is paid starvation wages, while a freshly arrived white man receives a higher salary with less work to do.

After receiving higher education in the parent state and obtaining degrees as doctors of medicine or of law, young native people cannot exercise their professions in their own country if they are not naturalized (and how many difficulties and humiliations a native must go through to obtain this naturalization!).

Dragged away from their countries and their homes, and pressganged into the army as 'volunteers,' the militarized natives are quick to savour the exquisite significance of this phantasmal 'equality' they are defending.

With the same rank, a white non-commissioned officer is almost always regarded as superior to his native colleague, who must salute and obey him.

This 'ethno-military' hierarchy is still more striking when white and coloured soldiers travel in the same train or ship.

Here is the most recent example.

In May the *S. S. Liger* left France for Madagascar with six hundred Malagasy soldiers on board.

The Malagasy non-commissioned officers were crowded into the holds, while their white colleagues were installed in comfortable cabins.

Ho Chi Minh, "Equality," *Selected Works of Ho Chi Minh* Vol. 1.

May our coloured brothers, warmed by the ship's boilers, if not by an ideal, awakened by the noise of the propellers, or by the voice of their conscience, think over and understand the fact that the good capitalism will always consider them as ordinary olo maloto.

The Battle of Omdurman

By Winston S. Churchill

Sir Winston Leonard Spencer-Churchill (1874–1965) was the son of an English lord and an American heiress. A graduate of the Royal Military College at Sandhurst, he chose to work as a war correspondent, covering the Cuban revolt against Spain (1895), and British campaigns in the Northwest Frontier of India (1897), the Sudan (1898) and South Africa during the Boer War (1899), authoring five books by the age of 26. His exciting reporting and his escape from a Boer prisoner of war camp won him fame and contributed to his election to Parliament where he spent some six decades. An unabashed proponent of the British Empire, Churchill's letters celebrate the 1898 campaign against Abdullah Ibn-Mohammed. Known as "The Khalifa" he was the successor to the Madhi, a messianic Muslim leader in the Sudan who had defeated the British in 1885. The British troops were eager to get revenge for this loss and for the death of Major-General "Chinese" Gordon, a hero of British campaigns in China.

Khartoum, 5 September

You see the address, my dear…, It is with a feeling of exultation that I write it big and black at the top of the page. The fact that a European can again in safety and confidence post a letter from such a situation has alone a deep significance. I am sure you will want to know how it all happened. Yet there is so much to tell that I hesitate where to begin. I told you in my last letter from Wad Habeshi Camp that I should probably have no opportunity of writing until after the event. Nor was I wrong. I should have liked to make your imagination march with the cavalry screen from Shabluka to Kerreri all through the thick scrub by the banks of the Nile, and peering cautiously for Dervishes under every bush. I should have liked to have described the

Winston Churchill, "The Battle of Omdurman," 1898.

reconnaissance and patrolling by day and the high zarebas and closely packed camps at night, where each man slept booted and belted with his weapon ready to his hand.

I would have tried to draw you some picture of the advance of the army. A long row of great brown masses of infantry with a fringe of cavalry dotting the plain for miles in front, with the Camel Corps—chocolate-coloured men on cream-coloured camels—stretching into the desert on the right and the gunboats stealing silently up river on the left, scrutinising the banks with their guns; while far behind the transport and baggage trailed away into the mirage, and far in front the telescope might discover the watching Dervish patrols. I would have written some account of our first contact with the enemy and of the expectations of war which we draw from that affair; but for all this you would not thank me, for the telegraph has already told you that tremendous events have taken place, and it is of these that you would have me write. Let me, then, begin at the 1st of September and describe the reconnaissance of Kerreri and the Battle of Khartoum which followed on the next day.

The whole army broke camp on the morning of the 1st and marched slowly towards the Kerreri position, which consisted of a line of low rocky hills at right angles to the river. In front were the cavalry and the Camel Corps, and these, pushing rapidly forward, soon interposed a distance of perhaps eight miles between them and the main force. The 21st Lancers were on the left nearest the Nile. The nine Egyptian squadrons curved backwards in a wide half-moon to protect the right flank.

We had not accomplished more than a mile when about a hundred enormous vultures joined us, and henceforth they accompanied the squadrons, flying or waddling lazily from bush to bush and always looking back at the horsemen. Officers and men alike were struck by this strange and unusual occurrence, and it was freely asserted that these birds of prey knew that two armies were approaching each other, and that this meant a battle and hence a feast. It would be difficult to assign limitations to the possibilities of instinct. The sceptic must at least admit that the vultures guessed right, even if they did not know. Yet we thought them wrong when we found the strong Kerreri Hills abandoned and the little Dervish camp, which had been shelled the day before, deserted and solitary.

The squadron of the 21st to which I have the pleasure of being attached halted at the foot of the hill. Colonel Martin and a few other officers ascended it, taking signallers with them. We waited. Then presently a message was sent down which filled us all with curiosity to look over the crest. The signal flag wagged tirelessly, and we spelt out the following words: 'Khartoum in sight.' More than thirteen years had passed since an Englishman could have said that with truth.

After a short halt the advance was resumed, and turning a shoulder of the hill I saw in the distance a yellow-brown pointed dome rising above the blurred horizon. It was the Mahdi's Tomb,* which stands in the very heart of Omdurman. From the high ground the field glass disclosed rows and rows of mud houses, making a dark patch on the brown of the plain. To the left, the river, steel-grey in the morning light, forked into two channels, and on the tongue of land between them the gleam of a white house showed among the trees. Then we knew that before us was Khartoum and the confluence of the Blue and White Niles.

A black, solitary hill rose between the Kerreri position and Omdurman. A long, low ridge running from it concealed the ground beyond. For the rest there was a wide, rolling, sandy plain of great extent, and patched with coarse, starveling grass. The river—the inevitable river—framed the picture on the left, and by its banks a straggling mud village stood. This, though we did not know it, was to be the field of Khartoum.

It was deserted. Not a living soul could be seen. And there were many who said at once that there would be no fight, for here we were arrived at the very walls of Omdurman and never any enemy to bar our path. Then, with our four squadrons looking very tiny on the broad expanse of ground, we moved steadily forward.

It was about three miles to the hill and ridge of which I have written—the last ridge which lay between us and the city. If there was a Dervish army, if there was to be a battle, if the Khalifa would maintain his boast and accept the arbitrament of war, much must be visible from that ridge. We looked over. At first nothing was apparent except the walls and houses of Omdurman and the sandy plain sloping up from the river to the distant hills. Then four miles away, on our right front, I perceived a long black line with white spots. It was the enemy. It seemed to me as we looked that there might be three thousand men behind a high dense zareba of thorn bushes. That, said the officers, was better than nothing. There would in any case be a skirmish.

I will not weary you with describing our tortuous movements towards the Dervish position. Looking at it, now from one point of view, now from another, but always edging nearer, the cavalry slowly approached it, and halted in the plain about two miles away, three great serpents of men—the light-coloured one, the 21st Lancers; a much longer and blacker one, the Egyptian squadrons; a mottled one, the Camel Corps and Horse Artillery.

From this distance a clearer view was possible, and we distinguished many horsemen riding about the flanks and front of the great dark line which crowned the crest of the slope. A few of these rode forward carelessly towards the watching squadrons to look at them. They were not apparently acquainted with the long range of the Lee-Metford carbine. Several troops were dismounted, and at eight hundred yards fire was made on them. Two were shot and fell to the ground. Their companions,

---

*Mohammed Ahmed (1848–1885).

dismounting, examined them, picked up one, let the other lie, and resumed their ride without acknowledging the bullets by even an increase of pace.

While this little incident passed so did the time. It was now nearly eleven o'clock. Suddenly the whole black line, which seemed to be zareba, began to move. It was made of men not bushes. Behind it other immense masses and lines of men appeared over the crest, and while we watched, amazed by the wonder of the sight, the whole face of the slope became black with swarming savages. Four miles from end to end, and in five great divisions, this mighty army advanced, and swiftly. The whole side of the hill seemed to move. Between the masses horsemen galloped continually. Before them many patrols dotted the plain, above them waved hundreds of banners, and the sun, glinting on perhaps forty thousand hostile spear-points, spread a sparkling cloud. It was, perhaps, the impression of a lifetime, nor do I expect ever again to see such an awe-inspiring and formidable sight. We estimated their number at not less than forty thousand men, and it is now certain fifty thousand would have been nearer the truth.

The steady and continuous advance of the great army compelled us to mount our horses and trot off to some safer point of view, while our patrols and two detached troops, engaging the Dervish scouts, opened a dropping fusillade. I was sent back to describe the state of affairs to the Sirdar, but as had he already witnessed the spectacle from the top of the black hill—Heliograph Hill I shall call it in future—you are the first to receive my account.

From the summit the scene was extraordinary. The great army of Dervishes was dwarfed by the size of the landscape to mere dark smears and smudges on the brown sand of the plain. Looking east another army was now visible—the British and Egyptian army. All three divisions had crossed the Kerreri position and now stood drawn up in formation for attack in a crescent, with their backs to the Nile. The transport and the houses of the village filled the enclosed space. I looked from one array to the other. That of the enemy was without doubt denser and longer. Yet there seemed a superior strength in the solid battalions, whose lines were so straight that they might have been drawn with a ruler. Neither force could see the other, though but five miles divided them.

At a quarter to two the Dervish army halted. Their drill appeared excellent, and they all stopped as by a single command. The nearest troops to them were the 21st Lancers, who were about a mile and a half away. We watched them anxiously, for if they continued to advance the action would have been brought on at once. No sooner had they halted than their riflemen discharged their rifles in the air with a great roar—a barbaric *feu-de-joie*. Then they all lay down on the ground, and it became evident that the matter would not be settled till the morrow.

We remained in our position among the sand hills of the ridge until the approach of darkness, and during the afternoon various petty encounters took place between our patrols and those of the enemy, resulting in a loss to them of about a dozen killed and wounded and to us of one man wounded and one horse killed. Then, as the light failed, we returned to the river to water and encamp, passing into the zareba through the ranks of the British division, whose officers and men, looking out steadfastly over the fading plain, asked us whether the enemy were coming and, if so, when. And it was with confidence and satisfaction that we replied and they heard: 'Probably at daylight.'

I have told you of one sight which I witnessed on the 1st of September, and I were but a poor chronicler if I were to forget or omit the other. At about eleven o'clock the gunboats had ascended the Nile and engaged the enemy's batteries on the river face of Omdurman. Throughout the day the loud reports of their guns could be heard, and looking from our position on the ridge we could see the white vessels steaming slowly forward against the current under clouds of black smoke from their furnaces, and amid other clouds of white smoke from their artillery. The forts replied vigorously, but the British aim was accurate and their fire crushing. The embrasures were smashed to bits, and many of the Dervish guns dismounted. Then the gunboats began to shell the Mahdi's Tomb, This part of the proceedings was so interesting that it distracted my attention at intervals from the advancing army.

The dome of the Tomb rose high and prominent above the mud houses of the city. A lyddite shell burst over it—a great flash, a white ball of smoke, and, after a pause, the dull thud of the distant explosion. Another and another followed. Presently, instead of the white smoke there was a prodigious cloud of red dust, and the whole Tomb disappeared. When this cleared away we saw that instead of being pointed it was now flat topped. Our shells continue to strike it with like effect, some breaking holes in the dome, others smashing off the cupolas, all enveloping it in dust, until I marvelled alike at the admirable precision and the wasteful folly of the practice. I feel inclined to write a little bitterly to you on this subject, because the mania to destroy this building cost me on the next day a good and gallant friend, and very nearly cost the country a skilful general.

When the gunboats had completed their bombardment, had sunk a Dervish steamer, had silenced all the hostile batteries, and had sorely battered the Mahdi's Tomb, they returned leisurely to the camp and lay moored close to the bank to lend the assistance of their guns in case of attack. And as the darkness became complete they threw their powerful searchlights over the plain and on to the distant hills, and all night long these dazzling beams disturbed, though they protected, the slumbers of the army.

The consciousness of the limitless possibilities of the morrow delayed the sleep which physical weariness invited, and a desire to inspect the precautions for defence led me around the perimeter of the zareba. The army had not formed a quadrilateral camp as on other nights, but lay down to rest in the formation for attack they had assumed in the afternoon. Every fifty yards behind the thorn bushes were double sentries. Every hundred yards a patrol with an officer was to be met. Fifty yards in rear of this line lay

the battalions, the men in all their ranks, armed and accoutred, but sprawled into every conceivable attitude which utter weariness could suggest or dictate. The full moon rising early displayed the whole scene. Imagination was stimulated, and I would set down some of my impressions for your private eye, did I not know you were a cynic, and would observe that others had thought the same on similar occasions before. So I shall end this letter here and now, and leave you, if I can, with some realisation of the solemnity and the significance of a night when two armies, one of fifty thousand, one of twenty-five thousand, both equally confident, and both equally brave, are waiting at five miles' distance for the coming of the morning and the settlement of their quarrel.
4 October, 1898

Khartoum, 6 September

The bugles all over the camp by the river began to sound at half-past four. The cavalry trumpets and the drums and fifes of the British division joined the chorus, and everyone awoke amid a confusion of merry or defiant notes. The moon was full, and by its light and that of lanterns we dressed ourselves—many with special care. Those who were callous, who had seen much war, or who were practical, set themselves to deliberately eat a substantial meal of such delicacies as 'porrig,' 'sausig,' ration biscuits, and 'bully' beef. Then it grew gradually lighter, and the cavalry mounted their horses, the infantry stood to arms, and the gunners went to their batteries, while the sun rising over the Nile displayed the wide plain, the dark rocky hills, and the waiting army. It was as if all the preliminaries were settled, the arena cleared, and nothing remained but the final act and the rigour of the game.

As soon as it was light enough to move, several squadrons of British and Egyptian cavalry were pushed swiftly forward to feign contact with the enemy and to learn his intentions. It was my fortune to be sent with an advanced patrol of the 21st Lancers, and though I know that it is of the battle that you wish to hear, and not of my personal experiences, I must describe events from my own standpoint. At half-past five the British and Egyptian army was drawn up in line, with its back to the river. Its flanks were secured by the gunboats, which were moored in the stream. Before it was the rolling sandy plain. To the right were the rocky hills of the Kerreri portion, near which the nine squadrons of Egyptian cavalry were massed. On the left the 21st Lancers were trotting towards Heliograph Hill, with their advanced patrols already cantering up its lower slopes. My patrol was, I think, the first to reach the top of the ridge and to look into the plain beyond. I had expected that the Dervish army would have retired to their original position, and could not believe that they would advance to the attack in daylight across open ground. Indeed, it seemed more probable that their hearts might have failed them in the night and that they had melted away into the deserts of

Kordofan. But these anticipations were immediately dispelled by the scene which was visible from the crest of the ridge.

It was a quarter to six. The light was dim, but growing stronger every minute. There in the plain lay the enemy, their numbers unaltered, their confidence and intentions apparently unshaken. Their front was nearly five miles long, and composed of great masses of men joined together by thinner lines. Behind and to the flanks were large reserves. They looked from where I stood dark blurs and streaks, relieved and diversified with odd-looking gleams of light from the spear points. After making the necessary reports I continued to watch the strange and impressive spectacle. As it became broad daylight, that is to say about ten minutes to six, I suddenly realised that all the masses were in motion and advancing swiftly. Their Emirs galloped about, among and before their ranks scouts and patrols began to scatter themselves all over the front. Then they began to cheer. They were still a mile away from the hill when a tremendous roar came up in waves of intense sound, like the tumult of the rising wind and sea before a storm.

The advance continued. The Dervish left began to stretch out across the Kerreri Plain—as I thought to turn to our right flank. Their centre, over which the black flag of the Khalifa floated high and remarkable, moved directly towards the hill. Their right pursued a line of advance south of Heliograph Hill, and would, I saw, pass over the ground on which I stood. This mass of men was the most striking of all. They could not have mustered less than seven thousand. Their array was perfect. They displayed a great number of flags—perhaps five hundred—which looked at the distance white, though they were really covered with texts from the Koran, which by their admirable alignment made the divisions of the Khalifa's army look like the old representations of the Crusaders in the Bayeux Tapestry. I called them at the moment 'the white flagmen' to distinguish them from the other masses, and that name will do as well as any other.

The attack developed. The left, under a famous Emir, appeared to have mistaken the squadrons of the Egyptian Cavalry for our main position. Ten thousand strong they toiled right up to the Kerreri hills, and did not come into action until later in the day. The centre deployed across the plain and marched straight towards the zareba. One small brigade of their great force—perhaps about two thousand strong—halted five hundred yards from my patrol, and perceiving the Lancers paid us the compliment of detaching a dozen riflemen to drive us from our point of observation. After awhile these began to shoot so straight that it "became expedient as well as desirable to move round the hill out of their fire. From this new position the centre was no longer visible, but the 'white flagmen' were of sufficient interest and importance to occupy the attention.

As the whole Dervish army continued to advance this division, which had until now been echeloned in rear of their right, moved up into the general line, and began to climb the southern slopes of Heliograph Hill. They, too, saluted us with musketry, but as the hill was within good artillery range of the zareba I knew that they would have something else to occupy their attention when they and their banners appeared over the shoulder and crest of the ridge, and we remained spectators, sheltering among the rocks about three hundred yards to their right flank.

Meanwhile yet another body of the enemy, who had been drawn up behind the 'white flagmen,' was moving slowly towards the Nile, echeloned still further behind their right, and not far from the suburbs of Omdurman. These men had evidently been posted to prevent the Dervish army being cut off from the city, and it was these that the 21st Lancers charged and drove back about two hours later. My attention was distracted from their movements by the loud explosion of artillery. The Dervish centre had come into range, and the batteries opened on them. Above the heads of the moving masses shells began to burst, dotting the air with smoke balls and the ground with bodies. But they were nearly two miles away, and the distance rendered me unsympathetic.

I looked back to the 'white flagmen.' They were very nearly over the crest. In another minute they would become visible to the batteries. Did they realise what would come to meet them? They were in a dense mass scarcely two thousand yards from the 32nd Field Battery and the gunboats. The ranges were known. It was a matter of machinery. The more distant cannonade passed unnoticed as the mind concentrated on the impending horror. I could see it coming. It was a matter of seconds, and then swift destruction would rush on these brave men.

They topped the crest and drew out into full view of the whole army. Their white flags made them conspicuous above all. As they saw the camp of their enemies they discharged their rifles with a great roar of musketry and quickened their pace, and I was alarmed to see a solitary British officer. Lieutenant Conolly of the Greys, attached to the 21st, galloping across their front at only a hundred yards distance. He had been sent out to take a final look behind the hill. Fortunately he returned safely, and with the necessary information. For a moment the white flags advanced in regular order, and the whole division crossed the crest and were exposed.

Forthwith the gunboats, and the 32nd Battery, and other guns from the zareba opened on them. I was but three hundred yards away, and with excellent glasses could almost see the faces of the Dervishes who met the fearful fire. About twenty shells struck them in the first minute. Some burst high in the air, others exactly in their faces. Others again plunged into the sand and exploding, dashed clouds of red dust, splinters, and bullets amid their ranks. The white flags toppled over in all directions. Yet they rose again immediately, as other men pressed forward to die for Allah's sacred cause and in the defence of the successor of the True Prophet of The Only God. It was a terrible sight, for as yet they had not hurt us at all, and it seemed an unfair advantage to strike thus cruelly when they could not reply.

From the purely military point of view I was not impressed with the effects of the shells. I had looked to see fifty men drop to each projectile. You read of these things in the text books on war, and you hear them stated every time you talk to an artillery officer. What soldier has not heard of the results of target practice? Eighty per cent of hits, etc. I watched most carefully, and from a close and excellent position. About five men on the average fell to each shell. Still, there were many shells. Under their influence the mass of the 'white flagmen' dissolved into thin lines of spearmen and skirmishers, and came on in altered formation and diminished numbers, but with unabated enthusiasm.

And now, the whole attack being thoroughly exposed, it became the duty of the cavalry to clear the front as quickly as possible and leave the further conduct of the debate to the infantry and the Maxim guns. We therefore retired into the zareba, and, taking advantage of the river bank, watered and fed our horses, while all the time the fusillade grew louder and more intense, and we wondered what progress the attack was making.

Of this I saw nothing, but it appears that the *debris* of the 'white flagmen' joined the centre, and that these continued their advance against the zareba gradually, spreading out and abandoning their dense formations, and gradually slowing down. At about eight hundred yards range of the British division the advance ceased, and they could make no further headway. Unable to advance, they were unwilling to retire, and their riflemen, taking advantage of the folds of the ground, opened and maintained an unequal combat. By 8:30 it was evident that the attack had been repulsed. The loss in the zareba did not exceed sixty killed and wounded. That of the enemy was not less than two thousand. Colonel F. Rhodes,[†] the *Times* correspondent, was unfortunately among the wounded, being shot through the shoulder as he sat on his horse near the Maxim guns.

The second phase of the action, or, as an excitable correspondent called it, 'the second battle' now began. Disregarding the presence of the Dervish left on and among the Kerreri Hills, the Sirdar gave the order for the army to march on towards Omdurman. The 21st Lancers moved out of the zareba and trotted over the ridge near Heliograph Hill. The whole of the British division made a left wheel, and faced south, their left on the river at right angles to the enemy's centre, and to their former front. The Egyptian and Sudanese divisions were echeloned on the right by brigades. Thus the army presented its flank to the Dervish centre, and its right rear to the Dervish left. Probably Sir Herbert Kitchener was anxious above all things to gain a moral advantage, and realised that if he could enter Omdurman the resistance of the enemy would collapse. Events, however, proved the movement to be premature. The Dervish left, who had started out in the morning confident of victory, and who had vainly toiled after the elusive cavalry and Camel Corps among the Kerreri Hills,

---

† Francis William Rhodes (1851–1905). Elder brother of Cecil Rhodes. Acted as special correspondent for *The Times* during the Sudan campaign, and afterwards edited *The River War* for Churchill.

now returned an exasperated but undefeated ten thousand. Infusing into the centre the encouragement of a reinforcement, they fell on General MacDonald's Sudanese Brigade, which was the rearmost of the echelon. That officer, who by personal prowess and military conduct has passed from the rank of private to that of general, faced about, and met the attack with a skill and determination which excited the admiration of all. General Lewis, with the Egyptian Brigade, also swung round, and thus the army assumed an A-shaped formation, the apex pointing west and away from the Nile, four brigades looking north-west towards the Dervish attack.

This was the critical moment of the engagement. The Sirdar, not the least disconcerted by the discovery of his mistake, immediately proceeded to rectify it. The movement of bringing up the right shoulders of the army ceased. Pivoting on the two brigades who were now hotly engaged, the British division and the whole south front of the A swung round until it became a straight line facing nearly west. Advancing in that direction the army steadily drove the Dervishes before them, away from the river, and as the left began to come up more and more threatened to cut their line of retreat.

Of this and all this I had but fleeting glances, for an event was taking place on the southern slopes of Heliograph Hill which absorbed my whole attention, and may perhaps invite yours. I will describe it at length and in detail, because I write as an eye witness, perhaps even as more, and you may read with interest. Everyone describes an action from his own point of view. Indeed, it is thence that we look at most things, human or divine. Why should I be or make an exception?

At about a quarter past eight the 21st Lancers moved out of the zareba, and occupied a position on the ridge of Heliograph Hill, whence a view of the ground right up to the walls of Omdurman was obtainable. Here we waited, dismounting a few troops to fire at the Dervish skirmishers on the higher slopes. At 840 orders reached us to advance, harass the enemy's right, and endeavour to cut him off from Omdurman. In pursuance of these orders Colonel Martin[‡] advanced his regiment in line of squadron columns slowly down the southern slopes of the ridge and hill, and continued across the plain in a south-westerly direction. In the distance large numbers of the enemy could be seen retreating into Omdurman. The whole plain was crossed by a continual stream of fugitives.

In the foreground about two hundred Dervishes were crouching in what appeared to be a small khor or crease in the plain. The duty of the cavalry to brush these away and proceed at once to the more numerous bodies in rear was plain. With a view to outflanking them the squadrons wheeled to the left into columns of troops, and, breaking into a trot, began to defile across their front. We thought them spearmen, for we were within three hundred yards and they had fired no shot. Suddenly, as

---

‡   Rowland Hill Martin (1848–1919). Commanding officer 21st Lancers 1892–8. Mentioned in despatches and awarded CB after Omdurman.

the regiment began to trot, they opened a heavy, severe, and dangerous fire. Only one course was now possible. The trumpets sounded 'right-wheel into line' and on the instant the regiment began to gallop in excellent order towards the riflemen. The distance was short, but before it was half covered it was evident that the riflemen were but a trifle compared to what lay behind. In a deep fold of the ground—completely concealed by its peculiar formation—a long, dense, white mass of men became visible. In length they were nearly equal to our front. They were about twelve deep. It was undoubtedly a complete surprise for us. What followed probably astonished them as much. I do not myself believe that they ever expected the cavalry to come on. The Lancers acknowledged the unexpected sight only by an increase of pace. A desire to have the necessary momentum to drive through so solid a line animated each man. But the whole affair was a matter of seconds.

At full gallop and in the closest order the squadron struck the Dervish mass. The riflemen, who fired bravely to the last, were brushed head over heel in the khor. And with them the Lancers jumped actually on to the spears of the enemy, whose heads were scarcely level with the horses knees.

It is very rarely that stubborn and unshaken infantry meet equally stubborn and unshaken cavalry. Usually, either the infantry run away and are cut down in flight, or they keep their heads and destroy nearly all the horsemen by their musketry. In this case the two living walls crashed together with a mighty collision. The Dervishes stood their ground manfully. They tried to hamstring the horses. They fired their rifles, pressing their muzzles into the very bodies of their opponents. They cut bridle-reins and stirrup-leathers. They would not budge till they were knocked over. They stabbed and hacked with savage pertinacity. In fact, they tried every device of cool determined men practised in war and familiar in cavalry. Many horses pecked on landing and stumbled in the press, and the man that fell was pounced on by a dozen merciless foes.

The regiment broke completely through the line everywhere, leaving sixty Dervishes dead and many wounded in their track. A hundred and fifty yards away they halted, rallied, and in less than five minutes were reformed and ready for a second charge. The men were anxious to cut their way back through their enemies. But some realisation of the cost of that wild ride began to come to all of us. Riderless horses galloped across the plain. Men, clinging on to their saddles, lurched hopelessly about, covered with blood from perhaps a dozen wounds. Horses streaming from tremendous gashes limped and staggered with their riders. In one hundred and twenty seconds five officers, sixty-six men, and one hundred and nineteen horses out of less than three hundred had been killed or wounded.

The Dervish line, broken and shattered by the charge, began to reform at once. They closed up, shook themselves together, and prepared with constancy and courage for another shock. The 21st, now again drawn up in line of squadron columns, wheeled and, galloping round the Dervish flank, dismounted and opened a heavy fire with their magazine carbines. Under the pressure of this fire the enemy changed front to meet the new attack, so that both sides were formed at right angles to their original lines. When the Dervish change of front was completed they began to advance against the dismounted men. But the fire was accurate, and there can be little doubt that the moral effect of the charge had been very great, and that these brave enemy were no longer unshaken. Be this as it may, the fact remains that they retreated swiftly, though in good order, towards the ridge of Heliograph Hill, where the Khalifa's black flag still waved, and the 21st Lancers remained in possession of the ground—and of their dead.

I have told you the story of the charge, but you will perhaps care to hear a few incidents. Colonel Martin, busy with the direction of his regiment, drew neither sword nor revolver, and rode through the press unarmed and uninjured. Major Crole Wyndham had his horse shot from under him by a Dervish who pressed his muzzle into the very hide. From out of the middle of that savage crowd the officer fought his way on foot and escaped in safety. Lieutenant Wormald, of the 7th Hussars, thrust at a man with his sword, and that weapon, by a well-known London maker, bent double and remained thus.

I saw myself Sergeant Freeman trying to collect his troops after the charge. His face was cut to pieces, and as he called on his men to rally, the whole of his nose, cheeks, and lips flapped amid red bubbles. Surely some place may be found in any roll of honour for such a man.

Lieutenant Nesham, of the 21st Lancers, had an even more extraordinary escape. Amid a crowd of men slashing and stabbing he remained in his saddle throughout. His left hand was nearly severed from his body by single stroke. He managed to twist the reins round his right wrist. The near bridle rein and the off stirrup-leather were both cut. The wounded officer reeled. His enemies closed around him. He received another deep cut in his right leg and a slighter one in his right arm. Yet his horse, pressing forward, carried him through the Dervishes to fall fainting among the rallying Squadrons.

I have written thus of others. You would ask me of my own experiences. You know my luck in these things. As on another occasion in the Indian Frontier, I came safe through—one of the very few officers whose saddlery, clothes, or horse were untouched, and without any incident that is worth while putting down here.

One impression only I will record. I remember no sound. The whole event seemed to pass in absolute silence. The yells of the enemy, the shouts of the soldiers, the firing of many shots, the clashing of sword and spear were unnoticed by the senses, unregistered by the brain. Others say the same. Perhaps it is possible for the whole of a man's faculties to be concentrated in eye, bridle-hand, and trigger-finger, and withdrawn from all other parts of the body.

It was not until after the squadrons had reformed that I heard of the death of Lieutenant Grenfell, of the 12th Lancers. This young officer, who to great personal charm and high courage added talents and industry which gave promise of a successful and even a famous military career, and who had earlier in the day reconnoitred the enemy, riding close up to their ranks under a hot fire in a manner that excited general admiration, had been cut down and killed. And at this shocking news the exhilaration of the gallop, the excitement of the moment, the joy and triumph of successful combat faded from the mind, and the realisation came home with awful force that war, disguise it as you may, is but a dirty, shoddy business, which only a fool would play at. Nor was it until the night when I saw Charles Neufeld[§] released from thirteen years of suffering and degradation that I again recognised that there are some things that have to be done, no matter what the cost may be. With this reflection, and with the knowledge that he felt probably little pain, certainly no fear, Robert Grenfell's friends, among whom I am sorrowfully proud to count myself, may—indeed must—be content.

The Lancers remained in possession of the dearly bought ground. There was not much to show that there had been a desperate fight. A quarter of a mile away nothing would have been noticed. Close to, the scene looked like a place where rubbish is thrown, or where a fair has recently been held. White objects, like dirty bits of newspaper, lay scattered here and there—the bodies of the enemy. Brown objects almost the colour of the earth, like bundles of dead grass or heaps of manure, were also dotted about—the bodies of soldiers. Among these were goat-skin water bottles, broken weapons, torn and draggled flags, cartridge cases. In the foreground lay a group of dead horses and several dead or dying donkeys. It was all litter.

We gathered reverently the poor remains of what had but a quarter of an hour before been the soldiers of a great and civilised Empire, and, horrified at their frightful wounds, laid them in a row. The wounded were sent with a small escort towards the river and hospitals. Then we remounted, and I observed, looking at my watch, that it was half-past-nine—only breakfast-time, that is to say, in distant, comfortable England. I dare say it occurred to others who were unhurt that there was yet plenty of time. At any rate, I deferred my thanks until a later hour.

I will not prolong this letter. If I am tired of writing, it reminds me that you may be weary of reading. Were I to continue I could not do justice to the subject, nor you to my efforts. Of the end of the battle, of the entry into Omdurman, and of the fight of the Khalifa I will write to-morrow. If this has amused your leisure, read further; if not, send my letter back unopened.

29 September, 1898

---

§   Charles (Karl) Neufeld (1856–1918). A Prussian explorer captured by the Khalifa in 1887 and kept in chains until he was found by Bennet Burleigh, special correspondent of the *Daily Telegraphy* and released after Omdurman.

Camp Omdurman, 3 September

Let me continue my account, my dear…, from the point where I was yesterday reminded that there are limits to your patience and my perseverance. By half-past nine the 21st Lancers were again trotting across the Plain of Omdurman towards the long lines of fugitives who streamed across it. With the experience of the past half-hour in our minds, and with the great numbers of the enemy in our front, it seemed to many that a bloody day lay before us. But we had not gone far when individual Dervishes began to walk towards the advancing squadrons, throwing down their weapons, holding up their hands and imploring mercy. It is doubtful what claim these had to clemency. The laws of war do not admit the right of a beaten enemy to quarter. The victor is not obliged to accept his surrender. Of his charity he may do so, but there is no obligation, provided of course that he make it clear to the suppliant that he must continue to fight. These were savages who had for many years afflicted the Sudan and cumbered the earth. We well knew the mercy they would have offered us had the fortunes of the day been reversed. The soldiers had seen their dead comrades hacked out of all semblance of humanity by the unimaginable ferocity of this same enemy who now asked for quarter, and consequent feeding and medical attendance. And there were some who would have said, 'Take up your arms and fight, for there is no mercy here.'

Yet it seems that those who use the powerful weapons of civilisation—the shrapnel shell, the magazine rifle, and the Maxim gun—can afford to bear all that the wild spearman may do without descending to retaliation. At any rate, I rejoice for the honour of the British cavalry when I reflect that they held their heads very high, and that the regiment that suffered by far the greatest loss took also the greatest number of prisoners.

As soon as it was apparent that the surrender of individuals was accepted the Dervishes began to come in and lay down their arms, at first by twos and threes, then by dozens and finally by scores. Meanwhile, those who were still intent on flight made a wide detour to avoid the cavalry, and streamed past our front at a mile's distance in uninterrupted succession. 'It looked,' to quote an officer's description, 'just like the people hurrying into Newmarket town after the Cambridgeshire.' The disarming and escorting of the prisoners delayed our advance, and many thousands of Dervishes escaped into Omdurman. To harry and annoy the fugitives a few troops were dismounted with carbines, and a constant fire was made on such as did not attempt to come in and surrender. Yet the crowds continued to run the gauntlet, and I myself saw at least twenty thousand men make good their escape from the field. Many of these were still ready to fight, and replied to our fire with bullets, fortunately at very long range. It would have been madness for two hundred Lancers to have galloped in among such masses, and we had to be content with the results of the carbine fire. The need of a fresh cavalry brigade was apparent. I could not help thinking of my Frontier friends, and of the effect which three smart regiments of Bengal Lancers would have produced. I write from the military and technical point of view. From any other it was evident that there had been enough killing that day.

Meanwhile the Sirdar, having made his army face nearly west, and having repulsed the attack of the Dervish left under Osman Sheikh-ud-Din, continued to advance away from the river, driving the Dervishes before him. But at about twelve o'clock he shut up his glasses and, remarking that the enemy had had 'a good dusting,' reverted to his previous intention of marching on Omdurman. This second attempt was in every way successful. The Dervishes were now thoroughly beaten. Their whole army had suffered great loss. All had been engaged. All had been defeated. To explain the movement briefly and clearly rather than correctly—the army which was advancing in line westwards suddenly went fours left and marched south in column, leaving the enemy to continue their flight at their pleasure and discretion.

At about two o'clock, and three miles from Omdurman, the whole force halted to rest by the banks of a khor. You will ask me to explain what a khor is. It is simply a hollow. When these hollows lie close to the flood Nile the waters of the river flow up them and give them the appearance of tributaries, whereas they are just the reverse. They are, indeed, similar to the subsidiary canals of an irrigation system. In the Punjab and in other parts of India the result is produced by artificial means. But the Nile is a natural irrigation system, and has found out all the engineering devices for itself. Whatever your idea of the khors may be, I can assure you that they are cool and convenient drinking-places.

To this khor the Lancers also made their way, and the thirsty horses plunged their noses in the water. The scene was a strange one. You must imagine a five hundred yards stretch of the Suez Canal. On the banks are crowds of men and animals. The whole of the British Infantry Division fills one side. Multitudes of khaki-clad men are sitting in rows on the slopes. Hundreds are standing by the brim or actually in the red, muddy water, drinking deeply. Two or three dead animals lying in the shallows show that the men must be thirsty rather than particular. Everywhere water bottles are being filled. It is the Nile that has come into the desert to refresh the tired animals and weary men—the Nile, which is the soul of the whole story, the spirit of the Sudan drama.

At four o'clock the march on Omdurman was resumed. The Egyptian cavalry, the 21st Lancers and the Camel Corps moved round the outskirts of the city, everywhere obstructed and delayed by the surrender of hundreds of prisoners. The infantry, the Sudanese in front, and the Sirdar at their head, entered the town. At first the route lay through the suburbs. A few shots were fired at the troops as they marched through the maze of mud houses, but no resistance was encountered. All the city was deserted and silent; not a Dervish was to be seen. Presently three men advanced slowly to meet the victorious General. They knelt in the roadway and presented him with the keys of the city itself and of the various public buildings—the prison and the arsenal. He accepted their surrender and spoke words of peace. Rising swiftly, they shouted out the good news, and thereupon from every house men, women and children appeared in the joy of relief from fear.

The march continued. Arrived at the great wall which divides the city proper from its suburbs the advance was checked. Though the wall had been breached in many places by the gunboats there were signs of resistance and many armed Dervishes were gathered on the parapets. It became necessary for the Maxim guns and a battalion of Sudanese to clear these defenders from the wall. But there was very little spirit in them, and a few minutes' firing sufficed.

Then the Sirdar rode towards the prison. The key would not fit the great door. The General, first and almost alone, rode through a narrow passage among the houses to a smaller entrance. This he was able to open, and the prisoners, over one hundred in number, were set at liberty. Of their names and conditions I will not write, because you will read these things in the newspapers. But the whole incident was intensely dramatic, and those who saw it carried away with them an impression which will live fresh and vivid in their minds for some years.

Meanwhile, behind the General came the army. On a broad front they entered the city and fired occasional volleys and, receiving occasional shots in return, they marched through Omdurman from end to end and returned to the suburbs to camp for the night.

Thus the occupation of Omdurman was accomplished, and only one sad and terrible accident marred the triumph. While the Sirdar with four guns with a battalion of infantry was taking possession of the ruins of the Mahdi's Tomb the red flag of the Headquarters Staff attracted the attention and drew the fire of two guns which had been left outside the town. I am told that their orders justify their action, and that they only carried out the instructions which the Sirdar had given. At any rate these facts are clear. Three shells burst in quick succession over the Staff and soldiers in the square in front of the Tomb. Another screamed overhead. Immediately everyone hurried from the spot in astonishment and alarm. But Mr. Hubert Howard, one of the correspondents of *The Times* newspaper, who was in the upper room of the Khalifa's house, which adjoined the Tomb, was killed by a fifth shell before he could follow.

Mr. Hubert Howard was a man of some reputation, and of much greater promise. The love of adventure had already led him several times to scenes of war and tumult. In 1895 he passed the Spanish lines in Cuba, and for six weeks fought and was hunted with the Cuban insurgents, whose privations and dangers he shared, and whose cause he afterwards pleaded warmly. At this time I was, as you know, with the Spanish forces witnessing their operations, and the fact that we had been on opposite sides proved a bond of union. Thereafter I saw him frequently. His profession—that of the Law—gave him more opportunities for travelling than fall to the lot of a subaltern of horse. On the outbreak of the Matabele War he hurried to South Africa, and in the attack on Sekombo's Kraal in the autumn of 1896 he acted as adjutant of Robertson's Cape Boys, and displayed military qualities which left no doubt in the minds of those who saw that he should have been a soldier, not only for his own sake, but for that of the army. Having, on his own initiative, captured a steep and nearly precipitous hill, which proved of considerable tactical value, he was severely wounded in the ankle. He refused to leave the field, and continued till the end of the day to drag himself about, directing and inspiriting his men. His services on this occasion, not less than his known abilities, obtained for him the position of Secretary to Lord Grey. The recrudescence of trouble in Mashonaland and Matabeleland in 1897 led him again to the field, and in many minor engagements—those unheeded skirmishes by which unknown men build up our Empire—he added to his reputation as a soldier and as a man.

On his return to England he passed without difficulty the needful examinations for admission to the Bar, and had been duly called. But war was in his blood. The great military expedition preparing on the Nile fascinated his imagination. His literary powers were known. He proceeded to Egypt a month ago—only a month ago—as joint correspondent of *The Times* with Colonel Rhodes.

I need not tell you how pleasant it was to ride with him on our long march up from the Atbara river, of the arguments and discussions which arose, of the plans for the future which were formed. You know how many times a week energetic and virile youth conquers the world in anticipation. You are familiar with the good fellowship of a camp, and know that the best of friends are made in the open air and when peril of life impends or exists.

A close and warm acquaintance was formed between him and the officers of the 21st Lancers. With their squadrons he witnessed the reconnaissance of Kerreri on the 1st of September. With all of us he rode out the charge on the morning of the 2nd. One of the first to force his way through the enemy's lines, he was the first to ride up and offer his congratulations to the colonel. But the firing behind the ridge attracted him, and as he aspired to share all the dangers he rode off in search of new adventure.

Of the occupation of Omdurman I saw nothing, for the cavalry hung on the flanks of the city until the night was far advanced, nor was it until eleven o'clock that we returned, hungry ourselves, and with weary horses, to bivouac near the 2nd British Brigade. There it was I heard the news. At first it seemed incredible. But there are no limits to the devilish ingenuity of malicious fortune, and the truth became certain that the man who had passed through many dangers, and who had that morning escaped unhurt from a charge where the casualties reached twenty-five per cent, had been killed by a British shell, the victim of an accident.

I would pay some tribute to his memory if words were of any avail. He was so brave a man that pity seems almost an insult, and the feeling grows that he will not have minded, whatever may lie beyond this world. It is of the type that I write. He was representative of those young men who, with famous names, and belonging to the only true aristocracy the world can now show, carry their brains and enthusiasm to the farthest corners of our wide Empire and infuse into the whole body the energy and vigour of progress. That force which in the national life of France and Germany is directed solely to military, and in the United States solely to commercial enterprises animates in our fortunate state all parts of the public service. Seeking for roads by which to advance the commonweal, men like Howard spread to our farthest provinces. Their graves, too, are scattered. His lies in the desert near the city of Omdurman. Thither his brother correspondents carried his body on the morning after the action, and General Hunter, passing at the moment, halted a Sudanese brigade to pay a last compliment to courage and resolution.

The complete destruction and dispersal of the Dervish army and the capture of their capital was accomplished with the loss of under five hundred soldiers. The great host which had risen in the morning confident of victory and nothing doubting were scattered in flight or death before night. Many thousand bodies lay about the plain and all along the line of retreat. The Khalifa, fearing the retribution which he was conscious of having deserved, fled on a swift camel, and with a small following made good his escape, using a route where the wells were small and far between. And the Sirdar, thoroughly satisfied with the issue of the event and wearied by the anxieties of the day, went to sleep in peace and security in the city of Omdurman.

I will write to you tomorrow if time allows, and tell you of the hoisting of the British flag, and of the scenes which the field of battle displayed. But I will not tell you all the horrors, as the taste for realism is one which should not be greatly encouraged. The desire to hear about dreadful things and the desire to see them are, after all, akin. Who shall say that the desire to do them is not also in the relationship? There will, however, be horrors enough.

29 September, 1898

Hun Speech

By Kaiser Wilhelm II

Kaiser Wilhelm II (1859–1941) became Emperor of Germany in 1888. Due to complications in childbirth, he suffered from a withered left arm. Perhaps to compensate for his handicap, he presented himself as a warrior, almost always appearing in uniform. He also adopted a very aggressive foreign policy, earning him the nickname of "a bull in a china shop." He dreamed of a colonial empire and expanded the German navy, angering and alienating France and England. Despite being Queen Victoria's grandson and related to the Russian Tsar, his reckless foreign policy eventually drove England, France, and Russia into an alliance against him. When the Boxer Rebellion threatened German interests he sent an expeditionary force. This is his farewell speech to the troops as they prepared to leave Bremerhaven.

Bremerhaven, July 27, 1900

Great overseas tasks have fallen to the new German Empire, tasks far greater than many of my countrymen expected. The German Empire has, by its very character, the obligation to assist its citizens if they are being set upon in foreign lands. The tasks that the old Roman Empire of the German nation was unable to accomplish, the new German Empire is in a position to fulfill. The means that make this possible is our army.

It has been built up during thirty years of faithful, peaceful labor, following the principles of my blessed grandfather. You, too, have received your training in accordance with these principles, and by putting them to the test before the enemy, you should see whether they have proved their worth in you. Your comrades in the navy have already passed this test; they have shown that the principles of your training are sound, and I

Kaiser Wilhelm II; Thomas Dunlap, trans., "Hun Speech," <germanhistorydocs.ghi-dc.org>. Copyright German Historical Institute. Reprinted with permission.

am also proud of the praise that your comrades have earned over there from foreign leaders. It is up to you to emulate them.

A great task awaits you: you are to revenge the grievous injustice that has been done. The Chinese have overturned the law of nations; they have mocked the sacredness of the envoy, the duties of hospitality in a way unheard of in world history. It is all the more outrageous that this crime has been committed by a nation that takes pride in its ancient culture. Show the old Prussian virtue. Present yourselves as Christians in the cheerful endurance of suffering. May honor and glory follow your banners and arms. Give the whole world an example of manliness and discipline.

You know full well that you are to fight against a cunning, brave, well-armed, and cruel enemy. When you encounter him, know this: no quarter will be given. Prisoners will not be taken. Exercise your arms such that for a thousand years no Chinese will dare to look cross-eyed at a German. Maintain discipline. May God's blessing be with you, the prayers of an entire nation and my good wishes go with you, each and every one. Open the way to civilization once and for all! Now you may depart! Farewell, comrades!

The unofficial but correct version of the crucial passage reads as follows:

Should you encounter the enemy, he will be defeated! No quarter will be given! Prisoners will not be taken! Whoever falls into your hands is forfeited. Just as a thousand years ago the Huns under their King Attila made a name for themselves, one that even today makes them seem mighty in history and legend, may the name German be affirmed by you in such a way in China that no Chinese will ever again dare to look cross-eyed at a German.

The Balinese Puputan (1906)

By Jhr. H. M. Van Weede

A puputan is a Balinese ritual suicide. There were several such incidents as the Dutch colonized this Hindu island. The Dutch arrived in the East Indies in the 1590s. Through a concerted effort and liberal doses of violence, the Dutch East India Company (the first corporation to be publicly traded on a stock market) built an empire based on a monopoly of the spice trade. Later the Dutch state took over these colonial possessions, promoting the development of rubber, coffee, and sugar plantations and taking control of more and more territory. From their base in Java, the Dutch sought to bring Bali under control in the early years of the twentieth century. In the event described here, a Dutch expeditionary force had landed on Sanur beach and was marching towards one of the royal palaces when it encountered the royal family in white funeral attire. The incident shocked and shamed the Dutch troops.

Because of our march to Sesetan we deceived the raja. He was convinced that we would attempt to invade his residence from the south and had ordered to install all his artillery on that side to prepare for a concentrated defense. When he realized his aberration it was too late to fortify the capital's north and east side. As a matter of fact the sharpened bombardment in the early morning of the 20th September had a major moral impact on his man folk; large numbers of warriors escaped to the northwest, and before we had reached our destination, no one could be found in the inner circle of the *puri* (temple), the *jro* (interior) residences of the nobility, and the area of Den Pasar with its neighborhoods, but the raja himself, his womenfolk, his relatives, his courtiers, and a band of loyal followers. Together with the old and demented king of Pamecutan in whose territory people were panic stricken, the raja

Jhr. H. M. Van Weede; Tineke Hellwig and Eric Tagliacozzo, eds., "The Balinese Puputan," *The Indonesia Reader: History, Culture, Politics*, pp. 262–264. Copyright © 2009 by Duke University Press. Reprinted with permission.

united no more than two thousand men in the army. As he was deserted by most of his men and faced the indignity of exile he decided, conforming to the customary law and his religion, that rather than surrender he would proceed to the *puputan*, that is a general attack with lances in which even women and children participate and all submit to death.

It must have been an impressive spectacle in the front court of the *puri* in the morning of the 20th September when a select crowd assembled in order to die in the sight of our ranks. The king and princes with their courtiers in their most magnificent garments had girded on krises whose golden hilts were shaped as Buddha images and were encrusted with precious stones. All were dressed in red or black, and they had combed their hair with care and moistened it with fragrant oil. The women, too, were dressed in their best outfits and jewelry; most of them wore their hair loose and all wore white cloaks. The king had ordered to burn down the puri and to destroy all breakables. When he was told at 9:00 a.m. that the enemy had penetrated into Den Pasar from the north, the tragic procession, two hundred and fifty persons in total, started to move. Every man and woman carried a kris or a long lance, children who were strong enough did so too, and infants were carried along. Hence they strode northward along the wide avenue with high trees on both sides, approaching their downfall. The raja went in front, according to tradition carried on the shoulders of one of his courtiers, and in silence they reached the intersection near the Baluan *jro* residences. On they walked until all of a sudden in curve of the road at the Tainsiap residences they could see the dark line of our infantry.

It was the 11th regiment that slowly moved forward from the north. One section, among who was Captain Schutstal van Woudenberg, followed the main road. When the magnificent procession appeared to them, the Balinese were approximately three hundred meters away from them. A small square was located between the two groups.

Immediately they were called a halt and Captain Schutstal commanded the translators with gesticulations and words to tell the approaching group to stop. This directive, however, was without success and in spite of repeated warnings the Balinese now changed their pace to a trot. Incessantly the captain and translators signaled, but in vain, and soon they had to admit that they were facing a crowd who were seeking their death. They allowed them to approach up to one hundred—eighty, seventy feet—but then they changed to a double-quick step with lances and krises raised, the raja still in front. For the safety of our troops it would be irresponsible to linger any longer and we fired the first salvo. A number of victims remained where they were. Among the first ones who fell was the raja and now one of the most horrific scenes took place that one can imagine. While those who were spared continued their attack and the fast firing on our side was necessary out of self defense, we saw how the lightly injured gave those who were seriously wounded the fatal stab. Women opened their chests to be killed or received their final blow between their shoulder blades. And when those who finished off others were hit by our shots, others—men and women—stood up to continue their bloody mission. Suicide too, took place on a large scale, and everyone yearned to die. Some women threw golden coins to our soldiers as a reward for the violent death they desired from them, and they positioned themselves in front of them, pointing to their hearts, as if they wanted to be hit there. If the soldiers did not fire, they stabbed themselves. An old man in particular paced busily over the corpses and stabbed with his kris the injured left and right until he was knocked out. An old woman took over his duty and underwent the same fate, but nothing would stop them, again and again others stood up to continue the extermination. Meanwhile it was important to remain alert because a second group of Balinese approached, commanded by the raja's half brother who was twelve years of age and could hardly carry his own lance, When summoned to halt by the captain and the translators, the boy seemed willing to obey for a split second, when his followers compelled him to continue. A fierce attack followed, and in the firing aimed at his followers, he, too, was slain by a bullet.

With exception of a few who withdrew in houses, and some injured who later recovered, the total crowd of heroes found the death they sought out. The corpses were piled up at the center of the square where the confrontation had taken place. The raja's wives had stabbed themselves with krises while stooped over him, and others, who were wounded, had dragged themselves to him in order to cover him. His body was buried under the corpses and from this mound here and there a gilded spearhead jutted out.

Imperialism: The Highest State of Capitalism (excerpts)

By V. I. Lenin

As a young man Vladimir Illich Ulyanov's (1870–1924) brother was executed for involvement in a plot to assassinate the tsar. This event helped to radicalize the 17-year-old, sending him down the path of revolution where he would take the nom de guerre "Lenin." Both an intellectual and an activist, Lenin sought to create strategy for revolution based upon the theoretical work of Karl Marx. Written in exile in 1916, Imperialism modified Marxism, claiming that the colonial world might be the place where a world revolution could begin.

We have seen that the economic quintessence of imperialism is monopoly capitalism. This very fact determines its place in history, for monopoly that grew up on the basis of free competition, and precisely out of free competition, is the transition from the capitalist system to a higher social-economic order. We must take special note of the four principal forms of monopoly, or the four principal manifestations of monopoly capitalism, which are characteristic of the epoch under review.

Firstly, monopoly arose out of the concentration of production at a very advanced stage of development. This refers to the monopolist capitalist combines, cartels, syndicates and trusts. We have seen the important part that these play in modern economic life. At the beginning of the twentieth century, monopolies acquired complete supremacy in the advanced countries. And although the first steps towards the formation of the cartels were first taken by countries enjoying the protection of high tariffs (Germany, America), Great Britain, with her system of free trade, was not far behind in revealing the same basic phenomenon, namely, the birth of monopoly out of the concentration of production.

Secondly, monopolies have accelerated the capture of the most important sources of raw materials, especially for the coal and iron industries, which are the basic and most

V.I. Lenin, "The Place of Imperialism in History," *Imperialism: The Highest Stage of Capitalism*, pp. 123–128. Copyright © 1993 by International Publishers. Reprinted with permission.

highly cartelised industries in capitalist society. The monopoly of the most important sources of raw materials has enormously increased the power of big capital, and has sharpened the antagonism between cartelised and non-cartelised industry.

Thirdly, monopoly has sprung from the banks. The banks have developed from modest intermediary enterprises into the monopolists of finance capital. Some three or five of the biggest banks in each of the foremost capitalist countries have achieved the "personal union" of industrial and bank capital, and have concentrated in their hands the disposal of thousands upon thousands of millions which form the greater part of the capital and income of entire countries. A financial oligarchy, which throws a close net of relations of dependence over all the economic and political institutions of contemporary bourgeois society without exception—such is the most striking manifestation of this monopoly.

Fourthly, monopoly has grown out of colonial policy. To the numerous "old" motives of colonial policy, finance capital has added the struggle for the sources of raw materials, for the export of capital, for "spheres of influence," *i.e.*, for spheres for profitable deals, concessions, monopolist profits and so on; in fine, for economic territory in general. When the colonies of the European powers in Africa, for instance, comprised only one-tenth of that territory (as was the case in 1876), colonial policy was able to develop by methods other than those of monopoly—by the "free grabbing" of territories, so to speak. But when nine-tenths of Africa had been seized (approximately by 1900), when the whole world had been divided up, there was inevitably ushered in a period of colonial monopoly and, consequently, a period of particularly intense struggle for the division and the redivision of the world.

The extent to which monopolist capital has intensified all the contradictions of capitalism is generally known. It is sufficient to mention the high cost of living and the oppression of the cartels. This intensification of contradictions constitutes the most powerful driving force of the transitional period of history, which began from the time of the definite victory of world finance capital.

Monopolies, oligarchy, the striving for domination instead of the striving for liberty, the exploitation of an increasing number of small or weak nations by an extremely small group of the richest or most powerful nations—all these have given birth to those distinctive characteristics of imperialism which compel us to define it as parasitic or decaying capitalism. More and more prominently there emerges, as one of the tendencies of imperialism, the creation of the "bondholding" (rentier) state, the usurer state, in which the bourgeoisie lives on the proceeds of capital exports and by "clipping coupons." It would be a mistake to believe that this tendency to decay precludes the possibility of the rapid growth of capitalism. It does not. In the epoch of imperialism, certain branches of industry, certain strata of the bourgeoisie and certain countries betray, to a more or less degree, one or other of these tendencies. On die whole, capitalism is growing far more rapidly than before. But this growth is not only becoming more and more uneven in general; its unevenness also manifests itself, in particular, in the decay of the countries which are richest in capital (such as, England).

In regard to the rapidity of Germany's economic development, Riesser, the author of the book on the big German banks, states:

> The progress of the preceding period (1848–70), which had not been exactly slow, stood in about the same ratio to the rapidity with which the whole of Germany's national economy, and with it German banking, progressed during this period (1870–1905) as the mail coach of the Holy Roman Empire of the German nation stood to the speed of the present-day automobile… which in whizzing past, it must be said, often endangers not only innocent pedestrians in its path, but also the occupants of the car.

In its turn, this finance capital which has grown so rapidly is not unwilling (precisely because it has grown so quickly) to pass on to a more "tranquil" possession of colonies which have to be seized—and not only by peaceful methods—from richer nations. In the United States, economic development in the last decades has been even more rapid than in Germany, and *for this very reason* the parasitic character of modern American capitalism has stood out with particular prominence. On the other hand, a comparison of, say, the republican American bourgeoisie with the monarchist Japanese or German bourgeoisie shows that the most pronounced political distinctions diminish to an extreme degree in the epoch of imperialism—not because they are unimportant in general, but because in all these cases we are discussing a bourgeoisie which has definite features of parasitism.

The receipt of high monopoly profits by the capitalists in one of the numerous branches of industry, in one of numerous countries, etc., makes it economically possible for them to corrupt certain sections of the working class, and for a time a fairly considerable minority, and win them to the side of the bourgeoisie of a given industry or nation against all the others. The intensification of antagonisms between imperialist nations for the division of the world increases this striving. And so there is created that bond between imperialism and opportunism, which revealed itself first and most clearly in England, owing to the fact that certain features of imperialist development were observable there much earlier than in other countries.

Some writers, L. Martov, for example, try to evade the fact that there is a connection between imperialism and opportunism in the labour movement—which is particularly striking at the present time—by resorting to "official optimistic" arguments (*à la* Kautsky and Huysmans) like the following: the cause of the opponents of capitalism would be hopeless if it were precisely progressive capitalism that led to the increase of opportunism, or, if it were precisely the best paid workers who were inclined towards opportunism, etc. We must have no illusion regarding "optimism" of this kind. It is optimism in regard to opportunism; it is optimism which serves to conceal opportunism. As a matter of fact the extraordinary rapidity and the particularly revolting character of the development of opportunism is by no means a guarantee that its victory will be durable: the rapid growth of a malignant abscess on a healthy body only causes it to burst more quickly and thus to relieve the body of it. The most dangerous people of all in this respect are those who do not wish to understand that the fight against imperialism is a sham and humbug unless it is inseparably bound up with the fight against opportunism.

From all that has been said in this book on the economic nature of imperialism, it follows that we must define it as capitalism in transition, or, more precisely, as moribund capitalism. It is very instructive in this respect to note that the bourgeois economists, in describing modern capitalism, frequently employ terms like "interlocking," "absence of isolation," etc., "in conformity with their functions and course of development," banks are "not purely private business enterprises; they are more and more outgrowing the sphere of purely private business regulation." And this very Riesser, who uttered the words just quoted, declares with all seriousness that the "prophecy" of the Marxists concerning "socialisation" has "not come true"!

What then does this word "interlocking" express? It merely expresses the most striking feature of the process going on before our eyes. It shows that the observer counts the separate trees, but cannot see the wood. It slavishly copies the superficial, the fortuitous, the chaotic. It reveals the observer as one who is overwhelmed by the mass of raw material and is utterly incapable of appreciating its meaning and importance. Ownership of shares and relations between owners of private property "interlock in a haphazard way." But the underlying factor of this interlocking, its very base, is the changing social relations of production. When a big enterprise assumes gigantic proportions, and, on the basis of exact computation of mass data, organises according to plan the supply of primary raw materials to the extent of two-thirds, or three-fourths of all that is necessary for tens of millions of people; when the raw materials are transported to the most suitable place of production, sometimes hundreds or thousands of miles away, in a systematic and organised manner; when a single centre directs all the successive stages of work right up to the manufacture of numerous varieties of finished articles; when these products are distributed according to a single plan among tens and hundreds of millions of consumers (as in the case of the distribution of oil in America and Germany by the American "oil trust")—then it becomes evident that we have socialisation of production, and not mere "interlocking"; that private economic relations and private property relations constitute a shell which is no longer suitable for its contents, a shell which must inevitably begin to decay if its destruction be delayed by artificial means; a shell which may continue in a state of decay for a fairly long period (particularly if the cure of the opportunist abscess is protracted), but which will inevitably be removed.

The enthusiastic admirer of German imperialism, Schulze-Gaevernitz, exclaims:

> Once the supreme management of the German banks has been entrusted to the hands of a dozen persons, their activity is even today more significant for the public good than that of the majority of the Ministers of State. (The "interlocking" of bankers, ministers, magnates of industry and rentiers is here conveniently forgotten.)... If we conceive of the tendencies of development which we have noted as realised to the utmost: the money capital of the nation united in the banks; the banks themselves combined into cartels; the investment capital of the nation cast in the shape of securities, then the brilliant forecast of Saint-Simon will be fulfilled: "The present anarchy of production caused by the fact that economic relations are developing without uniform regulation must make way for organisation in production. Production will no longer be shaped by isolated manufacturers, independent of each other and ignorant of man's economic needs, but by a social institution. A central body of management, being able to survey the large fields of social economy from a more elevated point of view, will regulate it for the benefit of the whole of society, will be able to put the means of production into suitable hands, and above all will take care that there be constant harmony between production and consumption. Institutions already exist which have assumed as part of their task a certain organisation of economic labour: the banks." The fulfilment of the forecasts of Saint-Simon still lies in the future, but we are on the way to its fulfilment—Marxism, different from what Marx imagined, but different only in form.[*]

A crushing "refutation" of Marx, indeed! It is a retreat from Marx's precise, scientific analysis to Saint-Simon's guesswork, the guesswork of a genius, but guesswork all the same.

January–July, 1916.

---

[*] Schulze-Gaevernitz, in *Grundriss der Socialökpnomik*, pp. 145–46.

Chapter 3
The First World War

Introduction

The First World War remains one of the key watersheds in World History. The war destroyed empires, ushered in revolution, and resulted in more than fifteen million casualties. Few expected such results when hostilities started in August, 1914. Conventional wisdom held that industrial technology would make it a rapid war that would end within a few months, likely by Christmas. Unfortunately, the reality of two armies equipped with machine guns meeting on the battlefield was an almost immediate stalemate. Both sides dug into the ground for protection and fired machine guns and artillery from behind their defenses, leaving a narrow strip of land ("No Man's Land") in between them. While the four-year conflict was primarily fought in the trenches of a small amount of territory in northeastern France and Belgium, there were other theaters of conflict around the globe. Furthermore, the French and English brought men from Africa and Asia to fight on the battlefields and to work in the munitions factories. The war shattered European self-confidence and the cultural myths that supported its hegemony, creating a "lost generation" of disillusioned and alienated rebels who rejected the pre-war order. As the war occupied the attention of the governments in Europe, it created the opportunity for Japan to engage in imperial expansion in China, Turkish nationalists to pursue genocidal policies of ethnic cleansing in Anatolia, and various conquered people to challenge colonial rule. All of the belligerent governments in Europe, even republican France, became increasingly authoritarian as the war dragged on, expanding government controls and suspending various civil liberties. The First World War was crucial in creating the necessary conditions for a series of revolutions, most notably the Bolshevik seizure of power in Russia, but also the rise of Fascism in post-war Italy. These documents show how the horrors of trench warfare destroyed the previous century's romantic notions of chivalry and honor, pushed some towards increased political radicalism, and dealt a devastating psychological blow to its survivors.

This chapter relates to sections 10.5, 10.6, and 10.7 of the History-Social Science Content Standards for California Public Schools.

For All We Have and Are (1914)

By Rudyard Kipling

At the start of the war, Kipling, the great bard of the British Empire, seemed to jump on the patriotic bandwagon that swept England, as it did France and Germany. He invokes the term "the Hun" for the Germans, reflecting a lingering reaction to the Kaiser's "Hun Speech" of 1900. Yet Kipling acknowledges that the war will require sacrifice.

For all we have and are,
For all our children's fate,
Stand up and take the war.
The Hun is at the gate!
Our world has passed away,
In wantonness o'er thrown.
There is nothing left to-day
But steel and fire and stone!
Though all we knew depart,
The old Commandments stand–
"In courage keep your heart,
In strength lift up your hand."
Once more we hear the word
That sickened earth of old–
"No law except the Sword
Unsheathed and uncontrolled."
Once more it knits mankind,
Once more the nations go
To meet and break and bind
A crazed and driven foe.

Rudyard Kipling, "For All We Have and Are," *The Works of Rudyard Kipling*, pp. 329–330.

Comfort, content, delight,
The ages' slow-bought gain,
They shrivelled in a night.
Only ourselves remain
To face the naked days
In silent fortitude,
Through perils and dismays
Renewed and re-renewed.
Though all we made depart,
The old Commandments stand–
"In patience keep your heart,
In strength lift up your hand."
No easy hope or lies
Shall bring us to our goal,
But iron sacrifice
Of body, will, and soul
There is but one task for all–
One life for each to give.
What stands if Freedom fall?
Who dies if England live?

V: The Soldier (1914)

By Rupert Brooke

Rupert Brooke (1887–1915) is best known for this saccharinely patriotic Petrarchan sonnet praising the British war effort. With strikingly boyish good looks, he became a darling of the early 20th century London literary scene. His naïve and Pollyanna-ish approach to what would turn out to be four years of industrialized mass murder captured the initial romanticism and optimism of 1914. However, this romanticism would not survive as the horrors of the war revealed themselves. Nor did Brooke survive. While on route to the disastrous Gallipoli he was bitten by a mosquito, contracted sepsis, and died on a French hospital ship in the Aegean. He got his wish and was buried in an olive grove on the island of Skyros, Greece, making it forever England.

If I should die, think only this of me:
That there's some corner of a foreign field
That is for ever England. There shall be
In that rich earth a richer dust concealed;
A dust whom England bore, shaped, made aware,
Gave, once, her flowers to love, her ways to roam,
A body of England's, breathing English air,
Washed by the rivers, blest by suns of home.

And think, this heart, all evil shed away,
A pulse in the eternal mind, no less
Gives somewhere back the thoughts by England given;
Her sights and sounds; dreams happy as her day;
And laughter, learnt of friends; and gentleness,
In hearts at peace, under an English heaven.

Rupert Brooke, "V: The Soldier."

In Flanders Fields (1915)

By John McCrae

John Alexander McCrae (1872–1918) was a Canadian physician who served in the British army as a surgeon in the war. After the 1915 death of what some say was a former student, he penned this poem and published it anonymously in the British journal Punch. It soon became widely popular. McCrae continued to serve until his death in 1918 from pneumonia. He was buried in Flanders.

In Flanders fields, the poppies blow
Between the crosses, row on row,
That mark our place; and in the sky
The larks, still bravely singing, fly
Scarce heard amid the guns below...
We are the Dead. Short days ago
We lived, felt dawn, saw sunset glow,
Loved, and were loved, and now we lie
In Flanders fields...
Take up our quarrel with the foe:
To you from failing hands, we throw
The torch; be yours to hold it high.
If ye break faith with us who die
We shall not sleep, though poppies grow
In Flanders fields...

John McCrae, "In Flanders Fields," Punch Magazine.

Chant of Hate

By Ernst Lissauer

Ernst Lissauer (1882–1937) was a German-Jewish poet and playwright who counted Stefan Zweig amongst his friends. A staunch nationalist, he coined the phrase "May God punish England." He wrote "Chant of Hate" in the heady days of 1914, but later came to regret its aggressive chauvinism.

French and Russian they matter not,
A blow for a blow and a shot for a shot;
We love them not, we hate them not,
We hold the Weichsel and Vosges-gate,
We have but one and only hate,
We love as one, we hate as one,
We have one foe and one alone.

He is known to you all, he is known to you all,
He crouches behind the dark grey flood,
Full of envy, of rage, of craft, of gall,
Cut off by waves that are thicker than blood,
Come, let us stand at the Judgment place,
An oath to swear to, face to face,
An oath of bronze no wind can shake,
An oath for our sons and their sons to take.
Come, hear the word, repeat the word,
Throughout the Fatherland make it heard.

We will never forego our hate,
We have but one single hate,

Ernst Lissauer, "Chant of Hate."

We love as one, we hate as one,
We have one foe, and one alone --
ENGLAND!

Take you the folk of the Earth in pay,
With bars of gold your ramparts lay,
Bedeck the ocean with bow on bow,
Ye reckon well, but not well enough now.
French and Russian, they matter not,
A blow for a blow, a shot for a shot,
We fight the battle with bronze and steel,
And the time that is coming Peace will seal.
You we will hate with a lasting hate,
We will never forego our hate,
Hate by water and hate by land,
Hate of the head and hate of the hand,
Hate of the hammer and hate of the crown,
Hate of seventy millions choking down.
We love as one, we hate as one,
We have one foe and one alone—
ENGLAND!

The War as the Catharsis of Italian Society

By Filippo Tommaso Marinetti

Filippo Tommaso Marinetti (1876–1944) was an Italian poet, editor, and fascist activist. He is most famous for founding the Futurist movement in 1909. The Futurists rejected what they saw as Italy's stale culture of relics and bourgeois values. They would later gravitate to Mussolini's cult of nationalism, masculinity, and risk-taking (captured in Il Duce's call to "live dangerously"). When war broke out in 1914, the Italian government did not honor its treaty obligations to Germany and Austria-Hungary. However, in 1915 Italy was lured into the war on the side of England, France, and Russia by promises of land annexations along the Adriatic coast. Marinetti, like other Futurists and future Fascists, welcome the war and saw it as a way to revive the Italian nation.

Italian students!

Since an illustrious past was crushing Italy and an infinitely more glorious future seethed in her breast, six years ago, under our all too voluptuous skies, Futurist energy was to be born, to organize itself, to be channelled, to find in us her motors, her vehicles of illumination and propagation. Italy, more than any other country, was in dire need of Futurism, because she was dying of pastism. The patient invented its own remedy. *We happen to be its doctors.* The remedy is valid for any country.

Our immediate programme was a relentless war against Italian pastism: archaeology, academicism, senilism, quietism, the obsession with sex, the tourist industry, etc. Our ultra-violent, anti-clerical, and anti-traditionalist nationalism is based on the inexhaustible vitality of Italian blood and the struggle against the ancestor-cult, which, far from cementing the race, makes it anaemic and putrid. But we were to move

Filippo T. Marinetti; Roger Griffin, ed., "The War as the Catharsis of Italian Society," *Fascism*, pp. 25-26. Copyright © 1995 by Oxford University Press.

beyond this immediate programme, already (partly) realized in six years of ceaseless battles. […]

Italian students!

Dynamic and aggressive, Futurism is now being fully realized in the great world war which it—alone—foresaw and glorified before it broke out. *The present war is the most beautiful Futurist poem which has so far been seen*; what Futurism signified was precisely the irruption of war into art, as embodied in the creation of the phenomenon of the Futurist Soiree (an extremely efficient means for propagating courage). Futurism was the militarization of innovating artists. Today we are witnessing an immense Futurist explosion of dynamic and aggressive contexts within which we soon wish to make our entrance and show what we are. […]

Fatherland = expansion + multiplication of the *ego*. Italian patriotism = to contain and feel in oneself the whole of Italy and all the Italians of tomorrow.

The War will sweep from power all her foes: diplomats, professors, philosophers, archaeologists, critics, cultural obsession, Greek, Latin, history, senilism, museums, libraries, the tourist industry. The War will promote gymnastics, sport, practical schools of agriculture, business, and industrialists. The War will rejuvenate Italy, will enrich her with men of action, will force her to live no longer off the past, off ruins and the mild climate, but off her own national forces.

21 Demands on China

By Japanese Government

During the First World War, as Europe's attention was taken off Africa and Asia, Japan saw an opportunity. During Prime Minister Okuma Shigenobu's second administration, the Japanese government presented the fragile Chinese republic with a series of demands. The measures would make Japan a hegemonic power in Northeast China. Weakened by the Western intervention (which included opium trafficking), economic chaos, and civil war, China was in no position to stand up to Japan. However, after the war, the United States and England pushed to annul the 21 Demands at the Washington Conference of 1921–22. Nonetheless, the demands were part of two generations of Japanese expansion in East Asia, which included the Sino-Japanese War (1894–1895), the Russo-Japanese War (1904–1905), the annexation of Korea (1910), the seizure of Manchuria (1931), the invasion of China (1937–1945), and finally the occupation of Southeast Asia (1941–1945).

GROUP I

The Japanese Government and the Chinese Government, being desirous to maintain the general peace in the Far East and to strengthen the relations of amity and good neighbourhood existing between the two countries, agree to the following articles:

Article 1

The Chinese Government engage to give full assent to all matters that the Japanese Government may hereafter agree with the German Government respecting the disposition of all the rights, interests and concessions, which, in virtue of treaties or otherwise, Germany possesses vis-à-vis China in relation to the province of Shantung.

"21 Demands on China."

Article 2

The Chinese Government engage that, within the province of Shantung or along its coast, no territory or island will be ceded or leased to any other Power, under any pretext whatever.

Article 3

The Chinese Government agree to Japan's building a railway connecting Chefoo or Lungkow with the Kiaochou Tsinanfu Railway.

Article 4

The Chinese Government engage to open of their own accord, as soon as possible, certain important cities and towns in the Province of Shantung for the residence and commerce of foreigners. The places to be so opened shall be decided upon in a separate agreement.

GROUP II

The Japanese Government and the Chinese Government, in view of the fact that the Chinese Government has always recognized the predominant position of Japan in South Manchuria and Eastern Inner Mongolia, agree to the following articles:

Article 1

The two contracting Parties mutually agree that the term of the lease of Port Arthur and Dairen and the term respecting the South Manchuria Railway and the Antung-Mukden Railway shall be extended to a further period of 99 years respectively.

Article 2

The Japanese subjects shall be permitted in South Manchuria and Eastern Inner Mongolia to lease or own land required either for erecting buildings for various commercial and industrial uses or for farming.

Article 3

The Japanese subjects shall have liberty to enter, reside, and travel in South Manchuria and Eastern Inner Mongolia, and to carry on business of various kinds commercial, industrial, and otherwise.

Article 4

The Chinese Government grant to the Japanese subjects the right of mining in South Manchuria and Eastern Inner Mongolia. As regards the mines to be worked, they shall be decided upon in a separate agreement.

Article 5

The Chinese Government agree that the consent of the Japanese Government shall be obtained in advance:

1. (1) whenever it is proposed to grant to other nationals the right of constructing a railway or to obtain from other nationals the supply of funds for constructing a railway in South Manchuria and Eastern Inner Mongolia, and (2) whenever a loan is to be made with any other Power, under security of the taxes of South Manchuria and Eastern Inner Mongolia.

Article 6

The Chinese Government engage that whenever the Chinese Government need the service of political, financial, or military advisers or instructors in South Manchuria or in Eastern Inner Mongolia, Japan shall first be consulted.

Article 7

The Chinese Government agree that the control and management of the Kirin-Chungchun Railway shall be handed over to Japan for a term of 99 years dating from the signing of this treaty.

GROUP III

The Japanese Government and the Chinese Government, having regard to the close relations existing between Japanese capitalists and the Han-Yeh-Ping Company and desiring to promote the common interests of the two nations, agree to the following articles:

Article 1

The two Contracting Parties mutually agree that when the opportune moment arrives the Han-Yeh-Ping Company shall be made a joint concern of the two nations, and that, without the consent of the Japanese Government, the Chinese Government shall not dispose or permit the Company to dispose of any right or property of the Company.

Article 2

The Chinese Government engage that, as a necessary measure for protection of the invested interests of Japanese capitalists, no mines in the neighbourhood of those owned by the Han-Yeh-Ping Company shall be permitted, without the consent of the said Company, to be worked by anyone other than the Said Company; and further that whenever it is proposed to take any other measure which may likely affect the interests of the said Company directly or indirectly, the consent of the said Company shall first be obtained.

GROUP IV

The Japanese Government and the Chinese Government, with the object of effectively preserving the territorial integrity of China, agree to the following article: The Chinese Government engage not to cede or lease to any other Power any harbour or bay on or any island along the coast of China.

GROUP V

Article 1

The Chinese Central Government to engage influential Japanese as political, financial, and military advisers.

Article 2

The Chinese Government to grant the Japanese hospitals, temples, and schools in the interior of China the right to own land.

Article 3

In the face of many police disputes which have hitherto arisen between Japan and China, causing no little annoyance the police in localities (in China), where such arrangement: are necessary, to be placed under joint Japanese and Chinese administration, or Japanese to be employed in police office in such localities, so as to help at the same time the improvement of the Chinese Police Service.

Article 4

China to obtain from Japan supply of a certain quantity of arms, or to establish an arsenal in China under joint Japanese and Chinese management and to be supplied with experts and materials from Japan.

Article 5

In order to help the development of the Nanchang-Kiukiang Railway, with which Japanese capitalists are so closely identified, and with due regard to the negotiations which have been pending between Japan and China in relation to the railway question in South China, China to agree to give to Japan the right of constructing a railway to connect Wuchang with the Kiukiang-Nanchang and Hangchou and between Nanchang and Chaochou.

Article 6

In view of the relations between the Province of Fukien and Formosa and of the agreement respecting the non-alienation of that province, Japan to be consulted first whenever foreign capital is needed in connection with the railways, mines, and harbour works (including dockyards) in the Province of Fukien.

Article 7

China to grant to Japanese subjects the right of preaching in China.

Chinese Reply to Japanese Ultimatum, 8 May 1915

On the 7th of this month, at three o'clock P.M., the Chinese Government received an Ultimatum from the Japanese Government together with an Explanatory Note of seven articles.

The Ultimatum concluded with the hope that the Chinese Government by six o'clock P.M. on the 9th of May will give a satisfactory reply, and it is hereby declared that if no satisfactory reply is received before or at the specified time, the Japanese Government will take steps she may deem necessary.

The Chinese Government with a view to preserving the peace of the Far East hereby accepts, with the exception of those five articles of Group V postponed for later negotiations, all the articles of Groups I, II, III, and IV and the exchange of notes in connection with Fukien Province in Group V as contained in the revised proposals presented on the 26th of April, and in accordance with the Explanatory Note of seven articles accompanying the Ultimatum of the Japanese Government with the hope that thereby all the outstanding questions are settled, so that the cordial relationship between the two countries may be further consolidated.

The Japanese Minister is hereby requested to appoint a day to call at the Ministry of Foreign Affairs to make the literary improvement of the text and sign the Agreement as soon as possible.

Report on the Deportation of Armenians from Zeitun, July 21, 1915

Henry Morgenthau

The following three documents are reports from the Armenian Genocide. The conventional dates for this genocide are 1915–1917, but this was merely a high point in some two decades of state-sponsored ethnic violence against several minority populations. By the advent of the First World War, the Ottoman Empire was a pale shadow of its previous glory. Ottoman territory in Europe had been lost to either the Austro-Hungarian or Russian Empires or had won independence. British, French, and Italians had colonized the Ottoman holdings in North Africa and during the war British agents (including the infamous T.E. Lawrence, aka "Lawrence of Arabia") encouraged various Arab tribes to revolt. Recognizing the need for reform and renovation, a faction of secular nationalists and army officers known as the Young Turks seized effective control of the government. As part of their program to strengthen the Turkish state, they sought to eliminate what they saw as troublesome minorities from the Anatolian Peninsula. Thus, there was an orchestrated campaign against Armenians, Greeks, Assyrians, and other smaller groups. The primary goal was to purge and purify the Turkish state. The attacks included expulsions, such as forcing Greeks across the border, and outright massacres. The Armenians suffered the most, with deaths estimated between one and one and a half million. The Turkish Republic that came to power after the post-war collapse of the empire has denied that the events were a genocide, going so far as to consider banning Arnold Schwarzenegger's movies from Turkish television in protest of the California governor's use of the term "genocide" and his declaration of "Days of Remembrance" in 2006.

Henry Morgenthau, "Report on the Deportation of Armenians from Zeitun, July 21, 1915."

American Embassy,
Constantinople
July 21, 1915
The Honorable
The Secretary of State,
Washington.

Sir:-

I have the honor to transmit herewith two copies of a report received from the American Consul General at Beirut relative to what has been going on in the Zeitoon region of Asiatic Turkey.

I have the honor to be, Sir,

Your obedient servant,

(signed) [U.S. Ambassador to the Ottoman Empire, Henry] Morgenthau

Enclosure: Two copies dated June 20.

Duplicate

A BRIEF STATEMENT OF THE PRESENT SITUATION OF THE ARMENIAN EXILES IN THIS REGION, JUNE 20, 1915.

The deportation began some six weeks ago, with 180 families from Zeitoon; since which time, all the inhabitants of that place and its neighboring villages have been deported: also most of the Christians in Albustan, many from Hadgin, Sis, Kars Pasar, Hassan Beyli and Deort Yol.

The numbers involved are approximately, to date, 26,500. Of these about 5,000 have been sent to the Konieh region, 5,500 are in Aleppo and surrounding towns and villages; and the remainder are in Der Zor, Racca, and various places in Mesopotamia, even as far as the neighborhood of Baghdad.

The process is still going on, and there is no telling how far it may be carried, the orders already issued will bring the number in this region up to 32,000, and there have been as yet none exiled from Aintab, and very few from Marash and Oorfah. The following is the text of the Government order covering the case. Art. 2nd. "The Commanders of the Army, of independent army corps and of divisions may, in case of military necessity and in case they suspect espionage or treason, send away, either or in mass, the inhabitants of villages and towns, and install them in other places."

The orders of Commanders may have been reasonably humane, but the execution of them has been for the most part unnecessarily harsh, and in many cases accompanied by horrible brutality to women and children, to the sick and the aged. Whole villages were deported at an hours notice, with no opportunity to prepare for the journey, not even in some cases to gather together the scattered members of the family, so that little children were left behind. At the mountain village of Geben the women were at the wash tub, and were compelled to leave their wet clothes in the water, and take the road barefooted and half clad just as they were. In some cases they were able to carry part of their scanty household furniture, or implements of agriculture, but for the most part they were neither to carry anything nor to sell it, even where there was time to do so.

In Hadgin well-to-do people, who had prepared food and bedding for the road, were obliged to leave it in the street, and afterward suffered greatly from hunger.

In many cases the men were (those of military age were nearly all in the army) bound tightly together with ropes or chains. Women with little children in their arms, or in the last days of pregnancy were driven along under the whip like cattle. Three different cases came under my knowledge where the woman was delivered on the road, and because her brutal driver hurried her along she died of hemorrhage. I also know of one case where the gendarme in charge was a humane man, and allowed the poor woman several hours rest and then procured a wagon for her to ride in. Some women became so completely worn out and hopeless that they left their infants beside the road. Many women and girls have been outraged. At one place the commander of the gendarmerie openly told the men to whom he consigned a large company, that they were at liberty to do what they choose with the women and girls.

As to subsistence, there has been a great difference in different places. In some places the Government has fed them, in some places it has permitted the inhabitants to feed them. In some places it has neither fed them nor permitted others to do so. There has been much hunger, thirst and sickness and some real starvation, and death.

These people are being scattered in small units, three or four families in a place, among a population of different race and religion, and speaking a different language. I speak of them as being composed of families, but four fifths of them are women and children, and what men there are for the most part old or incompetent.

If a means is not found to aid them through the next few months, until they get established in their new surroundings, two thirds or three fourths of them will die of starvation and disease.

First-Hand Account by a Turkish Army Officer on the Deportation of Armenians from Trebizond and Erzerum, December 26, 1916

By Lieutenant Sayied Ahmed Moukhtar Baas

In April 1915 I was quartered at Erzerum. An order came from Constantinople that Armenians inhabiting the frontier towns and village be deported to the interior. It was said then that this was only a precautional measure. I saw at that time large convoys of Armenians go through Erzerum. They were mostly old men, women and children. Some of the able-bodied men had been recruited in the Turkish Army and many had fled to Russia. The massacres had not begun yet. In May 1915 I was transferred to Trebizond. In July an order came to deport to the interior all the Armenians in the Vilayet of Trebizond. Being a member of the Court Martial I knew that deportations meant massacres.

The Armenian Bishop of Trebizond was ordered to proceed under escort to Erzerum to answer for charges trumped up against him. But instead of Erzerum he was taken to Baipurt and from there to Gumush-Khana. The Governor of the latter place was then Colonel Abdul-Kadar Aintabli of the General Staff. He is famous for his atrocities against the Armenians. He had the Bishop murdered at night. The Bishop of Erzerum was also murdered at Gumush-Khana.

Besides the deportation order referred to above an Imperial "Iradeh" was issued ordering that all deserters when caught, should be shot without trial. The secret order read "Armenians" in lieu of "deserters." The Sultan's "Iradeh" was accompanied by a "fatwa" from Sheikh-ul-Islam stating that the Armenians had shed Moslem blood

Lieutenant Sayied Ahmed Moukhtar Baas, "First-Hand Account by a Turkish Army Officer on the Deportation of Armenians from Trebizond and Erzerum, December 26, 1916."

and their killing was lawful. Then the deportations started. The children were kept back at first. The Government opened up a school for the grown up children and the American Consul of Trebizond instituted an asylum for the infants. When the first batches of Armenians arrived at Gumush-Khana all able-bodied men were sorted out with the excuse that they were going to be given work. The women and children were sent ahead under escort with the assurance by the Turkish authorities that their final destination was Mosul and that no harm will befall them. The men kept behind, were taken out of town in batches of 15 and 20, lined up on the edge of ditches prepared beforehand, shot and thrown into the ditches. Hundreds of men were shot every day in a similar manner. The women and children were attacked on their way by the ("Shotas") the armed bands organised by the Turkish Government who attacked them and seized a certain number. After plundering and committing the most dastardly outrages on the women and children they massacred them in cold blood. These attacks were a daily occurrence until every woman and child had been got rid of. The military escorts had strict orders not to interfere with the "Shotas."

The children that the Government had taken in charge were also deported and massacred.

The infants in the care of the American Consul of Trebizond were taken away with the pretext that they were going to be sent to Sivas where an asylum had been prepared for them. They were taken out to sea in little boats. At some distance out they were stabbed to death, put in sacks, and thrown into the sea. A few days later some of their little bodies were washed up on the shore at Trebizond.

In July 1915 I was ordered to accompany a convoy of deported Armenians. It was the last batch from Trebizond. There were in the convoy 120 men, 700 children and about 400 women. From Trebizond I took them to Gumish-Khana. Here the 120 men were taken away, and, as I was informed later, they were all killed. At Gumish-Khana I was ordered to take the women and children to Erzinjian. On the way I saw thousands of bodies of Armenians unburied. Several bands of "Shotas" met us on the way and wanted me to hand over to them women and children. But I persistently refused. I did leave on the way about 300 children with Moslem families who were willing to take care of them and educate them. The "Mutessarrif" of Erzinjian ordered me to proceed with the convoy to Kamack. At the latter place the authorities refused to take charge of the women and children. I fell ill and wanted to go back, but I was told that as long as the Armenians in my charge were alive I would be sent from one place to the other. However I managed to include my batch with the deported Armenians that had come from Erzerum. In charge of the latter was a colleague of mine Mohamed Effendi from the Gendarmerie. He told me afterwards that after leaving Kamach they came to a valley where the Euphrates ran. A band of Shotas sprang out and stopped the convoy. They ordered the escort to keep away and then shot every one of the Armenians and threw them in the river.

At Trebizond the Moslems were warned that if they sheltered Armenians they would be liable to the death penalty.

Government officials at Trebizond picked up some of the prettiest Armenian women of the best families. After committing the worst outrages on them they had them killed.

Cases of rape of women and girls even publicly are very numerous. They were systematically murdered after the outrage.

The Armenians deported from Erzerum started with their cattle and whatever possessions they could carry. When they reached Erzinjian they became suspicious seeing that all the Armenians had already been deported. The Vali of Erzerum allayed their fears and assured them most solemnly that no harm would befall them. He told them that the first convoy should leave for Kamach, the others remaining at Erzerum until they received word from their friends informing of their safe arrival to destination. And so it happened. Word came that the first batch had arrived safely at Kamach, which was true enough. But the men were kept at Kamach and shot, and the women were massacred by the Shotas after leaving that town.

The Turkish officials in charge of the deportation and extermination of the Armenians were: At Erzerum, Bihas Eddin Shaker Bey; At Trebizond; Naiil Bey, Tewfik Bey Monastirly, Colonel of Gendarmerie, The Commissioner of Police; At Kamach; The member of Parliament for Erzinjian. The Shotas headquarters were also at Kamach. Their chief was the Kurd Murzabey who boasted that he alone had killed 70,000 Armenians. Afterwards he was thought to be dangerous by the Turks and thrown into prison charged with having hit a gendarme. He was eventually executed in secret.

Report on the Massacre of Armenians in Cilicia Under French Administration, March 7, 1920

By Admiral de Robeck

Decypher, Admiral de Robeck, (Constantinople),

March 7th, 1920.
D. 4.20. p.m. March 7th. 1920.
R. 5.45. p.m. March 8th. 1920.
No. 200. (R).

Following for Mr. Aneurin Williams M.P. is transmitted at request of W.A. Kennedy. Message begins.

No. 5. Confirmation of news of Marash: 18,000 massacred in district: city burnt and without supplies and has not been relieved: 2,000 refugees have reached Adana: 13,000 women and children perished in snow-storm on way there: 8,000 Armenians still in Marash of whom many are wounded: Hadjia Zeitoun isolated: Adana, Tarsus not immediately threatened, but anxious and unsettled: no confidence of security in district. Message ends.

I submit any appearance of official confirmation of this message should be guarded against. We have no information other than that already telegraphed. French, as previously stated, are very reticent but take the line that loss of life is to be ascribed to casualties incident to hostilities and subsequent withdrawal rather than to <u>massacre</u>.

Admiral de Robeck, "Report on the Massacre of Armenians in Cilicia under French Administration, March 7, 1920."

The Junius Pamphlet: The Crisis of German Social Democracy (excerpts)

By Rosa Luxemburg

Rosa Luxemburg (1871–1919) was born to a Jewish family in the part of Poland under Russian imperial control until the First World War. Fleeing the repressive Russian regime, she immigrated to Switzerland where she studied law and political economy. Later she would marry a German to attain citizenship. As a young woman she encountered many revolutionary intellectuals living in exile or in the underground. Quickly she proved herself to be a formidable intellectual. Inspired by the work of Karl Marx, she published several well-regarded works including a critique of capitalism and imperialism that preceded Lenin's study of the subject. She joined the German Social Democratic Party but gravitated toward its far-left faction. She was openly suspicious and critical of Lenin's revolutionary methods, noting that his theory of party organization would make it authoritarian and undemocratic. When the war broke out in 1914 she was horrified that most socialists reneged on the previous pacifist pledge and supported the war. In disgust, Luxemburg and Karl Liebknecht formed a secret group called the Spartacus League. This 1915 pamphlet states her critique of international revolutionary socialism. In 1916 the Spartacus League staged an open protest against the war. German authorities promptly arrested Luxemburg and Liebknecht. In jail she continued to write. When she received news of the Bolshevik seizure of power, she condemned Lenin's use of military force. Released from prison in October 1918, she argued against staging a Bolshevik style coup by the league, which was soon to become the German Communist Party. While she lost the vote, she participated in the January, 1919 revolt against the new German government. Chancellor Friedrich Ebert, leader of the moderate Social Democratic Party, formed an alliance with the German army and paramilitary groups known as the Freikorps to quickly crush the rebellion. The Freikorps, precursors to the fascists, are believed to have murdered Luxemburg and Liebknecht, throwing her body in a Berlin canal. The 1919 events led to an irreparable schism between

Rosa Luxemburg; Dave Hollis, trans., *Selections from The Junius Pamphlet: The Crisis of German Social Democracy*. Licensed by the GNU Free Documentation License.

moderate socialists and the more radical communist movement, thus dividing the left until the rise of Adolf Hitler.

The scene has changed fundamentally. The six weeks' march to Paris has grown into a world drama. Mass slaughter has become the tiresome and monotonous business of the day and the end is no closer. Bourgeois statecraft is held fast in its own vise. The spirits summoned up can no longer be exorcised.

Gone is the euphoria. Gone the patriotic noise in the streets, the chase after the gold-colored automobile, one false telegram after another, the wells poisoned by cholera, the Russian students heaving bombs over every railway bridge in Berlin, the French airplanes over Nuremberg, the spy hunting public running amok in the streets, the swaying crowds in the coffee shops with ear-deafening patriotic songs surging ever higher, whole city neighborhoods transformed into mobs ready to denounce, to mistreat women, to shout hurrah and to induce delirium in themselves by means of wild rumors. Gone, too, is the atmosphere of ritual murder, the Kishinev air where the crossing guard is the only remaining representative of human dignity.

The spectacle is over. German scholars, those "stumbling lemurs," have been whistled off the stage long ago. The trains full of reservists are no longer accompanied by virgins fainting from pure jubilation. They no longer greet the people from the windows of the train with joyous smiles. Carrying their packs, they quietly trot along the streets where the public goes about its daily business with aggrieved visages.

In the prosaic atmosphere of pale day there sounds a different chorus—the hoarse cries of the vulture and the hyenas of the battlefield. Ten thousand tarpaulins guaranteed up to regulations! A hundred thousand kilos of bacon, cocoa powder, coffee-substitute—c.o.d., immediate delivery! Hand grenades, lathes, cartridge pouches, marriage bureaus for widows of the fallen, leather belts, jobbers for war orders—serious offers only! The cannon fodder loaded onto trains in August and September is moldering in the killing fields of Belgium, the Vosges, and Masurian Lakes where the profits are springing up like weeds. It's a question of getting the harvest into the barn quickly. Across the ocean stretch thousands of greedy hands to snatch it up.

Business thrives in the ruins. Cities become piles of ruins; villages become cemeteries; countries, deserts; populations are beggared; churches, horse stalls. International law, treaties and alliances, the most sacred words and the highest authority have been torn in shreds. Every sovereign "by the grace of God" is called a rogue and lying scoundrel by his cousin on the other side. Every diplomat is a cunning rascal to his colleagues in the other party. Every government sees every other as dooming its own people and worthy only of universal contempt. There are food riots in Venice, in Lisbon, Moscow, Singapore. There is plague in Russia, and misery and despair everywhere.

Violated, dishonored, wading in blood, dripping filth—there stands bourgeois society. This is it [in reality]. Not all spic and span and moral, with pretense to culture, philosophy, ethics, order, peace, and the rule of law—but the ravening beast, the witches' sabbath of anarchy, a plague to culture and humanity. Thus it reveals itself in its true, its naked form.

In the midst of this witches' sabbath a catastrophe of world-historical proportions has happened: International Social Democracy has capitulated. To deceive ourselves about it, to cover it up, would be the most foolish, the most fatal thing the proletariat could do. Marx says: "…the democrat (that is, the petty bourgeois revolutionary) [comes] out of the most shameful defeats as unmarked as he naïvely went into them; he comes away with the newly gained conviction that he must be victorious, not that he or his party ought to give up the old principles, but that conditions ought to accommodate him." The modern proletariat comes out of historical tests differently. Its tasks and its errors are both gigantic: no prescription, no schema valid for every case, no infallible leader to show it the path to follow. Historical experience is its only school mistress. Its thorny way to self-emancipation is paved not only with immeasurable suffering but also with countless errors. The aim of its journey—its emancipation depends on this—is whether the proletariat can learn from its own errors. Self-criticism, remorseless, cruel, and going to the core of things is the life's breath and light of the proletarian movement. The fall of the socialist proletariat in the present world war is unprecedented. It is a misfortune for humanity. But socialism will be lost only if the international proletariat fails to measure the depth of this fall, if it refuses to learn from it.

Letter to Wife

By Peter Hammerer

The following documents show the intense psychological stress suffered by many soldiers in the First World War. Trench warfare shattered the minds of men on both sides of the lines, leading to a new medical condition called "Shell Shock," which we now identify as "Post-Traumatic Stress Disorder."

Letter from Peter Hammerer (November 3, 1916) to his wife Rosina Hammerer in Haslach near Kempten (Allgau), Post Wertach

Written on November 3, 1916.

My dearest wife Rosina,

I'm letting you know I received your letter of October 23, 1916. Dear wife those things that that you sent through Michael Mayer sure tasted good. The big package. Dear wife don't send things so large any more as that is much too expensive. Dear Frau Rosina, I sent you a card on October 23 and those in the post office in Haslach have sent it back to me and written on it unknown. You are not in Haslach. Is that not a mean lot and they know you so well—you can see what sort of help you have there my dear wife. What sort of misery you are going to have when you go into childbed this month and I am not going to be there. No help but the children. And the devil's swindle doesn't stop. Although I think about it all the time, I running out of answers what to do as to you. Dear Frau Rosina, here the sons-of-bitches write you're getting so much help and get so much, the swindle nation. Dear wife, just like those crucifix bandits wrote that I wasn't doing anything—just getting drunk all the time.

I'm supposed to give my life here for such bandits. No, they shall give their own lives. I get nothing from them—only harm. Dear wife, let things go their own way—I've had enough. I stayed with you several extra days and now I have received two months jail. It's just as well. Dear Frau Rosina I know my own thoughts. I told it to them in the trial. I want to be let out. I don't want to have anything more to do with this misery. This must be the payment for the years when we were protecting the Big Capitalists, protecting their stuff. Let them protect it themselves and not send people out who have to go out and make a living. I have nothing from this and I want nothing more than to just come home to you. It's been over two years of trouble and misery now for you and the children and me. I have nothing to defend. Now I just want to make my own money, be on my own. I get nothing from them but hunger and misery. They don't give us nothing more to eat than goulash, and there's only potatoes in it—the rest of the goulash gets eaten by those who are behind the front. They hold their heads in a way that isn't pretty and get the big money on top of it. Dear wife, you can't imagine how bad it is here for us and every day it just keeps getting worse. It's the same inside and outside. You saw it in Kempten already. The Big Shots—they have more meat to gouge themselves on than a shepherd could jump over. And inside it's the same. Dear wife, let me just tell you, the ones in prison are much better off than we are here. It's said that he in the "field" deserves double rations and nothing to eat but potatoes and cabbage. It's because of them. They got big money and better food so that they can turn the crew into fools. But that's over. Everybody knows it's a lie, a swindle. Many warm greetings from your dear husband. I hope to see you soon.

[on a different piece of paper, same place and time:] Dear Frau Rosina, I am telling you again, let me know when you don't have a mark any more. If you should be really bad off I will come to you immediately no matter what happens. They should stop or let me go—either let me out or stop. They'll keep fighting for years because they are getting something out of it. Many of them have become rich through the war and there are still a lot that want to become rich and those are the ones we have to be there for and I am sick and tired of it. Let them go into the trenches themselves and not send us poor people in for them. One hears that at every front and everyone says the war is there only for the large capitalists so that their stuff doesn't go kaput and that these and no one else are the guilty ones for the war going on so long. Because they are profiting from it. They receive a cost of living allowance out here and at home the poor women with their children only receive a few marks. Why's that? If there was a God than he would have taken care of this long ago, but there isn't one—that's the conclusion—I guess that's what you got to think. I have seen enough and heard enough and stuck it out long enough and I, too, don't want no more third winter—I want to be let out."

Expert Medical Report by Senior Physician [*Oberarzt*] and Battalion Physician Dr. Kaindl of the First Battalion of the Twelfth Reserve Infantry Regiment concerning Soldier Peter Hammerer, April 21, 1916, to the First Battalion of the L.I.R. 12:

The examination of Reserve Soldier Peter Hammerer 1. Komp. Ldw. Inf. Rgts. No. 12 produced no evidence of either bodily ailments or phenomena indicating degenerative processes; nor did it show any deviations that would allow me to conclude that there was either a weakened nervous system or neurological deficiencies of any form.

Hammerer's physique is well-proportioned; his nutritional status and development is good; the sensory organs are without any noticeable defects. His knee reflexes showed themselves to be much faster than normal when tested, so that one can assume there are concealed irregularities in his nervous system. He is quite obviously easily excitable, with an accompanying reddening of the face. These are phenomena that would permit me to conclude that his nervous system has some blood congestion toward the head or toward the central nervous system.

He stated that he was not an alcoholic and that he has no contagious sexual diseases. Furthermore he explained that he already gets "wild" [*rapiadisch*] after a few beers.

He does not sleep well, often falling asleep only in the morning. He suffers often from nightmares. Often he suffers from vertigo, which is probably the result of the congestion mentioned above.

Clear indications for judging the mental condition of the soldier Hammerer can be derived from the family history of the accused.

The father of the accused—also a basket maker—is still alive and is supposedly an alcoholic who has repeatedly gotten into trouble with the law on account of fights.

His grandfather on his mother's side supposedly committed suicide; his grandmother was supposedly insane in her later years.

In summary, to conclude on the basis of the objective findings, and provided that the evidence given was true, it can be presumed that:

1. Hammerer received an insufficient and probably quite inadequate education and therefore does not possess the important character traits that are necessary to lead an ordered life.
2. Hammerer is a good example of a very excitable person who has no educative or moral footing, who is afflicted with a complete lack of self-control.
3. Hammerer has a genetic burden both from his father and his maternal grandparents.
4. On account of the nature of his occupation (an itinerant trade, which his father also practiced) and his insufficient education, Hammerer does not possess those ideal life characteristics that are absolutely necessary for a good soldierly spirit.

To put it briefly:

Hammerer is an inferior, weak-willed, weak-minded, easily excitable individual with few morals, and without any firm view of life or sense of duty. These characteristics need to be taken into consideration in making a judgment. They do not, however, allow him to be classified as beyond responsibility or mentally incompetent.

Dr. Kaindl.

Addenda:

I think it is worth mentioning in regard to making a judgment on Hammerer that already as a pupil who only went to school on the holidays [*Feiertagsschüler*] he had attacked his teacher and was therefore punished with expulsion.

Dr. Kaindl.

Dulce et Decorum Est (1917)

By Wilfred Owen

Wilfred Owen's (1893–1918) poetry stands in sharp contrast to the syrupy and patriotic verses of Rupert Brooke. Initially, Owen was an optimistic volunteer in 1915, but the reality of trench warfare shattered that attitude. After two harrowing events in the trenches, he was diagnosed with "Shell Shock" and hospitalized. As part of his therapy he wrote poetry about life in the trenches. He went back to the front in 1918, only to be shot and killed on November 4, 1918, exactly a week before the armistice ended hostilities.

BENT double, like old beggars under sacks,
Knock-kneed, coughing like hags, we cursed through sludge,
Till on the haunting flares we turned our backs
And towards our distant rest began to trudge.
Men marched asleep. Many had lost their boots
But limped on, blood-shod. All went lame; all blind;
Drunk with fatigue; deaf even to the hoots
Of gas-shells dropping softly behind.

Gas! GAS! Quick, boys!—An ecstasy of fumbling
Fitting the clumsy helmets just in time,
But someone still was yelling out and stumbling
And flound'ring like a man in fire or lime.—
Dim, through the misty panes and thick green light,
As under a green sea, I saw him drowning.

Wilfred Owen, "Dulce Et Decorum Est," Poems by Wilfred Owen.

In all my dreams before my helpless sight
He plunges at me, guttering, choking, drowning.

If in some smothering dreams you too could pace
Behind the wagon that we flung him in,
And watch the white eyes writhing in his face,
His hanging face, like a devil's sick of sin,
If you could hear, at every jolt, the blood
Come gargling from the froth-corrupted lungs,
Bitter as the cud
Of vile, incurable sores on innocent tongues,—
My friend, you would not tell with such high zest
To children ardent for some desperate glory,
The old Lie: *Dulce et decorum est*
Pro patria mori.

Disabled (1917)

By Wilfred Owen

Wilfred Owen's (1893–1918) poetry stands in sharp contrast to the syrupy and patriotic verses of Rupert Brooke. Initially, Owen was an optimistic volunteer in 1915, but the reality of trench warfare shattered that attitude. After two harrowing events in the trenches, he was diagnosed with "Shell Shock" and hospitalized. As part of his therapy he wrote poetry about life in the trenches. He went back to the front in 1918, only to be shot and killed on November 4, 1918, exactly a week before the armistice ended hostilities.

HE sat in a wheeled chair, waiting for dark,
And shivered in his ghastly suit of grey,
Legless, sewn short at elbow. Through the park
Voices of boys rang saddening like a hymn,
Voices of play and pleasure after day,
Till gathering sleep had mothered them from him.
About this time Town used to swing so gay
When glow-lamps budded in the light blue trees,
And girls glanced lovelier as the air grew dim,
—In the old times, before he threw away his knees.
Now he will never feel again how slim
Girls' waists are, or how warm their subtle hands.
All of them touch him like some queer disease.
There was an artist silly for his face,
For it was younger than his youth, last year.
Now, he is old; his back will never brace;
He's lost his colour very far from here,
Poured it down shell-holes till the veins ran dry,
And half his lifetime lapsed in the hot race,

Wilfred Owen, "Disabled," *Poems by Wilfred Owen.*

And leap of purple spurted from his thigh.
One time he liked a bloodsmear down his leg,
After the matches carried shoulder-high.
It was after football, when he'd drunk a peg,
He thought he'd better join. He wonders why . . .
Someone had said he'd look a god in kilts.

That's why; and maybe, too, to please his Meg,
Aye, that was it, to please the giddy jilts,
He asked to join. He didn't have to beg;
Smiling they wrote his lie; aged nineteen years.
Germans he scarcely thought of; and no fears
Of Fear came yet. He thought of jewelled hilts
For daggers in plaid socks; of smart salutes;
And care of arms; and leave; and pay arrears;
Esprit de corps; and hints for young recruits.
And soon, he was drafted out with drums and cheers.

Some cheered him home, but not as crowds cheer Goal.
Only a solemn man who brought him fruits
Thanked him; and then inquired about his soul.
Now, he will spend a few sick years in Institutes,
And do what things the rules consider wise,
And take whatever pity they may dole.
To-night he noticed how the women's eyes
Passed from him to the strong men that were whole.
How cold and late it is! Why don't they come
And put him into bed? Why don't they come?

Over There (1917)

By George M. Cohan

While George M. Cohan (1878–1942) was born on July 3, 1878, to an Irish Catholic family of vaudeville performers, he frequently claimed that he was born on the Fourth of July. A leading Tin Pan Alley lyricist, Cohan penned numerous catchy patriotic songs such as "Over There," "The Yankee Doodle Boy," and "You're a Grand Old Flag." This song epitomizes the naïve optimism of Americans as they entered the war. It is fitting that Dalton Trumbo's anti-war novel Johnny Got His Gun *references Cohan's ditty in its title.*

Johnnie, get your gun,
Get your gun, get your gun,
Take it on the run,
On the run, on the run.
Hear them calling, you and me,
Every son of liberty.
Hurry right away,
No delay, go today,
Make your daddy glad
To have had such a lad.
Tell your sweetheart not to pine,
To be proud her boy's in line.
(chorus sung twice)

Johnnie, get your gun,
Get your gun, get your gun,
Johnnie show the Hun
Who's a son of a gun.
Hoist the flag and let her fly,

George M. Cohan, "Over There."

Yankee Doodle do or die.
Pack your little kit,
Show your grit, do your bit.
Yankee to the ranks,
From the towns and the tanks.
Make your mother proud of you,
And the old Red, White and Blue.
(chorus sung twice)

Chorus
Over there, over there,
Send the word, send the word over there—
That the Yanks are coming,
The Yanks are coming,
The drums rum-tumming
Ev'rywhere.
So prepare, say a pray'r,
Send the word, send the word to beware.
We'll be over, we're coming over,
And we won't come back till it's over
Over there.

Common Form (1918)

By Rudyard Kipling

Kipling's couplet captures the disillusion of many after the reality of the war set in. Kipling may have felt a special guilt as he encouraged his son to join the army, only to have him die in battle. While Kipling was not of the post-war generation, this poem captures the cynical alienation of the "Lost Generation."

If any question why we died,
Tell them because our fathers lied.

Rudyard Kipling, "Common Form."

The Stab in the Back

By Paul von Hindenburg

Field Marshall Paul von Hindenburg (1847–1934) was an aristocratic Prussian army officer in the German Empire. During World War One, Hindenburg and his deputy, Erich Friedrich Wilhelm Ludendorff (1865–1937) became the de facto military rulers of Germany, dictating policy to the Kaiser and silencing civilian politicians. They oversaw the years of brutal trench warfare in which hundreds of thousands of men died for gains measured in merely a few kilometers. When Hindenburg and Ludendorff realized that the arrival of American troops would turn the tide in what had become a stagnant war of attrition, the officers encouraged the Kaiser to hand power over to a new civilian administration in the fall of 1918. Essentially Hindenburg and Ludendorff lost the war but set up the civilian politicians to take the blame for the loss. While a bitter dispute erupted between the two men, they both perpetuated the myth that the German army could have won the war but that it was "stabbed in the back" by civilians. In the 1920s Ludendorff was involved in conspiracies to overthrow the new Weimar Republic, including backing Hitler. Hindenburg, despite being a firm monarchist who distrusted democracy, successfully ran for president in 1925. While he was distrustful of Hitler, he did appoint him to be Chancellor in 1933. The "Stab in the Back" myth was central to NAZI propaganda.

Testimony delivered on November 18, 1919.

> *General Field Marshall v. Hindenburg*: History will render the final judgment on that about which I may give no further details here. At the time we still hoped that the *will to victory* would dominate everything else. When we assumed our post we made a series of proposals to the Reich leadership which aimed at combining all forces at the nation's disposal for a quick and favorable conclusion to the war; at the same time, they demonstrated to the government its enormous tasks. What finally became of our proposals,

Paul von Hindenburg; Anton Kaes, Martin Jay and Edward Dimendberg, eds.; Don Reneau, trans., "The Stab in the Back," *The Weimar Republic Sourcebook*, pp. 15–16. Copyright © 1994 by the University of California Press. Reprinted with permission.

once again partially because of the influence of the parties, is known. I wanted forceful and cheerful cooperation and instead encountered failure and weakness.

Chairman: That, too, is a value judgment, against which I must enter a definite protest.

von Hindenburg: The concern as to whether the homeland would remain resolute until the war was won, from this moment on, never left us. We often raised a warning voice to the Reich government. At this time, the secret *intentional mutilation of the fleet and the army* began as a continuation of similar occurrences in peace time. The effects of these endeavors were not concealed from the supreme army command during the last year of the war. The obedient troops who remained immune to revolutionary attrition suffered greatly from the behavior, in violation of duty, of their revolutionary comrades; they had to carry the battle the whole time.

(Chairman's bell. Commotion and shouting.)

Chairman: Please continue, General Field Marshall.

von Hindenburg: The intentions of the command could no longer be executed. Our repeated proposals for strict discipline and strict legislation were not adopted. Thus did our operations necessarily miscarry; the *collapse* was inevitable; the …

An English general said with justice: "The German army was stabbed in the back." No guilt applies to the good core of the army. Its achievements are just as admirable as those of the officer corps. Where the guilt lies has clearly been demonstrated. If it needed more proof, then it would be found in the quoted statement of the English general and in the boundless astonishment of our enemies at their victory.

That is the general trajectory of the tragic development of the war for Germany, after a series of brilliant, unsurpassed successes on many fronts, following an accomplishment by the army and the people for which no praise is high enough. This trajectory had to be established so that the military measures for which we are responsible could be correctly evaluated.

Chapter 4

Revolution and Counter-Revolution

Introduction

The devastation and disillusionment of the First World War sowed the seeds of revolution. On both the far left and the far right, the war radicalized political figures from Lenin to Mussolini. For Communists the war was proof of capitalism's internal contradictions and the human suffering it would tolerate in the name of profits. In the name of ending the injustices of industrial-capitalism, the Soviet Union sought to organize a global revolution along the lines of Marxist-Leninism. The Communists viewed the moderate socialists who had supported the war as contemptuous traitors, thus creating a serious divide amongst the leftist parties. For Fascists the war was a nationalist utopia where life had purpose and everyone had a place. During Hitler's rise to power, he actively promoted nostalgia for the Great War and argued that German men needed to literally fight the Communist threat in the streets. A cult of violence and masculinity was central to Fascism. Meanwhile in Asia, Mao Zedong turned to the peasantry and began to reinvent Communism with Chinese characteristics. Mao's radical departure from Marxist orthodoxy would be the model for Third World revolutions from Vietnam to Peru. Thus the war contained many of the origins of what Hannah Arendt would describe as "Totalitarianism." These selections demonstrate the variety and intensity of political forces unleashed in the aftermath of World War One.

This chapter relates to sections 10.3, 10.6, and 10.7 of the History-Social Science Content Standards for California Public Schools.

The Tasks of the Proletariat in the Present Revolution (The April Theses, 1917)

By V. I. Lenin

From 1900 to 1917, aside from a brief return after the Revolution of 1905, Lenin lived in exile in Switzerland, the Austro-Hungarian Empire, and France. When war broke out, he moved to Geneva in neutral Switzerland where, like Rosa Luxemburg, he condemned the socialist parties' pledge at the Second International to oppose a general war in Europe. However, he urged that the socialists work to transform what he saw as an imperialist war into civil wars that would lead to global revolution. When the Tsar Nicholas II was overthrown in 1917, emissaries from Hindenburg and Ludendorff offered him transport in a secret sealed train across Germany and to Finland where he could sneak into Russia. The scheme was designed to use Lenin as a political hand grenade that would weaken Russia from within, allowing for German victory on the Eastern Front. Lenin accepted the offer and played his role, announcing his April Thesis on his arrival at the Finland Station. In this document he calls for an opposition to the war and to the Provisional Government then headed by Lvov. He also urged that power should go to the people organized into councils known as "soviets."

Introduction

I did not arrive in Petrograd until the night of April 3, and therefore at the meeting on April 4, I could, of course, deliver the report on the tasks of the revolutionary proletariat only on my own behalf, and with reservations as to insufficient preparation.

The only thing I could do to make things easier for myself—and for *honest* opponents—was to prepare the theses *in writing*. I read them out, and gave the text to

V.I. Lenin, "The Tasks of the Proletariat in the Present Revolution (The April Thesis)," <http://www.marxists.org>.

Comrade Tsereteli. I read them *twice* very slowly: first at a meeting of Bolsheviks and then at a meeting of both Bolsheviks and Mensheviks.

I publish these personal theses of mine with only the briefest explanatory notes, which were developed in far greater detail in the report.

THESES

1) In our attitude towards the war, which under the new [provisional] government of Lvov and Co., unquestionably remains on Russia's part a predatory imperialist war owing to the capitalist nature of that government, not the slightest concession to "revolutionary defencism" is permissible.

The class-conscious proletariat can give its consent to a revolutionary war, which would really justify revolutionary defencism, only on condition: (a) that the power pass to the proletariat and the poorest sections of the peasants aligned with the proletariat; (b) that all annexations be renounced in deed and not in word; (c) that a complete break be effected in actual fact with all capitalist interests.

In view of the undoubted honesty of those broad sections of the mass believers in revolutionary defencism who accept the war only as a necessity, and not as a means of conquest, in view of the fact that they are being deceived by the bourgeoisie, it is necessary with particular thoroughness, persistence and patience to explain their error to them, to explain the inseparable connection existing between capital and the imperialist war, and to prove that without overthrowing capital *it is impossible* to end the war by a truly democratic peace, a peace not imposed by violence.

The most widespread campaign for this view must be organised in the army at the front.

Fraternisation

2) The specific feature of the present situation in Russia is that the country is *passing* from the first stage of the revolution—which, owing to the insufficient class-consciousness and organisation of the proletariat, placed power in the hands of the bourgeoisie—to its *second stage*, which must place power in the hands of the proletariat and the poorest sections of the peasants.

This transition is characterised, on the one hand, by a maximum of legally recognised rights (Russia is *now* the freest of all the belligerent countries in the world); on the other, by the absence of violence towards the masses, and, finally, by their unreasoning trust in the government of capitalists, those worst enemies of peace and socialism.

This peculiar situation demands of us an ability to adapt ourselves to the *special* conditions of Party work among unprecedentedly large masses of proletarians who have just awakened to political life.

3) No support for the Provisional Government; the utter falsity of all its promises should be made clear, particularly of those relating to the renunciation of annexations. Exposure in place of the impermissible, illusion-breeding "demand" that *this* government, a government of capitalists, should *cease* to be an imperialist government.

4) Recognition of the fact that in most of the Soviets of Workers' Deputies our Party is in a minority, so far a small minority, as against a *bloc of all* the petty-bourgeois opportunist elements, from the Popular Socialists and the Socialist-Revolutionaries down to the Organising Committee (Chkheidze, Tsereteli, etc.), Steklov, etc., etc., who have yielded to the influence of the bourgeoisie and spread that influence among the proletariat.

The masses must be made to see that the Soviets of Workers' Deputies are the *only possible* form of revolutionary government, and that therefore our task is, as long as *this* government yields to the influence of the bourgeoisie, to present a patient, systematic, and persistent explanation of the errors of their tactics, an *explanation* especially adapted to the practical needs of the masses.

As long as we are in the minority we carry on the work of criticising and exposing errors and at the same time we preach the necessity of transferring the entire state power to the Soviets of Workers' Deputies, so that the people may overcome their mistakes by experience.

5) Not a parliamentary republic—to return to a parliamentary republic from the Soviets of Workers' Deputies would be a retrograde step—but a republic of Soviets of Workers,' Agricultural Labourers' and Peasants' Deputies throughout the country, from top to bottom.

Abolition of the police, the army, and the bureaucracy.

The salaries of all officials, all of whom are elective and displaceable at any time, not to exceed the average wage of a competent worker.

6) The weight of emphasis in the agrarian programme to be shifted to the Soviets of Agricultural Labourers' Deputies.

Confiscation of all landed estates.

Nationalisation of *all* lands in the country, the land to be disposed of by the local Soviets of Agricultural Labourers' and Peasants' Deputies. The organisation of separate Soviets of Deputies of Poor Peasants. The setting up of a model farm on each of the large estates (ranging in size from 100 to 300 dessiatines, according to local and other conditions, and to the decisions of the local bodies) under the control of the Soviets of Agricultural Labourers' Deputies and for the public account.

7) The immediate union of all banks in the country into a single national bank, and the institution of control over it by the Soviet of Workers' Deputies.

8) It is not our *immediate* task to "introduce" socialism, but only to bring social production and the distribution of products at once under the *control* of the Soviets of Workers' Deputies.

9) Party tasks:

    (a) Immediate convocation of a Party congress;

    (b) Alteration of the Party Programme, mainly:

      (1) On the question of imperialism and the imperialist war,

      (2) On our attitude towards the state and *our* demand for a "commune state";

      (3) Amendment of our out-of-date minimum programme;

    (c) Change of the Party's name.

10. A new International.

We must take the initiative in creating a revolutionary International, an International against the *social-chauvinists* and against the "Centre."

In order that the reader may understand why I had especially to emphasise as a rare exception the "case" of honest opponents, I invite him to compare the above theses with the following objection by Mr. Goldenberg: Lenin, he said, "has planted the banner of civil war in the midst of revolutionary democracy" (quoted in No. 5 of Mr. Plekhanov's *Yedinstvo*).

Isn't it a gem?

I write, announce and elaborately explain: "In view of the undoubted honesty of those *broad* sections of the *mass* believers in revolutionary defencism … in view of the fact that they are being deceived by the bourgeoisie, it is necessary with *particular* thoroughness, persistence and *patience* to explain their error to them…."

Yet the bourgeois gentlemen who call themselves Social-Democrats, who *do not* belong either to the *broad* sections or to the *mass* believers in defencism, with serene brow present my views thus: "The banner[!] of civil war" (of which there is not a word in the theses and not a word in my speech!) has been planted(!) "in the midst [!!] of revolutionary democracy…."

What does this mean? In what way does this differ from riot-inciting agitation, from *Russkaya Volya*?

I write, announce and elaborately explain: "The Soviets of Workers' Deputies are the *only possible* form of revolutionary government, and therefore our task is to present a patient, systematic, and persistent *explanation* of the errors of their tactics, an explanation especially adapted to the practical needs of the masses."

Yet opponents of a certain brand present my views as a call to "civil war in the midst of revolutionary democracy"!

I attacked the Provisional Government for *not* having appointed an early date or any date at all, for the convocation of the Constituent Assembly, and for confining itself to promises. I argued that *without* the Soviets of Workers' and Soldiers' Deputies the convocation of the Constituent Assembly is not guaranteed and its success is impossible.

And the view is attributed to me that I am opposed to the speedy convocation of the Constituent Assembly!

I would call this "raving," had not decades of political struggle taught me to regard honesty in opponents as a rare exception.

Mr. Plekhanov in his paper called my speech "raving." Very good, Mr. Plekhanov! But look how awkward, uncouth and slow-witted you are in your polemics. If I delivered a raving speech for two hours, how is it that an audience of hundreds tolerated this "raving"? Further, why does your paper devote a whole column to an account of the "raving"? Inconsistent, highly inconsistent!

It is, of course, much easier to shout, abuse, and howl than to attempt to relate, to explain, to recall *what* Marx and Engels said in 1871, 1872 and 1875 about the experience of the Paris Commune and about the *kind* of state the proletariat needs. [See: The Civil War in France and Critique of the Gotha Programme]

Ex-Marxist Mr. Plekhanov evidently does not care to recall Marxism.

I quoted the words of Rosa Luxemburg, who on August 4, 1914, called *German* Social-Democracy a "stinking corpse." And the Plekhanovs, Goldenbergs and Co. feel "offended." On whose behalf? On behalf of the *German* chauvinists, because they were called chauvinists!

They have got themselves in a mess, these poor Russian social-chauvinists—socialists in word and chauvinists in deed.

The October Revolution

By Alexander Mosler

This eyewitness account by a Western diplomat shows the chaos of a revolutionary moment. Note that politics operates on several levels, including the high politics of Kerensky, the new head of the Provisional Government, and the popular level of the masses in the streets. Mosler identifies Kereneky's decision to continue the war as the crucial factor in his downfall and the success of the Bolsheviks. Confusion, anger, and fear dominate the streets of the Russian capital in the historic year of 1917.

From the balcony of the Swedish embassy one morning in July 1917, I saw warships and small boats filled with Kronstadt sailors and the Red Guard coming up the Neva.

To the sound of the "Marseillaise" and the loud hurrahs of Petersburg Bolsheviki gathered on the bank, the sailors left the ships at double-quick. Their intention was to take the Kerenski cabinet by surprise. Some of the Bolsheviki were armed only with a policeman's sword; others had carbines or muskets of various design. Many wore red scarves around their bodies or red cockades on their caps.

The embassy building was situated on the banks of the Neva, just below the first bridge over the river. Thus all ships coming from the Baltic or from Kronstadt which were too large to pass under the bridge had to anchor in front of the embassy.

Many angry looks were directed up at me from the crowd, who, seeing me on the balcony of a palatial house, took me for a hated bourgeois. A sailor called up to me, "We'll pay a visit to you this evening to find where you keep your money and whether you have any brandy in your cellars." However, the red-scarfed heroes came neither on that nor on the next evening.

They left the ships at double-quick; they came back spent, ragged, and dirty—singly, or in twos and threes. Without caps and without weapons they came looking for their

Alexander Mosler; Charles F. Horne, ed., "The October Revolution," *Source Records of the Great War*, vol. 5. Copyright © 1923 by American Legion. Reprinted with permission.

ships. Some carried their muskets concealed under their coats and only brought them out when the proximity of the boats made them feel safe from their pursuers.

Many had fallen during the adventure; a good third must have been taken prisoner; the survivors hastily weighed anchor and went silently down stream in the falling darkness.

While at the embassy I saw Kerenski and heard him speak. After the sailors' deputation with the ultimatum from Kronstadt had been arrested, he went on board a ship held by the mutineers.

I could observe him closely as he came down the street accompanied by his adjutant and some staff officers. He wore a black Russian blouse fastened high at the neck and hanging over his trousers and a black tasselled girdle around his hips. Officers and soldiers he greeted with a brief handshake; I heard plainly his curt "Good morning, comrades."

On board ship he spoke to the assembled sailors so impressively and convincingly that their mood changed completely. His last words were greeted with cheers; the black flag of anarchy which the ship was flying was hauled down, and in its place was raised the red flag of the Revolution. Ten minutes later the cruiser with Kerenski on board left its anchorage for Kronstadt.

Had Kerenski concluded peace earlier, had he in midsummer 1917 not given the order for a last attack upon the German lines, he would probably still sit upon the "golden chair." It was the military breakdown that caused his overthrow. During the fall of 1917, the situation slipped rapidly out of his control. I could draw a thousand pictures of the increasing anarchy; let a few such suffice.

On the street railways hubbub and license ruled. The cars were literally stuffed with soldiers, who of course paid no fare and whose behaviour was so insolent and speech so filthy that no respectable woman could think of riding with them.

At any moment a quarrel was likely to break out. When this occurred, the passengers instantly ranged themselves into two hostile camps, declaiming and arguing as in a popular mass meeting. From their talk I learned how embittered against the Bolsheviki were the greater part of the people of Petersburg.

Only the peasant soldiers, who had no conception of the meaning of Socialism, and the ragged, uneducated proletariat belonged to the Bolsheviki. The organized factory workers lined up with the Social Revolutionists. Non-commissioned officers and clerks also were opposed to the Bolsheviki, and the master craftsmen, the educated classes, and members of the Conservative and Liberal parties positively foamed with rage if one mentioned the Bolsheviki to them. As the peasant soldiers, however, possessed rifles and machine guns, the helpless majority had to nurse their rage in silence.

Among the passengers once standing in a car, I saw an officer of the Women's Battalion of Death. With a white fur cap saucily perched on her head, her hair combed high under it, and spurs on her boots, she was a sturdy and pleasing figure. Standing in front of her was a slovenly looking sailor, the band of his cap so loosely fastened that it hung almost over one eye. On it I read the name of his ship, the *Pamjat Asowa*, "In Memory of Asow," Asow, the revolutionist.

Soon the sailor began a conversation with the "lady soldier." "Well, my officer in petticoats, whom do you want to make war against now?" Receiving no answer, he broke out with "The devil take the wench" and other remarks unfit to print. The girl turned first red, then white; but the fellow kept up his stream of vile talk until she left the car. Not one of the onlookers took her part.

That happened in November. In the vicinity of the Winter Palace, where I got out, signs of the shooting which took place there at the time of Kerenski's fall were plainly visible. Thousands of rifle and machine gun bullets were lodged in the walls. The windows were almost all shattered and had paper stuck over the holes.

There were plenty of people on the street, but few among them that were well dressed. People in possession of good clothes had, indeed, good reason to stay inside their own four walls. In one of the cross streets of the Nevski Prospect, that is, in the very heart of the city, I myself saw three soldiers stop a lady and in spite of her tears and appeals for mercy take her shoes off her feet. The poor creature, still moaning, had to go home through the deep snow in her stocking feet, while the "comrades" sold their booty on the next street corner for two hundred roubles.

At about this time the contents of strong boxes in the banks were confiscated. Anxious throngs of people gathered before the doors of the banks, but no one was allowed to enter. Owners of buildings might not deposit their rents, but must turn them over to the Commissariat. Nor could a house owner keep more rooms for himself than there were members in his family.

Many days there was no electric light at all in dwellings or on the streets; or the lights went out at five o'clock in the afternoon.

Every court, every establishment, every community, was a little republic by itself. There was no general law or standard to which all men must conform. In the Petersburg district, for example, the head of the precinct decreed that government employees should receive a salary of three hundred roubles a month. This applied to everybody, from the man who checked overcoats and rubbers at the door to his own exalted self; not the productivity but the person was rewarded. In other public departments other regulations were laid down, each chief acting as he saw fit.

Among the soldiery, especially, turbulence and anarchy prevailed. All officers, from the commander of the regiment to the youngest lieutenant, were chosen by the soldiers. The men of a regiment met together, debated the matter excitedly, and then took a vote. Whoever received the most votes became the commander, whether or not he had the necessary education or ability for such a responsible post. The candidate who received the second largest number of votes became the second in command, and so on down.

Former officers if not re-elected were reduced to the rank and pay of private soldiers. No account was taken of their age or the families they might have dependent on them. So to escape starvation many ex-colonels, captains, and lieutenants took any work they could find to do. Officers of the Guard were to be seen acting as baggage men in the railway stations or as dock hands along the water front.

The soldiers passed their time playing cards and carrying on a small trade in cigarettes, spirits, and old clothing. Or they formed into bands and with fixed bayonets, "in the name of the law," entered and searched the houses of prosperous citizens. Everything which was not fastened down they carried off. At the slightest show of resistance they threatened the inmates with death. Men were killed like cattle on these occasions.

A lady told me later how these beasts in soldiers' uniforms had slowly tortured her husband to death before her own and her children's eyes. After chopping off his fingers one by one and putting out his eyes, they dragged him half conscious down the stairs and clubbed and bayoneted him to death. Then four soldiers stuck the bleeding corpse on their bayonets and carried it overhead as a panoply through the streets of Petersburg to the river. There they scraped the body off on the bridge railing and pitched it into the water.

I saw this family two days after the murder. The mother lay in bed out of her mind. The son, a university student, answered every question with the words, "They spitted him and threw him into the river." The seventeen-year-old daughter sat in a corner of the room on the floor weeping steadily, oblivious of what went on about her. Only the little sister, three years old, sat under the table and played with her doll.

Conditions of Admission to the Communist International (1920)

After seizing power in 1917, the Bolsheviks ended the war with Germany, fought a brutal civil war with the various enemies collectively known as the Whites (as opposed to the Communist Reds), and then sought to spread their revolutionary model around the world. Indeed, Lenin, Leon Trotsky (1879–1940), and other Bolsheviks believed that their revolution would only succeed if there was a world revolution. Lenin used his model for organizing a revolutionary party, as laid down in his 1902 What is to be Done?, to organize the international revolutionary organization known as the Third International or the Comintern (Communist International). Since radical socialists such as Lenin and Luxemburg had condemned the Second International since its failure to live up to the pledge to oppose a general war in Europe, Lenin proposed this new international organization of revolutionary socialist parties. He also established that the Comintern would be organized on the strict principles of discipline and centralized, perhaps authoritarian, control. Based in Moscow, the Comintern would dictate the party line to be followed around the world. This would lead some to criticize Comintern as an arm of Soviet foreign policy rather than an organic representation of the people's will in various revolutionary struggles.

Foreword

The First Congress of the Communist International did not draw up precise conditions for admission to the Communist International. Until the time the first congress was convened there were in most countries only Communist trends and

"Conditions of Admission to the Communist International."

groups. The Second Congress of the Communist International meets under different conditions. At the present time there are in most countries not only Communist trends and tendencies, but Communist parties and organizations.

Now parties and groups which have not in fact become communist often turn to the Communist International in the hope of joining it after recently belonging to the Second International. The Second International has been finally smashed to pieces. The parties in between and the 'centre' groups, which realize the hopelessness of the Second International, now try to lean upon the Communist International, which is becoming more and more powerful. In the process, however, they hope to retain an 'autonomy' that will permit them to continue their previous opportunist or 'centrist' policies. To a certain extent the Communist International is becoming fashionable.

The desire of certain leading 'centrist' groups to join the Communist International is an indirect confirmation of the fact that the Communist International has gained the sympathy of the overwhelming majority of class-conscious workers all over the world and that it is becoming a force that grows more powerful each day.

The Communist International is threatened by the danger of being watered down by elements characterized by vacillation and half measures, forces which have not yet finally discarded the ideology of the Second International.

Moreover, to this very day there remains in some big parties (Italy, Sweden, Norway, Yugoslavia, among others), whose majorities have adopted the standpoint of Communism, a significant reformist and social-pacifist wing which is only waiting for the opportunity to raise its head again, to start active sabotage of the proletarian revolution and thus to help the bourgeoisie and the Second International.

Not a single Communist may forget the lessons of the Hungarian Soviet Republic. The fusion of the Hungarian Communists with the so-called 'left' social democrats cost the Hungarian proletariat dear.

Consequently the Second Congress of the Communist International considers it necessary to establish quite precisely the conditions for the admittance of new parties and to point out to those parties that have been admitted to the Communist International the duties incumbent on them.

The Second Congress of the Communist International lays down the following conditions of membership of the Communist International:

1. All propaganda and agitation must bear a really Communist character and correspond to the programme and decisions of the Communist International. All the Party's press organs must be run by reliable Communists who have proved their devotion to the cause of the proletariat. The dictatorship of the proletariat must not be treated simply as a current formula learnt off by heart. Propaganda for it must be carried out in such a way that its necessity is comprehensible to every simple worker,

every woman worker, every soldier and peasant from the facts of their daily lives, which must be observed by our press and used day by day.

The periodical and other press and all the Party's publishing institutions must be subordinated to the Party leadership, regardless of whether at any given moment, the Party as a whole is legal or illegal. The publishing houses must not be allowed to abuse their independence and pursue policies that do not entirely correspond to the policies of the Party.

In the columns of the press, at public meetings, in the trades unions, in the co-operatives—wherever the members of the Communist International can gain admittance—it is necessary to brand not only the bourgeoisie but also its helpers, the reformists of every shade, systematically and pitilessly.

2. Every organization that wishes to affiliate to the Communist International must regularly and methodically remove reformists and centrists from every responsible post in the labour movement (Party organizations, editorial boards, trades unions, parliamentary factions, co-operatives, local government) and replace them with tested Communists, without worrying unduly about the fact that, particularly at first, ordinary workers from the masses will be replacing 'experienced' opportunists.

3. In almost every country in Europe and America the class struggle is entering the phase of civil war. Under such conditions the Communists can place no trust in bourgeois legality. They have the obligation of setting up a parallel organizational apparatus which, at the decisive moment, can assist the Party to do its duty to the revolution. In every country where a state of siege or emergency laws deprive the Communists of the opportunity of carrying on all their work legally, it is absolutely necessary to combine legal and illegal activity.

4. The duty of propagating Communist ideas includes the special obligation of forceful and systematic propaganda in the army. Where this agitation is interrupted by emergency laws it must be continued illegally. Refusal to carry out such work would be tantamount to a betrayal of revolutionary duty and would be incompatible with membership of the Communist International.

5. Systematic and methodical agitation is necessary in the countryside. The working class will not be able to win if it does not have the backing of the rural proletariat and at least a part of the poorest peasants, and if it does not secure the neutrality of at least a part of the rest of the rural population through its policies. Communist work in the countryside is taking on enormous importance at the moment. It must be carried out principally with the help of revolutionary Communist workers of the town and country who have connections with the countryside. To refuse to carry this work out, or to entrust it to unreliable, semi-reformist hands, is tantamount to renouncing the proletarian revolution.

6. Every party that wishes to belong to the Communist International has the obligation to unmask not only open social-patriotism but also the insincerity and hypocrisy

of social-pacifism, to show the workers systematically that, without the revolutionary overthrow of capitalism, no international court of arbitration, no agreement on the limitation of armaments, no 'democratic' reorganization of the League of Nations will be able to prevent new imperialist wars.

7. The parties that wish to belong to the Communist International have the obligation of recognizing the necessity of a complete break with reformism and 'centrist' politics and of spreading this break among the widest possible circles of their party members. Consistent Communist politics are impossible without this.

The Communist International unconditionally and categorically demands the carrying out of this break in the shortest possible time. The Communist International cannot tolerate a situation where notorious opportunists as represented by Turati, Modigliani, Kautsky, Hilferding, Hillquit, Longuet, MacDonald, etc., have the right to pass as members of the Communist International. This could only lead to the Communist International becoming something very similar to the wreck of the Second International.

8. A particularly marked and clear attitude on the question of the colonies and oppressed nations is necessary on the part of the Communist Parties of those countries where bourgeoisies are in possession of colonies and oppress other nations. Every party that wishes to belong to the Communist International has the obligation of exposing the dodges of its 'own' imperialists in the colonies, of supporting every liberation movement in the colonies not only in words but in deeds, of demanding that their imperialist compatriots should be thrown out of the colonies, of cultivating in the hearts of the workers in their own country a truly fraternal relationship to the working population in the colonies and to the oppressed nations, and of carrying out systematic propaganda among their own country's troops against any oppression of colonial peoples.

9. Every party that wishes to belong to the Communist International must systematically and persistently develop Communist activities within the trade unions, workers' and works councils, the consumer co-operatives and other mass workers' organizations. Within these organizations it is necessary to organize Communist cells the aim of which is to win the trades unions etc. for the cause of Communism by incessant and persistent work. In their daily work the cells have the obligation to expose everywhere the treachery of the social patriots and the vacillations of the 'centrists.' The Communist cells must be completely subordinated to the Party as a whole.

10. Every party belonging to the Communist International has the obligation to wage a stubborn struggle against the Amsterdam 'International' of scab trade union organizations. It must expound as forcefully as possible among trade unionists the idea of the necessity of the break with the scab Amsterdam International. It must support the International Association of Red Trades Unions affiliated to the Communist International, at present in the process of formation, with every means at its disposal.

11. Parties that wish to belong to the Communist International have the obligation to subject the personal composition of their parliamentary factions to review, to remove all unreliable elements from them and to subordinate these factions to the Party leadership, not only in words but also in deeds, by calling on every individual Communist member of parliament to subordinate the whole of his activity to the interests of really revolutionary propaganda and agitation.

12. The parties belonging to the Communist International must be built on the basis of the principle of democratic centralism. In the present epoch of acute civil war the Communist Party will only be able to fulfil its duty if it is organized in as centralist a manner as possible, if iron discipline reigns within it and if the Party centre, sustained by the confidence of the Party membership, is endowed with the fullest rights and authority and the most far-reaching powers.

13. The Communist Parties of those countries in which the Communists can carry out their work legally must from time to time undertake purges (re-registration) of the membership of their Party organizations in order to cleanse the Party systematically of the petty-bourgeois elements within it.

14. Every party that wishes to belong to the Communist International has the obligation to give unconditional support to every Soviet republic in its struggle against the forces of counter-revolution. The Communist Parties must carry out clear propaganda to prevent the transport of war material to the enemies of the Soviet republics. They must also carry out legal or illegal propaganda, etc., with every means at their disposal among troops sent to stifle workers' republics.

15. Parties that have still retained their old social-democratic programmes have the obligation of changing those programmes as quickly as possible and working out a new Communist programme corresponding to the particular conditions in the country and in accordance with the decisions of the Communist International.

As a rule the programme of every party belonging to the Communist International must be ratified by a regular Congress of the Communist International or by the Executive Committee. Should the Executive Committee of the Communist International reject a Party's programme, the Party in question has the right of appeal to the Congress of the Communist International.

16. All decisions of the Congresses of the Communist International and decisions of its Executive Committee are binding on all parties belonging to the Communist International. The Communist International, acting under conditions of the most acute civil war, must be built in a far more centralist manner than was the case with the Second International. In the process the Communist International and its Executive Committee must, of course, in the whole of its activity, take into account the differing conditions under which the individual Parties have to fight and work, and only take generally binding decisions in cases where such decisions are possible.

17. In this connection all those parties that wish to belong to the Communist International must change their names. Every party that wishes to belong to the Communist International must bear the name Communist Party of this or that country (Section of the Communist International). The question of the name is not formal, but a highly political question of great importance. The Communist International has declared war on the whole bourgeois world and on all scab social democratic parties. The difference between the Communist Parties and the old official 'social-democratic' or 'socialist' parties that have betrayed the banner of the working class must be clear to every simple toiler.

18. All the leading press of the Parties in every country have the duty of printing all the important official documents of the Executive Committee of the Communist International.

19. All Parties that belong to the Communist International or have submitted an application for membership have the duty of calling a special congress as soon as possible, and in no case later than four months after the Second Congress of the Communist International, in order to check all these conditions. In this connection all Party centres must see that the decisions of the Second Congress are known to all their local organizations.

20. Those parties that now wish to enter the Communist International but have not yet radically altered their previous tactics must, before they join the Communist International, see to it that no less than two thirds of the Central Committee and of all their most important central institutions consist of comrades who even before the Second Congress of the Communist International spoke out unambiguously in public in favour of the entry of the Party into the Communist International. Exceptions may be permitted with the agreement of the Executive Committee of the Communist International. The Executive Committee of the Communist International also has the right to make exceptions in relation to the representatives of the centrist tendency mentioned in paragraph 7.

21. Those Party members who fundamentally reject the conditions and Theses laid down by the Communist International are to be expelled from the Party.

The same will apply particularly to delegates to the special Party Congress.

Report on an Investigation of the Peasant Movement in Hunan (1927)

By Mao Zedong

If Lenin pushed Marxism by creating a revolutionary strategy out of Marx's theories and took liberties with it by seizing power in the name of the industrial working class in an overwhelmingly rural Russia, Mao Zedong (1893–1976) offered an even more radical interpretation. Karl Marx did not see the future coming from the countryside or from Asia. At one point he wrote of "the idiocy of rural life," showing his contempt for the peasantry, and his writings on India claimed that the West needed to modernize Asia before it could enter into a revolutionary stage. Mao took a contradictory position. He claimed that in China the peasants were a true revolutionary force. His Asian variant of Communism focused on mobilizing the peasantry to win the small villages and then, eventually, attack the cities. Initially the Comintern rejected Mao's ideas as too unorthodox and revisonist.

THE IMPORTANCE OF THE PEASANT PROBLEM

During my recent visit to Hunan I made a first-hand investigation of conditions in the five counties of Hsiangtan, Hsianghsiang, Hengshan, Liling, and Changsha. In the thirty-two days from January 4 to February 5, I called together fact-finding conferences in villages and county towns, which were attended by experienced peasants and by comrades working in the peasant movement, and I listened attentively to their reports and collected a great deal of material. Many of the hows and whys of the peasant movement were the exact opposite of what the gentry in Hankow and Changsha are saying. I saw and heard of many strange things of which I had hitherto

Mao Tse-Tung, "Report on An Investigation of the Peasant Movement in Hunan," *Selected Works of Mao Tse-Tung*, vol. 1. Copyright © 1975 by Foreign Languages Press.

been unaware. I believe the same is true of many other places, too. All talk directed against the peasant movement must be speedily set right. All the wrong measures taken by the revolutionary authorities concerning the peasant movement must be speedily changed. Only thus can the future of the revolution be benefited. For the present upsurge of the peasant movement is a colossal event. In a very short time, in China's central, southern and northern provinces, several hundred million peasants will rise like a mighty storm, like a hurricane, a force so swift and violent that no power, however great, will be able to hold it back. They will smash all the trammels that bind them and rush forward along the road to liberation. They will sweep all the imperialists, warlords, corrupt officials, local tyrants and evil gentry into their graves. Every revolutionary party and every revolutionary comrade will be put to the test, to be accepted or rejected as they decide. There are three alternatives. To march at their head and lead them? To trail behind them, gesticulating and criticizing? Or to stand in their way and oppose them? Every Chinese is free to choose, but events will force you to make the choice quickly.

FOURTEEN GREAT ACHIEVEMENTS

Most critics of the peasant associations allege that they have done a great many bad things. I have already pointed out that the peasants' attack on the local tyrants and evil gentry is entirely revolutionary behaviour and in no way blameworthy. The peasants have done a great many things, and in order to answer people's criticism we must closely examine all their activities, one by one, to see what they have actually done. I have classified and summed up their activities of the last few months; in all, the peasants under the leadership of the peasant associations have the following fourteen great achievements to their credit.

1. ORGANIZING THE PEASANTS INTO PEASANT ASSOCIATIONS

This is the first great achievement of the peasants. In counties like Hsiangtan, Hsianghsiang and Hengshan, nearly all the peasants are organized and there is hardly a remote corner where they are not on the move; these are the best places. In some counties, like Yiyang and Huajung, the bulk of the peasants are organized, with only a small section remaining unorganized; these places are in the second grade. In other counties, like Chengpu and Lingling, while a small section is organized, the bulk of the peasants remain unorganized; these places are in the third grade. Western Hunan, which is under the control of Yuan Tsu-ming, has not yet been reached by the associations' propaganda, and in many of its counties the peasants are completely unorganized; these form a fourth grade. Roughly speaking, the counties in central Hunan, with Changsha as the centre, are the most advanced, those in southern Hunan come second, and western Hunan is only just beginning to organize. According to the figures compiled by the provincial peasant association last November, organizations with a total membership of 1,367,727 have been set up in thirty-seven of the province's seventy-five counties. Of these members about one million were organized during October and November when the power of the associations rose high, while up to September the membership had only been 300,000–400,000. Then came the two months of December and January, and the peasant movement continued its brisk growth. By the end of January the membership must have reached at least two million. As a family generally enters only one name when joining and has an average of five members, the mass following must be about ten million. This astonishing and accelerating rate of expansion explains why the local tyrants, evil gentry and corrupt officials have been isolated, why the public has been amazed at how completely the world has changed since the peasant movement, and why a great revolution has been wrought in the countryside. This is the first great achievement of the peasants under the leadership of their associations.

2. HITTING THE LANDLORDS POLITICALLY

Once the peasants have their organization, the first thing they do is to smash the political prestige and power of the landlord class, and especially of the local tyrants and evil gentry, that is, to pull down landlord authority and build up peasant authority in rural society. This is a most serious and vital struggle. It is the pivotal struggle in the second period, the period of revolutionary action. Without victory in this struggle, no victory is possible in the economic struggle to reduce rent and interest, to secure land and other means of production, and so on. In many places in Hunan like Hsianghsiang, Hengshan and Hsiangtan Counties, this is of course no problem since the authority of the landlords has been overturned and the peasants constitute the sole authority. But in counties like Liling there are still some places (such as Liling's western and southern districts) where the authority of the landlords seems weaker than that of the peasants but, because the political struggle has not been sharp, is in fact surreptitiously competing with it. In such places it is still too early to say that the peasants have gained political victory; they must wage the political struggle more vigorously until the landlords' authority is completely smashed. All in all, the methods used by the peasants to hit the landlords politically are as follows:

Checking the accounts. More often than not the local tyrants and evil gentry have helped themselves to public money passing through their hands, and their books are not in order. Now the peasants are using the checking of accounts as an occasion to bring down a great many of the local tyrants and evil gentry. In many places committees for checking accounts have been established for the express purpose of settling financial scores with them, and the first sign of such a committee makes them shudder. Campaigns of this kind have been carried out in all the counties where the peasant movement is active; they are important not so much for recovering money as for publicizing the crimes of the local tyrants and evil gentry and for knocking them down from their political and social positions.

Imposing fines. The peasants work out fines for such offences as irregularities revealed by the checking of accounts, past outrages against the peasants, current activities which undermine the peasant associations, violations of the ban on gambling and refusal to surrender opium pipes. This local tyrant must pay so much, that member of the evil gentry so much, the sums ranging from tens to thousands of yuan Naturally, a man who has been fined by the peasants completely loses face.

Levying contributions. The unscrupulous rich landlords are made to contribute for poor relief, for the organization of co-operatives or peasant credit societies, or for other purposes. Though milder than fines, these contributions are also a form of punishment. To avoid trouble, quite a number of landlords make voluntary contributions to the peasant associations.

Minor protests. When someone harms a peasant association by word or deed and the offence is a minor one, the peasants collect in a crowd and swarm into the offender's house to remonstrate with him. He is usually let off after writing a pledge to "cease and desist," in which he explicitly undertakes to stop defaming the peasant association in the future.

Major demonstrations. A big crowd is rallied to demonstrate against a local tyrant or one of the evil gentry who is an enemy of the association. The demonstrators eat at the offender's house, slaughtering his pigs and consuming his grain as a matter of course. Quite a few such cases have occurred. There was a case recently at Machiaho, Hsiangtan County, where a crowd of fifteen thousand peasants went to the houses of six of the evil gentry and demonstrated; the whole affair lasted four days during which more than 130 pigs were killed and eaten. After such demonstrations, the peasants usually impose fines.

"Crowning" the landlords and parading them through the villages. This sort of thing is very common. A tall paper-hat is stuck on the head of one of the local tyrants or evil gentry, bearing the words "Local tyrant so-and-so" or "So-and-so of the evil gentry." He is led by a rope and escorted with big crowds in front and behind. Sometimes brass gongs are beaten and flags waved to attract people's attention. This form of punishment more than any other makes the local tyrants and evil gentry tremble. Anyone who has once been crowned with a tall paper-hat loses face altogether and can never again hold up his head. Hence many of the rich prefer being fined to wearing the tall hat. But wear it they must, if the peasants insist. One ingenious township peasant

association arrested an obnoxious member of the gentry and announced that he was to be crowned that very day. The man turned blue with fear. Then the association decided not to crown him that day. They argued that if he were crowned right away, he would become case-hardened and no longer afraid, and that it would be better to let him go home and crown him some other day. Not knowing when he would be crowned, the man was in daily suspense, unable to sit down or sleep at ease.

Locking up the landlords in the county jail. This is a heavier punishment than wearing the tall paper-hat. A local tyrant or one of the evil gentry is arrested and sent to the county jail; he is locked up and the county magistrate has to try him and punish him. Today the people who are locked up are no longer the same. Formerly it was the gentry who sent peasants to be locked up, now it is the other way round.

"Banishment." The peasants have no desire to banish the most notorious criminals among the local tyrants and evil gentry, but would rather arrest or execute them. Afraid of being arrested or executed, they run away. In counties where the peasant movement is well developed, almost all the important local tyrants and evil gentry have fled, and this amounts to banishment. Among them, the top ones have fled to Shanghai, those of the second rank to Hankow, those of the third to Changsha, and of the fourth to the county towns. Of all the fugitive local tyrants and evil gentry, those who have fled to Shanghai are the safest. Some of those who fled to Hankow, like the three from Huajung, were eventually captured and brought back. Those who fled to Changsha are in still greater danger of being seized at any moment by students in the provincial capital who hail from their counties; I myself saw two captured in Changsha. Those who have taken refuge in the county towns are only of the fourth rank, and the peasantry, having many eyes and ears, can easily track them down. The financial authorities once explained the difficulties encountered by the Hunan Provincial Government in raising money by the fact that the peasants were banishing the well-to-do, which gives some idea of the extent to which the local tyrants and evil gentry are not tolerated in their home villages.

Execution. This is confined to the worst local tyrants and evil gentry and is carried out by the peasants jointly with other sections of the people. For instance, Yang Chih-tse of Ninghsiang, Chou Chia-kan of Yuehyang and Fu Tao-nan and Sun Po-chu of Huajung were shot by the government authorities at the insistence of the peasants and other sections of the people. In the case of Yen Jung-chiu of Hsiangtan, the peasants and other sections of the people compelled the magistrate to agree to hand him over, and the peasants themselves executed him. Liu Chao of Ninghsiang was killed by the peasants. The execution of Peng Chih-fan of Liling and Chou Tien-chueh and Tsao Yun of Yiyang is pending, subject to the decision of the "special tribunal for trying local tyrants and evil gentry." The execution of one such big landlord reverberates through a whole county and is very effective in eradicating the remaining evils of feudalism. Every county has these major tyrants, some as many as several dozen and others at least a few, and the only effective way of suppressing the reactionaries is to execute at least a few in each county who are guilty of the most heinous crimes. When the local tyrants and evil gentry were at the height of their power, they literally slaughtered peasants without batting an eyelid. Ho Maichuan, for ten years head of the defence corps in the town of Hsinkang, Changsha County, was personally responsible for killing almost a thousand poverty-stricken peasants, which he euphemistically described as "executing bandits." In my native county of Hsiangtan, Tang Chun-yen and Lo Shu-lin who headed the defence corps in the town of Yintien have killed more than fifty people and buried four alive in the fourteen years since 1913. Of the more than fifty they murdered, the first two were perfectly innocent beggars. Tang Chunyen said, "Let me make a start by killing a couple of beggars!" and so these two lives were snuffed out. Such was the cruelty of the local tyrants and evil gentry in former days, such was the White terror they created in the countryside, and now that the peasants have risen and shot a few and created just a little terror in suppressing the counter-revolutionaries, is there any reason for saying they should not do so?

3. HITTING THE LANDLORDS ECONOMICALLY

Prohibition on sending grain out of the area, forcing up grain prices, and hoarding and cornering. This is one of the great events of recent months in the economic struggle of the Hunan peasants. Since last October the poor peasants have prevented the outflow of the grain of the landlords and rich peasants and have banned the forcing up of grain prices and hoarding and cornering. As a result, the poor peasants have fully achieved their objective; the ban on the outflow of grain is watertight, grain prices have fallen considerably, and hoarding and cornering have disappeared.

Prohibition on increasing rents and deposits; [...] agitation for reduced rents and deposits. Last July and August, when the peasant associations were still weak, the landlords, following their long-established practice of maximum exploitation, served notice one after another on their tenants that rents and deposits would be increased. But by October, when the peasant associations had grown considerably in strength and had all come out against the raising of rents and deposits, the landlords dared not breathe another word on the subject. From November onwards, as the peasants have gained ascendancy over the landlords they have taken the further step of agitating for reduced rents and deposits. What a pity, they say, that the peasant associations were not strong enough when rents were being paid last autumn, or we could have reduced them then. The peasants are doing extensive propaganda for rent reduction in the coming autumn, and the landlords are asking how the reductions are to be carried out. As for the reduction of deposits, this is already under way in Hengshan and other counties.

Prohibition on cancelling tenancies. In July and August of last year there were still many instances of landlords cancelling tenancies and re-letting the land. But after October nobody dared cancel a tenancy. Today, the cancelling of tenancies and the re-letting of land are quite out of the question; all that remains as something of a problem is whether a tenancy can be cancelled if the landlord wants to cultivate the land himself. In some places even this is not allowed by the peasants. In others the cancelling of a tenancy may be permitted if the landlord wants to cultivate the land himself, but then the problem of unemployment among the tenant-peasants arises. There is as yet no uniform way of solving this problem.

Reduction of interest. Interest has been generally reduced in Anhua, and there have been reductions in other counties, too. But wherever the peasant associations are powerful, rural money-lending has virtually disappeared, the landlords having completely "stopped lending" for fear that the money will be "communized." What is currently called reduction of interest is confined to old loans. Not only is the interest on such old loans reduced, but the creditor is actually forbidden to press for the repayment of the principal. The poor peasant replies, "Don't blame me. The year is nearly over. I'll pay you back next year."

4. OVERTHROWING THE FEUDAL RULE OF THE LOCAL TYRANTS AND EVIL GENTRY—SMASHING THE TU AND TUAN

The old organs of political power in the *tu* and *tuan (i.e.,* the district and the township), and especially at the *tu* level, just below the county level, used to be almost exclusively in the hands of the local tyrants and evil gentry. The *tu* had jurisdiction over a population of from ten to fifty or sixty thousand people, and had its own armed forces such as the township defence corps, its own fiscal powers such as the power to levy taxes per mou of land, and its own judicial powers such as the power to arrest, imprison, try and punish the peasants at will. The evil gentry who ran these organs were virtual monarchs of the countryside. Comparatively speaking, the peasants were not so much concerned with the president of the Republic, the provincial military governor or the county magistrate; their real "bosses" were these rural monarchs. A mere snort from these people, and the peasants knew they had to watch their step. As a consequence of the present revolt in the countryside the authority of the landlord class has generally been struck down, and the organs of rural administration dominated by the local tyrants and evil gentry have naturally collapsed in its wake. The heads of the *tu* and the *tuan* all steer clear of the people, dare not show their faces and push all local matters on to the peasant associations. They put people off with the remark, "It is none of my business!"

Whenever their conversation turns to the heads of the *tu* and the *tuan,* the peasants say angrily, "That bunch! They are finished!"

Yes, the term "finished" truly describes the state of the old organs of rural administration wherever the storm of revolution has raged.

5. OVERTHROWING THE ARMED FORCES OF THE LANDLORDS AND ESTABLISHING THOSE OF THE PEASANTS

The armed forces of the landlord class were smaller in central Hunan than in the western and southern parts of the province. An average of 600 rifles for each county would make a total of 45,000 rifles for all the seventy-five counties; there may, in fact, be more. In the southern and central parts where the peasant movement is well developed, the landlord class cannot hold its own because of the tremendous momentum with which the peasants have risen, and its armed forces have largely capitulated to the peasant associations and taken the side of the peasants; examples of this are to be found in such counties as Ninghsiang, Pingkiang, Liuyang, Changsha, Liling, Hsiangtan, Hsianghsiang, Anhua, Hengshan and Hengyang. In some counties such as Paoching, a small number of the landlords' armed forces are taking a neutral stand, though with a tendency to capitulate. Another small section are opposing the peasant associations, but the peasants are attacking them and may wipe them out before long, as, for example, in such counties as Yichang, Linwu, and Chiaho. The armed forces thus taken over from the reactionary landlords are all being reorganized into a "standing household militia" and placed under the new organs of rural self-government, which are organs of the political power of the peasantry. Taking over these old armed forces is one way in which the peasants are building up their own armed forces. A new way is through the setting up of spear corps under the peasant associations. The spears have pointed, double-edged blades mounted on long shafts, and there are now 100,000 of these weapons in the county of Hsianghsiang alone. Other counties like Hsiangtan, Hengshan, Liling, and Changsha have 70,000–80,000, or 50,000–60,000, or 30,000–40,000 each. Every county where there is a peasant movement has a rapidly growing spear corps. These peasants thus armed form an "irregular household militia." This multitude equipped with spears, which is larger than the old armed forces mentioned above, is a new-born armed power the mere sight of which makes the local tyrants and evil gentry tremble. The revolutionary authorities in Hunan should see to it that it is built up on a really extensive scale among the more than twenty million peasants in the seventy-five counties of the province, that every peasant, whether young or in his prime, possesses a spear, and that no restrictions are imposed as though a spear were something dreadful. Anyone who is scared at the sight of the spear corps is indeed a weakling! Only the local tyrants and evil gentry are frightened of them, but no revolutionaries should take fright.

6. OVERTHROWING THE POLITICAL POWER OF THE COUNTY MAGISTRATE AND HIS BAILIFFS

That county government cannot be clean until the peasants rise up was proved some time ago in Haifeng, Kwangtung Province. Now we have added proof, particularly in Hunan. In a county where power is in the hands of the local tyrants and evil gentry, the magistrate, whoever he may be, is almost invariably a corrupt official. In a county where the peasants have risen there is dean government, whoever the magistrate. In the counties I visited, the magistrates had to consult the peasant associations on everything in advance. In counties where the peasant power was very strong, the word of the peasant association worked miracles. If it demanded the arrest of a local tyrant in the morning, the magistrate dared not delay till noon; if it demanded arrest by noon, he dared not delay till the afternoon. When the power of the peasants was just beginning to make itself felt in the countryside, the magistrate worked in league with the local tyrants and evil gentry against the peasants. When the peasants' power grew till it matched that of the landlords, the magistrate took the position of trying to accommodate both the landlords and the peasants, accepting some of the peasant association's suggestions while rejecting others. The remark that the word of the peasant association "works miracles" applies only when the power of the landlords has been completely beaten down by that of the peasants. At present the political situation in such counties as Hsianghsiang, Hsiangtan, Liling and Hengshan is as follows:

(1) All decisions are made by a joint council consisting of the magistrate and the representatives of the revolutionary mass organizations. The council is convened by the magistrate and meets in his office. In some counties it is called the "joint council of public bodies and the local government," and in others the "council of county affairs." Besides the magistrate himself, the people attending are the representatives of the county peasant association, trade union council, merchant association, women's association, school staff association, student association and Kuomintang headquarters. At such council meetings the magistrate is influenced by the views of the public organizations and invariably does their bidding. The adoption of a democratic committee system of county government should not, therefore, present much of a problem in Hunan. The present county governments are already quite democratic both in form and substance. This situation has been brought about only in the last two or three months, that is, since the peasants have risen all over the countryside and overthrown the power of the local tyrants and evil gentry. It has now come about that the magistrates, seeing their

old props collapse and needing other props to retain their posts, have begun to curry favour with the public organizations.

(2) The judicial assistant teas scarcely any cases to handle. The judicial system in Hunan remains one in which the county magistrate is concurrently in charge of judicial affairs, with an assistant to help him in handling cases. To get rich, the magistrate and his underlings used to rely entirely on collecting taxes and levies, procuring men and provisions for the armed forces, and extorting money in civil and criminal lawsuits by confounding right and wrong, the last being the most regular and reliable source of income. In the last few months, with the downfall of the local tyrants and evil gentry, all the legal pettifoggers have disappeared. What is more, the peasants' problems, big and small, are now all settled in the peasant associations at the various levels. Thus the county judicial assistant simply has nothing to do. The one in Hsianghsiang told me, "When there were no peasant associations, an average of sixty civil or criminal suits were brought to the county government each day; now it receives an average of only four or five a day." So it is that the purses of the magistrates and their underlings perforce remain empty.

(3) The armed guards, the police and the bailiffs all keep out of the way and dare not go near the villages to practice their extortions. In the past the villagers were afraid of the townspeople, but now the townspeople are afraid of the villagers. In particular the vicious curs kept by the county government—the police, the armed guards and the bailiffs—are afraid of going to the villages, or if they do so, they no longer dare to practice their extortions. They tremble at the sight of the peasants' spears.

7. OVERTHROWING THE CLAN AUTHORITY OF THE ANCESTRAL TEMPLES AND CLAN ELDERS, THE RELIGIOUS AUTHORITY OF TOWN AND VILLAGE GODS, AND THE MASCULINE AUTHORITY OF HUSBANDS

A man in China is usually subjected to the domination of three systems of authority: (1) the state system (political authority), ranging from the national, provincial and county government down to that of the township; (2) the den system (clan authority), ranging from the central ancestral temple and its branch temples down to the head of the household; and (3) the supernatural system (religious authority), ranging from the King of Hell down to the town and village gods belonging to the nether world, and from the Emperor of Heaven down to all the various gods and spirits belonging to the celestial world. As for women, in addition to being dominated by these three systems of authority, they are also dominated by the men (the authority of the husband). These four authorities—political, clan, religious and masculine—are the embodiment of the whole feudal-patriarchal system and ideology, and are the four thick ropes binding the Chinese people, particularly the peasants. How the peasants have overthrown the political authority of the landlords in the countryside has been described above. The political authority of the landlords is the backbone of all the other systems of authority. With that overturned, the clan authority, the religious authority and the authority of the husband all begin to totter. Where the peasant association is powerful, the den elders and administrators of temple funds no longer dare oppress those lower in the clan hierarchy or embezzle clan funds. The worst clan elders and administrators, being local tyrants, have been thrown out. No one any longer dares to practice the cruel corporal and capital punishments that used to be inflicted in the ancestral temples, such as flogging, drowning and burying alive. The old rule barring women and poor people from the banquets in the ancestral temples has also been broken. The women of Paikno in Hengshan County gathered in force and swarmed into their ancestral temple, firmly planted their backsides in the seats and joined in the eating and drinking, while the venerable den bigwigs had willy-nilly to let them do as they pleased. At another place, where poor peasants had been excluded from temple banquets, a group of them flocked in and ate and drank their fill, while the local tyrants and evil gentry and other long-gowned gentlemen all took to their heels in fright. Everywhere religious authority totters as the peasant movement develops. In many places the peasant associations have taken over the temples of the gods as their offices. Everywhere they advocate the appropriation of temple property in order to start peasant schools and to defray the expenses of the associations, calling it "public revenue from superstition." In Liling County, prohibiting superstitious practices and smashing idols have become quite the vogue. In its northern districts the peasants have prohibited the incense-burning processions to propitiate the god of pestilence. There were many idols in the Taoist temple at Fupoling in Lukou, but when extra room was needed for the district headquarters of the Kuomintang, they were all piled up in a corner, big and small together, and no peasant raised any objection. Since then, sacrifices to the gods, the performance of religious rites and the offering of sacred lamps have rarely been practised when a death occurs in a family. Because the initiative in this matter was taken by the chairman of the peasant association, Sun Hsiao-shan, he is hated by the local Taoist priests. In the Lungfeng Nunnery in the North Third District, the peasants and primary school teachers chopped up the wooden idols and actually used the wood to cook meat. More than thirty idols in the Tungfu Monastery in the Southern District were burned by the students and peasants together, and only two small images of Lord Pao were snatched up by an old peasant who said, "Don't commit a sin !" In places where the power of the peasants is predominant, only the older peasants and the women still believe in the gods, the younger peasants no longer doing so. Since the latter control the associations, the overthrow of religious authority and the eradication of superstition are going on everywhere. As to the authority of the husband, this has always been weaker among the poor peasants because, out of economic necessity, their womenfolk have to do more manual labour than the women of the richer classes and therefore have more say and greater power of decision in family matters. With the increasing bankruptcy of the rural economy in recent years, the basis for men's domination over women has already been weakened. With the rise of the peasant movement, the women in many places have now begun to organize rural women's associations; the opportunity has come for them to lift up their heads, and the authority of the husband is getting shakier every day. In a word, the whole feudal-patriarchal system and ideology is tottering with the growth of the peasants' power. At the present time, however, the peasants are concentrating on destroying the landlords' political authority. Wherever it has been wholly destroyed, they are beginning to press their attack in the three other spheres of the clan, the gods and male domination. But such attacks have only just begun, and there can be no thorough overthrow of all three until the peasants have won complete victory in the economic struggle. Therefore, our present task is to lead the peasants to put their greatest efforts into the political struggle, so that the landlords' authority is entirely overthrown. The economic struggle should follow immediately, so that the land problem and the other economic problems of the poor peasants may be fundamentally solved. As for the den system, superstition, and inequality between men and women, their abolition will follow as a natural consequence of victory in the political and economic struggles. If too much of an effort is made, arbitrarily and prematurely, to abolish these things, the local tyrants and evil gentry will seize the pretext to put about such counter-revolutionary propaganda as "the peasant association has no piety towards ancestors," "the peasant association is blasphemous and is destroying religion" and "the peasant association stands for the communization of wives," all for the purpose of undermining the peasant movement. A case in point is the recent events at Hsianghsiang in Hunan and Yanghsin in Hupeh, where the landlords exploited the opposition of some peasants to smashing idols. It is the peasants who made the idols, and when the time comes they will cast the idols aside with their own hands; there is no need for anyone else to do it for them prematurely. The Communist Party's propaganda policy in such matters should be, "Draw the bow without shooting, just indicate the motions." It is for the peasants themselves to cast aside the idols, pull down the temples to the martyred virgins and the arches to the chaste and faithful widows; it is wrong for anybody else to do it for them.

While I was in the countryside, I did some propaganda against superstition among the peasants. I said:

"If you believe in the Eight Characters, you hope for good luck; if you believe in geomancy, you hope to benefit from the location of your ancestral graves. This year within the space of a few months the local tyrants, evil gentry and corrupt officials have all toppled from their pedestals. Is it possible that until a few months ago they all had good luck and enjoyed the benefit of well-sited ancestral graves, while suddenly in the last few months their luck has turned and their ancestral graves have ceased to exert a beneficial influence? The local tyrants and evil gentry jeer at your peasant association and say, 'How odd! Today, the world is a world of committeemen. Look, you can't even go to pass water without bumping into a committeeman!' Quite true, the towns and the villages, the trade unions and the peasant associations, the Kuomintang and the Communist Party, all without exception have their executive committee members—it is indeed a world of committeemen. But is this due to the Eight Characters and the location of the ancestral graves? How strange! The Eight Characters of all the poor wretches in the countryside have suddenly turned auspicious! And their ancestral graves have suddenly started exerting beneficial influences! The gods? Worship them by all means. But if you had only Lord Kuan and the Goddess of Mercy and no peasant association, could you have overthrown the local tyrants and evil gentry? The gods and goddesses are indeed miserable objects. You have worshipped them for centuries, and they have not overthrown a single one of the local tyrants or evil gentry for you! Now you want to have your rent reduced. Let me ask, how will you go about it? Will you believe in the gods or in the peasant association?"

My words made the peasants roar with laughter.

8. SPREADING POLITICAL PROPAGANDA

Even if ten thousand schools of law and political science had been opened, could they have brought as much political education to the people, men and women, young and old, all the way into the remotest corners of the countryside, as the peasant associations have done in so short a time? I don't think they could. "Down with imperialism!" "Down with the warlords!" "Down with the corrupt officials!" "Down with the local tyrants and evil gentry!"—these political slogans have grown wings, they have found their way to the young, the middle-aged and the old, to the women and children in countless villages, they have penetrated into their minds and are on their lips. For instance, watch a group of children at play. If one gets angry with another, if he glares, stamps his foot and shakes his fist, you will then immediately hear from the other the shrill cry of "Down with imperialism!"

In the Hsiangtan area, when the children who pasture the cattle get into a fight, one will act as Tang Sheng-chih, and the other as Yeh Kai-hsin; when one is defeated and runs away, with the other chasing him, it is the pursuer who is Tang Sheng-chih and the pursued Yeh Kai-hsin. As to the song "Down with the Imperialist Powers!" of course almost every child in the towns can sing it, and now many village children can sing it too.

Some of the peasants can also recite Dr. Sun Yat-sen's Testament. They pick out the terms "freedom," "equality," "the Three People's Principles," and "unequal treaties" and apply them, if rather crudely, in their daily life. When somebody who looks like one of the gentry encounters a peasant and stands on his dignity, refusing to make way along a pathway, the peasant will say angrily, "Hey, you local tyrant, don't you know the Three People's Principles?" Formerly when the peasants from the vegetable farms on the outskirts of Changsha entered the city to sell their produce, they used to be pushed around by the police. Now they have found a weapon, which is none other than the Three People's Principles. When a policeman strikes or swears at a peasant selling vegetables, the peasant immediately answers back by invoking the Three People's Principles and that shuts the policeman up. Once in Hsiangtan when a district peasant association and a township peasant association could not see eye to eye, the chairman of the township association declared, "Down with the district peasant association's unequal treaties!"

The spread of political propaganda throughout the rural areas is entirely an achievement of the Communist Party and the peasant associations. Simple slogans, cartoons and speeches have produced such a widespread and speedy effect among the peasants that every one of them seems to have been through a political school. According to the reports of comrades engaged in rural work, political propaganda was very extensive at the time of the three great mass rallies, the anti-British demonstration, the celebration of the October Revolution and the victory celebration for the Northern Expedition. On these occasions, political propaganda was conducted extensively wherever there were peasant associations, arousing the whole countryside with tremendous effect. From now on care should be taken to use every opportunity gradually to enrich the content and clarify the meaning of those simple slogans.

9. PEASANT BANS AND PROHIBITIONS

When the peasant associations, under Communist Party leadership, establish their authority in the countryside, the peasants begin to prohibit or restrict the things they dislike. Gaming, gambling and opium-smoking are the three things that are most strictly forbidden.

Gaming. Where the peasant association is powerful, mahjong, dominoes and card games are completely banned.

The peasant association in the 14th District of Hsianghsiang burned two basketfuls of mahjong sets.

If you go to the countryside, you will find none of these games played; anyone who violates the ban is promptly and strictly punished.

Gambling. Former hardened gamblers are now themselves suppressing gambling; this abuse, too, has been swept away in places where the peasant association is powerful.

Opium-smoking. The prohibition is extremely strict. When the peasant association orders the surrender of opium pipes, no one dares to raise the least objection. In

Liling County one of the evil gentry who did not surrender his pipes was arrested and paraded through the villages.

The peasants' campaign to 'disarm the opium-smokers!' is no less impressive than the disarming of the troops of Wu Pei-fu and Sun Chuan-fang by the Northern Expeditionary Army. Quite a number of venerable fathers of officers in the revolutionary army, old men who were opium-addicts and inseparable from their pipes, have been disarmed by the "emperors" (as the peasants are called derisively by the evil gentry). The "emperors" have banned not only the growing and smoking of opium, but also trafficking in it. A great deal of the opium transported from Kweichow to Kiangsi via the counties of Paoching, Hsianghsiang, Yuhsien and Liling has been intercepted on the way and burned. This has affected government revenues. As a result, out of consideration for the army's need for funds in the Northern Expedition, the provincial peasant association ordered the associations at the lower levels "temporarily to postpone the ban on opium traffic." This, however, has upset and displeased the peasants.

There are many other things besides these three which the peasants have prohibited or restricted, the following being some examples:

The flower drum. Vulgar performances are forbidden in many places.

Sedan-chairs. In many counties, especially Hsianghsiang, there have been cases of smashing sedan-chairs. The peasants, detesting the people who use this conveyance, are always ready to smash the chairs, but the peasant associations forbid them to do so. Association officials tell the peasants, "If you smash the chairs, you only save the rich money and lose the carriers their jobs. Will that not hurt our own people?" Seeing the point, the peasants have worked out a new tactic—considerably to increase the fares charged by the chair carriers so as to penalize the rich.

Distilling and sugar-making. The use of grain for distilling spirits and making sugar is everywhere prohibited, and the distillers and sugar-refiners are constantly complaining. Distilling is not banned in Futienpu, Hengshan County, but prices are fixed very low, and the wine and spirits dealers, seeing no prospect of profit, have had to stop it.

Pigs. The number of pigs a family can keep is limited, for pigs consume grain.

Chickens and ducks. In Hsianghsiang County the raising of chickens and ducks is prohibited, but the women object. In Hengshan County, each family in Yangtang is allowed to keep only three, and in Futienpu five. In many places the raising of ducks is completely banned, for ducks not only consume grain but also ruin the rice plants and so are worse than chickens.

Feasts. Sumptuous feasts are generally forbidden. In Shaoshan, Hsiangtan County, it has been decided that guests are to be served with only three kinds of animal food, namely, chicken, fish and pork. It is also forbidden to serve bamboo shoots, kelp and lentil noodles. In Hengshan County it has been resolved that eight dishes and no more may be served at a banquet. Only five dishes are allowed in the East Third District in

Liling County, and only three meat and three vegetable dishes in the North Second District, while in the West Third District New Year feasts are forbidden entirely. In Hsianghsiang County, there is a ban on all "egg-cake feasts," which are by no means sumptuous. When a family in the Second District of Hsianghsiang gave an "egg-cake feast" at a son's wedding, the peasants, seeing the ban violated, swarmed into the house and broke up the celebration. In the town of Chiamo, Hsianghsiang County, the people have refrained from eating expensive foods and use only fruit when offering ancestral sacrifices.

Oxen. Oxen are a treasured possession of the peasants. "Slaughter an ox in this life and you will be an ox in the next" has become almost a religious tenet; oxen must never be killed. Before the peasants had power, they could only appeal to religious taboo in opposing the slaughter of cattle and had no means of banning it. Since the rise of the peasant associations their jurisdiction has extended even to the cattle, and they have prohibited the slaughter of cattle in the towns. Of the six butcheries in the county town of Hsiangtan, five are now closed and the remaining one slaughters only enfeebled or disabled animals. The slaughter of cattle is totally prohibited throughout the county of Hengshan. A peasant whose ox broke a leg consulted the peasant association before he dared kill it. When the Chamber of Commerce of Chuchow rashly slaughtered a cow, the peasants came into town and demanded an explanation, and the chamber, besides paying a fine, had to let off firecrackers by way of apology.

Tramps and vagabonds. A resolution passed in Liling County prohibited the drumming of New Year greetings or the chanting of praises to the local deities or the singing of lotus rhymes. Various other counties have similar prohibitions, or these practices have disappeared of themselves, as no one observes them any more. The "beggar-bullies" or "vagabonds" who used to be extremely aggressive now have no alternative but to submit to the peasant associations. In Shaoshan, Hsiangtan County, the vagabonds used to make the temple of the Rain God their regular haunt and feared nobody, but since the rise of the associations they have stolen away. The peasant association in Huti Township in the same county caught three such tramps and made them carry clay for the brick kilns. Resolutions have been passed prohibiting the wasteful customs associated with New Year calls and gifts.

Besides these, many other minor prohibitions have been introduced in various places, such as the Liling prohibitions on incense-burning processions to propitiate the god of pestilence, on buying preserves and fruit for ritual presents, burning ritual paper garments during the Festival of Spirits and pasting up good-luck posters at the New Year At Kushui in Hsianghsiang County, there is a prohibition even on smoking water-pipes. In the Second District, letting off firecrackers and ceremonial guns is forbidden, with a fine of 1.20 yuan for the former and 2.40 yuan for the latter. Religious rites for the dead are prohibited in the 7th and 20th Districts. In the 18th

District, it is forbidden to make funeral gifts of money. Things like these, which defy enumeration, may be generally called peasant bans and prohibitions.

They are of great significance in two respects. First, they represent a revolt against bad social customs, such as gaming, gambling opium-smoking. These customs arose out of the rotten political environment of the landlord class and are swept away once its authority is overthrown. Second, the prohibitions are a form of self-defence against exploitation by city merchants; such are the prohibitions on feasts and on buying preserves and fruit for ritual presents. Manufactured goods are extremely dear and agricultural products are extremely cheap, the peasants are impoverished and ruthlessly exploited by the merchants and they must therefore encourage frugality to protect themselves. As for the ban on sending grain out of the area, it is imposed to prevent the price from rising because the poor peasants have not enough to feed themselves and have to buy grain on the market. The reason for all this is the peasants' poverty and the contradictions between town and country; it is not a matter of their rejecting manufactured goods or trade between town and country in order to uphold the so-called Doctrine of Oriental Culture. To protect themselves economically, the peasants must organize consumers' co-operatives for the collective buying of goods. It is also necessary for the government to help the peasant associations establish credit (loan) co-operatives. If these things were done, the peasants would naturally end the unnecessary ban on the outflow of grain as a method of keeping down the price, nor would they have to prohibit the inflow of certain manufactured goods in economic self-defence.

10. ELIMINATING BANDITRY

In my opinion, no ruler in any dynasty from Yu, Tang, Wen, and Wu down to the Ching emperors and the presidents of the Republic has ever shown as much prowess in eliminating banditry as have the peasant associations today. Wherever the peasant associations are powerful there is not a trace of banditry. Surprisingly enough, in many places even the pilfering of vegetables has disappeared. In other places there are still some pilferers. But in the counties I visited, even including those that were formerly bandit-ridden, there was no trace of bandits. The reasons are: First, the members of the peasant associations are everywhere spread out over the hills and dales, spear or cudgel in hand, ready to go into action in their hundreds, so that the bandits have nowhere to hide. Second, since the rise of the peasant movement the price of grain has dropped—it was six yuan a picul last spring but only two yuan last winter—and the problem of food has become less serious for the people. Third, members of the secret societies have joined the peasant associations, in which they can openly and legally play the hero and vent their grievances, so that there is no further need for the secret "mountain," "lodge," "shrine," and "river" forms of organization. In killing the pigs and shrine of the local tyrants and evil gentry and imposing heavy levies and fines, they have adequate outlets for their feelings against those who oppressed them. Fourth, the armies are recruiting large numbers of soldiers and many of the "unruly" have joined up. Thus the evil of banditry has ended with the rise of the peasant movement. On this point, even the well-to-do approve of the peasant associations. Their comment is, "The peasant associations? Well, to be fair, there is also something to be said for them."

In prohibiting gaming, gambling and opium-smoking, and in eliminating banditry, the peasant associations have won general approval.

11. ABOLISHING EXORBITANT LEVIES

As the country is not yet unified and the authority of the imperialists and the warlords has not been overthrown, there is as yet no way of removing the heavy burden of government taxes and levies on the peasants or, more explicitly, of removing the burden of expenditure for the revolutionary army. However, the exorbitant levies imposed on the peasants when the local tyrants and evil gentry dominated rural administration, e.g., the surcharge on each mou of land, have been abolished or at least reduced with the rise of the peasant movement and the downfall of the local tyrants and evil gentry. This too should be counted among the achievements of the peasant associations.

12. THE MOVEMENT FOR EDUCATION

In China education has always been the exclusive preserve of the landlords, and the peasants have had no access to it. But the landlords' culture is created by the peasants, for its sole source is the peasants' sweat and blood. In China 90 per cent of the people have had no education, and of these the overwhelming majority are peasants. The moment the power of the landlords was overthrown in the rural areas, the peasants' movement for education began. See how the peasants who hitherto detested the schools are today zealously setting up evening classes! They always disliked the "foreign-style school." In my student days, when I went back to the village and saw that the peasants were against the "foreign-style school," I, too, used to identify myself with the general run of "foreign-style students and teachers" and stand up for it, feeling that the peasants were somehow wrong. It was not until 1925, when I lived in the countryside for six months and was already a Communist and had acquired the Marxist viewpoint, that I realized I had been wrong and the peasants right. The texts used in the rural primary schools were entirely about urban things and unsuited to rural needs. Besides, the attitude of the primary school teachers towards the peasants was very bad and, far from being helpful to the peasants, they became objects of dislike. Hence the peasants preferred the old-style schools ("Chinese classes," as they called them) to the modern schools (which they called "foreign classes") and the old-style teachers to the ones in the primary schools. Now the peasants are enthusiastically establishing evening classes, which they call peasant schools. Some have already been opened, others are being organized, and on the average there is one school per township. The peasants are very enthusiastic about these schools, and regard them, and only them, as their own. The funds for the evening schools come from the "public revenue from superstition," from ancestral temple funds, and from other idle public funds or property. The county education boards wanted to use this money to establish primary schools, that is, "foreign-style schools" not suited to the needs of the peasants, while the latter wanted to use it for peasant schools, and the outcome of the dispute was that both got some of the money, though there are places where the peasants got it all. The development of the peasant movement has resulted in a rapid rise in their cultural level. Before long tens of thousands of schools will have sprung up in the villages throughout the province; this is quite different from the empty talk about "universal education," which the intelligentsia and the so-called "educationalists" have been bandying back and forth and which after all this time remains an empty phrase.

13. THE CO-OPERATIVE MOVEMENT

The peasants really need co-operatives, and especially consumers, marketing and credit co-operatives. When they buy goods, the merchants exploit them; when they sell their farm produce, the merchants cheat them; when they borrow money for rice, they are fleeced by the usurers; and they are eager to find a solution to these three problems. During the fighting in the Yangtze valley last winter, when trade routes were cut and the price of salt went up in Hunan, many peasants organized co-operatives to purchase salt. When the landlords deliberately stopped lending, there were many attempts by the peasants to organize credit agencies, because they needed to borrow money. A major problem is the absence of detailed, standard rules of organization. As these spontaneously organized peasant co-operatives often fail to conform to co-operative principles, the comrades working among the peasants are always eagerly enquiring about "rules and regulations." Given proper guidance, the co-operative movement can spread everywhere along with the growth of the peasant associations.

14. BUILDING ROADS AND REPAIRING EMBANKMENTS

This, too, is one of the achievements of the peasant associations. Before there were peasant associations the roads in the countryside were terrible. Roads cannot be repaired without money, and as the wealthy were unwilling to dip into their purses, the roads were left in a bad state. If there was any road work done at all, it was done as an act of charity; a little money was collected from families "wishing to gain merit in the next world," and a few narrow, skimpily paved roads were built. With the rise of the peasant associations orders have been given specifying the required width—three, five, seven or ten feet, according to the requirements of the different routes—and each landlord along a road has been ordered to build a section. Once the order is given, who dares to disobey? In a short time many good roads have appeared. This is no work of charity but the result of compulsion, and a little compulsion of this kind is not at all a bad thing. The same is true of the embankments. The ruthless landlords were always out to take what they could from the tenant-peasants and would never spend even a few coppers on embankment repairs; they would leave the ponds to dry up and the tenant-peasants to starve, caring about nothing but the rent. Now that there are peasant associations, the landlords can be bluntly ordered to repair the embankments. When a landlord refuses, the association will tell him politely, "Very well! If you won't do the repairs, you will contribute grain, a tou for each work-day." As this is a bad bargain for the landlord, he hastens to do the repairs. Consequently many defective embankments have been turned into good ones.

All the fourteen deeds enumerated above have been accomplished by the peasants under the leadership of the peasant associations. Would the reader please think it over and say whether any of them is bad in its fundamental spirit and revolutionary significance? Only the local tyrants and evil gentry, I think, will call them bad. Curiously enough, it is reported from Nanchang that Chiang Kai-shek, Chang Ching-chiang and other such gentlemen do not altogether approve of the activities of the Hunan peasants. This opinion is shared by Liu Yueh-chih and other right-wing leaders in Hunan, all of whom say, "They have simply gone Red." But where would the national revolution be without this bit of Red? To talk about "arousing the masses of the people" day in and day out and then to be scared to death when the masses do rise—what difference is there between this and Lord Sheh's love of dragons?

Hymn (1934)

By Louis Aragon

Louis Aragon (1897–1982) was a French poet and veteran of the First World War. He gravitated to the nihilistic Dada art movement after the war and then founded the Surrealist movement with André Breton. After the horrors of trench warfare, Aragon epitomized the "lost generation" of intellectuals who reject the society and culture that had created the war. His rebellion was both artistic and political, joining the French Communist Part in 1927. Here he devotes his poetic talents to exulting the Bolshevik Revolution.

They restored man to the earth
They said you will eat
And you will eat

They cast the heavens to the earth
They said The gods will perish
And the gods will perish

They made a building site of the earth
They said The weather will be beautiful
And the weather will be beautiful

They opened a hole on the earth
They said The flame will burst forth
And the flame will burst forth

Speaking to the masters of the earth
They said You will give way
And you will give way

Louis Aragon; Mitch Abidor, trans., "Hymn," <www.marxists.org>. Licensed by the GNU Free Documentation License.

They took in their hands the earth
They said The black shall be white
And the black shall be white

Glory on the lands and the earth
To the sun of Bolshevik days
And Glory to the Bolsheviks

Munich Speech of April 12, 1922

By Adolf Hitler

Adolf Hitler (1889–1945) was an ethnic German born in the Austro-Hungarian Empire. His early life was one of aimlessness; poor grades in school, an amateurish interest in German history, and a failed attempt to enter art school in Vienna left him homeless and living off an inheritance from his deceased parents. He frequently expressed his beliefs in German nationalism, hatred of Jews, and hostility to left-wing politics in rambling speeches to his various acquaintances. When war broke out in 1914, he went across the border and joined the German army. He served bravely in the war, receiving several decorations for valor. Hitler frequently noted that military service was the first time that he felt at home. In 1918 he was severely injured in a gas attack, losing his sight for some time. After the war, he served the army as a spy and infiltrated a small radical group, the German Workers Party, in 1919. He joined the party and quickly entered its inner circle of leadership. Soon the organization was known as the National Socialist Workers Party of Germany, or NAZI for short. With a platform for his ideas, he gave a series of speeches in which he railed against the Treaty of Versailles, socialists and communists, and a supposed international Jewish conspiracy. Hitler's rhetoric stressed the victimization of the German people by forces beyond their control. While often irrational and paranoid, his message did find traction with Germans who suspected some sort of betrayal at the end of the war. In the chaotic years of 1918–1923, Hitler and the NAZIs would be involved in a series of violent incidents including political street fighting and culminating in the failed 1923 Beer Hall Putsch (also known as the Hitler-Ludendorff-Putsch because of the former general's participation).

AFTER the War production had begun again and it was thought that better times were coming, Frederick the Great, after the Seven Years War, had as the result of superhuman efforts left Prussia without a penny of debt: at the end of the World War Germany was burdened with her own debt of some 7 or 8 milliards of marks

Adolf Hitler, "Munich Speech of April 12, 1922."

and beyond that was faced with the debts of 'the rest of the world'—the so-called 'reparations.' The product of Germany's work thus belonged not to the nation, but to her foreign creditors: 'it was carried endlessly in trains for territories beyond our frontiers.' Every worker had to support another worker, the product of whose labor was commandeered by the foreigner. 'The German people after twenty-five or thirty years, in consequence of the fact that it will never be able to pay all that is demanded of it, will have so gigantic a sum still owing that practically it will be forced to produce more than it does today.' What will the end be? and the answer to that question is 'Pledging of our land, enslavement of our labor-strength. Therefore, in the economic sphere, November 1918 was in truth no achievement, but it was the beginning of our collapse.' And in the political sphere we lost first our military prerogatives, and with that loss went the real sovereignty of our State, and then our financial independence, for there remained always the Reparations Commission so that 'practically we have no longer a politically independent German Reich, we are already a colony of the outside world. We have contributed to this because so far as possible we humiliated ourselves morally, we positively destroyed our own honor and helped to befoul, to besmirch, and to deny everything which we previously held as sacred.' If it be objected that the Revolution has won for us gains in social life: they must be extraordinarily secret, these social gains—so secret that one never sees them in practical life—they must just run like a fluid through our German atmosphere. Someone may say 'Well, there is the eight-hour day!' And was a collapse necessary to gain that? And will the eight-hour day be rendered any more secure through our becoming practically the bailiff and the drudge of the other peoples? One of these days France will say: "You cannot meet your obligations, you must work more." So this achievement of the Revolution is put in question first of all by the Revolution.

Then someone has said: "Since the Revolution the people has gained 'Rights.' The people governs!" Strange! The people has now been ruling three years and no one has in practice once asked its opinion. Treaties were signed which will hold us down for centuries: and who has signed the treaties? The people? No! Governments which one fine day presented themselves as Governments. And at their election the people had nothing to do save to consider the question: there they are already, whether I elect them or not. If we elect them, then they are there through our election. But since we are a self-governing people, we must elect the folk in order that they may be elected to govern us.

Then it was said, 'Freedom has come to us through the Revolution.' Another of those things that one cannot see very easily! It is of course true that one can walk down the street, the individual can go into his workshop and he can go out again: here and there he can go to a meeting. In a word, the individual has liberties. But in general, if he is wise, he will keep his mouth shut. For if in former times extraordinary care was taken that no one should let slip anything which could be treated as lèse-majesté, now a man must take much greater care that he doesn't say anything which might represent an insult to the majesty of a member of Parliament.

And if we ask who was responsible for our misfortune, then we must inquire who profited by our collapse. And the answer to that question is that 'Banks and Stock Exchanges are more flourishing than ever before.' We were told that capitalism would be destroyed, and when we ventured to remind one or other of these "famous statesmen" and said 'Don't forget that Jews too have capital,' then the answer was: 'What are you worrying about? Capitalism as a whole will now be destroyed, the whole people will now be free. We are not fighting Jewish or Christian capitalism, we are fighting every capitalism: we are making the people completely free.'

'Christian capitalism' is already as good as destroyed, the international Jewish Stock Exchange capital gains in proportion as the other loses ground. It is only the international Stock Exchange and loan-capital, the so-called 'supra-state capital,' which has profited from the collapse of our economic life, the capital which receives its character from the single supra-state nation which is itself national to the core, which fancies itself to be above all other nations, which places itself above other nations and which already rules over them.

The international Stock Exchange capital would be unthinkable, it would never have come, without its founders the supra-national, because intensely national, Jews.
…

The Jew has not grown poorer: he gradually gets bloated, and, if you don't believe me, I would ask you to go to one of our health-resorts; there you will find two sorts of visitors: the German who goes there, perhaps for the first time for a long while, to breathe a little fresh air and to recover his health, and the Jew who goes there to lose his fat. And if you go out to our mountains, whom do you find there in fine brand-new yellow boots with splendid rucksacks in which there is generally nothing that would really be of any use? And why are they there? They go up to the hotel, usually no further than the train can take them: where the train stops, they stop too. And then they sit about somewhere within a mile from the hotel, like blow-flies round a corpse.

These are not, you may be sure, our working classes: neither those working with the mind, nor with the body. With their worn clothes they leave the hotel on one side and go on climbing: they would not feel comfortable coming into this perfumed atmosphere in suits which date from 1913 or 1914. No, assuredly the Jew has suffered no privations! …

While now in Soviet Russia the millions are ruined and are dying, Chicherin—and with him a staff of over 200 Soviet Jews—travels by express train through Europe, visits the cabarets, watches naked dancers perform for his pleasure, lives in the finest hotels, and does himself better than the millions whom once you thought you must fight as 'bourgeois.' The 400 Soviet Commissars of Jewish nationality—they do not suffer; the thousands upon thousands of sub-Commissars—they do not suffer. No! all the treasures which the 'proletarian' in his madness took from the 'bourgeoise' in order to fight so-called capitalism—they have all gone into their hands. Once the worker appropriated the purse of the landed proprietor who gave him work, he took the rings, the diamonds and rejoiced that he had now got the treasures which before only the 'bourgeoisie' possessed. But in his hands they are dead things—they are veritable death-gold. They are no profit to him. He is banished into his wilderness and one cannot feed oneself on diamonds. For a morsel of bread he gives millions in objects of value. But the bread is in the hands of the State Central Organization and this is in the hands of the Jews: so everything, everything that the common man thought that he was winning for himself, flows back again to his seducers.

And now, my dear fellow-countrymen, do you believe that these men, who with us are going the same way, will end the Revolution? They do not wish the end of the Revolution, for they do not need it. For them the Revolution is milk and honey.

And further they cannot end the Revolution. For if one or another amongst the leaders were really not seducer but seduced, and today, driven by the inner voice of horror at his crime, were to step before the masses and make his declaration: 'We have all deceived ourselves: we believed that we could lead you out of misery, but we have in fact led you into a misery which your children and your children's children must still bear'—he cannot say that, he dare not say that, he would on the public square or in the public meeting be torn in pieces.

But amongst the masses there begins to flow a new stream—a stream of opposition. It is the recognition of the facts which is already in pursuit of this system, it already is hunting the system down; it will one day scourge the masses into action and carry the masses along with it. And these leaders, they see that behind them the anti-Semitic wave grows and grows; and when the masses once recognize the facts, that is the end of these leaders.

And thus the Left is forced more and more to turn to Bolshevism. In Bolshevism they see today the sole, the last possibility of preserving the present state of affairs. They realize quite accurately that the people is beaten so long as Brain and Hand can be kept apart. For alone neither Brain nor Hand can really oppose them. So long therefore as the Socialist idea is coined only by men who see in it a means for disintegrating a nation, so long can they rest in peace.

But it will be a sorry day for them when this Socialist idea is grasped by a Movement which unites it with the highest Nationalist pride, with Nationalist defiance, and thus places the Nation's Brain, its intellectual workers, on this ground. Then this system will break up, and there would remain only one single means of salvation for its supporters: viz. to bring the catastrophe upon us before their own ruin, to destroy the Nation's Brain, to bring it to the scaffold—to introduce Bolshevism.

So the Left neither can nor will help. On the contrary, their first lie compels them constantly to resort to new lies. There remains then the Right. And this party of the

Right meant well, but it cannot do what it would because up to the present time it has failed to recognize a whole series of elementary principles.

In the first place the Right still fails to recognize the danger. These gentlemen still persist in believing that it is a question of being elected to a Landtag or of posts as ministers or secretaries. They think that the decision of a people's destiny would mean at worst nothing more than some damage to their so-called bourgeois-economic existence. They have never grasped the fact that this decision threatens their heads. They have never yet understood that it is not necessary to be an enemy of the Jew for him to drag you one day, on the Russian model, to the scaffold. They do not see that it is quite enough to have a head on your shoulders and not to be a Jew: that will secure the scaffold for you.

In consequence their whole action today is so petty, so limited, so hesitating and pusillanimous. They would like to—but they can never decide on any great deed, because they fail to realize the greatness of the whole period.

And then there is another fundamental error: they have never got it clear in their own minds that there is a difference or how great a difference there is between the conception 'National' and the word 'dynastic' or 'monarchistic.' They do not understand that today it is more than ever necessary in our thoughts as Nationalists to avoid anything which might perhaps cause the individual to think that the National Idea was identical with petty everyday political views. They ought day by day to din into the ears of the masses: 'We want to bury all the petty differences and to bring out into the light the big things, the things we have in common which bind us to one another. That should weld and fuse together those who have still a German heart and a love for their people in the fight against the common hereditary foe of all Aryans. How afterward we divide up this State, friends—we have no wish to dispute over that! The form of a State results from the essential character of a people, results from necessities which are so elementary and powerful that in time every individual will realize them without any disputation when once all Germany is united and free.'

And finally they all fail to understand that we must on principle free ourselves from any class standpoint. It is of course very easy to call out to those on the Left, 'You must not be proletarians, leave your class-madness,' while you yourselves continue to call yourself 'bourgeois.' They should learn that in a single State there is only one supreme citizen—right, one supreme citizen—honor, and that is the right and the honor of honest work. They should further learn that the social idea must be the essential foundation for any State, otherwise no State can permanently endure.

Certainly a government needs power, it needs strength. It must, I might almost say, with brutal ruthlessness press through the ideas which it has recognized to be right, trusting to the actual authority of its strength in the State. But even with the most ruthless brutality it can ultimately prevail only if what it seeks to restore does truly correspond to the welfare of a whole people.

That the so-called enlightened absolutism of a Frederick the Great was possible depended solely on the fact that, though this man could undoubtedly have decided 'arbitrarily' the destiny—for good or ill—of his so-called 'subjects,' he did not do so, but made his decisions influenced and supported by one thought alone, the welfare of his Prussian people. It was this fact only that led the people to tolerate willingly, nay joyfully, the dictatorship of the great king.

AND THE RIGHT HAS FURTHER COMPLETELY FORGOTTEN THAT DEMOCRACY IS FUNDAMENTALLY NOT GERMAN: IT IS JEWISH. It has completely forgotten that this Jewish democracy with its majority decisions has always been without exception only a means towards the destruction of any existing Aryan leadership. The Right does not understand that directly every small question of profit or loss is regularly put before so-called 'public opinion,' he who knows how most skillfully to make this 'public opinion' serve his own interests becomes forthwith master in the State. And that can be achieved by the man who can lie most artfully, most infamously; and in the last resort he is not the German, he is, in Schopenhauer's words, 'the great master in the art of lying'—the Jew.

And finally it has been forgotten that the condition which must precede every act is the will and the courage to speak the truth—and that we do not see today either in the Right or in the Left.

There are only two possibilities in Germany; do not imagine that the people will forever go with the middle party, the party of compromises; one day it will turn to those who have most consistently foretold the coming ruin and have sought to dissociate themselves from it. And that party is either the Left: and then God help us! for it will lead us to complete destruction—to Bolshevism, or else it is a party of the Right which at the last, when the people is in utter despair, when it has lost all its spirit and has no longer any faith in anything, is determined for its part ruthlessly to seize the reins of power—that is the beginning of resistance of which I spoke a few minutes ago. Here, too, there can be no compromise—there are only two possibilities: either victory of the Aryan, or annihilation of the Aryan and the victory of the Jew.

It is from the recognition of this fact, from recognizing it, I would say, in utter, dead earnestness, that there resulted the formation of our Movement. There are two principles which, when we founded the Movement, we engraved upon our hearts: first, to base it on the most sober recognition of the facts, and second, to proclaim these facts with the most ruthless sincerity.

And this recognition of the facts discloses at once a whole series of the most important fundamental principles which must guide this young Movement which, we hope, is destined one day for greatness:

1. 'NATIONAL' AND 'SOCIAL' ARE TWO IDENTICAL CONCEPTIONS. It was only the Jew who succeeded, through falsifying the social idea and turning it into Marxism, not only in divorcing the social idea from the national, but in actually

representing them as utterly contradictory. That aim he has in fact achieved. At the founding of this Movement we formed the decision that we would give expression to this idea of ours of the identity of the two conceptions: despite all warnings, on the basis of what we had come to believe, on the basis of the sincerity of our will, we christened it 'National Socialist.' We said to ourselves that to be 'national' means above everything to act with a boundless and all-embracing love for the people and, if necessary, even to die for it. And similarly to be 'social' means so to build up the state and the community of the people that every individual acts in the interest of the community of the people and must be to such an extent convinced of the goodness, of the honorable straightforwardness of this community of the people as to be ready to die for it.

2. And then we said to ourselves: THERE ARE NO SUCH THINGS AS CLASSES: THEY CANNOT BE. Class means caste and caste means race. If there are castes in India, well and good; there it is possible, for there there were formerly Aryans and dark aborigines. So it was in Egypt and in Rome. But with us in Germany where everyone who is a German at all has the same blood, has the same eyes, and speaks the same language, here there can be no class, here there can be only a single people and beyond that nothing else. Certainly we recognize, just as anyone must recognize, that there are different 'occupations' and 'professions' [Stände]-there is the Stände of the watchmakers, the Stände of the common laborers, the Stände of the painters or technicians, the Stände of the engineers, officials, etc. Stände there can be. But in the struggles which these Stände have amongst themselves for the equalization of their economic conditions, the conflict and the division must never be so great as to sunder the ties of race.

And if you say 'But there must after all be a difference between the honest creators and those who do nothing at all'—certainly there must! That is the difference which lies in the performance of the conscientious work of the individual. Work must be the great connecting link, but at the same time the great factor which separates one man from another. The drone is the foe of us all. But the creators—it matters not whether they are brain workers or workers with the hand—they are the nobility of our State, they are the German people!

We understand under the term 'work' exclusively that activity which not only profits the individual but in no way harms the community, nay rather which contributes to form the community.

3. And in the third place IT WAS CLEAR TO US THAT THIS PARTICULAR VIEW IS BASED ON AN IMPULSE WHICH SPRINGS FROM OUR RACE AND FROM OUR BLOOD. We said to ourselves that race differs from race and, further, that each race in accordance with its fundamental demands shows externally certain specific tendencies, and these tendencies can perhaps be most clearly traced in their relation to the conception of work. The Aryan regards work as the foundation for the

maintenance of the community of people amongst its members. The Jew regards work as the means to the exploitation of other peoples. The Jew never works as a productive creator without the great aim of becoming the master. He works unproductively using and enjoying other people's work. And thus we understand the iron sentence which Mommsen once uttered: 'The Jew is the ferment of decomposition in peoples,' that means that the Jew destroys and must destroy because he completely lacks the conception of an activity which builds up the life of the community. And therefore it is beside the point whether the individual Jew is 'decent' or not. In himself he carries those characteristics which Nature has given him, and he cannot ever rid himself of those characteristics. And to us he is harmful. Whether he harms us consciously or unconsciously, that is not our affair. We have consciously to concern ourselves for the welfare of our own people.

4. And fourthly WE WERE FURTHER PERSUADED THAT ECONOMIC PROSPERITY IS INSEPARABLE FROM POLITICAL FREEDOM AND THAT THEREFORE THAT HOUSE OF LIES, 'INTERNATIONALISM,' MUST IMMEDIATELY COLLAPSE. We recognized that freedom can eternally be only a consequence of power and that the source of power is the will. Consequently the will to power must be strengthened in a people with passionate ardor. And thus we realized fifthly that

5. WE AS NATIONAL SOCIALISTS and members of the German Workers party—a Party pledged to work—MUST BE ON PRINCIPLE THE MOST FANATICAL NATIONALISTS. We realized that the State can be for our people a paradise only if the people can hold sway therein freely as in a paradise: we realized that a slave state will never be a paradise, but only—always and for all time—a hell or a colony.

6. And then sixthly we grasped the fact that POWER IN THE LAST RESORT IS POSSIBLE ONLY WHERE THERE IS STRENGTH, and that strength lies not in the dead weight of numbers but solely in energy. Even the smallest minority can achieve a mighty result if it is inspired by the most fiery, the most passionate will to act. World history has always been made by minorities. And lastly

7. If one has realized a truth, that truth is valueless so long as there is lacking the indomitable will to turn this realization into action!

These were the foundations of our Movement—the truths on which it was based and which demonstrated its necessity.

For three years we have sought to realize these fundamental ideas. And of course a fight is and remains a fight. Stroking in very truth will not carry one far. Today the German people has been beaten by a quite other world, while in its domestic life it has lost all spirit; no longer has it any faith. But how will you give this people once more firm ground beneath its feet save by the passionate insistence on one definite, great, clear goal?

Thus we were the first to declare that this peace treaty was a crime. Then folk abused us as 'agitators.' We were the first to protest against the failure to present this treaty to the people before it was signed. Again we were called 'agitators.' We were the first to summon men to resistance against being reduced to a continuing state of defenselessness. Once more we were 'agitators.' At that time we called on the masses of the people not to surrender their arms, for the surrender of one's arms would be nothing less than the beginning of enslavement. We were called, no, we were cried down as, 'agitators.' We were the first to say that this meant the loss of Upper Silesia. So it was, and still they called us 'agitators.' We declared at that time that compliance in the question of Upper Silesia MUST have as its consequence the awakening of a passionate greed which would demand the occupation of the Ruhr. We were cried down ceaselessly, again and again. And because we opposed the mad financial policy which today will lead to our collapse, what was it that we were called repeatedly once more? 'Agitators.' And today?

And finally we were also the first to point the people on any large scale to a danger which insinuated itself into our midst—a danger which millions failed to realize and which will nonetheless lead us all into ruin—the Jewish danger. And today people are saying yet again that we were 'agitators.' I would like here to appeal to a greater than I, Count Lerchenfeld. He said in the last session of the Landtag that his feeling 'as a man and a Christian' prevented him from being an anti-Semite. I SAY: MY FEELING AS A CHRISTIAN POINTS ME TO MY LORD AND SAVIOUR AS A FIGHTER. IT POINTS ME TO THE MAN WHO ONCE IN LONELINESS, SURROUNDED ONLY BY A FEW FOLLOWERS, RECOGNIZED THESE JEWS FOR WHAT THEY WERE AND SUMMONED MEN TO THE FIGHT AGAINST THEM AND WHO, GOD'S TRUTH! WAS GREATEST NOT AS SUFFERER BUT AS FIGHTER. In boundless love as a Christian and as a man I read through the passage which tells us how the Lord at last rose in His might and seized the scourge to drive out of the Temple the brood of vipers and of adders. How terrific was His fight for the world against the Jewish poison. Today, after two thousand years, with deepest emotion I recognize more profoundly than ever before—the fact that it was for this that He had to shed His blood upon the Cross. As a Christian I have no duty to allow myself to be cheated, but I have the duty to be a fighter for truth and justice. And as a man I have the duty to see to it that human society does not suffer the same catastrophic collapse as did the civilization of the ancient world some two thousand years ago—a civilization which was driven to its ruin through this same Jewish people.

Then indeed when Rome collapsed there were endless streams of new German bands flowing into the Empire from the North; but, if Germany collapses today, who is there to come after us? German blood upon this earth is on the way to gradual exhaustion unless we pull ourselves together and make ourselves free!

And if there is anything which could demonstrate that we are acting rightly, it is the distress which daily grows. For as a Christian I have also a duty to my own people. And when I look on my people I see it work and work and toil and labor, and at the end of the week it has only for its wage wretchedness and misery. When I go out in the morning and see these men standing in their queues and look into their pinched faces, then I believe I would be no Christian, but a very devil, if I felt no pity for them, if I did not, as did our Lord two thousand years ago, turn against those by whom today this poor people is plundered and exploited.

And through the distress there is no doubt that the people has been aroused. Externally perhaps apathetic, but within there is ferment. And many may say, 'It is an accursed crime to stir up passions in the people.' And then I say to myself: Passion is already stirred through the rising tide of distress, and one day this passion will break out in one way or another: AND NOW I WOULD ASK THOSE WHO TODAY CALL US 'AGITATORS': 'WHAT THEN HAVE YOU TO GIVE TO THE PEOPLE AS A FAITH TO WHICH IT MIGHT CLING?'

Nothing at all, for you yourselves have no faith in your own prescriptions.

That is the mightiest thing which our Movement must create: for these widespread, seeking and straying masses a new Faith which will not fail them in this hour of confusion, to which they can pledge themselves, on which they can build so that they may at least find once again a place which may bring calm to their hearts.

Horst Wessel Song (1929)

By Horst Wessel

Horst Wessel (1907–1930) was a German ultra-nationalist who joined the NAZI party in 1926. Wessel found a spot in Hitler's private paramilitary organization, the Sturmabteilung (SA), and engaged in the political street fighting that increased after the onset of the 1929 economic crisis. Opening the door to his flat one evening, he was shot in the face by an unknown assailant. The murder may have been political, and a local German Communist Party member (KPD) was found guilty of the crime, but it may have been a dispute over money or Wessel's live-in girlfriend, a young sex-worker. Regardless, the NAZI party turned this thuggish street fighter into a martyr. A marching song he penned became the party anthem and was used as a national song during the NAZI state (1933–1945). These lyrics show the NAZI obsession with strength, struggle, and being part of an organized force.

Flag high, ranks closed,
The SA marches with silent solid steps.
Comrades shot by the red front and reaction
march in spirit with us in our ranks.

The street free for the brown battalions,
The street free for the Storm Troopers.
Millions, full of hope, look up at the swastika;
The day breaks for freedom and for bread.

For the last time the call will now be blown;
For the struggle now we all stand ready.
Soon will fly Hitler-flags over every street;
Slavery will last only a short time longer.

Horst Wessel, "Horst Wessel Song." Reprinted with permission.

Flag high, ranks closed,
The SA marches with silent solid steps.
Comrades shot by the red front and reaction
march in spirit with us in our ranks.

Law to Remove the Distress of the People and the State (The Enabling Act) (1933)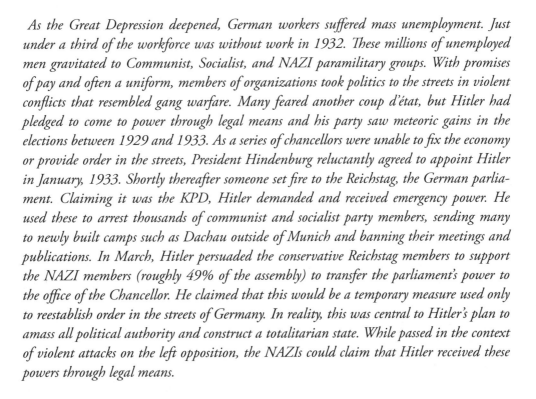

As the Great Depression deepened, German workers suffered mass unemployment. Just under a third of the workforce was without work in 1932. These millions of unemployed men gravitated to Communist, Socialist, and NAZI paramilitary groups. With promises of pay and often a uniform, members of organizations took politics to the streets in violent conflicts that resembled gang warfare. Many feared another coup d'état, but Hitler had pledged to come to power through legal means and his party saw meteoric gains in the elections between 1929 and 1933. As a series of chancellors were unable to fix the economy or provide order in the streets, President Hindenburg reluctantly agreed to appoint Hitler in January, 1933. Shortly thereafter someone set fire to the Reichstag, the German parliament. Claiming it was the KPD, Hitler demanded and received emergency power. He used these to arrest thousands of communist and socialist party members, sending many to newly built camps such as Dachau outside of Munich and banning their meetings and publications. In March, Hitler persuaded the conservative Reichstag members to support the NAZI members (roughly 49% of the assembly) to transfer the parliament's power to the office of the Chancellor. He claimed that this would be a temporary measure used only to reestablish order in the streets of Germany. In reality, this was central to Hitler's plan to amass all political authority and construct a totalitarian state. While passed in the context of violent attacks on the left opposition, the NAZIs could claim that Hitler received these powers through legal means.

The Reichstag has passed the following law, which is, with the approval of the Reichsrat, herewith promulgated, after it has been established that it meets the requirements for legislation altering the Constitution.

"Law to Remove the Distress of the People and the State (The Enabling Act)," *National Socialism: Basic Principles, their Application by the Nazi Party's Foreign Organizations, and the Use of Germans Abroad for Nazi Aims*, pp. 217-218.

Article 1. National laws can be enacted by the Reich Cabinet as well as in accordance with the procedure established in the Constitution. This also applies to the laws referred to in Article 85, Paragraph 2, and in Article 87 of the Constitution.

Article 2. The national laws enacted by the Reich Cabinet may deviate from the Constitution as long as they do not affect the position of the Reichstag and the Reichsrat. The powers of the President remain undisturbed.

Article 3. The national laws enacted by the Reich Cabinet shall be prepared by the Chancellor and published in the *Reichsgesetzblatt*. They come into effect, unless otherwise specified, the day after their publication. Articles 68–77 of the Constitution do not apply to the laws enacted by the Reich Cabinet.

Article 4. Treaties of the Reich with foreign states which concern matters of national legislation do not require the consent of the bodies participating in legislation. The Reich Cabinet is empowered to issue the necessary provisions for the implementation of these treaties.

Article 5. This law becomes effective on the day of its publication. It becomes invalid on April 1, 1937; it also becomes invalid if the present Reich Cabinet is replaced by another.

Reich President von Hindenburg
Reich Chancellor Adolf Hitler
Reich Minister of the Interior Frick
Reich Minister for Foreign Affairs Baron von Neurath
Reich Minister of Finances Count Schwerin von Krosigk

Present Status of the Anti-Semitic Movement in Germany, September 21, 1933

By George Messersmith

As American Consul General in Berlin, George S. Messersmith (1883–1960) was able to observe Hitler's rise to power. He was one of the first voices to clearly warn of the violence to come should the NAZI movement go unchecked. Importantly, other prominent Americans such as Henry Ford and Charles Lindberg (both rabid anti-Semites) saw Hitler as restoring order to a chaotic Germany.

American Consul General
Berlin, Germany, September 21, 1933
Subject: The present status of the anti-Semitic movement in Germany
The Honorable
The Secretary of State
Washington

Sir:

I have the honor to refer to my confidential despatch No. 1330 of May 23, on the status of the anti-Semitic movement in Germany at that time, and to my confidential despatch No. 1369 of June 17, giving a resume of the then social, economic and political status of the Jews in Germany. In the present despatch, I shall endeavor to bring the Department a resume of developments since my last despatch.

George Messersmith, "Report to the State Department on the Present Status of the Anti-Semitic Movement in Germany, September 21, 1933."

Dr. Achim Gercke is the expert for racial questions in the Ministry of the Interior of the Reich. There is transmitted herewith, as of primary interest in connection with the situation of the Jews in Germany, a translation of a confidential memorandum prepared by Dr. Gercke on fundamental principles with respect to the "Mischlingefrage," that is, [the] question of racial inter-mixture. This memorandum was not intended for publication and came to me through a confidential source. It is worthy of the Department's attention as practically all laws and regulations affecting the Jews in Germany pass through Dr. Gercke as the racial expert of the Ministry of the Interior of the Reich, and this memorandum is particularly interesting as showing the attitude of Dr. Gercke on fundamental aspects of the problem. I quote below only a few of the significant statements made in the memorandum.

"A person is not to be considered Aryan, one of whose grandparents is Jewish; only those persons are to be considered Aryans who have no Jewish ancestors whatsoever. [...] The Jewish question and the question of mixed blood must therefore be solved on a social plane. It must again become an ethical rule that persons of German blood may only contract marriages with persons of their own kind. [...] Now as to the fundamental principles: It would be contrary to all principles of racial health if one would, without hesitation, look upon an admixture of Jewish blood in the second, third, or fourth generation as non-existent or negligible. Experience on the contrary tells us that no number of generations can be definitely determined which would be necessary to extinguish the influence of a blood mixture which has once taken place."

There is also transmitted herewith a translation of an article which appeared in the June number of the "National-Socialistische Monatshefte" by Dr. Gercke. This article is also of particular interest as showing the basic attitude of the man who acts as the racial expert of the Ministry of the Interior. The following are significant quotations from this article.

"Through the victory of the National-Socialist revolution, also those who have never before worked or fought for its solution have recognized the Jewish question as a national problem. Everyone has acknowledged that the present situation is untenable. The unrestricted expansion and the equal treatment of Jews lead to unfair competition on the part of the Jews and to the surrender of the important positions of German spiritual and material value to those of a strange race. [...] This distortion of the Jewish problem must not be supported even by outward appearance, all the more as it would be political insanity if the national regulation of the Jewish question were mingled with questions of foreign policy. [...] All propositions which intended to create a permanent condition or a permanent regulation for the Jews in Germany do not solve the Jewish question, as they do not detach the Jew from Germany. And that is the main thing. The Jews, if they can live eternally as parasites in the nations which offer them their hospitality, will always remain a source of political danger where the open destructive fire of Bolshevism can again and again be set ablaze. [...] We must build up our country without the Jews; they can only remain strangers without nationality and may not occupy any legal and legitimate permanent position within the structure of the country. Only in this way will Ahasverus be forced to reach for his staff for the last time and exchange it for the axe and the spade."

Since I last addressed a despatch to the Department on this subject, there has been no alleviation what[so]ever of the situation of the Jews in Germany. On the contrary their condition is growing steadily worse. The situations described in previous despatches continue to exist and in the time which has elapsed it is possible to see even more definitely the implacability with which the various laws and regulations affecting the Jews in practically all conditions of life in Germany are carried through. That this should be so was to be expected, for those who control the National Socialist movement and the Government have not changed their views with respect to the treatment of the Jews. I am informed that the Chancellor, Mr. Hitler, and the Minister of Propaganda, Dr. Goebbels, among the higher leaders of the Party are the ones who remain adamant on this question. Outstanding Americans and foreigners who have in the past months had an opportunity to talk with the Chancellor and who believed it would be important to give him the view of the outside world on the Jewish question have, I am informed, found it entirely impossible to speak to him on this question. If they endeavored to make any remarks on the Jewish question the Chancellor interrupted them and delivered his point of view, which, I am told reliably, has remained entirely the same from the outset. I am informed also from reliable and confidential sources that Mr. Keppler, who is the most intimate of the Chancellor's economic advisors, Dr. Schmitt, the Minister of Commerce, and Dr. Schacht, the President of the Reichsbank, are not able to talk with the Chancellor on this subject and as soon as they endeavor to bring to him certain points of view, he refuses to listen to anything they have to say on this subject. This information comes to me from such creditable sources that I believe it may be taken as correct. Dr. Goebbels, the Minister of Propaganda, who is still the principal spokesman of the Government on the Jewish question, will listen to what others say to him, but without comment, and apparently so far without any change in his opinions being effected. My conversations with various people closely connected with the Government and with the Party, some of them occupying responsible positions in the various Ministries, would indicate that these [individuals] would be very happy if a more mild Jewish policy could be carried through; but it is obvious that they are powerless as long as the opinions of the highest leaders of the Party remain unchanged.

Dr. Rosenberg, the head of the Foreign Office of the National Socialist Party, who has been considerably in eclipse since his visit to London several months ago, came prominently into the press again on August 24 when he commented on the Zionist Congress held in Prague. According to the "Voelkische Beobachter," Dr. Rosenberg expressed himself as follows:

"The fact that Germany as the first of the great nations decided recently to remember its origin and its right to individuality in the formation of its political life, has, in spite of strong opposition, not failed to make a deep impression on the rest of the world. [...] National Socialism did not start this problem; but it has been its fate to have this problem forced upon it for solution, and in spite of what Jewry has done to Germany in the last fourteen years, the great movement of National Socialism has avoided taking vengeance on them in the legal way, taking into consideration the participation of the Jews in the war, and their deed, to avoid hardships as far as possible.[...]"

In this same article Dr. Rosenberg brought out that if the plan of the Prague Zionist Congress to help all the Jews emigrate from Germany were carried through, this would make it impossible for the German Government to take action against those Jews who remained in the country for the offensive action of those who had left. He said that the position of Germany in the future towards the whole problem would be determined by [the] results of the Congress at Prague and by the leaders of Jewry throughout the world. In other words, he made the threat that if the action of Jewish world leaders was objectionable to the German Government, it would only result in greater hardships for the Jews in Germany.

In the issue of August 26 of "Der Deutsche," which is the personal organ of Dr. Ley, the leader of the Deutsche Arbeitsfront, this paper comments that it would be a very happy solution if all Jews in Germany could be got out of the country as the Zionist Congress in Prague was planning, and that Germany would place no obstacle in the way of Jews leaving as this would only make more room for Germans now without work. This article comments, however, that "to clear up this problem, there remains the question of how much in the way of property the Jews leaving Germany will be permitted to take with them."

During the Nuremberg Party convention, the Chancellor and Dr. Goebbels both made significant speeches on the Jewish question. As the Department has, I believe, received copies of these speeches with appropriate comment, it does not seem necessary to comment on them further, except to state that these speeches indicated clearly that the Chancellor and Dr. Goebbels remain as implacable on the Jewish question as from the outset of the movement and place such stress on the question that, at the most important meeting the Party has ever held, their principal speeches are on racial questions.

It is, however, interesting to quote the following from the close of one of Goebbels' speeches at the Nuremberg convention:

"Let me say at the close a few words concerning the measures which we have taken against the dangers of the world propaganda which is directed against us. It is quite clear that such a well-planned campaign against Germany's peace and safety cannot remain unanswered by us. World propaganda against us will be answered by world propaganda for us. What propaganda is, and what might it has, and with what measures and methods it can be combated, that we know. We have not learned this in theory, but in practice, and have mastered it in our everyday work."

If the principal spokesman of the Party, and its highest leaders and the racial expert of the Government in the Ministry of the Interior hold the views set forth in the speeches referred to above and in the memoranda hereto appended, it is not difficult to understand that the racial question has not become in any sense easier.

The establishment of so-called "racial offices" is to take place throughout Germany. As early as May 4 the "Berliner Tageblatt," evening issue, carried an article to the effect that a racial office was being established in Dortmund under the head of the Kommissar for health. According to this article the racial records for the eighty thousand school children in Dortmund were to be made up as rapidly as possible in view of the importance of the new generation.

On June 28 a meeting took place in the Ministry of the Interior of the Reich, at which Dr. Frick addressed the committee of experts on population and race problems, when he stated that "in addition to the threatening increase of hereditarily inferior persons, the Government must follow with equal care the increasing mixture of races." He indicated that a law would soon be issued prohibiting [the] marriage of Germans with Jews.

The question as to who is Aryan and non-Aryan has been one which since the Party came into power has been creating considerable discussion. The matter is one of primary interest under the so-called "Reichsbeamtengesetz," that is, [the] law governing the officials of the Reich. According to this law persons of Jewish blood are to be prohibited from holding any office in the country, with certain exceptions, the principal exception being the "Frontkaempfer," that is, Jews who fought at the front during the war. The basic principles are laid down somewhat as follows:

1. He is to be considered non-Aryan who has Jewish parents or grandparents. It is sufficient if one parent or grandparent is non-Aryan.
2. Anyone who is called to be an official of the Reich has to show that he and his wife are of Aryan origin. Every official of the Reich who wishes to marry has to show that the person whom he wishes to marry is of Aryan origin. This proof is to be in the form of birth certificates and marriage certificates.
3. The basic principles laid down are to apply to the officials of the Reich, the states, the communes, the communal organizations and other bodies, institutions and foundations having official status.

According to the "Berliner Tageblatt" of September 16, the Ministry of the Interior of the Reich has issued a further explanatory statement in connection with the office-holders law to clear up the term "non-Aryan." In this declaration it is stated that if one of the grandparents of the official is Jewish or of Jewish origin, the official shall be considered Jewish under law. The Minister emphasizes that in interpreting the law, Aryan origin does not depend upon religion, but upon race and blood.

It is obvious from the foregoing that all persons with Jewish parents or grandparents are excluded from being officials or from holding any official position in Germany.

With respect to citizenship, the laws planned which are to disfranchise the Jews are for the most part still in preparation. From the best information available, it is apparently still the intention that practically all the Jews in Germany are to be disfranchised. The Jews are to be given the status of "foreigners" in Germany even though the family may have been in Germany for generations. This is the attitude of the radical element of the Party and unless there is a considerable change, the laws, when they appear, will be very drastic. Under the law of July 14, 1933, the Minister of the Interior of the Reich already has the authority to deprive persons of their citizenship without giving any reason for such action, and to confiscate the property of such persons. The "Berliner Tageblatt" of August 25 and other newspapers carry of a list of thirty-three German citizens who were deprived of their citizenship under this law by the Minister of the Interior. Among the names in these lists are those of George Bernhard, Leon Feuchtwanger, Heinrich Mann, and Philip Schneidemann.

The laws governing the prohibition of mixed marriages have not yet been issued; but such marriages have been almost as effectively stopped already by the other measures in effect as they could be by law. The Department is aware from previous reports that Party members can no longer marry a person who is not of Aryan origin, and if there is any Party member who has a non-Aryan wife or husband, he or she must be excluded from the Party. According to the "Beamtengesetz" many persons of Aryan origin who are married to non-Aryans have been compelled to give up their positions. It is no exaggeration to state that thousands of marriages which had been planned between Aryans and non-Aryans are not taking place as the marriage would ruin the career or the possible chance of making a livelihood of the one or the other party. The non-Aryan wives of Aryan officials have to my knowledge voluntarily left their husbands in order that they might continue in their careers. The wife of an Aryan professor recently informed me that she was leaving for the United States and separating from her husband as he had a position with a Government office in Stuttgart, and as she was of Jewish origin she was leaving him in order that he might be able to continue to make his living. As I happen to know that this was a happy marriage, I merely cite this as an isolated instance of the human tragedies daily taking place.

The "cleaning-out" in the universities of Jewish professors and those who have any non-Aryan ancestors according to the "Beamtengesetz" is continuing. There is, I understand, only one professor of Jewish origin left in the University of Berlin. On September 9 the Reichstatthalter of Saxony, in accordance with a decision of the Saxon Ministry of Education and the "Beamtengesetz," ordered the separation of six former

Professors from the University of Leipzig, of whom five were of Jewish origin. In other universities the "cleaning out" process has been completed for some time.

In this connection it may be interesting for the Department to know that a few days ago I had a conversation in the Ministry of the Interior of the Reich with the Ministerialdirektor Dr. Buttsman, whom I had gone to see with regard to an American physician in Germany, and he insisted on talking on the Jewish question. He told me the usual defence, which is made in various Ministries and in the press and which we hear constantly from all sides, and stressed particularly that in solving the Jewish problem Germany was doing a service for our country and for the rest of the world as well. He said that in carrying through the various laws affecting Jewish professors and professional men, it had been endeavored to avoid all hardships, and that in applying the *numerus clausus* the German government was following the only possible course. I told him that I did not want to discuss the Jewish question but that since he had raised the matter I should be interested in knowing how many Jewish professors there were left under the *numerus clausus* in the University of Berlin. He then gave me the impression that very few of the professors has been disturbed, and when I told him that so far I could learn only one was left, if he were still there, he had nothing to say. I then asked him how many Jewish professors were left in the University of Leipzig and he said that most of them were undisturbed. When I brought to his attention that five had been let out one at a time less than two weeks ago and that I understood no non-Aryan professor was left in Leipzig, he had nothing to say. I merely mention this to indicate that there is a remarkable insincerity which one finds in high-ranking officers of the Government. As Dr. Buttsman is apparently one of the high-ranking officers of the Government to whom American and foreign professors are directed for information when they come to Germany, it is quite possible to understand why some of the professional men who come to Germany leave it with such an incorrect picture of the situation.

The position of the Jewish physicians in Germany is becoming more difficult continually. They have been excluded from the physicians' organizations in which membership is a necessity if the physician is to enjoy any of the ordinary privileges of his career. They are excluded from the hospitals and clinics, except from those which are Jewish. They are for the most part not permitted to treat patients belonging to the various insurance organizations, public and private, unless they be purely Jewish organizations. The only exceptions in this connection which have been made are those in favor of Jewish physicians who served at the front during the war. Such war service, however, is no guarantee of privilege. I transmit herewith two clippings taken from a newspaper in Nuremberg. In the first clipping are given the names of eleven Jewish physicians in Nuremberg who have been re-admitted to practice with the sick benefit insurance organizations in the city; but the newspaper, in order to show its readers its regret that this official re-admission to practice has taken place, surrounds the item with a black border. The second clipping is from the same newspaper of the following day and refers to the previous article. The head of the Physicians' organization in Nuremberg, Dr. Strock, publishes the same list of eleven physicians and says that this publication of their re-admission was made without his knowledge and consent. He goes on to warn all people not to in any way consult or use these physicians in spite of the fact that they have been re-admitted. The "Vossiche Zeitung" of August 24 carries an article to the effect that the new "Academy of Physicians" has been established and that no physician of non-Aryan origin is to be admitted to the Academy.

The situation of the Jewish lawyers in Germany has in no sense become better. A general depression prevails among the majority of lawyers who have been re-admitted. Dr. Max Alsberg, one of the most distinguished lawyers at the Berlin Bar and who was only 56 years of age, committed suicide in a sanatorium in the Engadin some days ago. The "Berliner Tageblatt" of September 13 carries an article of considerable length, commenting on Dr. Alsberg's professional reputation, stating that he died of a heart attack from which he had suffered for some time. I am informed from a reliable source that Dr. Alsberg took his own life as a result of the depression from which he was suffering.

There is transmitted herewith a copy of the questionnaire which must be filled in by all persons who desire to be appointed to any public office in Germany or to hold an office in an official or semi-official organization. The interesting questions are found on page 4 where the applicant is required to give very detailed information with regards to his parents and grandparents. All German officials, high and low, are being required to fill in this form and they are carefully examined. Those who cannot prove their Aryan origin by supporting documents or who are not accepted under the "Beamtengesetz" are separated from their office.

As an indication of the extent to which the anti-Semitic movement is carried, it is interesting to note that a new telephone alphabet has been published by the German Post Office, which is to be effective throughout the country. It was customary when spelling names on the telephone, to use "Samuel" for the letter S, but this must now be "Siegfried"; and instead of "Nathan" for N, it must now be "Nordpol."

The Department is aware of the steps which have been taken in various universities and throughout the various cities in Germany to exclude from the libraries books written by Jewish authors. In this connection the following order issued by the appropriate Prussian Ministry to universities, high schools, etc., is of interest:

"For scientific libraries, the confiscation or destruction of Jewish or Marxistic books does not come in question. The lending, however, of such books is to be carried on with the greatest care in the future. Such books can only be given out when the lender can show that he needs the books for serious scientific investigational work."

As indicative of the popular sentiment, I wish to bring to the Department's attention a meeting which took place in the Sport Palast in Berlin on the evening of

September 18. The meeting was addressed by Dr. Habicht, whose speech was reported in a number of the Berlin newspapers. He was followed by Schultze Wechsungen, who is the National Socialist propaganda chief for the Berlin district. Some 6,000 persons were present at this meeting and listened with interest and enthusiasm to the speech which Mr. Wechsungen made attacking the Jews. He advocated increasing the total of 40,000 persons now in the concentration camps by sending there large number of Jews, as this would help the unemployment problem. He demanded the further persecution of the Jews in Germany and advocated the beating of German women who dared to appear in public with Jews. He states that far too many who belong in the concentration camps are still free but one by one they will go there. He added that the Jews have good reason to thank their God that Hitler is the National Socialist leader. If Hitler were not their leader the Jews in Germany would no longer exist. He went on to say that as propaganda chief of the Berlin district he decreed that in the future every Aryan German girl who is seen in a restaurant or on the street with a Jew, must be given a good beating. "The municipal administration must keep the drainage system working. The Storm Troopers of the National Socialist Party have to take care of the other purifying measures." This speech was so outrageous that not a single newspaper in Berlin carried an account of it and only one newspaper made any mention at all that Wechsungen had spoken at the meeting. A correspondent of the New York Herald Tribune and [a correspondent] of the International News Service were present at the meeting and took stenographic notes of Wechsungen's speech.

In various dispatches I have informed the Department that the period of physical persecution of the Jews may be considered as over. This I think still holds, but isolated instances of physical outrages committed on Jews continually take place. About three weeks ago the son of one of the most prominent Jewish families in Germany was delivered dead to his wife, and the family allowed to bury the body but not to see it, except one side of the face. The mother of this Jew is one of the most philanthropic women in Germany and has contributed during the war and since then, freely from her considerable fortune, to the relief of suffering. Her son, who was obviously brutally murdered, was five times wounded during the first war and after the first time that he was wounded would not have been under the necessity of returning to the front. After the war, being impaired in health as a result of his wounds and enjoying an ample fortune, he bought an estate about 40 miles from Berlin where he devoted himself to training young men to be good farmers. He gained the enmity of a father and son living on his estate, who were continually making difficulty, but who, as National Socialists, after March 5 saw that this Jew was put into a concentration camp where he was severely mistreated. On account of the position of his family and his own good works and those of his mother, he was released from the concentration camp. After leaving the concentration camp he came to live with his wife in Berlin as it was no longer safe for him on the estate. About three weeks ago on a Saturday morning, he was notified by the police of his district to appear at the police station to register. He went to the police station and when he arrived there was told a telegram had just come requiring his arrest and he was detained. He was permitted to send word to his wife, who came and brought his luncheon to the police station. This was the last time he was seen live by any of his family. On the Wednesday evening following, a policeman came to the home of his wife and said that if she would come to the police station she would have good news of her husband. In the meantime prominent persons had used all their influence in an endeavor to learn where the young man was; but he could not be located even with the assistance of high-ranking members of the Government in Berlin. The wife went to the police station and when she arrived there was informed that her husband was dead. She was taken to the mortuary and a cloth was lifted from one side of the face of the young man so that she could identify him. The body was delivered to the family for burial but they were not permitted to see it. The police gave out that he had committed suicide by throwing himself in front of a truck while being taken to the concentration camp. The fact is that the same two men, father and son, who had previously caused his being placed in a concentration camp through the S.A. and the assistance of the police, had got him into their hands. How he was actually killed remains a mystery, beyond that his dead body was delivered to the police at the police station by the S.A., who had received him alive at the same station. The facts in this case as above recited, horrible and unbelievable as they may seem, come to me from sources which are unimpeachable.

That incidents of the above nature are becoming more and more isolated is undoubtedly correct; but it is equally true that they are still continuing to take place and that the perpetrators, even though it is possible for the authorities to locate them, remain entirely unpunished.

I have gone into the present status of the Jews in Germany at this length as I believe it is essential that the Department be informed as to details. The Minister of Propaganda, Dr. Goebbels, repeated in his speech on the racial question at Nuremberg the phrase heard so often, that not a hair on the head of a Jew had been harmed since the 5th of March. If such statements are made by responsible officers of the Government, it is necessary that the real facts appear in the record.

Respectfully yours,

George S. Messersmith
American Consul General

Description of Anti-Semitic Persecution and Kristallnacht and its Aftereffects in the Stuttgart Region

By Samuel Honaker

Another American Consul, Samuel Honaker, observed NAZI anti-Semitic violence first-hand in 1938, and reported it to George S. Messersmith, then Assistant to the Secretary of State. After a German Jewish emigrant assassinated a German diplomat in Paris, Hitler ordered Goebbels to use the SA and SS to organize a widespread and coordinated attack on German Jews. The NAZIs claimed the violence was spontaneous, but this document shows otherwise. November 11, 1938 became known as Kristallnacht, "the Night of Broken Glass." Thousands of synagogues, Jewish shops, and homes were attacked and burned and an unknown number of German Jews were beaten, raped, and murdered.

I. Letter to Hugh R. Wilson, American Embassy, Berlin

American Consulate
Stuttgart, Germany, November 12, 1938
No. 307
Subject: Anti-Semitic Persecution in the Stuttgart Consular District
The Honorable Hugh R. Wilson, American Ambassador, Berlin

Sir:

Samuel Honaker, "American Consul Samual Honaker's Description of Anti-Semitic Persecution and Kristallnacht and its Aftereffects in the Stuttgart Region."

I have the honor to report that the Jews of Southwest Germany have suffered vicissitudes during the last three days which would seem unreal to one living in an enlightened country during the twentieth century if one had not actually been a witness of their dreadful experiences, or if one had not had them corroborated by more than one person of undoubted integrity. To the anguish of mind to which the Jews of this consular district have been subjected for some time, and which suddenly became accentuated on the morning and afternoon of the tenth of November, were added the horror of midnight arrests, of hurried departures in a half-dressed state from their homes in the company of police officers, of the wailing of wives and children suddenly left behind, of imprisonment in crowded cells, and the panic of fellow prisoners.

These wholesale arrests were the culmination of a day of suffering on the part of the Jews. The desecration and burning of synagogues started before daylight and should have proved a warning signal of what was to come during the course of the next few hours. At 10:30 A.M. about twenty-five leaders of the Jewish community were arrested by a joint squad of policemen and plain clothes men. The arrested persons ranged from thirty-five to sixty-five years of age and were taken from their community officer (*Israelitischer Oberrat*) to the police station in two motor vehicles. As the victims passed from the building to the motor cars bystanders cursed and shouted at them.

Other arrests took place in various parts of Stuttgart. While this city was the scene of many anti-Semitic demonstrations during the course of the day, similar events were taking place all over Württemberg and Baden. Jews were attacked here and there. So great had become the panic of the Jewish people in the meantime that, when the consulate opened after Armistice Day, Jews from all sections of Germany thronged into the office until it was overflowing with humanity, begging for an immediate visa or some kind of letter in regard to immigration which might influence the police not to arrest or molest them. Women over sixty years of age pleaded on behalf of husbands imprisoned in some unknown place. American mothers of German sons invoked the sympathy of the Consulate. Jewish fathers and mothers with children in their arms were afraid to return to their homes without some document denoting their intention to immigrate at an early date. Men in whose homes old, rusty revolvers had been found during the last few days cried aloud that they did not dare ever again to return to their places of residence or business. In fact, it was a mass of seething, panic-stricken humanity.

Burning of Synagogues

Early on the morning of November 10th practically every synagogue—at least twelve in number—in Württemberg, Baden, and Hohenzollern was set on fire by well-disciplined and apparently well-equipped young men in civilian clothes. The procedure was practically the same in all cities of this district, namely, Stuttgart, Karlsruhe,

Freiburg, Heidelberg, Heilbronn, et cetera. The doors of the synagogues were forced open. Certain sections of the building and furnishings were drenched with petrol and set on fire. Bibles, prayer books, and other sacred things were thrown into the flames. Then the local fire brigades were notified. In Stuttgart, the city officials ordered the fire brigade to save the archives and other written material having a bearing on vital statistics. Otherwise, the fire brigades confined their activities to preventing the flames from spreading. In a few hours the synagogues were, in general, heaps of smoking ruins.

Devastation of Jewish Shops

Practically all the Jewish shops in the Stuttgart consular district are reported to have been attacked, ransacked, and devastated. These actions were carried out by young men and half-grown boys. It was easy to recognize under the civilian clothes of the former trained and disciplined S.A. or S.S. men, while in the case of the latter the Hitler Youth uniform was evident in some instances. The young men set about their task in most cases quietly and efficiently. They first smashed windows, destroyed furnishings, and then began to throw merchandise into the street. Throughout these actions the police looked on, either smilingly or unconcernedly.

Most of the Jewish shops in Stuttgart are situated in the main business section of the city. On the Königsstrasse, the principal business street, no looting was observed, but in the side streets looting was noticed in a number of cases. In front of one shop people were seen trying on shoes which had been thrown into the street. Before the Café Heimann was demolished, people helped themselves to cake and so forth.

The following is a list of Jewish shops in Stuttgart which were badly damaged:

Name of Firm	Address	Principal Business
Bamberger & Hertz	2 Poststrasse	Clothing
Bloch	1 Rotbühlstrasse	Restaurant
Jacobs	32 Hauptstätterstrasse	Radios
Katz	6 Leonhardsplatz	Shoes
Robert	8 Marktstrasse	Clothing
Salberg	56 Königstrasse	Photographer
Scheinmann	45 Königstrasse	Shoes
Speier	58 Königstrasse	Shoes
Speier	4 Marktplatz	Shoes
Tanne	6 Tübingerstrasse	Department store
Ika	21 Königstrasse	Lingerie

Arrests and Other Persecutive Activities

It has been learned from reliable sources that practically the entire male Jewish population of the city of Stuttgart, ranging from the age of eighteen to sixty-five years, has been arrested by authorities representing the police. In most cases the arrests are reported to have been effected by two policemen wearing civilian clothes. These arrests included many prominent Jewish businessmen and several consuls of foreign states, among whom the most notable is the Danish Consul General for Württemberg. All of the arrested persons were immediately conducted to police headquarters and then placed in cells. During the course of November 11th some of the persons arrested were transported to Welzheim, which is the most important concentration camp in Württemberg. Arrests were also made as late as 10 A.M. on Saturday, the 12th of November. It is understood that the latter arrests consisted very largely of young men living in rural districts, who have since been brought to police headquarters in Stuttgart.

In several small places in Württemberg, notably in Rexingen, Buttenhausen, and Laupheim, Jews have been prohibited from leaving their homes since the 10th of November. They are not permitted to receive or send mail. Unconfirmed reports are even to the effect that these persons are having difficulty in securing food, and in some cases it has been reported that farmers have been slipping food to them through the back doors of their homes.

In Heilbronn an order was issued Friday (November 11th) prohibiting Jews from entering cinemas in that city. Early on the morning of the 10th of November a number of Jews who had been arrested were forced to march in the streets of Kehl two by two, reporting in chorus: "We are guilty of the murder in Paris and we are traitors to Germany." Among there were ex-servicemen, some of whom had been wounded during the Great War, and some of whom had received war decorations.

At the time of writing this report it seems as if arrests in rural districts have not been as widespread as in the city of Stuttgart. Many Jewish men, some of whom are of excellent business standing, are reported to have left their homes on Thursday and to have disappeared in the meantime. Their friends assume that they are wandering about, in the hope that possibly the storm will blow itself out and they will be left unmolested. It is reported that, in such cases, the police have left word with their families that the missing men should report to police headquarters as soon as they appear at their homes. Naturally, there are rumors of many suicides, especially of elderly Jewish men, but so far reports of this kind have not been confirmed.

Although the writer has spoken with the proprietors of homes which have been demolished in other parts of Germany during the last few days, no attacks on private houses and apartments occupied by Jews in Württemberg have been reported in the case of Stuttgart, with the exception of two isolated instances. It is known, however, that the Jewish State Orphans' Asylum in Esslingen, which is only about six miles from

Stuttgart, has been forcibly evacuated and the children chased out into the streets. Many families, the males of which have been arrested, are without any money and are now being assisted by more fortunate Jewish families. Jewish organizations have not been able to extend aid during the last few days, for their offices have been closed and their funds sequestered.

After a period of three days during which persecutive measures against the Jews have been unprecedented in this part of Germany, depression among this section of the population has become indescribable. Many Jewish women are afraid that the worst is yet to be experienced. They look forward with dread to the day on which Herr von [sic] Roth will be buried. Apprehension is prevalent in Jewish circles that a large number of the Jews already in prison will be kept by the authorities as hostages. They are hoping that Jews in foreign countries and the foreign Press will not give occasion to the German authorities to make more severe their persecution and apprehension as regards the future.

Reaction of the People to the Events Described

There is a strong belief among many conservative people in Stuttgart that the violent action against the Jews which has taken place during the last three days was planned and in practically no way spontaneous as the German Press would like to have everyone believe. It became quickly known in Stuttgart that action against the Jews in Württemberg and Hohenzollern had taken place more or less simultaneously. It was just as quickly known that three measures were being executed throughout this section of Germany:

    (a) the burning of synagogues;

    (b) the smashing of windows and the forced closing of all Jewish shops; and

    (c) the wholesale arrests of Jewish men.

These actions have caused a great part of the population to feel very uneasy and quickly to give expression to their lack of agreement with such practices. Reactions on the part of the populace have, however, shown a division of sentiment. The vast majority of the non-Jewish population, perhaps as much as 80 percent, have given evidence of complete disagreement with these violent demonstrations against the Jews. Many people, in fact, are hanging their heads with shame. On the other hand, possibly 20 percent of the population has shown satisfaction as a result of the application of radical measures.

Respectfully yours,
Samuel Honaker,
American Consul General

II. Letter to George S. Messersmith, Department of State, Washington, DC

American Consulate
Stuttgart, Germany, November 15, 1938
The Honorable George S. Messersmith
Assistant to the Secretary of State
Washington, DC

Dear Mr. Messersmith:

Appreciating your keen interest in German matters I believe that you will wish to have a first-hand account of the reprisals which have been taken against the Jews in this section of Germany during the last few days. Therefore, I am enclosing for ready reference a copy of my report no. 307, of November 12, 1938, entitled "Anti-Semitic Persecution in the Stuttgart Consular District." After careful investigation and personal knowledge this report was very hurriedly written so that it could reach the Embassy at Berlin at the earliest practicable date. You may wish to have additional information on the subject.

Of all the places in this section of Germany, the Jews in Rastatt, which is situated near Baden-Baden, have apparently been subjected to the most ruthless treatment. Many Jews in this section were cruelly attacked and beaten and the furnishings of their homes almost totally destroyed. Practically all male Jews in that city were arrested and transported either to prisons or to concentration camps. Those that escaped arrest are hiding in the woods or have sought refuge with friends. Similar developments occurred in other places, and there were doubtless many outrages of which I have not yet heard.

Even Jews directing charitable organizations were seriously molested, although it must have been apparent to the authorities that these Jews could have rendered much necessary relief had they been allowed to remain at liberty and retain the use of funds which were immediately confiscated. In the meantime, Aryan doctors in Stuttgart have been refusing to render medical aid to Jews greatly needing their services, unless evidence is furnished that no Jewish doctor is available. An old Jew living in Bad Cannstatt, a suburb of Stuttgart, suffered a heart collapse on Friday (November 11th) and, when a member of his family called a well-known heart specialist in Stuttgart, the latter is reported to have replied that "as long as there is a Jewish doctor still at liberty I cannot come." So far as I have been able to learn, all Jewish doctors in Stuttgart, except Dr. Einstein, a child specialist of over sixty-five years of age, have been arrested in spite of the overwhelming demand for medical treatment on account of ruthless action most apparently inspired by the German authorities.

All Jewish automobiles are systematically being confiscated. As a rule, two men in civilian clothes with police authority visit the homes of Jewish owners of automobiles and demand the keys of their garages and cars. Upon request receipts are usually given for the automobiles, and these receipts are signed "by the Criminal Police."

A few Aryan people have been arrested for giving too open expression to their disgust over the events of the last few days. Many persons secretly sympathizing with the Jews or discountenancing such ruthless treatment of helpless people are becoming more and more afraid to give expression to their feelings. However, I have heard of many instances where Aryans are rendering secret service to afflicted Jewish families and are even providing them with money and food.

Even consideration of religion has not prevented the arrest of persons of the Jewish race who were born and baptized as Christians. A typical example of this character is the arrest in Stuttgart of Dr. Gabriel, who until 1933 was the head of the Bureau of Academic Information at the University of Cologne. It is understood that Dr. Gabriel, who is said to have collaborated for some time with Professor Sprague of Columbia University, has been placed in a concentration camp at Welzheim, Württemberg.

So far as Stuttgart is concerned, I can state confidently that these so-called reprisals against the Jews were not a spontaneous movement originating from the people as a whole. In any event, the movement clearly seems to have been well organized and planned and carried out by persons having the confidence of the authorities. For instance, the fire brigade was stationed in the vicinity of the synagogue in Bad Cannstatt before the building was ever set on fire. Again, on Thursday morning (November 10th) while the demolition of Jewish shops was in full swing at Stuttgart, a new 12-cylinder Mercedes automobile carrying high S.S. officials drove up in front of the shops under devastation. These men made an inspection of what was going on, and apparently after giving their approval drove pompously away while the destruction continued.

Dr. Max Immanuel, a member of the board of the Berlin Credit Investment Company, who is said to have collaborated closely in the past with Herr Schacht, has informed me that all the interior furnishings of his sister's home in Nuremberg were completely destroyed. Nuremberg seems to have been the scene of much destruction and ill-treatment.

Only yesterday (Sunday, the 13th of November) the wife of a prominent Jew in Nuremberg whom I have known well for several years, and who has been of much assistance to me in connection with certain reports, called at my home in the hope that I could render some assistance in obtaining the release of her husband who was arrested [at] about 3.30 o'clock on the morning of November 10th. This lady told me that she had been awakened [at] about 1 o'clock by rude knocking and [the] ringing of her door bell. Men in S.A. uniform entered abruptly when the door was opened and immediately began to destroy the furnishings of the drawing room and dining room. Leather chairs were cut and stabbed with knives to such an extent that they are now practically worthless. China was thrown on the floor and broken. Not a piece of glassware was left unbroken in the apartment. When these men left, the interior of the building, except the bedrooms which they did not enter, were a mass of ruins.

This destruction did not satisfy the people responsible for it, for at approximately 4 a.m. two men dressed in civilian clothes and representing the police again called at her home and rudely demanded that her husband dress immediately. Her husband was placed under arrest and transported to prison. Although this lady is a person of some influence and has contact with the police at Nuremberg, she has not yet been able to ascertain to what prison or concentration camp her husband has been transported.

During the course of the day two people reported to me that the Jewish Old People's Home in Neustadt, Palatinate, had been burned to the ground and that about sixty inmates, all of whom were old people, and some of whom were ill and crippled and some just merely infirm from age, had been removed to the Jewish Old People's Home at Mannheim. There was really no accommodation for them in the latter institution and apparently they have been lying on the floor here and there in the building.

There are many similar stories, but I feel that you will be sufficiently informed to wish me now to turn to the immediate experiences which I have had during the past few days as the officer in charge of the Consulate at Stuttgart.

In a figurative sense, my home has been bombarded by visitors and telephone calls giving evidence of the distressing circumstances in which many people are finding themselves. Hundreds are appealing for help and encouragement, and with husbands in concentration camps many are without funds. Late last night an American woman of over sixty years of age begged for assistance in ascertaining the whereabouts of her aged and sick husband who had been rounded up with the German Jews. I have strong hopes that he will be at her side again within a few hours. Many other Americans are appealing on behalf of their Jewish relatives.

The Consulate received almost one hundred telegrams yesterday and almost as many today. Many of these have been from the United States and have expressed the utmost interest in their relatives in Germany. In the majority of cases the male members of the families concerned were ascertained to be in concentration camps. Even up to this minute arrests have been made in Stuttgart and telegrams are constantly being received, although it is late at night.

For more than five days the office has been inundated with people. Each day a larger and larger crowd has besieged the Consulate, filling all the rooms and overflowing into the corridor of a building six stories high. Today there were several thousand. Each person has been handled with the greatest possible consideration and each person must have felt that he or she had been as courteously and sympathetically handled as the enormous crowd would permit.

The entire staff has responded most loyally and efficiently to the demands with which we have been faced. Of the officers, all of whom have worked well under trying conditions, I wish especially to mention, first, Consul L'Heureux, and secondly, Vice Consul Spalding. Of the clerks, Mr. Morton Bernath has been outstanding.

These situations are not entirely new to us at Stuttgart. While this one is on a much greater scale, we have been experiencing similar but minor situations during the past three years, some of which appear retrospectively to have been much more difficult and to have required much more ingenuity. In reality, I have handled many protection cases, with the able assistance of Morton Bernath, which have involved arrests for political offences, exchange infractions, et cetera, and I am glad to report to you that we have been uniformly successful. At the present time matters involving the transfer of money on behalf of American citizens in the United States are proving unusually difficult features of our work on account of the attitude of the German Government. Only a few days ago, however, we were successful in prevailing upon the German Government to release its claim on the entire fortune of an aged Jewish woman of American nationality.

I trust that the foregoing description will, in addition to the political reports of this office, with which the Embassy seems to be very pleased, give you a concrete idea of the situation which has been confronting us from time to time over the last three years, and will especially depict the conditions which are immediately confronting us.

Sincerely yours,
[signed: Samuel Honaker]

Chapter 5

Anti-Colonialism and Nationalism

Introduction

While from the very first conquests there had been some form of resistance to European colonialism, in the twentieth century this opposition began to take shape as modern nationalism. Political leaders realized that they could mobilize a mass base within the colony and that, once mobilized, these leaders could direct the population in sustained campaigns to reform or remove European colonial rule. Yet anti-colonialism and nationalism were not monolithic, one-size-fits-all ideologies. Indeed, there were countless varieties of strategies and theories. Some, like Ho Chi Minh, linked the global class struggle of Marxist-Leninism to the struggle to be free of foreign control. Others, like Jomo Kenyatta and Lépold Sédar Senghor and the Négritude poets acknowledged the psychological impact of colonization. They wanted the colonized people to reject the culture of the colonizers, embracing and celebrating the value of their native traditions. With regard to tactics, we can see the stark contrast between Gandhi's deep and profound commitment to non-violence and Fanon's belief that anti-colonial violence would allow the colonized to retain their dignity. These documents reveal the variety of anti-colonial movements in the twentieth century.

This chapter relates to sections 10.4, 10.9, and 10.10 of the History-Social Science Content Standards for California Public Schools.

Some Considerations on the Colonial Question

By Ho Chi Minh

While Ho Chi Minh was a committed nationalist fighting for the cause of Vietnam's independence from France, he was also a communist and founding member of the French Communist Party. Here he gives a frank assessment of the difficulties in merging the anti-colonial and world-revolutionary movements.

Since the French Party has accepted Moscow's 'twenty-one conditions' and joined the Third International, among the problems which it has set itself is a particularly ticklish one—colonial policy. Unlike the First and Second Internationals, it cannot be satisfied with purely sentimental expressions of position leading to nothing at all, but must have a well defined working programme, an effective and practical policy.

On this point, more than on others, the Party faces many difficulties, the greatest of which are the following:

1. The great size of the colonies

Not counting the new 'trusteeships' acquired after the war, France possesses:

In Asia, 450,000 square kilometres, in Africa 3,541,000 square kilometres, in America, 108,000 square kilometres and in Oceania 21,600 square kilometres, or a total area of 4,120,000 square kilometres (eight times its own territory), with a population of 48,000,000 souls. These people speak over twenty different languages. This diversity of tongues does not make propaganda easy, for, except in a few old colonies, a French propagandist can make himself understood only through an interpreter. However, translations are of limited value, and in these countries of administrative despotism, it is rather difficult to find an interpreter to translate revolutionary speeches.

Ho Chi Minh, "Some Considerations on the Colonial Question," *Selected Works of Ho Chi Minh*, vol. 1. Copyright © by Foreign Languages Publishing House.

There are other drawbacks: though the natives of all the colonies are equally oppressed and exploited, their intellectual, economic and political development differs greatly from one region to another. Between Annam and the Congo, Martinique and New Caledonia, there is absolutely nothing in common, except poverty.

2. The indifference of the proletariat of the mother country towards the colonies

In his theses on the colonial question, Lenin clearly stated that 'the workers of colonizing countries are bound to give the most active assistance to the liberation movements in subject countries.' To this end, the workers of the mother country must know what a colony really is, they must be acquainted with what is going on there, and with the suffering—a thousand times more acute than theirs—endured by their brothers, the proletarians in the colonies. In a word, they must take an interest in this question.

Unfortunately, there are many militants who still think that a colony is nothing but a country with plenty of sand underfoot and of sun overhead; a few green coconut palms and coloured folk, that is all. And they take not the slightest interest in the matter.

3. The ignorance of the natives

In colonized countries—in old Indo-China as well as in new Dahomey—the class struggle, and proletarian strength, are unknown factors for the simple reason that there are neither big commercial and industrial enterprises, nor workers' organizations. In the eyes of the natives, Bolshevism—a word which is the more vivid and expressive because frequently used by the bourgeoisie—means either the destruction of everything or emancipation from the foreign yoke. The first sense given to the word drives the ignorant and timorous masses away from us; the second leads them to nationalism. Both senses are equally dangerous. Only a tiny section of the intelligentsia knows what is meant by communism. But these gentry, belonging to the native bourgeoisie and supporting the bourgeois colonialists, have no interest in the communist doctrine being understood and propagated. On the contrary, like the dog in the fable, they prefer to bear the mark of the collar and to have their piece of bone. Generally speaking, the masses are thoroughly rebellious, but completely ignorant. They want to free themselves, but do not know how to go about doing so.

4. Prejudices

The mutual ignorance of the two proletariats gives rise to prejudices. The French workers look upon the native as an inferior and negligible human being, incapable of understanding and still less of taking action. The natives regard all the French as wicked exploiters. Imperialism and capitalism do not fail to take advantage of this mutual suspicion and this artificial racial hierarchy to frustrate propaganda and divide forces which ought to unite.

5. Fierceness of repression

If the French colonialists are unskillful in developing colonial resources, they are masters in the art of savage repression and the manufacture of loyalty made to measure. The Gandhis and the de Valeras would have long since entered heaven had they been born in one of the French colonies. Surrounded by all the refinements of courts martial and special courts, a native militant cannot educate his oppressed and ignorant brothers without the risk of falling into the clutches of his civilizers.

Faced with these difficulties, what must the Party do?

Intensify propaganda to overcome them.

Facing Mount Kenya (excerpts)

By Jomo Kenyatta

Jomo Kenyatta (1894–1978) is considered by many to be the founding father of the Kenyan nation. Born to a Kikuyu family, his given name was Kamau wa Muigai but he changed it to Johnstone Kamau when he was baptized but later took the name Kenyatta to refer to a traditional Kikuyu belt. In the 1930s he again changed his name to Jomo Kenyatta, Jomo meaning "burning spear." In the late 1920s he became active in Kenyan politics and published a paper that preached national self-improvement. In 1929 Kenyatta was sent to England to testify in favor of Kikuyu rights. He returned to England again in 1931 but stayed in Europe for almost 15 years. Under Comintern sponsorship he spent two years studying economics at Moscow State University and then studied anthropology under Bronisław Malinowski at the London School of Economics. Kenyatta published his thesis as Facing Mount Kenya in 1938, a defense of Kikuyu tradition, ritual, and culture. In England he had close connection with a variety of Pan-Africanists such as W.E.B. Du Bois and Kwame Nkrumah. After World War Two, he returned to Kenya to struggle for independence. Kenyatta served as Kenya's first president until his death in 1978.

THE CUSTOM of clitoridectomy of girls, which we are going to describe here, has been strongly attacked by a number of influential European agencies—missionary, sentimental pro-African, Government, educational and medical authorities. We think it necessary to give a short historical background of the method employed by these bodies in attacking the custom of clitoridectomy of girls.

In 1929, after several attempts to break down the custom, the Church of Scotland Mission to Gikuyu issued an order demanding that all their followers and those who wish their children to attend schools should pledge themselves that they will not in any way adhere to or support this custom, and that they will not let their children

Jomo Kenyatta, *Selections from Facing Mt. Kenya*, pp. 125–129, 297–306. Copyright © 1965 by Random House Inc. Reprinted with permission.

undergo the initiation rite. This raised a great controversy between the missionaries and the Gikuyu. The matter was taken up seriously by both educated and uneducated Gikuyu. Children of those who did not denounce the custom were debarred from attending the missionary schools. People petitioned the Government and educational authorities. During the petitioning period many of these deserted schools and churches were used for storing maize and potatoes. A "gentlemen's agreement" was reached between the Government and the missionaries. The ban on children attending the schools was lifted but the missionaries maintained that teachers must be only those who had denounced the custom, for they hoped that teachers with this qualification would be able to mould the children in the way favourable to the missionary attitude. People were indignant about this decision and at once demanded the right to establish their own schools where they could teach their children without interference with the group custom. The cry for schools was raised high, and the result was the foundation of Gikuyu independent schools and Kareng'a schools. These schools are entirely free from missionary influence, both in educational and religious matters.

In 1930 the question of the custom of clitoridectomy was raised in the House of Commons and a committee of Members of Parliament was appointed to investigate the matter. The members of the committee included the Duchess of Atholl, Colonel Josiah Wedgwood, C. R. Buxton and others. The writer was invited to attend the committee meeting and give the Gikuyu's point of view. It was then agreed that the best way to tackle the problem was through education and not by force of an enactment, and that the best way was to leave the people concerned free to choose what custom was best suited to their changing conditions.

In 1931 a conference on African children was held in Geneva under the auspices of the Save the Children Fund. In this conference several European delegates urged that the time was ripe when this "barbarous custom" should be abolished, and that, like all other "heathen" customs, it could be abolished at once by law. It was the duty of the Conference, for the sake of the African children, to call upon the Governments, under which the customs of this nature were practised, to pass laws making it a criminal offence for anyone who should be found guilty of practising the custom of clitoridectomy.

However, this urge for abolishing a people's social custom by force of law was not wholeheartedly accepted by the majority of the delegates in the Conference. General opinion was for education which would enable the people to choose what customs to keep and which ones they would like to get rid of.

It should be pointed out here that there is a strong community of educated Gikuyu opinion in defence of this custom. In the matrimonial relation, the *rite de passage* is the deciding factor. No proper Gikuyu would dream of marrying a girl who has not been circumcised, and vice versa. It Is taboo for a Gikuyu man or woman to have sexual relations with someone who has not undergone this operation. If it happens, a man or woman must go through a ceremonial purification, *korutwo thahu or gotahikio megiro*—namely, ritual vomiting of the evil deeds. A few detribalised Gikuyu, while they are away from home for some years, have thought fit to denounce the custom and to marry uncircumcised girls, especially from coastal tribes, thinking that they could bring them back to their fathers' homes without offending the parents. But to their surprise they found that their fathers, mothers, brothers and sisters, following the tribal custom, are not prepared to welcome as a relative-in-law anyone who has not fulfilled the ritual qualifications for matrimony. Therefore a problem has faced these semi-detribalised Gikuyu when they wanted to return to their homeland. Their parents have demanded that if their sons wished to settle down and have the blessings of the family and the clan, they must divorce the wife married outside the rigid tribal custom and then marry a girl with the approved tribal qualifications. Failing this, they have been turned out and disinherited.

In our short survey we have mentioned how the custom of clitoridectomy has been attacked on one side, and on the other how it has been defended. In view of these points the important problem is an anthropological one: it is unintelligent to discuss the emotional attitudes of either side, or to take violent sides in the question, without understanding the reasons why the educated, intelligent Gikuyu still cling to this custom.

The real argument lies not in the defence of the surgical operation or its details, but in the understanding of a very important fact in the tribal psychology of the Gikuyu—namely, that this operation is still regarded as the very essence of an institution which has enormous educational, social, moral, and religious implications, quite apart from the operation itself. For the present it is impossible for a member of the tribe to imagine an initiation without clitoridectomy. Therefore the abolition of the surgical element in this custom means to the Gikuyu the abolition of the whole institution.

The real anthropological study, therefore, is to show that clitoridectomy, like Jewish circumcision, is a mere bodily mutilation which, however, is regarded as the *conditio sine qua non* of the whole teaching of tribal law, religion, and morality.

The initiation of both sexes is the most important custom among the Gikuyu. It is looked upon as a deciding factor in giving a boy or girl the status of manhood or womanhood in the Gikuyu community. This custom is adhered to by the vast majority of African peoples and is found in almost every part of the continent. It is therefore necessary to examine the facts attached to this widespread custom in order to have some idea why the African peoples cling to this custom which, in the eyes of a good many Europeans, is nothing but a "horrible" and "painful" practice, suitable only to barbarians.

In the first place it is necessary to give the readers a clear picture of why and how this important sociobiological custom is performed.

NAME OF THE CUSTOM

The Gikuyu name for this custom of *rite de passage* from childhood to adulthood is *irua*, i.e. circumcision, or trimming the genital organs of both sexes. The dances and songs connected with the initiation ceremony are called *mambura*, i.e. rituals or divine services. It is important to note that the moral code of the tribe is bound up with this custom and that it symbolises the unification of the whole tribal organisation. This is the principal reason why *irua* plays such an important part in the life of the Gikuyu people.

The *irua* marks the commencement of participation in various governing groups in the tribal administration, because the real age-groups begin from the day of the physical operation. The history and legends of the people are explained and remembered according to the names given to various age-groups at the time of the initiation ceremony. For example, if a devastating famine occurred at the time of the initiation, that particular *irua* group would be known, as "famine" (*ng'aragu*). In the same way, the Gikuyu have been able to record the time when the European introduced a number of maladies, such as syphilis, into Gikuyu country, for those initiated at the time when this disease first showed itself are called *gatego*, i.e. syphilis. Historical events are recorded and remembered in the same manner. Without this custom a tribe which had no written records would not have been able to keep a record of important events and happenings in the life.

CONCLUSION

IN CONCLUDING this study we cannot too strongly emphasise that the various sides of Gikuyu life here described are the parts of an integrated culture. No single part is detachable; each has its context and is fully understandable only in relation to the whole. The reader who has begun at the beginning and read through will appreciate this for himself, but it is worthwhile to point out briefly some of the implications.

The key to this culture is the tribal system, and the bases of the tribal system are the family group and the age-grades, which between them shape the character and determine the outlook of every man, woman, and child in Gikuyu society. According to Gikuyu ways of thinking, nobody is an isolated individual. Or rather, his uniqueness is a secondary fact about him: first and foremost he is several people's relative and several people's contemporary. His life is founded on this fact spiritually and economically, just as much as biologically; the work he does every day is determined by it, and it is the basis of his sense of moral responsibility and social obligation. His personal needs, physical and psychological, are satisfied incidentally while he plays his part as member of a family group, and cannot be fully satisfied in any other way. The fact that in Gikuyu language individualism is associated with black magic, and that a man or woman is honoured by being addressed as somebody's parent, or somebody's uncle or aunt, shows how indispensably kinship is at the root of Gikuyu ideas of good and evil.

This vital reality of the family group is an important thing for Europeans to bear in mind, since it underlies the whole social and economic organisation of the Gikuyu. It means, for instance, that the authority of the tribe is different in kind from that of the European national State. The Gikuyu does not think of his tribe as a group of individuals organised collectively, for he does not think of himself as a social unit. It is rather the widening-out of the family by a natural process of growth and division. He participates in tribal affairs through belonging to his family, and his status in the larger organisation reflects his status in the family circle. The average European observer, not being trained in comparative sociology, takes his own fundamental assumptions for granted without realising that he is doing so. He thinks of the tribe as if it must be analogous to the European Sovereign State, and draws the conclusion that the executive authority for that sovereignty must be vested in the Chief, as if he were a Prime Minister or a President. In doing so he makes a huge mistake, which makes it impossible for him to enter into intelligible relations with the Gikuyu people. They simply do not know where he gets his ideas from, since to them the family rather than the larger unit is the primary reality on which power is based.

The visible symbol of this bond of kinship is the family land, which is the source of livelihood and the field of labour. In an agricultural community the whole social organisation must derive from the land, and without understanding the system on which it is held and worked it will be impossible to see the meaning of other aspects of life. In Gikuyu society the system of land tenure can only be understood by reference to the ties of kinship. It is no more true to say that the land is collectively owned by the tribe than that it is privately owned by the Individual. In relation to the tribe, a man is the owner of his land, and there is no official and no committee with authority to deprive him of it or to levy a tax on his produce. But in so far as there are other people of his own flesh and blood who depend on that land for their daily bread, he is not the owner, but a partner, or at the most a trustee for the others. Since the land is held in trust for the unborn as well as for the living, and since it represents his partnership in the common life of generations, he will not lightly take upon himself to dispose of it. But in so far as he is cultivating a field for the maintenance of himself and his wives and children, he is the undisputed owner of that field and all that grows in it. In the same way a woman is the owner of her land and her hut as far as outside people, even her husband's other wives, are concerned, and in her management of her property she expresses her initiative as well as contributes to the family budget. But her ownership is not irresponsible; her chief function in the group is the bringing up of her own children, and it would not occur to her that the land was hers for any other purpose.

At the same time, since the Gikuyu outlook is essentially social, there are certain mutual claims which are generally assumed. Relatives help and consult one another in matters of common concern; anyone who is in need will go to his nearest prosperous kinsman as a matter of course, and hospitality is taken for granted. These things are a matter of good breeding and custom rather than of legal enactment, but to understand their gradations in detail would be to understand the real bonds which hold Gikuyu society together.

Economic life, of course, depends on the land. Certain things have to be done, some of them collectively and some of them by individuals, and the stages of life and division of labour are regulated by these necessities. Traditional usage has allotted to every person at every age the tasks best suited to him and the group with whom to work, and in every collective activity certain jobs are taken over by men and others by women, while children undertake the responsibilities for which their strength and experience are suited. Thus there is no master-and-man relationship in economic life, and there need be little or no argument about the division of labour; people grow up to know what is expected of them and what are the limits of their obligations.

For such a complex community life a careful training is required and the Gikuyu educational system supplies it. On its technical side it is practical from the earliest years. The Gikuyu child does not need Montessori exercises or class-room lessons in manual dexterity, for with plenty of space to tumble about in, and with older people around him doing interesting manual jobs, he will naturally learn by real experiments. There is work for him to do as soon as he has acquired the skill to do it properly, and he hardly distinguishes work from play. As he grows older the age-group gives him the democratic companionship of equals, and he learns by competition with other children the keenness of sense and agility of limb which will equip him for his life, as well as skill in the various operations of agricultural and pastoral work. He learns these things by imitation and free exercise, and to some extent at his own risk, and in doing so he learns how to behave to his seniors and how to get along with comrades of his own age. And since there is plenty of necessary activity, of a kind suited for every age, the steps of his education are not just exercises for his own improvement, but real contributions to the needs of the group life.

It is therefore difficult to separate cultural from technical training, but something must be said about the cultural side. The Gikuyu child does not go to school to acquire his tribal education, because he does not need to do so. In the first place the normal life of the community is a healthy environment for him to grow and learn in, and the family scheme has room for him; it is not necessary, either for his own good or for his parents' convenience, to keep him in a special sheltered reservation. Secondly, detachment from the family is no part of the Gikuyu scheme of training. In a European's life the school is usually the first big influence which takes him away from his parents and brings him as an individual into a separate relationship with the State, but Gikuyu boys and girls do not have to make this break. They naturally learn their tribal traditions and moral values from their parents and grandparents, so that they grow up with a simple family allegiance through which they come to understand their duties to the rest of the world. At the same time a great deal of their life and activity is carried on with their own age-group, through whom they learn the lessons of equality and co-operation. By going through their initiation rites together, Gikuyu boys and girls are given an understanding in common, which in some ways is like that of Englishmen who graduate from a college in the same year, though it is much more sacred and binding, and is a vital element in Gikuyu government.

In trying to understand these initiation ceremonies, one must bear in mind the difference between Gikuyu and European culture. The latter is mainly literary; every English child is compelled by law to go through several years of schooling, after which he is expected to be able to read at least his Bible, his ballot-paper, and his newspaper, and thus pick up his social inheritance. The Gikuyu does not use printed books: instead, his social education is imparted to him by image and ritual, the rhythm of the dance and the words of the ceremonial song. For every stage of life there is an appropriate course of instruction through these means, and it is made as unforgettably dramatic as possible. At adolescence especially, when boys and girls begin to take their place as responsible members of the community, it is necessary to impress upon them exactly what is expected of them in their new station in life, and what new obligations are imposed on them by the development of their sexual powers, as well as of their general mental and physical growth.

Again, sexual practices have to be related to the economic life of a community. Children are a social responsibility, and in agricultural life a man cannot afford a wife and family until he has a hut and land and the power to cultivate it. Therefore, sexual intercourse must be restricted, but for the individual's health and happiness it must not be altogether frustrated. On reaching the proper age, the young initiates are given the benefit of tribal experience and taught how to strike the right balance. If there are breaches of the code, or adjustments to be made between one and another, there is the age-group to take the matter in hand and impress the young offender with a proper sense of the importance of public opinion.

Before entering on marriage, they must again be instructed in the new duties which belong to this new advance in status. For marriage has two sides; it is a free choice of one another by the boy and girl, and this side of it is their own affair. The choice is not a complete leap in the dark, for the freedom of association and physical intercourse which has been allowed to them before marriage ought to have made each of them competent to select a mate with good judgment. But beyond this, it means the linking of two families in bonds which are social and economic as well as biological, and which are, in fact, the connecting-links of tribal life. The code which regulates the behaviour of relations by marriage is, therefore, a most important matter in its bearing on the whole of social life, and has to be very carefully learnt and punctiliously followed.

Marriage, and especially parenthood, gives a man his full share in the common happiness and qualifies him to think for the common good. It is not till he has a son or daughter entering on adolescence that he is regarded as really mature enough to take part in the tribal government, and here again we see that the guiding principles are his family experience, and the opinion of him which his contemporaries have formed. It is not until he has a family growing up that he has had a chance to show his capacity for wise administration and for dealing intelligently and justly with other people, and what he can do in the family group he is expected to do on a larger scale in the interests of the community as a whole. Among his equals in age a man may be selected as a leader or spokesman by reason of his innate gifts and understanding, for the age-group system gives the Gikuyu a good grasp of the principles of democratic selection. If so, he will be marked out by the elders as one who will play an important part in public affairs later on, but not until he has passed successive age-grades and acquired the experience of life which will qualify him to take full responsibility in tribal matters. By that time he is probably the leader of almost a miniature tribe of his own relatives, as well as his age-grade, and his family life will give evidence of his ability in government.

When we come to religion, we see again that Gikuyu religion is integrated with the whole of Gikuyu life. Religion is a dramatisation of belief, and belief is a matter of social experience of the things that are most significant to human life. In Gikuyu life the earth is so visibly the mother of all things animate, and the generations are so closely linked together by their common participation in the land, that agricultural ritual, and reverence for ancestral spirits, must naturally play the foremost part in religious ceremonial.

The new religious movement is interesting because of its bearing on the question of social change. It is not reasonable to expect the Gikuyu to assimilate Christianity whole as the European missionary expounds it. Its language and its traditions have no relation to his daily life, its ceremony is meaningless to him, and its moral code, with its insistence on monogamy, for which Gikuyu economy is not planned, and its objection to the central rituals of his own society, strikes him as subversive of all intelligible social values. But the new religious movement does show that Africans, under the influence of new forces, are not incapable of a spontaneous adaptation. It is an effort from within, to assimilate what seems to them valuable in the Christian code and the culture of which it is a part, while at the same time adapting it to the needs of Gikuyu life.

Lastly, we come to magical practices and see how they, like religion, are inspired by the daily economic and social activities of the people, and how they run through and fertilise these activities and refer them to the mysterious forces which surround human life. Even here it is clear how everything good comes from the collective life of the community, while the wizard practises his works of darkness alone. And when a man has been convicted of the capital crime of anti-social wizardry, his offence is against the whole of society, but it is one of his own kinsmen who has to pass final judgment against him by lighting the fire of his execution.

It is all these different aspects of life together that make up a social culture. And it is the culture which he inherits that gives a man his human dignity as well as his material prosperity. It teaches him his mental and moral values and makes him feel it worthwhile to work and fight for liberty.

But a culture has no meaning apart from the social organisation of life on which it is built. When the European comes to the Gikuyu country and robs the people of their land, he is taking away not only their livelihood, but the material symbol that holds family and tribe together. In doing this he gives one blow which cuts away the foundations from the whole of Gikuyu life, social, moral, and economic. When he explains, to his own satisfaction and after the most superficial glance at the issues involved, that he is doing this for the sake of the Africans, to "civilise" them, "teach them the disciplinary value of regular work," and "give them the benefit of European progressive ideas," he is adding insult to injury, and need expect to convince no one but himself.

There certainly are some progressive ideas among the Europeans. They include the ideas of material prosperity, of medicine, and hygiene, and literacy which enables people to take part in world culture. But so far the Europeans who visit Africa have not been conspicuously zealous in imparting these parts of their inheritance to the Africans, and seem to think that the only way to do it is by police discipline and armed force. They speak as if it was somehow beneficial to an African to work for them instead of for himself, and to make sure that he will receive this benefit they do their best to take away his land and leave him with no alternative. Along with his land they rob him of his government, condemn his religious ideas, and ignore his fundamental conceptions of justice and morals, all in the name of civilisation and progress.

If Africans were left in peace on their own lands, Europeans would have to offer them the benefits of white civilisation in real earnest before they could obtain the African labour which they want so much. They would have to offer the African a way of life which was really superior to the one his fathers lived before him, and a share in the prosperity given them by their command of science. They would have to let the African choose what parts of European culture could be beneficially transplanted, and how they could be adapted. He would probably not choose the gas bomb or the armed police force, but he might ask for some other things of which he does not get so much to-day. As it is, by driving him off his ancestral lands, the Europeans have robbed him of the material foundations of his cultures and reduced him to a state of serfdom incompatible with human happiness. The African is conditioned, by the cultural and social institutions of centuries, to a freedom of which Europe has little conception, and it is not in his nature to accept serfdom for ever. He realises that he must fight unceasingly for his own complete emancipation; for without this he is doomed to remain the prey of rival Imperialisms, which in every successive year will drive their fangs more deeply into his vitality and strength.

Shooting an Elephant (1936)

By George Orwell

Eric Arthur Blair (1903–1950) is best known by his nom de plume, George Orwell, and best known for his dystopic novel 1984. While his mother had grown up in Burma and Orwell was born in British India, he spent his childhood in England. After graduating from Eton he lacked the funds for a college education so he joined the colonial police force in 1922. He chose Burma as a posting because his grandmother still lived there. After five years in country he contracted dengue fever and was allowed to return to England. He then decided to leave the police force and pursue a career as a writer. Always a free thinker, he was critical of colonialism, capitalism, and communism.

In Moulmein, in Lower Burma, I was hated by large numbers of people—the only time in my life that I have been important enough for this to happen to me. I was sub-divisional police officer of the town, and in an aimless, petty kind of way anti-European feeling was very bitter. No one had the guts to raise a riot, but if a European woman went through the bazaars alone somebody would probably spit betel juice over her dress. As a police officer I was an obvious target and was baited whenever it seemed safe to do so. When a nimble Burman tripped me up on the football field and the referee (another Burman) looked the other way, the crowd yelled with hideous laughter. This happened more than once. In the end the sneering yellow faces of young men that met me everywhere, the insults hooted after me when I was at a safe distance, got badly on my nerves. The young Buddhist priests were the worst of all. There were several thousands of them in the town and none of them seemed to have anything to do except stand on street corners and jeer at Europeans.

All this was perplexing and upsetting. For at that time I had already made up my mind that imperialism was an evil thing and the sooner I chucked up my job and got out of it the better. Theoretically—and secretly, of course—I was all for the Burmese and all against their oppressors, the British. As for the job I was doing, I hated it more

George Orwell, "Shooting an Elephant," *A Collection of Essays*, pp. 148–156. Copyright © 1970 by Estate of Sonia Brownwell Orwell. Reprinted with permission.

bitterly than I can perhaps make clear. In a job like that you see the dirty work of Empire at close quarters. The wretched prisoners huddling in the stinking cages of the lock-ups, the grey, cowed faces of the long-term convicts, the scarred buttocks of the men who had been flogged with bamboos—all these oppressed me with an intolerable sense of guilt. But I could get nothing into perspective. I was young and ill-educated and I had had to think out my problems in the utter silence that is imposed on every Englishman in the East. I did not even know that the British Empire is dying, still less did I know that it is a great deal better than the younger empires that are going to supplant it. All I knew was that I was stuck between my hatred of the empire I served and my rage against the evil-spirited little beasts who tried to make my job impossible. With one part of my mind I thought of the British Raj as an unbreakable tyranny, as something clamped down, in saecula saeculorum, upon the will of prostrate peoples; with another part I thought that the greatest joy in the world would be to drive a bayonet into a Buddhist priest's guts. Feelings like these are the normal by-products of imperialism; ask any Anglo-Indian official, if you can catch him off duty.

One day something happened which in a roundabout way was enlightening. It was a tiny incident in itself, but it gave me a better glimpse than I had had before of the real nature of imperialism—the real motives for which despotic governments act. Early one morning the sub-inspector at a police station the other end of the town rang me up on the phone and said that an elephant was ravaging the bazaar. Would I please come and do something about it? I did not know what I could do, but I wanted to see what was happening and I got on to a pony and started out. I took my rifle, an old .44 Winchester and much too small to kill an elephant, but I thought the noise might be useful *in terrorem*. Various Burmans stopped me on the way and told me about the elephant's doings. It was not, of course, a wild elephant, but a tame one which had gone 'must.' It had been chained up, as tame elephants always are when their attack of 'must' is due, but on the previous night it had broken its chain and escaped. Its mahout, the only person who could manage it when it was in that state, had set out in pursuit, but had taken the wrong direction and was now twelve hours' journey away, and in the morning the elephant had suddenly reappeared in the town. The Burmese population had no weapons and were quite helpless against it. It had already destroyed somebody's bamboo hut, killed a cow and raided some fruit-stalls and devoured the stock; also it had met the municipal rubbish van and, when the driver jumped out and took to his heels, had turned the van over and inflicted violences upon it.

The Burmese sub-inspector and some Indian constables were waiting for me in the quarter where the elephant had been seen. It was a very poor quarter, a labyrinth of squalid bamboo huts, thatched with palmleaf, winding all over a steep hillside. I remember that it was a cloudy, stuffy morning at the beginning of the rains. We began questioning the people as to where the elephant had gone and, as usual, failed to get any definite information. That is invariably the case in the East; a story always sounds clear enough at a distance, but the nearer you get to the scene of events the vaguer it becomes. Some of the people said that the elephant had gone in one direction, some said that he had gone in another, some professed not even to have heard of any elephant. I had almost made up my mind that the whole story was a pack of lies, when we heard yells a little distance away. There was a loud, scandalized cry of 'Go away, child! Go away this instant!' and an old woman with a switch in her hand came round the corner of a hut, violently shooing away a crowd of naked children. Some more women followed, clicking their tongues and exclaiming; evidently there was something that the children ought not to have seen. I rounded the hut and saw a man's dead body sprawling in the mud. He was an Indian, a black Dravidian coolie, almost naked, and he could not have been dead many minutes. The people said that the elephant had come suddenly upon him round the corner of the hut, caught him with its trunk, put its foot on his back and ground him into the earth. This was the rainy season and the ground was soft, and his face had scored a trench a foot deep and a couple of yards long. He was lying on his belly with arms crucified and head sharply twisted to one side. His face was coated with mud, the eyes wide open, the teeth bared and grinning with an expression of unendurable agony. (Never tell me, by the way, that the dead look peaceful. Most of the corpses I have seen looked devilish.) The friction of the great beast's foot had stripped the skin from his back as neatly as one skins a rabbit. As soon as I saw the dead man I sent an orderly to a friend's house nearby to borrow an elephant rifle. I had already sent back the pony, not wanting it to go mad with fright and throw me if it smelt the elephant.

The orderly came back in a few minutes with a rifle and five cartridges, and meanwhile some Burmans had arrived and told us that the elephant was in the paddy fields below, only a few hundred yards away. As I started forward practically the whole population of the quarter flocked out of the houses and followed me. They had seen the rifle and were all shouting excitedly that I was going to shoot the elephant. They had not shown much interest in the elephant when he was merely ravaging their homes, but it was different now that he was going to be shot. It was a bit of fun to them, as it would be to an English crowd; besides they wanted the meat. It made me vaguely uneasy. I had no intention of shooting the elephant—I had merely sent for the rifle to defend myself if necessary—and it is always unnerving to have a crowd following you. I marched down the hill, looking and feeling a fool, with the rifle over my shoulder and an ever-growing army of people jostling at my heels. At the bottom, when you got away from the huts, there was a metalled road and beyond that a miry waste of paddy fields a thousand yards across, not yet ploughed but soggy from the first rains and dotted with coarse grass. The elephant was standing eight yards from the road, his left side towards us. He took not the slightest notice of the crowd's approach. He was tearing up bunches of grass, beating them against his knees to clean them and stuffing them into his mouth.

I had halted on the road. As soon as I saw the elephant I knew with perfect certainty that I ought not to shoot him. It is a serious matter to shoot a working elephant—it is comparable to destroying a huge and costly piece of machinery—and obviously one ought not to do it if it can possibly be avoided. And at that distance, peacefully eating, the elephant looked no more dangerous than a cow. I thought then and I think now that his attack of 'must' was already passing off; in which case he would merely wander harmlessly about until the mahout came back and caught him. Moreover, I did not in the least want to shoot him. I decided that I would watch him for a little while to make sure that he did not turn savage again, and then go home.

But at that moment I glanced round at the crowd that had followed me. It was an immense crowd, two thousand at the least and growing every minute. It blocked the road for a long distance on either side. I looked at the sea of yellow faces above the garish clothes—faces all happy and excited over this bit of fun, all certain that the elephant was going to be shot. They were watching me as they would watch a conjurer about to perform a trick. They did not like me, but with the magical rifle in my hands I was momentarily worth watching. And suddenly I realized that I should have to shoot the elephant after all. The people expected it of me and I had got to do it; I could feel their two thousand wills pressing me forward, irresistibly. And it was at this moment, as I stood there with the rifle in my hands, that I first grasped the hollowness, the futility of the white man's dominion in the East. Here was I, the white man with his gun, standing in front of the unarmed native crowd—seemingly the leading actor of the piece; but in reality I was only an absurd puppet pushed to and fro by the will of those yellow faces behind. I perceived in this moment that when the white man turns tyrant it is his own freedom that he destroys. He becomes a sort of hollow, posing dummy, the conventionalized figure of a sahib. For it is the condition of his rule that he shall spend his life in trying to impress the 'natives,' and so in every crisis he has got to do what the 'natives' expect of him. He wears a mask, and his face grows to fit it. I had got to shoot the elephant. I had committed myself to doing it when I sent for the rifle. A sahib has got to act like a sahib; he has got to appear resolute, to know his own mind and do definite things. To come all that way, rifle in hand, with two thousand people marching at my heels, and then to trail feebly away, having done nothing—no, that was impossible. The crowd would laugh at me. And my whole life, every white man's life in the East, was one long struggle not to be laughed at.

But I did not want to shoot the elephant. I watched him beating his bunch of grass against his knees, with that preoccupied grandmotherly air that elephants have. It seemed to me that it would be murder to shoot him. At that age I was not squeamish about killing animals, but I had never shot an elephant and never wanted to. (Somehow it always seems worse to kill a *large* animal.) Besides, there was the beast's owner to be considered. Alive, the elephant was worth at least a hundred pounds; dead, he would only be worth the value of his tusks, five pounds, possibly. But I had got to act quickly.

I turned to some experienced-looking Burmans who had been there when we arrived, and asked them how the elephant had been behaving. They all said the same thing: he took no notice of you if you left him alone, but he might charge if you went too close to him.

It was perfectly clear to me what I ought to do. I ought to walk up to within, say, twenty-five yards of the elephant and test his behavior. If he charged, I could shoot; if he took no notice of me, it would be safe to leave him until the mahout came back. But also I knew that I was going to do no such thing. I was a poor shot with a rifle and the ground was soft mud into which one would sink at every step. If the elephant charged and I missed him, I should have about as much chance as a toad under a steam-roller. But even then I was not thinking particularly of my own skin, only of the watchful yellow faces behind. For at that moment, with the crowd watching me, I was not afraid in the ordinary sense, as I would have been if I had been alone. A white man mustn't be frightened in front of 'natives'; and so, in general, he isn't frightened. The sole thought in my mind was that if anything went wrong those two thousand Burmans would see me pursued, caught, trampled on and reduced to a grinning corpse like that Indian up the hill. And if that happened it was quite probable that some of them would laugh. That would never do.

There was only one alternative. I shoved the cartridges into the magazine and lay down on the road to get a better aim. The crowd grew very still, and a deep, low, happy sigh, as of people who see the theatre curtain go up at last, breathed from innumerable throats. They were going to have their bit of fun after all. The rifle was a beautiful German thing with cross-hair sights. I did not then know that in shooting an elephant one would shoot to cut an imaginary bar running from ear-hole to ear-hole. I ought, therefore, as the elephant was sideways on, to have aimed straight at his ear-hole, actually I aimed several inches in front of this, thinking the brain would be further forward.

When I pulled the trigger I did not hear the bang or feel the kick—one never does when a shot goes home—but I heard the devilish roar of glee that went up from the crowd. In that instant, in too short a time, one would have thought, even for the bullet to get there, a mysterious, terrible change had come over the elephant. He neither stirred nor fell, but every line of his body had altered. He looked suddenly stricken, shrunken, immensely old, as though the frightful impact of the bullet had paralysed him without knocking him down. At last, after what seemed a long time—it might have been five seconds, I dare say—he sagged flabbily to his knees. His mouth slobbered. An enormous senility seemed to have settled upon him. One could have imagined him thousands of years old. I fired again into the same spot. At the second shot he did not collapse but climbed with desperate slowness to his feet and stood weakly upright, with legs sagging and head drooping. I fired a third time. That was the shot that did for him. You could see the agony of it jolt his whole body and knock the last remnant of strength from his legs. But in falling he seemed for a moment to rise, for as his hind legs collapsed beneath him he seemed to tower upward like a huge rock toppling, his trunk reaching skyward like a tree. He trumpeted, for the first and only time. And then down he came, his belly towards me, with a crash that seemed to shake the ground even where I lay.

I got up. The Burmans were already racing past me across the mud. It was obvious that the elephant would never rise again, but he was not dead. He was breathing very rhythmically with long rattling gasps, his great mound of a side painfully rising and falling. His mouth was wide open—I could see far down into caverns of pale pink throat. I waited a long time for him to die, but his breathing did not weaken. Finally I fired my two remaining shots into the spot where I thought his heart must be. The thick blood welled out of him like red velvet, but still he did not die. His body did not even jerk when the shots hit him, the tortured breathing continued without a pause. He was dying, very slowly and in great agony, but in some world remote from me where not even a bullet could damage him further. I felt that I had got to put an end to that dreadful noise. It seemed dreadful to see the great beast Lying there, powerless to move and yet powerless to die, and not even to be able to finish him. I sent back for my small rifle and poured shot after shot into his heart and down his throat. They seemed to make no impression. The tortured gasps continued as steadily as the ticking of a clock.

In the end I could not stand it any longer and went away. I heard later that it took him half an hour to die. Burmans were bringing dash and baskets even before I left, and I was told they had stripped his body almost to the bones by the afternoon.

Afterwards, of course, there were endless discussions about the shooting of the elephant. The owner was furious, but he was only an Indian and could do nothing. Besides, legally I had done the right thing, for a mad elephant has to be killed, like a mad dog, if its owner fails to control it. Among the Europeans opinion was divided. The older men said I was right, the younger men said it was a damn shame to shoot an elephant for killing a coolie, because an elephant was worth more than any damn Coringhee coolie. And afterwards I was very glad that the coolie had been killed; it put me legally in the right and it gave me a sufficient pretext for shooting the elephant. I often wondered whether any of the others grasped that I had done it solely to avoid looking a fool.

The Party Comes to Phu-Rieng

By Tran Tu Binh

Pham Văn Phu (1907–1967) changed his name to Tran Tu Binh, meaning "one who will die for peace." He hailed from a poor family in a Catholic village in the north of Vietnam. In 1927 he signed up to work on a Michelin rubber plantation in the mountains of southern Vietnam. Tran witnessed the brutal conditions of near-slavery and joined the Indochinese Communist Party in 1929. In 1930 he helped to lead a revolt of thousands of Vietnamese plantation workers against the Michelin company. The French colonial state brutally repressed the revolt and sentenced Tran to ten years on the infamous Con Son Island prison. There he met other party members and began to rise through the ranks. After his release became a prominent activist and, later, one of the first generals of the Democratic Republic of Vietnam (the northern communist regime). The Red Earth was published during the struggle against the American backed regime in southern Vietnam.

Our struggles drew the attention of Ngo Gia Tu, one of the first Communists in Viet Nam. Brother Tu had come south to work in 1927. In 1928 he delegated Nguyen Xuan Cu, alias Vinh, one of his comrades, to go up to Phu-rieng to work in the rubber workers movement and to build up an infrastructure for the Revolutionary Youth League. Cu was from the North, a student at the Buoi school (now the Chu Van An school). Though he had student roots, brother Cu understood that if he wanted to make revolution he would have to go among the worker and peasant masses and learn from them to be able to fulfill his responsibility. He came to Phu-rieng and asked to work as houseboy for the overseer Lebonne, chief of Village 3.

At the time the French hated and suspected me and transferred me to the clinic to clean up and do the laundry. They wanted to cut me off from the old Ha-nam workers who really believed in me. So, from then on, I had to live at the clinic. The work was hard and complex, but I learned what I could from it. After only a few months

Tran Tu Binh; David G. Marr, ed.; John Spragens, Jr., trans., "The Party Comes to Phu-Rieng," *The Red Earth: A Vietnamese Memoir of Life on a Colonial Rubber Plantation*, pp. 47–63. Copyright © 1985 by the Ohio University Press. Reprinted with permission.

working at the clinic I knew how to give intramuscular and intravenous injections. I also knew how to use the common drugs. The head nurse, whose name was Phong, was short with very dark skin. He would laugh maliciously while he stared evenly at you. Phong beat the patients resoundingly, and whenever any women workers were ill and came to the clinic, he always raped them. Many times I stopped him, he beat me, and I hit back. I had long been famous at the plantation for my obstinacy, and I was not about to submit to him.

Brother Cu heard of my attitude and of all the struggles I had been involved in before, so he held me in high esteem. He sought me out to make friends. He invited me back to his room and we exchanged confidences. He was very poised, and every time he explained something to me he went slowly, explaining each detail so I had a thorough understanding of all he had said.

Cu also worked cautiously. Before he propagandized anyone, he researched and investigated the person carefully. Within a short time the number of people he had propagandized and brought into the Revolutionary Youth League had risen to four, including me and three other comrades: Ta, Hong and Hoa. Cu's style of work had a great influence on me after that.

The things that Cu explained to us were very practical. They were in direct response to the impasse we faced at the time. They helped us discover the reasons for the failure of our previous efforts, and at the same time gave each person confidence in the new methods of struggle. For the first time I understood how revolutionary theory was related to the revolutionary movement. The teachings of the old masters of Marxism penetrated my heart still more deeply: "Without revolutionary theory there is no revolutionary movement," and "When theory thrusts deep into reality it becomes a material strength." Nevertheless I really only understood the principles which lay behind these slogans a long time later, after I had passed through the "university" of the revolution, in prison. At the time I simply knew that, thanks to Cu's explanations, I was like a person groping his way along a rugged road who suddenly sees a sheaf of blazing torches brilliantly lighting the way.

Cu passed on to us a great many experiences and concrete methods of struggle. He helped us to understand what an organized struggle is, how to select the crucial slogans, how to set up a leadership committee, how to organize our defenses, how much food to set aside, and so forth. We were hearing most of this for the very first time.

Comrade Cu had our complete affection and confidence. He had not been with us for long, yet the rubber workers were drawn to him as iron to a magnet. I still remember how we would gather after we had eaten in the evenings to hear Cu speak. On cool evenings when the moon was bright, we would go out in the yard together and sit on the ground. At that hour the manager, assistant manager, and overseers had their heads buried in their fancy, proper houses, having a good time with their wives and children. So no one discovered our activities. We sat and listened, entranced. After talking about struggle experiences, Cu would tell us about the Soviet Union, about the land where workers like us had taken complete control, about the struggles of workers around the world.

Often the hour grew quite late, but there was not one of us who wanted to be the first to leave. Anyone who had the misfortune to be sick and could not come to hear Cu speak was very sorry. Gradually our zest for life grew. A sense of confidence in the coming struggle, and in our lives afterward, rose in our hearts.

While he was propagandizing the workers at Phu-rieng, Cu maintained close contact with Ngo Gia Tu, who was then in Cho-lon. The person who took up the task of liaison at that time was Ty, a woman worker who came from the village of Chi-lai, An-lao District, Kien-an Province. Sister Ty was tiny and elegant. She had large round eyes which glowed an expressive black, mirroring the determination and courage in her heart. She kept up her work until the big 1930 struggle.

On a couple of occasions Cu had me go to Cho-lon. Cu had a special affection for me. In part it was because I was direct and loyal by nature, and in part it was because I was the first person he had recruited. Besides this sense of spontaneous comradeship, we shared the vows of brotherhood we had taken. After our exchanges of thoughts about the tyranny the capitalist owners were imposing on the plantation, our hostility toward them increased. We asked two men who worked in the machine shop to forge two hatchet blades with the word "justice" engraved on the face of each. Cu and I exchanged these two finely honed hatchets. It revealed my immaturity, yet at the same time it expressed our intent.

Before we realized it, Cu had been at Phu-rieng for the better part of a year. The number of people grouped around us grew daily. At the time the labor movement in our country was seething. In those circumstances the working class had an urgent need for their own party, a tightly organized party with a system of leadership from top to bottom, a party with the correct theoretical direction to be able to lead the movement to victory.

Thus, on the basis of the Revolutionary Youth League and the New Viet Nam Revolutionary Party, three Communist groups—the Indochinese Communist party, the Communist party of An-nam, and the Indochinese Communist League—were formed within the space of a few months. These were the revolutionary organizations of our working class which were later, on 3 February 1930, unified by Nguyen Ai Quoc into the Vietnamese Communist party (later changed to the Indochinese Communist party), the vanguard party of the working class and of our nation.

During this period, before the unification of the Indochinese Communist party, all the communist groups were engaged in positive activities, building bases among the masses, organizing new branches, pushing forward the movement among workers and laboring people in every quarter, building an unprecedentedly powerful revolutionary movement.

Ngo Gia Tu was one of the people in the Revolutionary Youth League who actively pushed those first efforts to build a party of the working class. Brother Tu gave Nguyen Xuan Cu the task of founding a branch of the Indochinese Communist party at Phu-rieng. Cu gave the rules and regulations of the party to a number of workers at Phu-rieng to study. I was one of them.

The Phu-rieng branch was officially founded one night in October 1929. In all, six of us went together into the forest behind Village 3 for the founding ceremony. We lit some candles and hung a hammer and sickle flag on a large tree, wrapping it around the trunk. It was a clear, bright moonlit night and the weather was quite chilly, yet I felt hot all over. You could tell from his face how moved Cu was as he announced, on behalf of his superiors, the reason for the meeting. Our right hands clenched tightly, we raised them above our heads in a salute to the flag.

After the salute, Cu read the oath. It was so long ago that I cannot remember exactly what the words were, but I still remember quite clearly the spirit of the oath. It included the following points:

- To be loyal to our class and to the party until death.
- To preserve party secrets to the end. If we were captured by the enemy we were not to confess, even if it meant we were tortured to death.
- To integrate ourselves into the masses, and to stand shoulder to shoulder in struggle.
- To set aside every other faith and believe only in communism.
- To combine our strength in the struggle, first for the national liberation revolution and afterwards for the socialist revolution, advancing towards a world of great harmony.

We all raised our hands in the air and took the vow. After the oath, we all shook hands and called each other "comrade." It is hard to describe how I felt at that moment. At that hour I had officially come into the family of Communists, of revolutionaries. There was something about being called "comrade" for the first time that gave me an extraordinary feeling of warmth and affection. I felt as if my strength had doubled. From then on, the minds and hands of these comrades would help me and lead me forward. My heart felt light, floating, as if I were being lifted up. My ears grew hot, and my eyes were so misty I could not see my comrades clearly.

So it was that the Phu-rieng branch was founded. The four comrades besides me and Cu were Ta, Hong, Hoa, and Doanh. Cu was the secretary. I was assigned the task of organizing youth for a Red Guards unit. Ta was responsible for Village 2. He was a tall man from Ha-noi, very poised, and the workers had great confidence in him.

At that time Hong was a driver at the car garage, so he was given responsibility for the labor union. Hong was quite courageous, but he was quiet and gentle like a girl. When he exchanged confidences with us, he often expressed the wish that the village of Thi-cau in Bac-ninh, his home village, could have a party branch, too. Doanh was the leader of Village 3. In contrast to Hong, Doanh was tall and walked with great self-assurance. He was bold, a hearty eater, and a loud talker. Hoa also worked at the car garage and helped Hong in the task of mobilizing the drivers and machine shop workers there. Afterwards, whenever the branch met we usually used an empty room in the overseer's house where Cu worked or the pharmacy at the clinic where I worked.

The work at that time was still rather helter-skelter, but it was very practical. The branch paid attention to the workers' food and living quarters and to each person's family life in order to work out problems quickly and settle them peacefully.

Because sister Ty carried out her communications work so well, Ngo Gia Tu was in regular contact with us. He secretly sent books and newspapers for us to read. The newspapers were Thanh nien giai phong (Liberation Youth) and *Humanité*, the official publication of the French Communist party. *Humanité* was written in French, and since I had some knowledge of that language I was responsible for translating the main articles for the others to read—articles on the world situation, the situation in France, and experiences and lessons from struggle. We learned a great deal from *Humanité*. The French Communists were our brothers, comrades with a common enemy: the capitalists, the colonialists, the imperialists who were ruling us. Their newspaper reached us at just the right time and was precious spiritual food for us, since we party members at Phu-rieng had a low level of theoretical understanding and lacked experience in struggle.

The party's line and course of action at that time were for the most part laid out for us by Cu. Among the major components of the party course of action which Cu explained, there was only one which bothered me. Cu had spoken about the problem of fields and farmers in our country. He had emphasized the necessity of confiscating all the land held by religious organizations. I felt it was correct to take back factories and mines for the workers and to take back land from the landlords for the farmers. But why should we also take religious land holdings to divide among the people? Those lands belonged to God. What did the crops and interest used to pay for religious services have to do with the revolution? Indeed, it was the lessons inculcated in me during those years in church schools which made me wonder about this.

I asked Cu about it. Right away he asked me how I had lived when I was at the Hoang Nguyen seminary. I answered that it had been a very hard life. Then he asked me what kind of life the tenant farmers around the mission seemed to have. I responded that their lives seemed even harsher than mine. Cu laughed quietly, then explained to me who a landlord was and who a farmer was. He said that the nature of rent paid to the mission was no different from the nature of rent paid to a landlord. He emphasized that it was necessary to reclaim that religious land and divide it among the farmers, though naturally a certain amount of land would be left for pagodas and churches to use for their services. But it would be absolutely forbidden to use this land to exploit the poor. Cu's clear, simple, concrete explanation dissolved my doubts. From then on I believed him with all my heart and mind, without the slightest ambiguity.

Since we had just been enlightened, those of us in the branch were extremely enthusiastic. Secret party organizations—the trade union and the Red Guards unit—were set up. The party branch competed with the owners for control of mass organizations. Many legal organizations—the mutual aid and assistance association, sports and art groups—were set up under branch control. Work went on at a fast pace.

In general every struggle was under party direction. Yet there were many ultra-left activities, too, and I myself was involved in some of them. At that time there was a French nurse named Vaillant at the clinic. He had originally been a sailor and knew nothing at all about medicine. He did not even know how to give an injection. He was a highly paid idiot. On the job all he did was sit and wave his hand to tell us what to do. If something displeased him in the least, he would launch into loud curses and denunciations. Once he called me "savage." I was furious at him. Vaillant sprang threateningly toward me. That is how the fight broke out. I put up my hand to ward off his slap, then took advantage of the situation to land a blow on Vaillant's jaw. He fell, smashing one of the clinic beds. Then he sprang up and ran into the office to get a gun. I fled. Vaillant fired several shots into the air but did not dare chase me. It was evening before I returned.

By that time the movement at Phu-rieng had gained strength. The imperialists were looking for some way to calm the movement, so Vaillant did not dare behave too fiercely. He just docked my pay four dong and pretended to patch up relations by saying, "The higher-ups like you, so they have decided not to throw you in prison!" I gave an evasive answer and thought to myself, "Your mother! Just try something and see what happens." There were a lot of incidents like that during this period.

Cu was exhausted from his efforts to shape the struggle in the proper way. From time to time Cu went back to Sai-gon to report to Ngo Gia Tu on the situation. Once Cu took me along with him. I got to meet Tu at his quarters on Lagrandière Street.

At that time, toward the end of 1929, the Indochinese Communist party was continuing to push the task of proletarianizing its cadres and party members. Tu was working as a coolie in Cho-lon, both to make a living and to establish a base for his activities. He lived in a tiny, cramped room with only a broken-down bed and a few changes of worn clothes. Yet within a few minutes after I met him, I could see that he was an extraordinarily warm-hearted person. On the outside there was nothing noteworthy about him. If anything, he was rather ugly, squat, and heavy-set with a round face and small eyes. But his manner of speaking was very unaffected and intimate. Tu's attitude toward younger comrades like me was open and friendly, leading everyone to love and trust him at once.

His way of speaking was very practical, not the least bit literary. "If we want to liberate ourselves," he told me, "we must liberate our class first. We are all members of that social class."

"To struggle for class liberation," he advised me, "we must integrate ourselves with the proletarian masses; we must be proletarianized."

Ngo Gia Tu's words moved me greatly. The more we talked, the fonder I became of him. I learned a great many useful things from this visit with him. He had a concrete understanding of the workers struggle. He very carefully read the newspaper which we published secretly at Phu-rieng and especially liked the column on workers' activities. In that column we satirized certain bad habits and customs like gambling, drunkenness, and wife snatching. "This is good!" Tu said. "Our workers must give up these bad habits and customs. You are pointing the way for the masses to develop a new morality. These bad habits and customs are the mores of the capitalists. We are the revolutionary working class. How can we let ourselves be infected with these evils?"

Like Cu, Tu paid attention to straightening out our aberrations and passed on to us some very concrete struggle lessons. He told us of his experiences when mobilizing the masses and the workers in Bac-ninh, Ha-noi, Hai-phong, and other places. I felt those experiences were particularly helpful. Afterwards I also utilized Tu's experiences when mobilizing the workers at Phu-rieng to struggle with the enemy.

Brother Tu also pulled a few comrades out of Phu-rieng and other bases, trained them, then sent them to other plantations to mobilize the workers. His work kept him extremely busy. During the day he had his exhausting work as a coolie. At night, when he came home, he met members of the organization and cadres from various locations, to hear about the situation and to offer his opinions. Even so, he always had time to visit with people in the neighborhood and was highly esteemed by them. His mass stand was very good, and it was that fact that caused me to change many of my weak points and made me feel even greater affection for him.

Afterwards, when I was sent out to Con-son, I met Tu again. Being near him for so long I understood his spirit still better and had still greater faith in him and esteem for him. Then, a short time afterwards, he escaped from Con-son only to encounter a typhoon and be lost. I was depressed for months by the sorrow of losing Tu, my revolutionary mentor.

Toward the end of 1929, Cu came to be suspected by the imperialists. The turncoat Duong Hac Dinh had fingered him, but because they did not have a shred of solid evidence, the imperialists could not imprison him. They deported him to the North.

The Phu-rieng branch gave me the responsibility of secretary. From then on I had to shoulder that heavy responsibility. It was a great honor, but I could not rid myself of the worry that, although I had been trained through years of struggle, I still did not have very much experience. All the same, I continued my activities with a firm spirit because of the uninterrupted liaison between me and brother Tu provided by the clever work of sister Ty, the worker with the big, round, deep black intelligent eyes who was so courageous.

THE HOUR BEFORE THE STORM

From the time Vasser arrived, the capitalist owners softened their repressive policies. But it was only a matter of form rather than substance. They saw clearly that if they relied solely on beatings they could never force the workers to make great profits for them.

Vasser now combined cruel beatings and pay docking with shrewd cajolery. He paid for costumes for the cheo group, for sports equipment, instruments, and drums. The party branch position was to take advantage of that opportunity to organize mutual aid associations, sports teams, and arts groups to bring the masses together and to win them over to us.

The workers formed three cheo groups in Villages 9, 3, and 2. As soon as they had a group set up, they would ask Vasser to allocate money to buy costumes and drums. The person in charge of all the cheo groups was comrade Quy, a member of the secret rubber workers union. Quy was active and very enthusiastic. He had a slight, slender build and an oval face, so that in the cheo plays he usually took female roles like Dieu Thuyen and Tay Thi.

Cheo plots were taken from ancient stories of The Three Kingdoms and Heroic State of Eastern Chu. At the time, each cheo group had as many as seven or eight plays. The most famous were The Deception of Chou Yu, Pledge in the Peach Orchard, The Romance of La Bo and Dieu Thuyen, and Pham Lai and Tay Thi. In general the plays were self-written and self-produced, chosen with subjects emphasizing personal loyalty, filial piety, feminine virtue, and righteousness. We were not yet able to perform new plays with a revolutionary content, but those plays stimulated our patriotic spirit.

Every Saturday night, when the cheo drums sounded, the workers would come in great numbers from all the villages around. In the moments just before a cheo performance began, the executive committee of the labor union would skillfully guide the masses in new directions of struggle and explain the situation on the plantation.

In sports, we asked Vasser to let us start a soccer team. When evening came, the players took the ball out to the practice field. On Sunday they went out together to neighboring plantations for games. And there were many who went along to cheer them on. So while the players were contending on the field, the members of the labor union and members of the party branch were trying to make contact with the secret infrastructure from the other plantation to discuss the situation at the two places or to exchange experiences. And we took advantage of those times when team members went to Sai-gon for friendship matches to make contact with Ngo Gia Tu and to bring leaflets and secret newspapers back to the plantation.

We set up a dragon dance group, too. The group went around to all the villages on the plantation on festival days and at Tet. Members of the dragon dance group were all strong and healthy youth chosen from the Red Guards unit. They wrapped red scarves around their heads and wore red shirts. We were very fond of that color with its revolutionary significance. The dragon dance group practiced every evening. Taking advantage of that part of the dance where the dragon jousts with warriors wielding wooden weapons, the members of the group took wooden swords and staves and practiced the dance together. The truth was, we were practicing the martial arts all evening long. I was the "fighting master" who taught them to use the staves. Later, during the big struggles, the Red Guards were able to use sticks and poles well for this very reason.

We also organized mutual aid and assistance societies. When someone was sick, we would go to visit and take medicines. If anyone had the misfortune to die, we would take them out and bury them properly.

The non-Catholic workers had a Spring and Autumn society which, in keeping with the old customs, burned votive offerings to their ancestors or organized visits to shrines several times a year. Each time, they found a bit of wine and meat to set out for a pleasant meal together. The Catholics had a St. Joseph society. When someone died, the society would ask for a mass for them and pray for the soul of the unfortunate person. I was in charge of this society. Actually the religious activities of these two societies were very weak. They were simply legal mass organizations intended to bring together large numbers of people and to lead them to more advanced forms of struggle. We skillfully held on to the leadership positions of these public, legal organizations in order to smash Vasser's schemes of cajoling the masses and of trying to put them to sleep.

There were also the secret organizations, which included, besides the party branch which was the nerve center, a secret labor union and a unit of Red Guards. Comrade Hong, a party member, was secretary of the secret rubber workers union. Among the activists were Ta, Chuong from Ninh-binh, and Mo from Vinh-bao in Hai-duong Province. Chuong was later sent out to Con-son where he died of dysentery.

The executive committee of the labor union met once a month to assess the situation and to set out the general direction for the next month's struggles. The union published a monthly paper called Giai thoat [Emancipation]. There was no editorial board. Hong took direct charge of chasing down articles from members of the branch and from the union's executive committee. It was printed at night out in the forest by one of the workers. Although that newspaper was very rudimentary, duplicated by the gelatin block technique, it was quite practical and in close touch with the situation at Phu-rieng. Ngo Gia Tu himself praised the paper and liked reading it very much. The paper had columns on workers' daily activities and the union's operations. For international politics, it used excerpts from the Paris paper *Humanité*, and for news of struggles at home it carried selections from *Giai-phong* [Liberation], at that time the paper of the Indochinese Communist party.

When Tran Van Cung was arrested, the paper Giai-thoat carried an article in the name of the secret union demanding that the imperialists release him. Brother Cung was one of seven members of the Revolutionary Youth League who founded the first branch of the Indochinese Communist party.

Our union had a large membership. It could be said that an absolute majority of the workers belonged. It was indeed a broad-based mass, class organization of the party. The workers enthusiastically took part in its every activity. It was precisely because of this organization that the nerve center—the Phu-rieng party branch with less than a dozen members—was able to lead all the struggles there, from the smallest to the most massive.

The Red Guards were the party's armed organization. To be precise, the name of the group at the time was the Young Red Guards [Thanh nien xich ve doi]. I myself was the unit leader. In every village we organized a squad of about thirty people under the command of a squad leader. At the time the squad leader in Village 9 was comrade Nguyen Manh Hong, now [1971] deputy chief of the Forestry Service. Then, however, comrade Manh Hong was still quite young. From his short, plump, fair-skinned appearance, no one would have suspected that Manh Hong was an activist. And yet Hong worked irrepressibly for the party and his class, even though he had just turned sixteen. Hong and I were very well matched. Once I went to live for a month in Village 9 to talk with Manh Hong about our work. At night, like two brothers sharing the same bed, we fell asleep with our legs flopping one against the other.

The Young Red Guards had a very specific responsibility. They were the armed forces of the party branch and had the task of protecting the party and protecting the struggle. During strikes, the Red Guards always went along to guard the workers who were negotiating with the owners. In ordinary times, the Red Guards shielded the villages against the secret agents of the owners and the imperialists. These lackeys frequently hung around eavesdropping, spying on the workers to try to pick up news. Whenever the Red Guards discovered one, they would beat him until he was barely able to crawl away, all the time shouting that he was a thief.

Discipline at that time was very strict. I devised rules for the members of the Red Guards unit to follow. Members had to pledge absolute loyalty to the party and the union and pledge to obey every order received. In dealing with secret agents, with foremen and with the owners, the Red Guards had to oppose them to the end in order to protect the workers representatives, the members of the union executive committee, and the comrades of the party branch. All members had to give absolute obedience to their squad leaders and to the Red Guards commander. Besides that, the Red Guards were responsible for maintaining order on those nights when there were cheo performances and on days when there were soccer games.

All the Red Guards activities were half public, half secret. As far as the owners were concerned, they were just workers like any others. From our side, however, the branch gave them every task which called for maintaining order and security, or for armed confrontation with the owners. I took advantage of the dragon dance group to teach them the martial arts. At the time, I did not even know the word "military," and had yet to give any thought to practice with guns, crawling and creeping as our soldiers do nowadays. The main thing we did was practice the dance with staves. I had always been quite good with staves, ever since the time I studied at the Hoang Nguyen seminary, so I now taught the others. Every festive day they took the dragon's head around to dance. They all appeared most imposing with red scarves wrapped around their heads, unbuttoned shirts tied at the waist with a sash, and staves in their hands.

The unit's weapons were still extremely rudimentary. We mainly used staves and hatchets. All these hatchets were simple tree-cutting tools, but they were forged of good steel. They were honed sharp and bright as a mirror, so it seemed that one light stroke would be enough to split an enemy's head right in two.

Since 1928, when Cu came to be with us, and especially since the founding of the Phu-rieng party branch, the workers' organization at Phu-rieng had grown tighter every day. Struggles were a lively mixture of legal and illegal forms. One of the first things we did was take a position of opposition to the docking of workers' pay and to corporal punishment. If someone was beaten, we took action immediately.

I still remember the incident when comrade Cao was hit on the head with a hoe by a French foreman because he had not finished clearing grass from an assigned plot of ground in time. All the workers laid down their tools. A hundred of us went to the manager's bungalow to present our case. The manager tried to pacify us. We did not listen, but continued our strike, demanding that the French foreman be expelled from the plantation and that the manager guarantee that workers would not be beaten any more. As for comrade Cao, we asked that he be given treatment until he recovered. While he was in the clinic and unable to return to work, the plantation was to continue to pay him. Our struggle was resolute. In the end the owners had to concede. We waited until they agreed to resolve the main problems before we returned to the work area.

Having won once, we pushed on to strike yet another blow. This time the union selected workers' representatives to go ask the manager to distribute good rice, meat that was not all gristle, and fish that was not rotten. The representatives argued that when workers ate such bad food, they became ill and could not go out to work. While the representatives were bargaining with the owners, workers who were sick with diarrhea, stomach ailments, or any one of a hundred other diseases went to the nurse. It took about half an hour for each person, and since there was a total of at least one hundred people who came, the plantation lost scores of labor hours each day. The struggle thus had many facets, coordinated in tight synchronization. At first Vasser was unyielding, but after he had added it all up and seen that there was no way he could win, he resigned himself to resolving the problems we raised.

Gradually we pushed on to demand that women receive paid maternity leave and that rice be distributed to them while they were lying-in. Previously any woman who was giving birth and could not work was given no pay and no rice ration. Afterwards Vasser permitted them to receive two months rice but still would not pay them, using the excuse that the contract did not provide for that. We did not yet press our demand for lying-in women to be paid.

At that time there were struggles at many different levels. Sometimes only one group would strike, sometimes a team, and sometimes two or three villages stopped work at the same time. Vasser looked one way and then the other trying to find a way to deal with us. He made a show of going by the contract and sweetly proclaimed: "Whoever finishes early, come on back and rest, or play soccer and practice cheo."

On the surface it sounded like a good deal, but in fact the terms of the contract he offered were quite harsh. The workers responded by doing their work in a plodding, evenly paced manner. If they were digging holes to plant trees, they would spread out in a long line across the work area, watching each other as they dug. Each person would wait until everyone else had finished digging a hole before going on to the next row. Thus the holes they dug wound up in straight lines with no one ahead and no one behind. The other tasks, such as planting saplings, clearing ground and hoeing, were done in the same way, with everyone keeping to the pace of the weakest member of the group. Not knowing what to do, Vasser was forced to reduce our quotas, and so we won. From that time on all completed their quota a half hour or an hour early, stopped work, and returned to take care of their private affairs. In short, we kept the pressure on Vasser so that he could not breathe easily. Every scheme, every artifice advanced by that renegade priest met with defeat.

One other thing needs to be said, though. In spite of our many victories, our daily life really did not improve a great deal. One detail will make that clear. Because of living conditions at Phu-rieng, all pregnancies resulted in stillbirths. Few women workers could carry their children even as long as the fourth month. That is sufficient to show what living conditions existed even then.

Gradually the rights we were able to demand increased. The daily regimen and the treatment at the clinic became less deplorable. The owners had to buy more medicine and set up more beds. We struggled against the cruelest of the nurses until they were sent elsewhere. The workers who did the most strenuous work and grew ill were also allowed some injections of vitamins. And women workers could sometimes dare to come up to the clinic for they did not beat us as much, and when they did, they dared not give such terrible beatings as they had in the past.

Then we advanced to the demand for hot water to drink while working. The clause concerning water was very important to us. At that time, when workers grew tired and thirsty, they would simply find a hole in the ground and drink the water standing there. In the bad climate, with so many malaria mosquitoes and a low level of sanitation, drinking standing water could be extremely dangerous. Malaria and dysentery were common at Phu-rieng.

We appointed a representative to demand that they assign one person in the morning and one in the evening to spare hot water for the workers to drink in the work area. We had a very good rationale. With hot water to drink, the workers would not get sick; a full day's work would be profitable for the plantation; and the workers would benefit from improved health. Finally the owners had to go along. So every morning and every afternoon each work group chose one person to boil water for the group to drink. There was no shortage of firewood in the forest. And when someone was sick or feeling weak, they would be assigned to that job. In this way we were able to give an extra day's work to people who otherwise would have had to stay home from work without pay.

Vasser was on the one hand using blandishments and cajolery, and on the other hand making every effort to repress us severely. But he did not beat us in person the way Triai had. Vasser always used lackeys like the overseers Durandet and the brothers. Durandet's beatings were no less severe than those of Monte. And he raped much as Barre. Once he tried to make sister Nguyen Thi X from him. She refused. He laughed provocatively, then tied her to a stake and beat her on the buttocks. When he had finished beating her, he asked if she was ready to go with him yet, but she was still determined not to do what he said. He forced her down on the ground at once, then used a great bamboo cane to beat her dozens of times on the soles of her feet. When he got tired of beating her, he threw her back into the workers' village as one throws out an old torn rag. The flesh of her feet was shredded, and you could see the white bones in the mass of bloody, sticky flesh.

Durandet was in charge of Village 9, but he went out raping in Villages 2, 4, and 6. To this day I still remember the stooped form of that deadly ape. In a fit of passion he would go through the rubber forest as the late afternoon sun's rays slanted down, searching for a mate, looking truly loathsome.

At that time the LeBonne brothers were still overseers for Village 9. The two were exactly alike in their faces and physical appearance and also in their temperament. The LeBonne brothers had heads fat and round as soccer balls, with red, squinting eyes and shiny, greasy skin. I do not know how long they had lived in Indochina, but they could sound off in Vietnamese like corn popping. They cursed and swore all the day long: "Mother fucker," "Father fucker"—the most despicable kind of profanity. As soon as the older brother finished beating in one location, the younger brother would come over with his cane on his shoulder. In the work area of the laborers from Village 9 you could always hear the sound of the LeBonne brothers quacking out their curses and the heartrending cries of those being caned.

While Durandet and the LeBonne brothers were beating the workers with such a vengeance, the manager Vasser shut his ears and pretended to know nothing. Whenever Vasser came out to the forest to watch the workers on the job, that crew just controlled themselves so that they seemed gentle as lambs. If they did get angry, they simply spoke testily. At such times, if a stranger were to come by, he would have thought that we could breathe easily at Phu-rieng; that laborers could work however they wanted; that the Vietnamese and French foremen did not beat or curse; and that the manager Vasser was as good as the earth, a carved silver crucifix with the figure of Jesus Christ nailed to the cross hanging around his neck. A stranger would have had the impression, too, that labor was carried out according to contract, that a worker could go back when he finished the work set out for him, that at night we could meet for cheo performances and other pasttimes, and in the afternoon divide up for pleasant games of soccer. Phu-rieng was "heaven" indeed!

At the beginning of 1929, Michelin again changed the manager and some of the overseers. Vasser left and Soumagnac came. He was an air force captain, and even brought his French wife to Phu-rieng. Soumagnac was about thirty years old, a thoroughbred capitalist who owned many shares in Michelin. By this time the rubber forests at Phu-rieng had some trees which were almost three years old—nearly big enough for the first sap collection. The Michelin company felt they should select some trustworthy individuals with authority in the company to come oversee the work at Phu-rieng. Soumagnac met those criteria perfectly. He was a tall man and quite handsome. He always wore gold-rimmed glasses and spoke with a voice sweet as sugar.

In all of 1929 Soumagnac was only around Phu-rieng watching things about half the time. The other six months he took his wife off on pleasure trips to Da-lat, Sai-gon, Cap St. Jacques, and other places. Although he was seldom at Phu-rieng, we got a clear idea of what he was like. He was dissolute in some bestial fashion. He always had six or seven servants at his bungalow, as drivers, house servants, cooks, secretaries, and the like. Soumagnac selected each person with great care. They had to be handsome, strong, and young before he would take them. Any man who went to work in Soumagnac's bungalow had to spread his buttocks to satisfy the manager's carnal passions. Soumagnac kept this up until a person was haggard and pale, then turned him out and replaced him with someone else.

The wife took after her husband. Soumagnac's wife was only about twenty-one or twenty-two years old, devilishly beautiful and unbelievably passionate. She had a lover who was indeed a second Paris. But besides her Paris, Soumagnac's wife made the servants and cooks come up to satisfy her, too. It could be said that as soon as the master belched, the mistress got hungry, and vice versa. After only two months workers who were called to serve in the bungalow were exhausted, their faces pale yellow, their bodies always warm and feverish, sweat drenching the backs of their shirts.

The assistant manager was this Paris who took care of the paperwork in the office, and who always clung to the skirts of Soumagnac's wife. Yet Soumagnac remained calm and let them be. The ethics, the morals of the colonialists were truly incredible!

The overseers under Soumagnac's authority still included Durandet from the old crew, and there was a man named Boudy who was in charge of Village 2. Boudy was famous for his cruel beatings. He would strike a blow which split the flesh of the person being beaten, bend down to examine the wound oozing blood, eyeing it like a craftsman inspecting his work, and then suddenly raise his hand and bring down another blow on top of the old wound, not a centimeter away, always keeping a perfectly straight face.

Under Soumagnac the method of setting quotas and the partially relaxed activities for workers continued as under the renegade priest Vasser. But by this time the policies of cajolery could no longer deceive us, no matter how treacherous they might be. Since 1929 Phu-rieng had had a Communist party branch. All the military executioners and renegade priests, all the policies of savage repression and two-faced cajolery mixed with torture, however cunning, had been unmasked.

We remembered when we had just arrived at Phu-rieng, the silence of the forests weighing so heavily on our hearts, making us homesick, causing us to long for our wives and children, stirring a hundred confused emotions. Everything was deserted, desolate, yet we had to live with this gang of beasts in human guise, who might beat us or bind us at any time. We had no way of knowing whether we would live or die.

But where there is repression there is struggle. The more savage the repression, the stronger the struggle. We rubber workers had resisted the capitalist masters right from the time we first left home. Were we to allow them to straddle our necks, tear out our livers and sip our blood?

In general, struggles such as those described above were aimed at demanding material benefits. They were primarily economic, but they also had clear political content. The workers of Phu-rieng had become a force, with tight organization, with leadership for struggle, with a head to direct it. It had all the characteristics of a self-conscious working class. This was clear evidence of the truth that a workers' struggle movement combined with Marxist-Leninist theory will give birth to a Communist party. After the founding of the party, the working class will advance from a "class of itself" to a "class for itself."

The Phu-rieng party branch had indeed guided the struggles from lower forms to higher forms. After the branch was formed, every struggle incorporated political slogans as well as economic ones. For instance, we demanded an end to the head tax, demanded release of political prisoners, and specifically demanded that Tran Van Cung be freed.

The more we struggled, the more we won. And the more we won, the more we struggled. The more we won, the more the masses believed in and gathered around the party branch. Gradually we learned to martial our forces, to protect ourselves when we were on the defensive, and to strike boldly when we were on the attack.

The movement had grown. By the end of 1929 it could be said that the party branch at Phu-rieng had the support of the majority of workers at the plantation. The others were also influenced by the branch through the broad membership of the union.

It was also at this same time that the whole movement of workers throughout the country was rising—weavers in Nam-dinh, cement workers in Hai-phong, workers in the Ben-thuy match factory, and others. The ferment was everywhere. The Phu-rieng party branch prepared for a new round of struggles to be waged on a greater scale as far as both ends and means were concerned.

It was right at this time that brother Cu was betrayed. The ruling clique deported him to the North. When Cu left, he turned over the task of secretary of the Phu-rieng branch to me. From that time I carried a heavy responsibility with virtually no theoretical understanding and with only a limited amount of experience.

THE 1930 STRUGGLE OF THE PHU-RIENG RUBBER WORKERS

Since before Tet in 1930 the Phu-rieng party branch had been making both material and spiritual preparations for the large-scale strike about to come.

From *Humanité* the branch learned that French workers making preparations for a strike paid great attention to the problem of food supplies. Studying that experience, the branch was careful to discuss and resolve the food problem before the strike broke out. To prepare for sufficient food supplies in case the strike should drag on for a long time, union members were instructed to set aside rice, salt, and dried fish. Each village selected a person to go into the forest, choose a well-hidden place, and make a shelter to hide the food. The cache had to be secure against rain and against plundering by rats or other vermin. In addition, it had to be safe from the eyes of the foremen and undercover lackeys of the plantation owners. The food stores were gradually built up over a period of months, a little bit each day. The branch also gave one unit of the Red Guards the task of finding some way to take over the plantation's rice stores when the strike broke out, then carrying the rice out to forest hiding places.

Hasty preparations were also made to secure weapons. Those in the blacksmith group at the garage machine shop used wrecked jeeps and automobiles to make a number of daggers and long knives for the workers. Whoever had a hatchet had to keep it sharply honed at all times. And each person had to make ready a sturdy pole and two torches.

The branch and the executive committee of the union also met many times to discuss the goals of the struggle. At the time, the workers at Phu-rieng had both common demands and particular demands for each village. For the workers of the plantation as a whole, the following rights were to be demanded:

- A prohibition on beatings.
- A prohibition on docking pay.
- Exemption from taxes.
- Maternity leave for women workers.
- An eight-hour work day, including the time spent going to the work area and returning to the barracks.
- Compensation for workers injured in accidents on the job.

In addition to these, there was one political slogan: Free Tran Van Cung.

There was another major point for the workers in Villages 2 and 3, those who had arrived in the same wave as I had. Those of us who had survived three years at Phu-rieng and were now about to complete our contracts demanded to be returned to our homes. The owners were to bear the cost of transportation and all other expenses. That was very reasonable and sensible.

At that time there were also a number of our compatriots from the mountain tribes who had been captured by the French and brought in to do forced labor. The French were absolutely merciless toward them. They were given only rice and dried fish and got no pay at all. We often had to help them treat intestinal worms and malaria, so the ties between us became quite close. Besides, I had already taken a vow with the oldest man in the village that we would regard each other as members of the same family. We definitely needed a positive response from them to our coming strike. We immediately talked to them about it.

They understood at once, and said, "Right. The big man makes us do forced labor for days, months, even years yet gives us no land to farm. And the big man gives us no money. The big man has taken all our land. Now we have to tell the big man not to capture us for forced labor any more. The big man must give us farmland so we can take care of our elders and children."

One person spoke to another. Finally they promised us that if the workers went on strike to demand that the big man give more money, they would also stay at home and not come to the plantation to work any more. And if the workers fled, they would show them the way through the forest. Taking advantage of the coming lunar New Year, they would quit work. They promised that if we kept them informed every day, then they would help us if anything happened.

We were quite moved by their sympathy for us. We warned them not to guide the French or join the French army. On the 27th day of the last lunar month we saw them off. They went straight back to their villages that night.

We were very happy with this response from the mountain people. Our struggle would not be isolated. When it became too fierce, we would have a place to take shelter. There were individuals among them who had been to lower Laos and even all the way to Thailand and knew the trails. If necessary, we could flee. In only one evening the hundreds of mountaineers brought in by the French for forced labor at Phu-rieng had returned home, every last one of them. That also meant that when our strike broke out, the plantation owners would not be able to find a single worker to replace us.

On the night of the 28th day of the last lunar month, the executive committee of the Phu-rieng rubber workers union implemented the party branch directive to call together in the forest a conference of representatives of the five workers' villages. A great many workers came to the conference. The meeting progressed in secret, but with great excitement and enthusiasm. A drizzle was falling, the night was black as ink, and the torches we lit were barely enough to illuminate and warm a small corner of the forest, far from the villages and barracks. The delegates sat around in clusters, shivering from the cold. Nevertheless, glancing around at their eyes and listening to their ebullient voices was enough to make one aware of the zeal of all of Phu-rieng. The major points proposed by the branch were all approved by the delegates. They accepted responsibility for returning to their villages and urgently completing tasks not yet finished.

The atmosphere in all the workers' villages at the time was very animated. Although the branch only intended to stage a strike, the workers prepared weapons as if they were getting ready for an uprising. There was a good side to that, but in another sense it was not correct, and one of our shortcomings was not to have resolved and calmed down that phenomenon in time. Indeed I must confess that in the bottom of our hearts we, too, were very moved by the tumultuous atmosphere. It was as if a tempest were about to break over the forests. Anyone who had witnessed how we workers were forced for all these years to grit our teeth, twist and turn, and endure the tyranny of the enemy would have found it hard to escape the kind of emotions I felt as I watched us now turn around and stand up.

The legal newspapers of the day reported that our strike began 3 February 1930, in other words the fifth day of the first month of the year Tan Mao [the Year of the Cat]. In fact our struggle began on the first day of the lunar New Year, in other words 30 January 1930. A few days before, the manager, Soumagnac, had gotten wind that something was about to happen. As we did not yet have much experience, our preparations were pretty much out in the open. Soumagnac had his lackeys pass the word to the workers to come up to welcome the New Year with him on the morning of the first day of Tet. Soumagnac said he would give everyone a bonus. He wanted to calm us down, to use the joyous atmosphere of Tet to buy us off. We used his lackeys to send word back to Soumagnac that on that first day we would indeed all come up to celebrate Tet.

And that is what happened. Beginning early in the morning, workers in all the villages formed up in ranks according to the directions of the Red Guards squad leaders and marched on Soumagnac's bungalow. They were boisterous but very well organized. There was no uproar, no jostling. Each person held a long staff ready in his hand.

In keeping with the customs at Phu-rieng during previous Tet celebrations, our dragon dance group led the way. The members of the dragon dance group were all fighters chosen from the Red Guards. Each had a red scarf wrapped around his head and red shirt and blue trousers belted at the waist by a sash. A group carrying clubs and hatchets went along on both sides to protect the dragon dance group. The farther we went, the longer the procession became. Each time we passed a village we gained several hundred more people. In the end, five thousand workers from all parts of the Phu-rieng plantation arrived in Soumagnac's front yard.

He knew something was happening, but he still made a show of bravery and came out to greet us from his veranda. His face still wore an arrogant expression and he puffed on a cigarette which dangled carelessly from his mouth. However, it was easy to tell from the way his green eyes darted about that his stomach was churning. There were so many of us, and the atmosphere was quite different from previous years.

Following our plan, the workers surrounded the yard and sat in perfect order to watch the dragon dance group.

Ahimsa, Satyagraha, and Swaraj

By Gandhi

After his experience in South Africa, Gandhi returned to India to struggle for swaraj, *or "home-rule." He explicitly rejected armed struggle and terrorism in favor of a strategy and ideology he called* satyagraha, *or "truth/soul force." Based upon the South Asian religious concept of* ahimsā, *or non-violence to sentient beings, he organized a series of protests against British rule. Many of these protests were met with brutal repression from the British. These passages define the philosophy and techniques of his movement.*

A votary of *ashimā* cannot subscribe to the utilitarian formula greatest good of the greatest number. He will strive for the greatest good of all and die in the attempt to realize the ideal. He will therefore be willing to die, so that the others may live. He will serve himself with the rest, by himself dying. The greatest good of all inevitably includes the good of the greatest number, and, therefore, he and the utilitarian will converge in many points in their career but there does come a time when they must part company, and even work in opposite directions. The utilitarian to be logical will never sacrifice himself. The absolutist will even sacrifice himself. *17*

Young India, December 9, 1926

You might of course say that there can be no nonviolent rebellion and there has been none known to history. Well, it is my ambition to provide an instance, and it is my dream that my country may win its freedom through nonviolence. And, I would like to repeat to the world times without number, that I will not purchase my country's freedom at the cost of nonviolence. My marriage to nonviolence is such an absolute thing that I would rather commit suicide than be deflected from my position. I have not mentioned truth in this connexion, simply because truth cannot be expressed except by nonviolence. 18

Mohandas K. Gandhi, Selections from *All Men Are Brothers: Autobiographical Reflections*, pp. 81–83, 91–97. Copyright © 2005 by Navajivan Trust. Reprinted with permission.

Young India, November 12, 1931

The accumulated experience of the past thirty years, the first eight of which were in South Africa, fills me with the greatest hope that in the adoption of nonviolence lies the future of India and the world. It is the most harmless and yet equally effective way of dealing with the political and economic wrongs of the down-trodden portion of humanity. I have known from early youth that nonviolence is not a cloistered virtue to be practised by the individual for the peace and final salvation, but it is a rule of conduct for society if it is to live consistently with human dignity and make progress towards the attainment of peace for which it has been yearning for ages past.   19

Gandhiji's Correspondence with the Government, 1942–44

Up to the year 1906, I simply relied on appeal to reason. I was a very industrious reformer. I was a good draftsman, as I always had a close grip of facts which in its turn was the necessary result of my meticulous regard for truth. But I found that reason failed to produce an impression when the critical moment arrived in South Africa. My people were excited; even a worm will and does sometimes turn—and there was talk of wreaking vengeance. I had then to choose between allying myself to violence or finding out some other method of meeting the crisis and stopping the rot and it came to me that we should refuse to obey legislation that was degrading and let them put us in jail if they liked. Thus came into being the moral equivalent of war. I was then a loyalist, because I implicitly believed that the sum total of the activities of the British Empire was good for India and for humanity. Arriving in England soon after the outbreak of the war I plunged into it and later when I was forced to go to India as a result of the pleurisy that I had developed, I led a recruiting campaign at the risk of my life, and to the horror of some of my friends. The disillusionment came in 1919 after the passage of the Black Row-Latt Act* and the refusal of the government to give the simple elementary redress of proved wrongs that we had asked for. And so, in 1920, I became a rebel. Since then the conviction has been growing upon me, that things of fundamental importance to the people are not secured by reason alone but have to be purchased with their suffering. Suffering is the law of human beings; war is the law of the jungle. But suffering is infinitely more powerful than the law of the jungle for converting the opponent and opening his ears, which are otherwise shut, to the voice of reason. Nobody has probably drawn up more petitions or espoused more forlorn causes than I and I have come to this fundamental conclusion that if you want something really important to be done you must not merely satisfy the reason, you must move the heart also. The appeal of reason is more to the head but the penetration of the heart comes from suffering. It opens up the inner understanding in man. Suffering is the badge of the human race, not the sword. 20

---

1. *Act depriving Indians of some fundamental civil liberties.

Young India, November 4, 1931

Nonviolence is a power which can be wielded equally by all—children, young men and women or grown up people—provided they have a living faith in the God of Love and have therefore equal love for all mankind. When nonviolence is accepted as the law of life it must pervade the whole being and not be applied to isolated acts.   21

Harijan, September 5, 1936

If we are to be nonviolent, we must then not wish for anything on this earth which the meanest or the lowest of human beings cannot have.   22

With Gandhiji in Ceylon, published in 1928

The principle of nonviolence necessitates complete abstention from exploitation in any form.   23

Harijan, November 11, 1939

My resistance to war does not carry me to the point of thwarting those who wish to take part in it. I reason with them. I put before them the better way and leave them to make the choice.   24

Harijan, January 18, 1942

I would say to my critics to enter with me into the sufferings, not only of the people of India but of those, whether engaged in the war or not, of the whole world. I cannot look at this butchery going on in the world with indifference. I have an unchangeable faith that it is beneath the dignity of man to resort to mutual slaughter. I have no doubt that there is a way out.   25

Hindustan Standard, July 20, 1944

Perfect nonviolence is impossible so long as we exist physically, for we would want some space at least to occupy. Perfect nonviolence whilst you are inhabiting the body is only a theory like Euclid's point or straight line, but we have to endeavour every moment of our lives.   26

Harijan, July 21, 1940

In life, it is impossible to eschew violence completely. Now the question arises, where is one to draw the line? The line cannot be the same for every one. For, although, essentially the principle is the same, yet everyone applies it in his or her own way. What is one man's food can be another's poison. Meat-eating is a sin for me. Yet, for another person, who has always lived on meat and never seen anything wrong in it, to give it up, simply in order to copy me, will be a sin.

If I wish to be an agriculturist and stay in a jungle, I will have to use the minimum unavoidable violence, in order to protect my fields. I will have to kill monkeys, birds and insects, which eat up my crops. If I do not wish to do so myself, I will have to engage someone to do it for me. There is not much difference between the two. To allow crops to be eaten up by animals, in the name of *ahimsā*, while there is a famine in the land, is certainly a sin. Evil and good are relative terms. What is good under certain conditions can become an evil or a sin, under a different set of conditions.

Man is not to drown himself in the well of the *shāstras*, but he is to dive in their broad ocean and bring out pearls. At every step he has to use his discrimination as to what is *ahimsā* and what is *himsā*. In this, there is no room for shame or cowardice. The poet had said that the road leading up to God is for the brave, never for the cowardly.   64

Mahatma, VII, 1946

To say or write a distasteful word is surely not violent especially when the speaker or writer believes it to be true. The essence of violence is that there must be a violent intention behind a thought, word, or act, i.e., an intention to do harm to the opponent so-called.

False notions of propriety or fear of wounding susceptibilities often deter people from saying what they mean and ultimately land them on the shores of hypocrisy. But if nonviolence of thought is to be evolved in individuals or societies or nations, truth has to be told, however harsh or unpopular it may appear to be for the moment. 65

Harijan, December 19, 1936

Never has anything been done on this earth without direct action. I reject the word 'passive resistance' because of its insufficiency and its being interpreted as a weapon of the weak.   66

Young India, May 12, 1920

Nonviolence presupposes ability to strike. It is a conscious, deliberate restraint put upon one's desire for vengeance. But vengeance is any day superior to passive, effeminate and helpless submission. Forgiveness is higher still. Vengeance too is weakness. The desire for vengeance comes out of fear of harm, imaginary or real. A man who fears no one on earth would consider it troublesome even to summon up anger against one who is vainly trying to injure him.   67

Young India, August 12, 1926

Nonviolence and cowardice go ill together. I can imagine a fully armed man to be at heart a coward. Possession of arms implies an element of fear, if not cowardice. But true nonviolence is an impossibility without the possession of unadulterated fearlessness.   68

Harijan, July 15, 1939

My creed of nonviolence is an extremely active force. It has no room for cowardice or even weakness. There is hope for a violent man to be some day nonviolent, but there is none for a coward. I have therefore said more than once in these pages that if we do not know how to defend ourselves, our women and our places of worship by the force of suffering, i.e., nonviolence, we must, if we are men, be at least able to defend all these by fighting.   69

Young India, June 16, 1927

The people of a village near Bettia told me that they had run away whilst the police were looting their houses and molesting their womenfolk. When they said that they had run away because I had told them to be nonviolent, I hung my head in shame. I assured them that such was not the meaning of my nonviolence. I expected them to intercept the mightiest power that might be in the act of harming those who were under their protection, and draw without retaliation all harm upon their own heads even to the point of death, but never to run away from the storm centre. It was manly enough to defend one's property, honour, or religion at the point of the sword. It was manlier and nobler to defend them without seeking to injure the wrong-doer. But it was unmanly, unnatural and dishonourable to forsake the post of duty and, in order to save one's skin, to leave property, honour or religion to the mercy of the wrong-doer. I could see my way of delivering *ahimsā* to those who knew how to die, not to those who were afraid of death.   70

Gandhiji in Indian Villages, published in 1927

I would risk violence a thousand times than the emasculation of a whole race. 71

Young India August 4, 1920

My nonviolence does not admit of running away from danger and leaving dear ones unprotected. Between violence and cowardly flight, I can only prefer violence to cowardice. I can no more preach nonviolence to a coward than I can tempt a blind man to enjoy healthy scenes. Nonviolence is the summit of bravery. And in my own experience, I have had no difficulty in demonstrating to men trained in the school of violence the superiority of nonviolence. As a coward, which I was for years, I harboured violence. I began to prize nonviolence only when I began to shed cowardice.   72

Young India, May 28, 1924

Nonviolence cannot be taught to a person who fears to die and has no power of resistance. A helpless mouse is not nonviolent because he is always eaten by pussy. He would gladly eat the murderess if he could, but he ever tries to flee from her. We do not call him a coward, because he is made by nature to behave no better than he does. But a man who, when faced by danger, behaves like a mouse, is rightly called a coward. He harbours violence and hatred in his heart and would kill his enemy if he could without hurting himself. He is a stranger to nonviolence. All sermonizing on it will be lost on him. Bravery is foreign to his nature. Before he can understand nonviolence he has to be taught to stand his ground and even suffer death, in the attempt to defend himself against the aggressor who bids fair to overwhelm him. To do otherwise would be to confirm his cowardice and take him farther away from nonviolence. Whilst I may not actually help anyone to retaliate, I must not let a coward seek shelter behind nonviolence so-called. Not knowing the stuff of which nonviolence is made, many have honestly believed that running away from danger every time was a virtue compared to offering resistance, especially when it was fraught with danger to one's life. As a teacher of nonviolence I must, so far as it is possible for me, guard against such an unmanly belief.   73

Harijan July 20, 1935

No matter how weak a person is in body, if it is a shame to flee, he will stand his ground and die at his post. This would be nonviolence and bravery. No matter how weak he is, he will use what strength he has in inflicting injury on his opponent, and die in the attempt. This is bravery, but not nonviolence. If, when his duty is to face danger, he flees, it is cowardice. In the first case the man will have love or charity in him. In the second and third case, there would be a dislike or distrust and fear.   74

Harijan, August 17, 1935

Supposing I was a Negro, and my sister was ravished by a white or lynched by a whole community, what would be my duty? I ask myself. And the answer comes to me: I must not wish ill to these, but neither must I co-operate with them. It may be that ordinarily I depend on the lynching community for my livelihood. I refuse to co-operate with them, refuse even to touch the food that comes from them, and I refuse to co-operate with even my brother Negroes who tolerate the wrong. That is the self-immolation I mean. I have often in my life resorted to the plan. Of course, a mechanical act of starvation will mean nothing. One's faith must remain undimmed whilst life ebbs out, minute by minute. But I am a very poor specimen of the practice of nonviolence, and my answer may not convince you. But I am striving very hard, and even if I do not succeed fully in this life, my faith will not diminish.   75

Mahatma, IV, 1936

In this age of the rule of brute force, it is almost impossible for anyone to believe that anyone else could possibly reject the law of the final supremacy of brute force. And so I receive anonymous letters advising me that I must not interfere with the progress of the non-co-operation movement even though popular violence may break out. Others come to me and, assuming that secretly I must be plotting violence, inquire when the happy moment for declaring open violence is to arrive. They assure me that the English will never yield to anything but violence, secret or open. Yet others, I am informed, believe that I am the most rascally person living in India because I never give out my real intention and that they have not a shadow of a doubt that I believe in violence just as much as most people do.

Such being the hold that the doctrine of the sword has on the majority of mankind, and as success of non-cooperation depends principally on absence of violence during its pendency, and as my views in this matter affect the conduct of a large number of people, I am anxious to state them as clearly as possible.

I do believe that, where there is only a choice between cowardice and violence, I would advise violence. Thus when my eldest son asked me what he should have done, had he been present when I was almost fatally assaulted in 1908, whether he should have run away and seen me killed or whether he should have used his physical force which he could and wanted to use, and defend me, I told him that it was his duty to defend me even by using violence. Hence it was that I took part in the Boer War, the so-called Zulu Rebellion and the late war. Hence also do I advocate training in arms for those who believe in the method of violence. I would rather have India resort to arms in order to defend her honour than that she should in a cowardly manner become or remain a helpless witness to her own dishonour.

But I believe that nonviolence is infinitely superior to violence, forgiveness is more manly than punishment. Forgiveness adorns a soldier. But abstinence is forgiveness only when there is the power to punish; it is meaningless when it pretends to proceed from a helpless creature. A mouse hardly forgives a cat when it allows itself to be torn to pieces by her. I, therefore, appreciate the sentiment of those who cry out for the condign punishment of General Dyer and his ilk. They would tear him to pieces if they could. But I do not believe India to be a helpless creature. Only I want to use India's and my strength for a better purpose.

Let me not be misunderstood. Strength does not come from physical capacity. It comes from an indomitable will. An average Zulu is anyway more than a match for an average Englishman in bodily capacity. But he flees from an English boy, because he fears the boy's revolver or those who will use it for him. He fears death and is nerveless in spite of his burly figure. We in India may in a moment realize that one hundred thousand Englishmen need not frighten three hundred million human beings. A definite forgiveness would, therefore, mean a definite recognition of our strength. With enlightened forgiveness must come a mighty wave of strength in us, which would make it impossible for a Dyer and a Frank Johnson to heap affront on India's devoted head. It matters little to me that for the moment I do not drive my point home. We feel too downtrodden not to be angry and revengeful. But I must not refrain from saying that India can gain more by waiving the right of punishment. We have better work to do, a better mission to deliver to the world.

I am not a visionary. I claim to be a practical idealist. Religion of nonviolence is not meant merely for the *rishis* and saints. It is meant for the common people as well. Nonviolence is the law of our species as violence is the law of the brute. The spirit lies dormant in the brute, and he knows no law but that of physical might. The dignity of man requires obedience to a higher law, to the strength of the spirit.

I have ventured to place before India the ancient law of self-sacrifice. For *Satyāgraha* and its offshoots, non-co-operation and civil resistance, are nothing but new names for the law of suffering. The *rishis*, who discovered the law of nonviolence in the midst of violence, were greater geniuses than Newton. They were themselves greater warriors than Wellington. Having themselves known the use of arms, they realized their uselessness and taught a weary world that its salvation lay not through violence but through nonviolence.

Nonviolence in its dynamic condition means conscious suffering. It does not mean meek submission to the will of the evil-doer, but it means putting of one's whole soul against the will of the tyrant. Working under this law of our being, it is possible for a single individual to defy the whole might of an unjust empire to save his honour, his religion, his soul, and lay the foundation for that empire's fall or its regeneration.

And so I am not pleading for India to practise nonviolence because it is weak. I want her to practise nonviolence being conscious of her strength and power. No training in arms is required for realization of her strength. We seem to need it, because we seem to think that we are but a lump of flesh. I want to recognize that she has a soul that cannot perish and that can rise triumphant above every physical weakness and defy the physical combination of a whole world. … If India takes up the doctrine of the sword, she may gain momentary victory. Then India will cease to be the pride of my heart. I am wedded to India because I owe my all to her. I believe absolutely that she has a mission for the world. She is not to copy Europe blindly. India's acceptance of the doctrine of the sword will be the hour of my trial. I hope I shall not be found wanting. My religion has no geographical limits. If I have a living faith in it, it will transcend my love for India herself. My life is dedicated to the service of India through the religion of nonviolence which I believe to be the root of Hinduism. *76*

Mahatma, II, Young India, August 11, 1920

I must continue to argue till I convert opponents or I own defeat. For my mission is to convert every Indian, even Englishmen and finally the world, to nonviolence for regulating mutual relations whether political, economic, social or religious. If I am accused of being too ambitious, I should plead guilty. If I am told that my dream can never materialize, I would answer 'that is possible,' and go my way. I am a seasoned soldier of nonviolence, and I have evidence enough to sustain my faith. Whether, therefore, I have one comrade or more or none, I must continue my experiment. *77*

Mahatma, V, Harijan, January 13, 1940

It has been suggested by American friends that the atom bomb will bring in *ahimsā*, as nothing else can. It will, if it is meant that its destructive power will so disgust the world, that it will turn it away from violence for the time being. And this is very like a man glutting himself with the dainties to the point of nausea, and turning away from them only to return with redoubled zeal after the effect of nausea is well over. Precisely in the same manner will the world return to violence with renewed zeal, after the effect of disgust is worn out.

Often does good come out of evil. But that is God's, not man's plan. Man knows that only evil can come out of evil, as good out of good. … The moral to be legitimately drawn from the supreme tragedy of the atom bomb is that it will not be destroyed by counter bombs, even as violence cannot be by counter violence. Mankind has to go out of violence only through nonviolence. Hatred can be overcome only by love. Counter hatred only increases the surface, as well as the depth of hatred.

I am aware that I am repeating what I have many times stated before and practised to the best of my ability and capacity. What I first stated was itself nothing new. It was as old as the hills. Only I recited no copy-book maxim but definitely announced what

I believed in every fibre of my being. Sixty years of practice in various walks of life has only enriched the belief which the experience of friends fortified. It is, however, the central truth by which one can stand alone without flinching. I believe in what Max Muller said years ago, namely, that truth needed to be repeated, as long as there were men who disbelieved it.   78

Mahatma, VII, Harijan, July 1946

If India makes violence her creed, and I have survived, I would not care to live in India. She will cease to evoke any pride in me. My patriotism is subservient to my religion. I cling to India like a child to its mother's breast, because I feel that she gives me the spiritual nourishment I need. She has the environment that responds to my highest aspiration. When that faith is gone, I shall feel like an orphan without hope of ever finding a guardian.   79

Young India, April 6, 1921

Prayer to the Masks (1945)

By Léopold Sédar Senghor

Léopold Sédar Senghor (1906–2001) was one of the most prominent African intellectuals of the 20th century. The first African elected to the prestigious Académie Française, he was educated in Dakar, Senegal, and Paris, France. Working as a professor in the 1930s, he and Aimé Césaire developed the literary movement négritude. Négritude fought French racism by celebrating an essential African identity and urging blacks to take pride in themselves as they were. While not anti-white, the movement argued that Sub-Saharan African culture was more sophisticated than what Europeans were willing to acknowledge. He thus stressed the importance of dialogue and exchange between white and black culture. He served in World War Two and spent time in various prisoner of war camps. After the war, he entered politics, representing Senegal in the French parliament and then becoming independent Senegal's first president from 1960 to 1980.

Masks! O Masks!
Black mask red mask you white-and-black masks,
Masks at the four points the Spirit breathes from,
I salute you in silence!
And not you last, lion-headed Ancestor,
You guard this place from any woman's laughter, any fading smile,
Distilling this eternal air in which I breathe my Forebears.
Basks of maskless faces, stripped of every dimple as of every wrinkle,
You who have arranged this portrait, this face of mine bent above this altar of white paper
In your image, hear me!
Now dies the Africa of empires—the dying of a pitiable princess
And Europe's too, to whom we're linked by the umbilicus.
Fix your immutable eyes on your subjugated children,

Léopold Sedar Senghor; Ellen Conroy Kennedy, ed. and trans., "Prayer to the Masks," *The Negritude Poets: An Anthology of Translations from the French*. Copyright © 1989 by Ellen Conroy Kennedy.

Who relinquish their lives as the poor their last garments.

May we answer present at the world's rebirth,

Like the yeast white flour needs.

For who would teach rhythm to a dead world of cannons and machines?

Who would give the shout of joy at dawn to wake the dead and orphaned?

Tell me, who would restore the memory of life to men whose hopes are disemboweled?

They call us men of cotton, coffee, oil.

They call us men of death.

We are men of dance, whose feet take on new strength from stamping the hard ground.

Indonesia Raya

By Wage Rudolf Supratman

Wage Rudolf Supratman (1903–1938) was an Indonesian songwriter who penned this nationalist call for unity in the Dutch East Indies in 1927. The song was part of the Indonesian nationalist movement's argument that all of the more than 17,000 islands (some joke 18,000 at low tide) claimed by the Dutch should be part of a united and independent nation. These nationalists had a serious obstacle in the region's amazing diversity that included a variety of religions and over 350 different languages. The call for a "greater Indonesia" was more than a romantic celebration of the land, it was part of an effort to create a united front against Dutch colonial rule.

"Indonesia Raya"
Indonesia, my homeland
The land where I shed my blood
Right there, I stand
To be a scout of my motherland
Indonesia, my nationality
My nation and my homeland
Let us exclaim
"Indonesia unites!"
Long live my land, long live my state
My nation, my people, entirely
Let us build its soul, let us build its body
For the Great Indonesia
Great Indonesia, independent & sovereign!
My land, my country which I love
Great Indonesia, independent & sovereign!
Long live Great Indonesia!

Great Indonesia, independent & sovereign!
My land, my country which I love
Great Indonesia, independent & sovereign!
Long live Great Indonesia!
Indonesia, a noble land
Our wealthy land
Right there, I stand
Forever and ever
Indonesia, a hereditary land
A heritage of ours
Let us pray
"To Indonesians' happiness!"
Fertile may its soil, flourish may its soul
Its nation, its people, entirely
Aware may its heart, aware may its mind
For the Great Indonesia
Indonesia, a sacred land
Our victorious land
Right there, I stand
To guard the pure motherland
Indonesia, a radiant land
A land which I adore
Let us pledge
"Indonesia is eternal!"
Safe may its people, safe may its children
Its islands, its seas, entirely
The state progresses, its scouts advance
For the Great Indonesia

"On Violence" from *The Wretched of the Earth* (1961)

By Frantz Fanon

Frantz Fanon (1925–1961) was born in Fort-de-France, Martinique, and was a student of Césaire. Fanon is regarded as one of the key theorists of post-colonialism, combining Marxist, existentialism, and an analysis of race. When France fell to the NAZIs and the collaborationist Vichy regime came to power, Fanon joined De Gaulle's Free French Forces. He fought in battles in France, but he and other colonial troops were pulled out of their units before crossing the Rhine into German territory. After the war, he briefly returned to Martinique to help with Césaire's mayoral campaign and then studied psychiatry in France. He practiced in Normandy before being transferred to Algeria in 1953. When the Algerian war for independence broke out, he soon joined the Algerian National Liberation Front. Nonetheless, he treated both French and Algerian patients suffering from the trauma of guerilla combat, torture, and terrorism that characterized this brutal war. After his expulsion from Algeria, Fanon worked with the independence movement from their base in neighboring Tunisia. He published several books theorizing the struggle for decolonization before his sudden death from leukemia in 1961. In his most famous work, he argued, in contrast to Gandhi, that the violence of de-colonization could have a purifying and healing impact on the colonized.

CONCERNING VIOLENCE

National liberation, national renaissance, the restoration of nationhood to the people, commonwealth: whatever may be the headings used or the new formulas introduced decolonization is always a violent phenomenon. At whatever level we study it—relationship between individuals, new names for sports clubs, the human

Frantz Fanon, "Concerning Violence," *The Wretched of the Earth*, pp. 35-46. Copyright © 1963 by Présence Africaine. Reprinted with permission of Grove/Atlantic, Inc.

admixture at cocktail parties, in the police, on the directing boards of national or private banks—decolonization is quite simply the replacing of a certain "species" of men by another "species" of men. Without any period of transition, there is a total, complete, and absolute substitution. It is true that we could equally well stress the rise of a new nation, the setting up of a new state, its diplomatic relations, and its economic and political trends. But we have precisely chosen to speak of that kind of *tabula rasa* which characterizes at the outset all decolonization. Its unusual importance is that it constitutes, from the very first day, the minimum demands of the colonized. To tell the truth, the proof of success lies in a whole social structure being changed from the bottom up. The extraordinary importance of this change is that it is willed, called for, demanded. The need for this change exists in its crude state, impetuous and compelling, in the consciousness and in the lives of the men and women who are colonized. But the possibility of this change is equally experienced in the form of a terrifying future in the consciousness of another "species" of men and women: the colonizers.

Decolonization, which sets out to change the order of the world, is, obviously, a program of complete disorder. But it cannot come as a result of magical practices, nor of a natural shock, nor of a friendly understanding. Decolonization, as we know, is a historical process: that is to say that it cannot be understood, it cannot become intelligible nor clear to itself except in the exact measure that we can discern the movements which give it historical form and content. Decolonization is the meeting of two forces, opposed to each other by their very nature, which in fact owe their originality to that sort of substantification which results from and is nourished by the situation in the colonies. Their first encounter was marked by violence and their existence together—that is to say the exploitation of the native by the settler—was carried on by dint of a great array of bayonets and cannons. The settler and the native are old acquaintances. In fact, the settler is right when he speaks of knowing "them" well. For it is the settler who has brought the native into existence and who perpetuates his existence. The settler owes the fact of his very existence, that is to say, his property, to the colonial system.

Decolonization never takes place unnoticed, for it influences individuals and modifies them fundamentally. It transforms spectators crushed with their inessentiality into privileged actors, with the grandiose glare of history's floodlights upon them. It brings a natural rhythm into existence, introduced by new men, and with it a new language and a new humanity. Decolonization is the veritable creation of new men. But this creation owes nothing of its legitimacy to any supernatural power; the "thing" which has been colonized becomes man during the same process by which it frees itself.

In decolonization, there is therefore the need of a complete calling in question of the colonial situation. If we wish to describe it precisely, we might find it in the well-known words: "The last shall be first and the first last." Decolonization is the putting into practice of this sentence. That is why, if we try to describe it, all decolonization is successful.

The naked truth of decolonization evokes for us the searing bullets and blood-stained knives which emanate from it. For if the last shall be first, this will come to pass after a murderous and decisive struggle between the two protagonists. That affirmed intention to place the last at the head of things, and to make them climb at a pace (too quickly, some say) the well-known steps which characterize an organized society, can only triumph if we use all means to turn the scale, including, of course, that of violence.

You do not turn any society, however primitive it may be, upside down with such a program if you have not decided from the very beginning, that is to say from the actual formulation of that program, to overcome all the obstacles that you will come across in so doing. The native who decides to put the program into practice, and to become its moving force, is ready for violence at all times. From birth it is clear to him that this narrow world, strewn with prohibitions, can only be called in question by absolute violence.

The colonial world is a world divided into compartments. It is probably unnecessary to recall the existence of native quarters and European quarters, of schools for natives and schools for Europeans; in the same way we need not recall apartheid in South Africa. Yet, if we examine closely this system of compartments, we will at least be able to reveal the lines of force it implies. This approach to the colonial world, its ordering and its geographical layout will allow us to mark out the lines on which a decolonized society will be reorganized.

The colonial world is a world cut in two. The dividing line, the frontiers, are shown by barracks and police stations. In the colonies it is the policeman and the soldier who are the official, instituted go-betweens, the spokesmen of the settler and his rule of oppression. In capitalist societies the educational system, whether lay or clerical, the structure of moral reflexes handed down from father to son, the exemplary honesty of workers who are given a medal after fifty years of good and loyal service, and the affection which springs from harmonious relations and good behavior—all these aesthetic expressions of respect for the established order serve to create around the exploited person an atmosphere of submission and of inhibition which lightens the task of policing considerably. In the capitalist countries a multitude of moral teachers, counselors and "bewilderers" separate the exploited from those in power. In the colonial countries, on the contrary, the policeman and the soldier, by their immediate presence and their frequent and direct action maintain contact with the native and advise him by means of rifle butts and napalm not to budge. It is obvious here that the agents of government speak the language of pure force. The intermediary does not lighten the oppression, nor seek to hide the domination; he shows them up and puts them into practice with the clear conscience of an upholder of the peace; yet he is the bringer of violence into the home and into the mind of the native.

The zone where the natives live is not complementary to the zone inhabited by the settlers. The two zones are opposed, but not in the service of a higher unity. Obedient to the rules of pure Aristotelian logic, they both follow the principle of reciprocal exclusivity. No conciliation is possible, for of the two terms, one is superfluous. The settlers' town is a strongly built town, all made of stone and steel. It is a brightly lit town; the streets are covered with asphalt; and the garbage cans swallow all the leavings, unseen, unknown and hardly thought about. The settler's feet are never visible, except perhaps in the sea; but there you're never close enough to see them. His feet are protected by strong shoes although the streets of his town are clean and even, with no holes or stones. The settler's town is a well-fed town, an easygoing town; its belly is always full of good things. The settlers' town is a town of white people, of foreigners.

The town belonging to the colonized people, or at least the native town, the Negro village, the medina, the reservation, is a place of ill fame, peopled by men of evil repute. They are born there, it matters little where or how; they die there, it matters not where, nor how. It is a world without spaciousness; men live there on top of each other, and their huts are built one on top of the other. The native town is a hungry town, starved of bread, of meat, of shoes, of coal, of light. The native town is a crouching village, a town on its knees, a town wallowing in the mire. It is a town of niggers and dirty Arabs. The look that the native turns on the settler's town is a look of lust, a look of envy; it expresses his dreams of possession—all manner of possession: to sit at the settler's table, to sleep in the settler's bed, with his wife if possible. The colonized man is an envious man. And this the settler knows very well; when their glances meet he ascertains bitterly, always on the defensive, "They want to take our place." It is true, for there is no native who does not dream at least once a day of setting himself up in the settler's place.

This world divided into compartments, this world cut in two is inhabited by two different species. The originality of the colonial context is that economic reality, inequality, and the immense difference of ways of life never come to mask the human realities. When you examine at close quarters the colonial context, it is evident that what parcels out the world is to begin with the fact of belonging to or not belonging to a given race, a given species. In the colonies the economic substructure is also a superstructure. The cause is the consequence; you are rich because you are white, you are white because you are rich. This is why Marxist analysis should always be slightly stretched every time we have to do with the colonial problem.

Everything up to and including the very nature of precapitalist society, so well explained by Marx, must here be thought out again. The serf is in essence different from the knight, but a reference to divine right is necessary to legitimize this statutory difference. In the colonies, the foreigner coming from another country imposed his rule by means of guns and machines. In defiance of his successful transplantation, in spite of his appropriation, the settler still remains a foreigner. It is neither the act of owning factories, nor estates, nor a bank balance which distinguishes the governing classes. The governing race is first and foremost those who come from elsewhere, those who are unlike the original inhabitants, "the others."

The violence which has ruled over the ordering of the colonial world, which has ceaselessly drummed the rhythm for the destruction of native social forms and broken up without reserve the systems of reference of the economy, the customs of dress and external life, that same violence will be claimed and taken over by the native at the moment when, deciding to embody history in his own person, he surges into the forbidden quarters. To wreck the colonial world is henceforward a mental picture of action which is very clear, very easy to understand and which may be assumed by each one of the individuals which constitute the colonized people. To break up the colonial world does not mean that after the frontiers have been abolished lines of communication will be set up between the two zones. The destruction of the colonial world is no more and no less that the abolition of one zone, its burial in the depths of the earth or its expulsion from the country.

The natives' challenge to the colonial world is not a rational confrontation of points of view. It is not a treatise on the universal, but the untidy affirmation of an original idea propounded as an absolute. The colonial world is a Manichean world. It is not enough for the settler to delimit physically, that is to say with the help of the army and the police force, the place of the native. As if to show the totalitarian character of colonial exploitation the settler paints the native as a sort of quintessence of evil.* Native society is not simply described as a society lacking in values. It is not enough for the colonist to affirm that those values have disappeared from, or still better never existed in, the colonial world. The native is declared insensible to ethics; he represents not only the absence of values, but also the negation of values. He is, let us dare to admit, the enemy of values, and in this sense he is the absolute evil. He is the corrosive element, destroying all that comes near him; he is the deforming element, disfiguring all that has to do with beauty or morality; he is the depository of maleficent powers, the unconscious and irretrievable instrument of blind forces. Monsieur Meyer could thus state seriously in the French National Assembly that the Republic must not be prostituted by allowing the Algerian people to become part of it. All values, in fact, are irrevocably poisoned and diseased as soon as they are allowed in contact with the colonized race. The customs of the colonized people, their traditions, their myths—above all, their myths—are the very sign of that poverty of spirit and of their constitutional depravity. That is why we must put the DDT which destroys parasites, the bearers of disease, on the same level as the Christian religion which wages war on embryonic heresies and instincts, and on evil as yet unborn. The recession of yellow fever and the advance of evangelization form part of the same balance sheet. But the triumphant *communiqués* from the missions are in fact a source of information concerning the implantation of foreign influences in the core of the colonized people. I speak of the Christian religion, and no one need be astonished. The Church in the colonies is the white people's Church, the foreigner's Church. She does not call the native to God's ways but to the ways of the white man, of the master, of the oppressor. And as we know, in this matter many are called but few chosen.

At times this Manicheism goes to its logical conclusion and dehumanizes the native, or to speak plainly, it turns him into an animal. In fact, the terms the settler uses when he mentions the native are zoological terms. He speaks of the yellow man's reptilian motions, of the stink of the native quarter, of breeding swarms, of foulness, of spawn, of gesticulations. When the settler seeks to describe the native fully in exact terms he constantly refers to the bestiary. The European rarely hits on a picturesque style; but the native, who knows what is in the mind of the settler, guesses at once what he is thinking of. Those hordes of vital statistics, those hysterical masses, those faces bereft of all humanity, those distended bodies which are like nothing on earth, that mob without beginning or end, those children who seem to belong to nobody, that laziness stretched out in the sun, that vegetative rhythm of life—all this forms part of the colonial vocabulary. General de Gaulle speaks of "the yellow multitudes" and François Mauriac of the black, brown, and yellow masses which soon will be unleashed. The native knows all this, and laughs to himself every time he spots an allusion to the animal world in the other's words. For he knows that he is not an animal; and it is precisely at the moment he realizes his humanity that he begins to sharpen the weapons with which he will secure its victory.

As soon as the native begins to pull on his moorings, and to cause anxiety to the settler, he is handed over to well-meaning souls who in cultural congresses point out to him the specificity and wealth of Western values. But every time Western values are mentioned they produce in the native a sort of stiffening or muscular lockjaw. During the period of decolonization, the native's reason is appealed to. He is offered definite values, he is told frequently that decolonization need not mean regression, and that he must put his trust in qualities which are well-tried, solid, and highly esteemed. But it so happens that when the native hears a speech about Western culture he pulls out his knife—or at least he makes sure it is within reach. The violence with which the supremacy of white values is affirmed and the aggressiveness which has permeated the victory of these values over the ways of life and of thought of the native mean that, in revenge, the native laughs in mockery when Western values are mentioned in front of him. In the colonial context the settler only ends his work of breaking in the native when the latter admits loudly and intelligibly the supremacy of the white man's values. In the period of decolonization, the colonized masses mock at these very values, insult them, and vomit them up.

This phenomenon is ordinarily masked because, during the period of decolonization, certain colonized intellectuals have begun a dialogue with the bourgeoisie of the colonialist country. During this phase, the indigenous population is discerned only as an indistinct mass. The few native personalities whom the colonialist bourgeois have come to know here and there have not sufficient influence on that immediate discernment to give rise to nuances. On the other hand, during the period of liberation, the colonialist bourgeoisie looks feverishly for contacts with the elite and it is with these elite that the familiar dialogue concerning values is carried on. The colonialist bourgeoisie, when it realizes that it is impossible for it to maintain its domination over the colonial countries, decides to carry out a rearguard action with regard to culture, values, techniques, and so on. Now what we must never forget is that the immense majority of colonized peoples is oblivious to these problems. For a colonized people the most essential value, because the most concrete, is first and foremost the land: the land which will bring them bread and, above all, dignity. But this dignity has nothing to do with the dignity of the human individual: for that human individual has never heard tell of it. All that the native has seen in his country is that they can freely arrest him, beat him, starve him: and no professor of ethics, no priest has ever come to be beaten in his place, nor to share their bread with him. As far as the native is concerned, morality is very concrete; it is to silence the settler's defiance, to break his flaunting violence—in a word, to put him out of the picture. The well-known principle that all men are equal will be illustrated in the colonies from the moment that the native claims that he is the equal of the settler. One step more, and he is ready to fight to be more than the settler. In fact, he has already decided to eject him and to take his place; as we see it, it is a whole material and moral universe which is breaking up. The intellectual who for his part has followed the colonialist with regard to the universal abstract will fight in order that the settler and the native may live together in peace in a new world. But the thing he does not see, precisely because he is permeated by colonialism and all its ways of thinking, is that the settler, from the moment that the colonial context disappears, has no longer any interest in remaining or in co-existing. It is not by chance that, even before any negotiation* between the Algerian and French governments has taken place, the European minority which calls itself "liberal" has already made its position clear: it demands nothing more nor less than twofold citizenship. By setting themselves apart in an abstract manner, the liberals try to force the settler into taking a very concrete jump into the unknown. Let us admit it, the settler knows perfectly well that no phraseology can be a substitute for reality.

Thus the native discovers that his life, his breath, his beating heart are the same as those of the settler. He finds out that the settler's skin is not of any more value than a native's skin; and it must be said that this discovery shakes the world in a very necessary

---

*   Fanon is writing in 1961.—*Trans.*

manner. All the new, revolutionary assurance of the native stems from it. For if, in fact, my life is worth as much as the settler's, his glance no longer shrivels me up nor freezes me, and his voice no longer turns me into stone. I am no longer on tenterhooks in his presence; in fact, I don't give a damn for him. Not only does his presence no longer trouble me, but I am already preparing such efficient ambushes for him that soon there will be no way out but that of flight.

We have said that the colonial context is characterized by the dichotomy which it imposes upon the whole people. Decolonization unifies that people by the radical decision to remove from it its heterogeneity, and by unifying it on a national, sometimes a racial, basis. We know the fierce words of the Senegalese patriots, referring to the maneuvers of their president, Senghor: "We have demanded that the higher posts should be given to Africans; and now Senghor is Africanizing the Europeans." That is to say that the native can see clearly and immediately if decolonization has come to pass or not, for his minimum demands are simply that the last shall be first.

But the native intellectual brings variants to this petition, and, in fact, he seems to have good reasons: higher civil servants, technicians, specialists—all seem to be needed. Now, the ordinary native interprets these unfair promotions as so many acts of sabotage, and he is often heard to declare: "It wasn't worth while, then, our becoming independent…"

Chapter 6

World War II

Introduction

As its name might indicate, the Second World War had many of its origins in the First World War. Indeed, it is nearly impossible to imagine Hitler coming to power without the punitive terms of the Treaty of Versailles to serve as a rallying point. One could even make the argument that the drive for empire (in Eastern Europe for Germany, China and Southeast Asia for Japan, and the Balkans and Africa for Italy) was a central cause for the two wars. Historian A.J.P. Taylor has gone so far to suggest that 1914-1945 was really a second Thirty Years War, with a fragile armistice in the middle. Yet, the world did not enter into the second global conflict with the same naïve enthusiasm of 1914. The horrors of total war were now well known and the new conventional wisdom held that due to technological advances a return to total war would be even worse. Such predictions were correct as four to five times as many people died in the second war as in the first. Even more shocking, new weapons allowed for long-range aerial bombardment of cities, leading to civilian deaths accounting for half of those lost. If genocide was introduced with the Turkish persecution of the Armenians in the World War One, the NAZI mass murder of Jews, Roma and Sinti (Gypsies), homosexuals, and political prisoners raised genocide to a still unimaginable intensity. The Asian theater was not without its excesses, including the "Rape of Nanking" and the firebombing of most of Japan's cities. Wartime propaganda aside, there was a more somber sense of duty and foreboding in the popular culture of World War Two. These selected documents guide the reader through the key moments in the largest war the world has yet seen.

This chapter relates to section 10.8 of the History-Social Science Content Standards for California Public Schools.

September 1, 1939

By W.H. Auden

W.H. Auden (1907–1973) was born in England but later received American citizenship. One of the more prominent English language writers of the mid-20th century, his work is known for its innovative style as well as its engagement with serious moral issues. Having traveled in China during the Japanese invasion (1937–1945) and publishing Journey to a War *(1939) with Christopher Isherwood, Auden may have been more aware than others of the horrors that would be unleashed upon Hitler's invasion of Poland and the official start of World War Two (of course, the war had been raging in Asia years prior to this). The poem is complex, obviously filled with dread about the coming war with Germany; it also critiques the alienation he felt as a gay man in conservative American society. Despite its bleakness, the poem ends on an optimistic note.*

I sit in one of the dives
On Fifty-second Street
Uncertain and afraid
As the clever hopes expire
Of a low dishonest decade:
Waves of anger and fear
Circulate over the bright
And darkened lands of the earth,
Obsessing our private lives;
The unmentionable odour of death
Offends the September night.

Accurate scholarship can
Unearth the whole offence
From Luther until now

That has driven a culture mad,
Find what occurred at Linz,
What huge imago made
A psychopathic god:
I and the public know
What all schoolchildren learn,
Those to whom evil is done
Do evil in return.

Exiled Thucydides knew
All that a speech can say
About Democracy,
And what dictators do,
The elderly rubbish they talk
To an apathetic grave;
Analysed all in his book,
The enlightenment driven away,
The habit-forming pain,
Mismanagement and grief:
We must suffer them all again.

Into this neutral air
Where blind skyscrapers use
Their full height to proclaim
The strength of Collective Man,
Each language pours its vain
Competitive excuse:
But who can live for long
In an euphoric dream;
Out of the mirror they stare,
Imperialism's face
And the international wrong.
Faces along the bar
Cling to their average day:
The lights must never go out,
The music must always play,
All the conventions conspire
To make this fort assume
The furniture of home;
Lest we should see where we are,

Lost in a haunted wood,
Children afraid of the night
Who have never been happy or good.

The windiest militant trash
Important Persons shout
Is not so crude as our wish:
What mad Nijinsky wrote
About Diaghilev
Is true of the normal heart;
For the error bred in the bone
Of each woman and each man
Craves what it cannot have,
Not universal love
But to be loved alone.

From the conservative dark
Into the ethical life
The dense commuters come,
Repeating their morning vow;
'I will be true to the wife,
I'll concentrate more on my work,'
And helpless governors wake
To resume their compulsory game:
Who can release them now,
Who can reach the dead,
Who can speak for the dumb?
All I have is a voice
To undo the folded lie,
The romantic lie in the brain
Of the sensual man-in-the-street
And the lie of Authority
Whose buildings grope the sky:
There is no such thing as the State
And no one exists alone;
Hunger allows no choice
To the citizen or the police;
We must love one another or die.

Defenseless under the night
Our world in stupor lies;
Yet, dotted everywhere,
Ironic points of light
Flash out wherever the Just
Exchange their messages:
May I, composed like them
Of Eros and of dust,
Beleaguered by the same
Negation and despair,
Show an affirming flame.

All Captives Slain

By F. Tillman Durdin

As a New York Times correspondent, F. Tilman Durdin (1907–1998) reported on one of the most brutal massacres of the war. Importantly, the war crime occurred years before the more famous NAZI atrocities in Europe.

Aboard the U.S.S. Oahu at Shanghai, Dec. 17 [1937]

Through wholesale atrocities and vandalism at Nanking the Japanese Army has thrown away a rare opportunity to gain the respect and confidence of the Chinese inhabitants and of foreign opinion there. …

The killing of civilians was widespread. Foreigners who traveled widely through the city Wednesday found civilian dead on every street. Some of the victims were aged men, women and children.

Policemen and firemen were special objects of attack. Many victims were bayoneted and some of the wounds were barbarously cruel.

Any person who ran because of fear or excitement was likely to be killed on the spot as was any one caught by roving patrols in streets or alleys after dark. Many slayings were witnessed by foreigners.

The Japanese looting amounted almost to plundering of the entire city. Nearly every building was entered by Japanese soldiers, often under the eyes of their officers, and the men took whatever they wanted. The Japanese soldiers often impressed Chinese to carry their loot. …

The mass executions of war prisoners added to the horrors the Japanese brought to Nanking. After killing the Chinese soldiers who threw down their arms and surrendered, the Japanese combed the city for men in civilian garb who were suspected of being former soldiers.

In one building in the refugee zone 400 men were seized. They were marched off, tied in batches of fifty, between lines of riflemen and machine gunners, to the execution ground.

Just before boarding the ship for Shanghai the writer watched the execution of 200 men on the Bund [dike]. The killings took ten minutes. The men were lined against a wall and shot. Then a number of Japanese, armed with pistols, trod nonchalantly around the crumpled bodies, pumping bullets into any that were still kicking.

The army men performing the gruesome job had invited navy men from the warships anchored off the Bund to view the scene. A large group of military spectators apparently greatly enjoyed the spectacle.

When the first column of Japanese troops marched from the South Gate up Chungshan Road toward the city's Big Circle, small knots of Chinese civilians broke into scattering cheers, so great was their relief that the siege was over and so high were their hopes that the Japanese would restore peace and order. There are no cheers in Nanking now for the Japanese.

By despoiling the city and population the Japanese have driven deeper into the Chinese a repressed hatred that will smolder through tears as forms of the anti-Japanism that Tokyo professes to be fighting to eradicate from China.

The capture of Nanking was the most overwhelming defeat suffered by the Chinese and one of the most tragic military debacles in the history of modern warfare. In attempting to defend Nanking the Chinese allowed themselves to be surrounded and then systematically slaughtered. …

The flight of the many Chinese soldiers was possible by only a few exits. Instead of sticking by their men to hold the invaders at bay with a few strategically placed units while the others withdrew, many army leaders deserted, causing panic among the rank and file.

Those who failed to escape through the gate leading to Hsiakwan and from there across the Yangtze were caught and executed. …

When the Japanese captured Hsiakwan gate they cut off all exit from the city while at least a third of the Chinese Army still was within the walls.

Because of the disorganization of the Chinese a number of units continued fighting Tuesday noon, many of these not realizing the Japanese had surrounded them and that their cause was hopeless. Japanese tank patrols systematically eliminated these.

Tuesday morning, while attempting to motor to Hsiakwan, I encountered a desperate group of about twenty-five Chinese soldiers who were still holding the Ningpo Guild Building on Chungahan Road. They later surrendered.

Thousands of prisoners were executed by the Japanese. Most of the Chinese soldiers who had been interned in the safety zone were shot in masses. The city was combed in a systematic house-to-house search for men having knapsack marks on their shoulders or other signs of having been soldiers. They were herded together and executed.

Many were killed where they were found, including men innocent of any army connection and many wounded soldiers and civilians. I witnessed three mass executions of prisoners within a few hours Wednesday. In one slaughter a tank gun was turned on a group of more than 100 soldiers at a bomb shelter near the Ministry of Communications.

A favorite method of execution was to herd groups of a dozen men at entrances of dugout and to shoot them so the bodies toppled inside. Dirt then was shoveled in and the men buried.

Since the beginning of the Japanese assault on Nanking the city presented a frightful appearance. The Chinese facilities for the care of army wounded were tragically inadequate, so as early as a week ago injured men were seen often on the streets, some hobbling, others crawling along seeking treatment.

Civilian casualties also were heavy, amounting to thousands. The only hospital open was the American managed University Hospital and its facilities were inadequate for even a fraction of those hurt.

Nanking's streets were littered with dead. Sometimes bodies had to be moved before automobiles could pass.

The capture of Hsiakwan Gate by the Japanese was accompanied by the mass killing of the defenders, who were piled up among the sandbags, forming a mound six feet high. Late Wednesday the Japanese had not removed the dead, and two days of heavy military traffic had been passing through, grinding over the remains of men, dogs and horses.

The Japanese appear to want the horrors to remain as long as possible, to impress on the Chinese the terrible results of resisting Japan.

Chungahan Road was a long avenue of filth and discarded uniforms, rifles, pistols, machine guns, fieldpieces, knives and knapsacks. In some places the Japanese had to hitch tanks to debris to clear the road.

What Is Guerrilla Warfare? (1937)

By Mao Zedong

Faced with the Japanese invasion and the inability of Ching Kai-Sheck's republican army to stand up to the invaders, Mao and the Chinese Communist Party took the initiative to defend China. Crucially, Mao's decision to turn to guerilla warfare was both practical and ideological. Lacking the arms to fight the Japanese Imperial Army in conventional battles, Mao recognized that small-scale attacks by irregular bands on vulnerable supply lines was the only possible tactic. Mao also saw that guerilla warfare was a way to mobilize and politicize the masses, particularly the peasantry. Thus, the tactical and ideological came together. Considering that the communists had been in decade long struggle with Chiang Kai-Shek's nationalist forces, guerilla warfare would also be a way to build a base for the coming civil war once the Japanese left.

IN A WAR OF REVOLUTIONARY CHARACTER, guerrilla operations are a necessary part. This is particularly true in a war waged for the emancipation of a people who inhabit a vast nation. China is such a nation, a nation whose techniques are undeveloped and whose communications are poor. She finds herself confronted with a strong and victorious Japanese imperialism. Under these circumstances, the development of the type of guerrilla warfare characterized by the quality of mass is both necessary and natural. This warfare must be developed to an unprecedented degree and it must coordinate with the operations of our regular armies. If we fail to do this, we will find it difficult to defeat the enemy.

These guerrilla operations must not be considered as an independent form of warfare. They are but one step in the total war, one aspect of the revolutionary struggle. They are the inevitable result of the clash between oppressor and oppressed when the latter reach the limits of their endurance. In our case, these hostilities began at a

Mao Zedong (Mao Tse-Tung); Samuel B. Griffith II, trans., "What is Guerrilla Warfare?" *On Guerrilla Warfare*, pp. 41–50. Copyright © 2000 by the University of Illinois Press. Reprinted with permission.

time when the people were unable to endure any more from the Japanese imperialists. Lenin, in *People and Revolution*, said: "A people's insurrection and a peoples revolution are not only natural but inevitable." We consider guerrilla operations as but one aspect of our total or mass war because they, lacking the quality of independence, are of themselves incapable of providing a solution to the struggle.

Guerrilla warfare has qualities and objectives peculiar to itself. It is a weapon that a nation inferior in arms and military equipment may employ against a more powerful aggressor nation. When the invader pierces deep into the heart of the weaker country and occupies her territory in a cruel and oppressive manner, there is no doubt that conditions of terrain, climate, and society in general offer obstacles to his progress and may be used to advantage by those who oppose him. In guerrilla warfare, we turn these advantages to the purpose of resisting and defeating the enemy.

During the progress of hostilities, guerrillas gradually develop into orthodox forces that operate in conjunction with other units of the regular army. Thus the regularly organized troops, those guerrillas who have attained that status, and those who have not reached that level of development combine to form the military power of a national revolutionary war. There can be no doubt that the ultimate result of this will be victory.

Both in its development and in its method of application, guerrilla warfare has certain distinctive characteristics. We first discuss the relationship of guerrilla warfare to national policy. Because ours is the resistance of a semi-colonial country against an imperialism, our hostilities must have a clearly defined political goal and firmly established political responsibilities. Our basic policy is the creation of a national united anti-Japanese front. This policy we pursue in order to gain our political goal, which is the complete emancipation of the Chinese people. There are certain fundamental steps necessary in the realization of this policy, to wit:

1. Arousing and organizing the people.
2. Achieving internal unification politically.
3. Establishing bases.
4. Equipping forces.
5. Recovering national strength.
6. Destroying enemy's national strength.
7. Regaining lost territories.

There is no reason to consider guerrilla warfare separately from national policy. On the contrary, it must be organized and conducted in complete accord with national anti-Japanese policy. It is only those who misinterpret guerrilla action who say, as does Jen Ch'i Shan, "The question of guerrilla hostilities is purely a military matter and not a political one." Those who maintain this simple point of view have lost sight of the political goal and the political effects of guerrilla action. Such a simple point of view will cause the people to lose confidence and will result in our defeat.

What is the relationship of guerrilla warfare to the people? Without a political goal, guerrilla warfare must fail, as it must if its political objectives do not coincide with the aspirations of the people and their sympathy, cooperation, and assistance cannot be gained. The essence of guerrilla warfare is thus revolutionary in character. On the other hand, in a war of counterrevolutionary nature, there is no place for guerrilla hostilities. Because guerrilla warfare basically derives from the masses and is supported by them, it can neither exist nor flourish if it separates itself from their sympathies and cooperation. There are those who do not comprehend guerrilla action, and who therefore do not understand the distinguishing qualities of a people's guerrilla war, who say: "Only regular troops can carry on guerrilla operations." There are others who, because they do not believe in the ultimate success of guerrilla action, mistakenly say: "Guerrilla warfare is an insignificant and highly specialized type of operation in which there is no place for the masses of the people" (Jen Ch'i Shan). Then there are those who ridicule the masses and undermine resistance by wildly asserting that the people have no understanding of the war of resistance (Yeh Ch'ing, for one). The moment that this war of resistance dissociates itself from the masses of the people is the precise moment that it dissociates itself from hope of ultimate victory over the Japanese.

What is the organization for guerrilla warfare? Though all guerrilla bands that spring from the masses of the people suffer from lack of organization at the time of their formation, they all have in common a basic quality that makes organization possible. All guerrilla units must have political and military leadership. This is true regardless of the source or size of such units. Such units may originate locally, in the masses of the people; they may be formed from an admixture of regular troops with groups of the people, or they may consist of regular army units intact. And mere quantity does not affect this matter. Such units may consist of a squad of a few men, a battalion of several hundred men, or a regiment of several thousand men.

All these must have leaders who are unyielding in their policies—resolute, loyal, sincere, and robust. These men must be well educated in revolutionary technique, self-confident, able to establish severe discipline, and able to cope with counterpropaganda. In short, these leaders must be models for the people. As the war progresses, such leaders will gradually overcome the lack of discipline, which at first prevails; they will establish discipline in their forces, strengthening them and increasing their combat efficiency. Thus eventual victory will be attained.

Unorganized guerrilla warfare cannot contribute to victory and those who attack the movement as a combination of banditry and anarchism do not understand the nature of guerrilla action. They say: "This movement is a haven for disappointed militarists, vagabonds and bandits" (Jen Ch'i Shan), hoping thus to bring the movement into disrepute. We do not deny that there are corrupt guerrillas, nor that there are people who under the guise of guerrillas indulge in unlawful activities. Neither do we deny that the movement has at the present time symptoms of a lack of organization, symptoms that might indeed be serious were we to judge guerrilla warfare solely by the corrupt and temporary phenomena we have mentioned. We should study the corrupt phenomena and attempt to eradicate them in order to encourage guerrilla warfare, and to increase its military efficiency. "This is hard work, there is no help for it, and the problem cannot be solved immediately. The whole people must try to reform themselves during the course of the war. We must educate them and reform them in the light of past experience. Evil does not exist in guerrilla warfare but only in the unorganized and undisciplined activities that are anarchism," said Lenin, in *On Guerrilla Warfare**.

What is basic guerrilla strategy? Guerrilla strategy must be based primarily on alertness, mobility, and attack. It must be adjusted to the enemy situation, the terrain, the existing lines of communication, the relative strengths, the weather, and the situation of the people.

In guerrilla warfare, select the tactic of seeming to come from the east and attacking from the west; avoid the solid, attack the hollow; attack; withdraw; deliver a lightning blow, seek a lightning decision. When guerrillas engage a stronger enemy, they withdraw when he advances; harass him when he stops; strike him when he is weary; pursue him when he withdraws. In guerrilla strategy, the enemy's rear, flanks, and other vulnerable spots are his vital points, and there he must be harassed, attacked, dispersed, exhausted and annihilated. Only in this way can guerrillas carry out their mission of independent guerrilla action and coordination with the effort of the regular armies. But, in spite of the most complete preparation, there can be no victory if mistakes are made in the matter of command. Guerilla warfare based on the principles we have mentioned and carried out over a vast extent of territory in which communications are inconvenient will contribute tremendously towards ultimate defeat of the Japanese and consequent emancipation of the Chinese people.

A careful distinction must be made between two types of guerrilla warfare. The fact that revolutionary guerrilla warfare is based on the masses of the people does not in itself mean that the organization of guerrilla units is impossible in a war of counterrevolutionary character. As examples of the former type we may cite Red guerrilla hostilities during the Russian Revolution; those of the Reds in China; of the Abyssinians against the Italians for the past three years; those of the last seven years in Manchuria, and the vast anti-Japanese guerrilla war that is carried on in China today. All these struggles have been carried on in the interests of the whole people or the greater part of them; all had a broad basis in the national manpower, and all have been in accord with the laws of historical development. They have existed and will continue to exist, flourish, and develop as long as they are not contrary to national policy.

---

* Presumably, Mao refers here to the essay that has been translated into English under the title "Partisan Warfare." See *Orbis*, II (Summer, 1958), No. 2, 194–208.—S.B.G.

The second type of guerrilla warfare directly contradicts the law of historical development. Of this type, we may cite the examples furnished by the White Russian guerrilla units organized by Denikin and Kolchak; those organized by the Japanese; those organized by the Italians in Abyssinia; those supported by the puppet governments in Manchuria and Mongolia, and those that will be organized here by Chinese traitors. All such have oppressed the masses and have been contrary to the true interests of the people. They must be firmly opposed. They are easy to destroy because they lack a broad foundation in the people.

If we fail to differentiate between the two types of guerrilla hostilities mentioned, it is likely that we will exaggerate their effect when applied by an invader. We might arrive at the conclusion that "the invader can organize guerrilla units from among the people." Such a conclusion might well diminish our confidence in guerrilla warfare. As far as this matter is concerned, we have but to remember the historical experience of revolutionary struggles.

Further, we must distinguish general revolutionary wars from those of a purely "class" type. In the former case, the whole people of a nation, without regard to class or party, carry on a guerrilla struggle that is an instrument of the national policy. Its basis is, therefore, much broader than is the basis of a struggle of class type. Of a general guerrilla war, it has been said: "When a nation is invaded, the people become sympathetic to one another and all aid in organizing guerrilla units. In civil war, no matter to what extent guerrillas are developed, they do not produce the same results as when they are formed to resist an invasion by foreigners" (*Civil War in Russia*).[†]* The one strong feature of guerrilla warfare in a civil struggle is its quality of internal purity. One class may be easily united and perhaps fight with great effect, whereas in a national revolutionary war, guerrilla units are faced with the problem of internal unification of different class groups. This necessitates the use of propaganda. Both types of guerrilla war are, however, similar in that they both employ the same military methods.

National guerrilla warfare, though historically of the same consistency, has employed varying implements as times, peoples, and conditions differ. The guerrilla aspects of the Opium War, those of the fighting in Manchuria since the Mukden incident, and those employed in China today are all slightly different. The guerrilla warfare conducted by the Moroccans against the French and the Spanish was not exactly similar to that which we conduct today in China. These differences express the characteristics of different peoples in different periods. Although there is a general similarity in the quality of all these struggles, there are dissimilarities in form. This

---

† Presumably, Mao refers here to *Lessons of Civil War*, by S. I. Gusev; first published in 1918 by the Staff Armed Forces, Ukraine; revised in 1921 and published by GIZ, Moscow; reprinted in 1958 by the Military Publishing House, Moscow.—S.B.G.

fact we must recognize. Clausewitz wrote, in *On War* : "Wars in every period have independent forms and independent conditions, and, therefore, every period must have its independent theory of war." Lenin, in *On Guerrilla Warfare*, said: "As regards the form of fighting, it is unconditionally requisite that history be investigated in order to discover the conditions of environment, the state of economic progress, and the political ideas that obtained, the national characteristics, customs, and degree of civilization." Again: "It is necessary to be completely unsympathetic to abstract formulas and rules and to study with sympathy the conditions of the actual fighting, for these will change in accordance with the political and economic situations and the realization of the people's aspirations. These progressive changes in conditions create new methods."

If, in today's struggle, we fail to apply the historical truths of revolutionary guerrilla war, we will fall into the error of believing with T'ou Hsi Sheng that under the impact of Japan's mechanized army, "the guerrilla unit has lost its historical function." Jen Chi Shan writes: "In olden days, guerrilla warfare was part of regular strategy but there is almost no chance that it can be applied today." These opinions are harmful. If we do not make an estimate of the characteristics peculiar to our anti-Japanese guerrilla war, but insist on applying to it mechanical formulas derived from past history, we are making the mistake of placing our hostilities in the same category as all other national guerrilla struggles. If we hold this view, we will simply be beating our heads against a stone wall and we will be unable to profit from guerrilla hostilities.

To summarize: What is the guerrilla war of resistance against Japan? It is one aspect of the entire war, which, although alone incapable of producing the decision, attacks the enemy in every quarter, diminishes the extent of area under his control, increases our national strength, and assists our regular armies. It is one of the strategic instruments used to inflict defeat on our enemy. It is the one pure expression of anti-Japanese policy, that is to say, it is military strength organized by the active people and inseparable from them. It is a powerful special weapon with which we resist the Japanese and without which we cannot defeat them.

Day of Infamy Speech

By Franklin D. Roosevelt

President Roosevelt's (1882–1945) speech after the Japanese attack notes the shock and anger felt by many Americans. However, the speech notes that not only was the Hawaiian naval base a target, but there were simultaneous Japanese strikes against multiple British and American colonial possessions in Southeast Asia. This belies the fact that Japanese strategy was not to invade the United States, but rather to weaken the American ability to project power across the Pacific Ocean, thus giving the Japanese a free hand in Southeast Asia. Japanese wars aims lay in Southeast Asia as it was a source of oil, food, and war material for the ongoing campaign in China. Thus, the Pacific theater of the war was really a Japanese effort to destroy the Western colonial empires and create what was to be the Greater East Asia Co-Prosperity Sphere. In theory this would be an "Asia for Asians," but in practice is was an Asia for Japan's use.

December 8, 1941

Yesterday, December 7, 1941—a date which will live in infamy—the United States of America was suddenly and deliberately attacked by naval and air forces of the Empire of Japan.

The United States was at peace with that nation and, at the solicitation of Japan, was still in conversation with its Government and its Emperor looking toward the maintenance of peace in the Pacific. Indeed, one hour after Japanese air squadrons had commenced bombing in Oahu, the Japanese Ambassador to the United States and his colleague delivered to the Secretary of State a formal reply to a recent American message. While this reply stated that it seemed useless to continue the existing diplomatic negotiations, it contained no threat or hint of war or armed attack.

It will be recorded that the distance of Hawaii from Japan makes it obvious that the attack was deliberately planned many days or even weeks ago. During the intervening

Franklin D. Roosevelt, "Franklin D. Roosevelt's Infamy Speech."

time the Japanese Government has deliberately sought to deceive the United States by false statements and expressions of hope for continued peace.

The attack yesterday on the Hawaiian Islands has caused severe damage to American naval and military forces. Very many American lives have been lost. In addition American ships have been reported torpedoed on the high seas between San Francisco and Honolulu.

Yesterday the Japanese Government also launched an attack against Malaya. Last night Japanese forces attacked Hong Kong. Last night Japanese forces attacked Guam. Last night Japanese forces attacked the Philippine Islands. Last night the Japanese attacked Wake Island. This morning the Japanese attacked Midway Island.

Japan has, therefore, undertaken a surprise offensive extending throughout the Pacific area. The facts of yesterday speak for themselves. The people of the United States have already formed their opinions and well understand the implications to the very life and safety of our nation.

As Commander-in-Chief of the Army and Navy, I have directed that all measures be taken for our defense.

Always will we remember the character of the onslaught against us. No matter how long it may take us to overcome this premeditated invasion, the American people in their righteous might will win through to absolute victory.

I believe I interpret the will of the Congress and of the people when I assert that we will not only defend ourselves to the uttermost but will make very certain that this form of treachery shall never endanger us again.

Hostilities exist. There is no blinking at the fact that our people, our territory and our interests are in grave danger.

With confidence in our armed forces—with the unbounded determination of our people—we will gain the inevitable triumph—so help us God.

I ask that the Congress declare that since the unprovoked and dastardly attack by Japan on Sunday, December seventh, a state of war has existed between the United States and the Japanese Empire.

Remember Pearl Harbor (1941)

By Sammy Kaye

This jingoistic American song stands in contrast to "The White Cliffs of Dover."

History in ev'ry century
Records an act that lives forevermore.
We'll recall, as into line we fall
The thing that happened on Hawaii's shore

Let's remember Pearl Harbor
As we go to meet the foe
Let's remember Pearl Harbor
As we did the Alamo.

We will always remember
how they died for Liberty
Let's remember Pearl Harbor
And go on to victory.

Let's remember Pearl Harbor
As we go to meet the foe
Let's remember Pearl Harbor
As we did the Alamo.

We will always remember
How they died for Liberty
Let's remember Pearl Harbor
And go on to victory

Sacred War (1941)

By Vasily Lebedev-Kumach

This popular Soviet song combined Russian patriotism with an ideological struggle against fascism.

Rise up, huge country,
Rise up for a fight to the death!
With the dark fascist force,
With the damned horde.

Refrain x 2:

Let noble fury
Boil up like a wave
The people's war is going on,
The sacred war!

We'll give repulse to oppressors
Of all fervent ideas,
Rapists, robbers,
Tormentors of people.

Refrain

Black wings don't dare
To fly over the homeland;
Her vast fields
The enemy doesn't dare to trample.

Vasily Lebedev-Kumach, "Sacred War."

Refrain

To the rotten fascist scum
We'll drive a bullet into the forehead,
For the rabble of humanity
We'll knock together a solid casket!

Refrain x 2

Der Fuehrer's Face (1942)

By Oliver Wallace

This gimmicky American song was used in a Donald Duck cartoon to lampoon the NAZI party and the German war effort. After each "heil" the band would do a "Bronx Cheer."

CHORUS
When der fuehrer says we is de master race
We heil heil right in der fueher's face.
Not to love der fuehrer is a great disgrace,
So we heil heil right in der fuehrer's face.

When Herr Goebbels says we own the world and space
We heil heil right in Herr Goebbels' face.
When Herr Goring says they'll never bomb dis place
We heil heil right in Herr Goring's face.
Are we not the supermen Aryan pure supermen?
Ja we are the supermen (super duper supermen)
Is this Nutsy land so good?
Would you leave it if you could?
Ja this Nutsy land is good.
We would leave it if we could.
We bring the world to order.
Heil Hitler's world to order.
Everyone of foreign race
Will love der fuehrer's face
When we bring to the world dis order.

Minutes of a Meeting at Hitler's Headquarters (July 16, 1941)

By Martin Bormann

Martin Bormann (1900–1945) was a high-ranking NAZI official who served as Hitler's personal secretary. Privy to most meetings of the regime's inner circle, he often took minutes and notes at significant discussions. This document details Hitler's plans for Eastern Europe in the first month of the invasion of the Soviet Union. This evidence indicates that Hitler's goal was to colonize the land to the east, creating a massive German empire where ethnic Germans would rule over other subservient nationalities. It is worth noting that he compares his plans with those of the British in India.

Top Secret

Führer's Headquarters, July 16, 1941

A conference attended by Reichsleiter Rosenberg, Reich Minister Lammers, Field Marshal Keitel, the Reichsmarschall [Göring], and me was held today by order of the Führer at 3:00 p.m. in his quarters. The conference began at 3.00 p.m. and, including a break for coffee, lasted until about 8.00 p.m.

By way of introduction the Führer emphasized that he wished first of all to make some basic statements. Various measures were now necessary; this was confirmed, among other events, by an assertion made in an impudent Vichy newspaper that the war against the Soviet Union was Europe's war and that therefore it had to be conducted for Europe as a whole. Apparently the Vichy paper meant to say by these hints that it ought not to be the Germans alone who benefited from this war, but that all European states ought to benefit from it.

Martin Bormann, "Minutes of a Meeting at Hitler's Headquarters (July 16, 1941)."

It was essential that we should not proclaim our aims before the whole world; also, this was not necessary, but the chief thing was that we ourselves should know what we wanted. In no case should our own way be made more difficult by superfluous declarations. Such declarations were superfluous because we could do everything wherever we had the power, and what was beyond our power we would not be able to do anyway.

What we told the world about the motives for our measures ought to be conditioned, therefore, by tactical reasons. We ought to proceed here in exactly the same way as we did in the cases of Norway, Denmark, Holland and Belgium. In these cases too we said nothing about our aims, and if we were clever we would continue in the same way.

We shall then emphasize again that we were forced to occupy, administer and secure a certain area; it was in the interest of the inhabitants that we should provide order, food, traffic, etc., hence our measures. It should not be recognizable that thereby a final settlement is being initiated! We can nevertheless take all necessary measures— shooting, resettling, etc.—and we shall take them.

But we do not want to make any people into enemies prematurely and unnecessarily. Therefore we shall act as though we wanted to exercise a mandate only. It must be clear to *us*, however, that we shall never withdraw from these areas.

Accordingly we should act:

1. To do nothing which may obstruct the final settlement, but to prepare for it only in secret;

2. To emphasize that we are liberators.

In particular:

The Crimea has to be evacuated by all foreigners and to be settled by Germans only.

In the same way the former Austrian part of Galicia will become Reich territory.

Our relations with Romania are presently good, but one does not know what our relations will be at any future time. This we have to consider and we have to draw our frontiers accordingly. One ought not to be dependent on the good will of other people; we have to arrange our relations with Romania in accordance with this principle.

In principle we have now to face the task of cutting up the giant cake according to our needs, in order to be able: first, to dominate it; second, to administer it; and third, to exploit it.

The Russians have now given an order for partisan warfare behind our front. This partisan war again has some advantage for us; it enables us to exterminate everyone who opposes us.

Principles:

Never again must it be possible to create a military power west of the Urals, even if we have to wage war for a hundred years in order to attain this goal. All successors of the Führer must know: Security for the Reich exists only if there are no foreign military forces west of the Urals; it is Germany who undertakes the protection of this area against all possible dangers. Our iron principle must be and must remain:

We must never permit anybody but the Germans to carry arms!

This is especially important; even when it seems easier at first to enlist the armed support of foreign, subjugated nations, it is wrong to do so. This will prove some day to be to our disadvantage absolutely and unavoidably. Only the German may carry arms, not the Slav, nor the Czech, nor the Cossack, nor the Ukrainian!

On no account should we apply a wavering policy such as was done in Alsace before 1918. What distinguishes the Englishman is his constant and consistent following of *one* line and *one* aim. In this respect we must learn absolutely from him. Therefore we ought never to base our actions on individual contemporary personalities; here again the conduct of the British in India towards the Indian princes, etc., ought to be an example: It is always the soldier who has to consolidate the regime!

We have to create a Garden of Eden in the newly won eastern territories; they are vitally important to us; as compared with them colonies play only an entirely subordinate part.

Even if we divide up certain areas at once, we shall always proceed in the role of protectors of the law and of the population. The terms which are necessary at this time should be selected in accordance with this principle: We shall not speak of new Reich territory, but of the task which became necessary because of the war.

[…]

The Führer emphasizes that the entire Baltic area must become Reich territory.

Likewise the Crimea, including a considerable hinterland (the area north of the Crimea) must become Reich territory; the hinterland must be as large as possible.

[…]

The Führer emphasizes further that the Volga colony, too, will have to become Reich territory, also the district around Baku; the latter will have to become a German concession (military colony).

[…]

The annexation of Finland as a federated state should be prepared with great caution. The area around Leningrad is wanted by the Finns; the Führer will have Leningrad razed to the ground in order to hand it over to the Finns.

[…]

The Reichsmarschall, however, emphasized the most important criteria which for the time being must be exclusively decisive for us: securing food supplies, and as far as necessary, of the economy; securing of the roads, etc.

[…]

Reichsleiter Rosenberg then broached the question of providing for the security of the administration.

[…]

Field Marshal Keitel emphasizes that the inhabitants themselves ought to be made responsible for their affairs because it was of course impossible to put a sentry in front of every shed or railway station. The inhabitants had to understand that anybody who did not perform his duties properly would be shot, and that they would be held responsible for every offense.

[...]

After the break the Führer emphasized that we had to understand that the Europe of today was nothing but a geographical term; in reality, Asia extended up to our frontiers.

[...]

Description of the Execution of Jews Outside Riga on December 1, 1941

By Major General Bruns

As the NAZI invasion swept through Eastern Europe and the Soviet Union, Hitler's elite SS organized a systematic campaign of mass murder of Jews, Roma and Sinti (Gypsies), and members of the Communist Party. Know as Einsatzgruppen, these SS units worked in close coordination with army and battalions of reserve police officers. The SS also found local anti-Semitic collaborators. In the space of six months the Einsatzgruppen murdered more than 700,000 people. The primary method of execution was to round up men, women, and children, march them to a nearby clearing in the woods, and then to shoot them with machine guns and rifles. This brutal strategy of taking the killers to the victims was eventually deemed imperfect in the eyes of the NAZIs as some Jews escaped and it took a serious psychological toll on the killers. The history of the Einsatzgruppen illustrates the horrific violence of the war in the East, encouraged by NAZI ideology that viewed the local population of racially inferior (in contrast to the west and north of Europe where the occupation was not as ruthless).

Top Secret
C.S.D.I.C. (U.K.)
G.G. Report
S.R.G.G. 1158 (C)
The following conversation took place between:—
CS/1952—Generalmajor BRUNS (Heeres-Waffenmeisterschule I, BERLIN), Capt'd GÖTTINGEN (8 Apr 45) and other Senior Officer PW[s] whose voices could not be identified.

Major General Bruns, "Description of the Execution of Jews Outside Riga on December 1, 1941, Surreptitiously Taped Conversation."

Information received: 25 Apr 45

TRANSLATION:

BRUNS: As soon as I heard those Jews were to be shot on Friday I went to a 21-year-old boy and said that they had made themselves very useful in the area under my command, besides which the Army MT park had employed 1,500 and the 'Heeresgruppe' 800 women to make underclothes of the stores we captured in RIGA; besides which about 1,200 women in the neighborhood of RIGA were turning millions of captured sheepskins into articles we urgently required: ear-protectors, fur caps, fur waistcoats, etc. Nothing had been provided, as of course the Russian campaign was known to have come to a victorious end in October 1941. In short, all those women were employed in a useful capacity. I tried to save them. I told that fellow ALTENMEYER(?) whose name I shall always remember and who will be added to the list of war criminals: "Listen to me, they represent valuable man-power." "Do you call Jews valuable human beings, sir?" I said: "Listen to me properly, I said 'valuable man-power.' I didn't mention their value as human beings." He said: "Well, they're to be shot in accordance with the FÜHRER's orders. I said: "FÜHRER's orders?" "Yes," whereupon he showed me his orders. This happened at SKIOTAWA(?), 8 km. from RIGA, between SIAULAI and JELGAVA, where 5,000 BERLIN Jews were suddenly taken off the train and shot. I didn't see that myself, but what happened at SKIOTAWA(?)—to cut a long story short, I argued with the fellow and telephoned to the General at HQ, to JAKOBS and ABERGER(?), and to a Dr. SCHULTZ who was attached to the Engineer General, on behalf of these people; I told him: "Granting that the Jews have committed a crime against the other peoples of the world, at least let them do the drudgery; send them to throw earth on the roads to prevent our heavy lorries skidding." "Then I'd have to feed them." I said: "The little amount of food they receive, let's assume 2 million Jews—they got 125 gr. of bread a day—if we can't even manage that, the sooner we end the war the better." Then I telephoned, thinking it would take some time. At any rate on Sunday morning I heard that they had already started on it. The Ghetto was cleared and they were told: "You're being transferred; take along your most essential things." Incidentally it was a happy release for those people, as their life in the Ghetto was a martyrdom. I wouldn't believe it and drove there, to have a look.

? [Unidentified P.O.W.]: Everyone abroad knew about it; only we Germans were kept in ignorance.

BRUNS: I'll tell you something: some of the details may have been correct, but it was remarkable that the firing squad detailed that morning—six men with tommy-guns were posted at each pit; the pits were 24 m in length and 3 m in breadth—they had to lie down like sardines in a tin, with their heads in the centre. Above them were six men with tommy-guns who gave them the coup de grace. When I arrived, those pits were so full that the living had to lie down on top of the dead; then they were shot and, in order to save room, they had to lie down neatly in layers. Before this, however, they were stripped of everything at one of the stations—here at the edge of the wood were the three pits they used that Sunday and here they stood in a queue 1½ km long which approached step by step—a queuing up for death. As they drew nearer they saw what was going on. About here they had to hand over their jewelry and suitcases. All good stuff was put into the suitcases and the remainder thrown on a heap. This was to serve as clothing for our suffering population—and then, a little further on they had to undress and, 500 m in front of the wood, strip completely; they were only permitted to keep on a chemise or knickers. They were all women and small two-year-old children. Then all those cynical remarks. If only I had seen those tommy-gunners, who were relieved every hour because of over-exertion, carry out their task with distaste, but no, nasty remarks like: "Here comes a Jewish beauty." I can still see it all in my memory: a pretty woman in a flame-colored chemise. Talk about keeping the race pure: at RIGA they first slept with them and then shot them to prevent them from talking. Then I sent two officers out there, one of whom is still alive, because I wanted eye-witnesses. I didn't tell them what was going on, but said: "Go out to the forest of SKIOTAWA(?), see what's up there and send me a report." I added a memorandum to their report and took it to JAKOBS myself. He said: "I have already two complaints sent me by Engineer 'Bataillone' from the UKRAINE." There they shot them on the brink of large crevices and let them fall down into them; they nearly had an epidemic of plague, at any rate a pestilential smell. They thought they could break off the edges with picks, thus burying them. That loss there was so hard that two Engineer 'Bataillone' were required to dynamite the edges; those 'Bataillone' complained. JAKOBS had received that complaint. He said: "We didn't quite know how to tell the FÜHRER. We'd better do it through CANARIS." CANARIS had the unsavory task of waiting for the favorable moment to give the FÜHRER certain gentle hints. A fortnight later I visited the 'Oberbürgermeister' or whatever he was called then, concerning some other business. ALTENMEYER(?) triumphantly showed me: "Here is an order, just issued, prohibiting mass-shootings on that scale from taking place in future. They are to be carried out more discreetly." From warnings given me recently I knew that I was receiving still more attention from spies.

? [Unidentified P.O.W.]: A wonder you're still alive.

BRUNS: At GÖTTINGEN I expected to be arrested every day.

Conditions in Germany and the Warsaw Ghetto Uprising (July 9, 1943)

By Count Helmuth James von Moltke

Count Helmuth James Graf von Moltke (1907–1945) was a lawyer who was drafted into the German counter-intelligence bureau. Coming from a prestigious Prussian military family, he turned against the NAZI state because of its numerous human-rights abuses. Von Moltke used his office to aid victims of NAZI persecution and strengthen the admittedly weak resistance movements. He was arrested in 1944, tried in a kangaroo court, and executed in January, 1945.

Air Bombardments of Western Germany

The statements made in Allied broadcasts to the effect that German war production has dropped by 25–30% up to now as a result of bombardments of Germany's armament centres are entirely erroneous. The decline of production is relatively light. It appears that the aerial photographs brought back by Allied reconnaissance aircraft are used far more extensively as bases for the judgment of damage inflicted than first-hand reports. Such photographs may well show the destruction of entire work-shops, but they give no indication as to the actual extent of [the] destruction of machine equipment. It has been established that even when work-shops are completely smashed, the machine tool equipment generally suffers only minor damage unless destroyed by direct hits. The intact machines are then put back into operation 3–4 weeks after the bombardment, when the debris has been cleared away; while

Count Helmuth James von Moltke, "Conditions in Germany and the Warsaw Ghetto Uprising (July 9, 1943)."

the shop-buildings themselves are reconstructed only so far as is necessary for the routine of production, in order to conserve the appearance to the aerial observer of heavy damage and stoppage of work. Exceptions to this rule are naturally those plants which from their character are paralyzed entirely by direct hits in any vital part, such as boiler houses, power stations, chemical factories, refineries, etc.

A circumstance that very seriously interferes with industrial production, and one that has not been fully appreciated as yet by the Allies, is the destruction of residences. As a result of the extensive destruction of workers' settlements and residential quarters in the Ruhr, housing accommodation for workers has become so scarce that a more appreciable direct effect in lowering rates of production is traceable to this circumstance than to any direct damage to centres of production. The acute shortage of building materials and construction workers makes it impossible to cope effectively with this situation. The remedy of evacuating from areas subject to air attack all inhabitants whose presence is not essential to armament production cannot be applied because it would involve other serious dislocations, especially of the transport system.

No Decentralization in Germany's Administrative System

Contrary to the belief current among the Allies that German administration has been partially decentralized, it must be emphasized that the entire administrative mechanism of the Reich and the Nazi Party continues to be centred in Berlin and the other traditional administrative centres, and that, moreover, no preparations are being made for any future decentralization. The recurring remonstrances made by the High Command of the Wehrmacht are met by Party Headquarters with the argument that it would injure the prestige of the Party if the centres of administration were to be moved elsewhere, and that the potential influence of such preparatory measures upon the morale of the home front made it imperative to avoid them. Consequently, a concentrated bombardment and possible destruction of the central administrative authorities, which are all still housed in the traditional public buildings, would very effectively paralyze Germany's administrative system.

U-Boat Warfare

As regards the abortive Doenitz Offensive, it is true that it represents a major German defeat; but although the U-Boats were indeed recalled late in June this must not be regarded as a purely defensive measure, but must be interpreted in connection with the evolution of new offensive tactics as a rejoinder to the improved Allied defence. The

OKW (High Command of the Wehrmacht) confidently anticipates new great U-boat successes in August as a result of a novel offensive strategy.

Foreign Workers

The foreign workers in Germany represent the most serious problem of internal security. In most factories the percentage of foreign workers is already greater than that of the German personnel. This foreign labour is a hostile element, dissatisfied to a degree, and almost without exception communist by conviction and, it appears, guided by communist organizations. (German labour, on the other hand, seems hardly to show any communist tendencies.) The OKW realizes that in the case of a revolution the foreign workers will also have arms at their disposal, and that an armed [up]rising of this numerically powerful element might have serious, even decisive consequences.

The General Situation

The Gestapo and SS are complete masters of the situation. Despite all symptoms of strong opposition there is nothing to indicate that in the near future internal difficulties might arise which would precipitate or give a chance for an [up]rising. The Wehrmacht is passing more and more into the service of the Party, which has shown great skill and psychological insight in winning over for its purposes the most influential generals by bestowing upon them huge estates and manors as tokens of "the nation's" admiration and gratitude for their military exploits. This procedure is designed to involve the Wehrmacht irretrievably in the Party's responsibilities, and make any change of front, on the former's part, impossible. The majority of the marshals, generals, and high officers thus honoured see things only as they want them to be for the sake of conserving their new wealth and influence. This makes them blind to certain self-evident facts; contrary to Allied suppositions, the major part of the officer corps of the OKW and the Wehrmacht generally, who are in a position to listen in on Allied broadcasts in safety, do not avail themselves of this possibility. They have acquired—and this applies to lower ranks also—a fullness of wealth, affluence, and personal power unheard of in the history of military castes, and opportunities for action of every kind such as professional soldiers dream of all their lives. This accounts for the fact that the Wehrmacht, with insignificant exceptions, backs up the Party and supports its strategy and policies. The number of clear-thinking men in the OKW and in the armed forces is small. This section is positive in its opinion that a total and unmitigated military defeat is necessary to destroy once and for all German Militarism and the myth of Germany's invincibility in the field, and to make Germany as a nation fit for a lasting peace.

Allied Broadcasts

It must be pointed out that only reports of bare and unadorned facts have any effect upon German listeners, [with] every exaggeration or "talking down" jeopardizing the success of the entire propaganda effort. Even commentaries to the bare news bulletins should be abstained from, because in this way it is left to the people themselves to form their own judgment—a thing that has been consistently denied them by their own propaganda.

The Munich Student Riots

Reports concerning the recent student riots at Munich University indicate that they were on a far larger scale than the first accounts that reached the outside world had suggested. The ruthless measures taken by the Gestapo are due to the dangerous extent of the disorders. Prof. Huber of Munich University has not been shot or beheaded as reported in British broadcasts; he is still alive, and is slowly tortured to death by the Gestapo.

The Catholic Movement in Germany

The Catholic revival in Germany is spreading in an astonishing manner. Attendance of Divine Service is the only way of registering a silent protest, and the churches can hardly contain the huge congregations. The German bishops enjoy a tremendous popularity, especially Count Preysing, who is given similar ovations as Count Galen.

It is highly significant that according to recent reports an average of 30% of Catholic schoolboys about to take their school certificates (Abiturium), when asked in the customary way what careers they propose to enter, state that they wish to study Theology and become priests. Special attention is drawn to one case which occurred at a Stettin gymnasium (Classical High School for Boys), where except for three young men who had decided to go in for Law, Agriculture, and the Army, respectively, all stated that they wished to read Theology and take orders. As a result, all members of the gymnasium have been arrested and detained by order of the Gestapo. These cases concern boys of ages from 15 to 17. These are not local occurrences, but similar accounts come from all parts of the Reich.

The Battle in the Ghetto of Warsaw

Concerning the fighting that took place in the Ghetto of Warsaw last May the following details are now available:

Approximately 30,000–35,000 Jews interned in the Warsaw Ghetto had for months been working tenaciously to transform their barracks and stone houses into a defensive system, and had dug subterranean passages connecting the Ghetto with the outer city, in preparation for the expected arrival of SS "annihilation squads" for the partial or total liquidation of the Ghetto. Through underground ducts and dug-out connecting passages to the surrounding parts of the city, the Jews had succeeded with the help of Polish partisans and German soldiers in transporting food, building materials, and arms into the Ghetto. The most modern equipment, from light automatic weapons to the heaviest arms, had been secured—in some cases bought—out of army and SS stores and secretly accumulated in the Ghetto. Several hundred German deserters had also taken refuge in the Ghetto and worked on the makeshift fortifications together with the Jews.

Late in April, 2 platoons of the regular German garrison of Warsaw received orders to conduct a certain transport of Jews from the Ghetto to one of the nearby railway stations, where they were to be taken over by SS guards and consigned to one of the "annihilating institutes" which have been set up in Poland.

These two platoons did not return. Two further platoons which were sent out to find out what had become of them, and to execute the order, did not return either. It has been ascertained that both units met with armed resistance, that a large part of them went over to the defenders with all arms and equipment, while the rest were overcome and taken prisoners. These events, it is important to note, were preceded by a protest by officers of the regular army against their employment for tasks unconnected with the military service of warfare.

Early in May, motorized units were brought up to crush the resistance of the Ghetto. A regular battle began, during which the assault troops had occasion to convince themselves that the Jews were equipped with the most up-to-date weapons, automatic guns, field guns, even antitank and anti-aircraft guns, and were entrenched in veritable fortified bunkers. Up to the middle of May, many hundred officers and men from the companies charged with breaking the resistance of the Ghetto deserted or went over with their arms to help the defenders, until on May 16 the regular companies had to be retired to be replaced by mechanized SS [Waffen-SS]. Bitter fighting then went on between the defenders and large detachments of SS troops, during which several thousand German Officers and men were killed or wounded. The resistance of the Ghetto was almost entirely broken down by heavy tanks and dive-bombers, and the Ghetto itself all but razed to the ground. Only a few thousand of the 30,000 odd interned Jews are reported to have survived the battle; they have been transferred to new camps where they have probably been "liquidated" by now. Only a few Jews and a small number of the defending German soldiers are said to have succeeded in escaping to the city by way of the underground passages. The extensive investigations started by the Gestapo, SD (Sicherheits-Dienst), and SS (Security Service) have brought to light the fact that in addition to several hundred German deserters about 1,200–1,500 German officers and men had gone over and helped in the defence of the Ghetto. The defence was conducted under the command of a German colonel, who is reported to have made this escape during the last days of the fighting.

The proceedings instituted in the matter have been kept a close secret, and the Gestapo has done everything in its power to keep the news from leaking through even to the OKW and the Party. Hundreds of arrests, deportations, and executions are said to have taken place in order to confine the circle of those informed of the occurrences to the most trusted members of the Gestapo, SD, and SS. According to a secret report of the German Sicherheitsdienst, the motive of the German officers and men in taking action against the "liquidation" of the internees of the Ghetto has been their refusal to take any further part in the perpetration of massacres and atrocities, from their conviction that the German soldier's duty was to defend the German people against an external enemy, if the interest of the State demanded it, but not to assist in senseless and inhuman cruelties against innocent and helpless men and women by order of a party which professed to act in the name of the German people.

U.S. War Effort

Party circles still detect some chances for a successful termination of the War for Germany, if it can be drawn out. It is argued in this connection that time is working for Germany; this belief has been strengthened lately by the impression that America is showing signs of moral disintegration and war-weariness which, it is felt, will become more and more pronounced as the War drags on. The argument is based upon the long-drawn and constantly recurring strikes, and upon signs of wavering and symptoms of a revival of Isolationism which are given publicity in some American journals.

It is incomprehensible why the American Labour troubles are incessantly dwelt upon in British broadcasts. The effect of this can be studied with profit in the German press of the last weeks, which devoted a special campaign to gloating over the strikes and drawing encouraging conclusions from them.

Sentences Passed upon Catholic Priests

Among the many recent cases of prosecution of Catholic priests, a particularly interesting case is that of the Dean of St. Hedwig's Church, Berlin. Because of the solicitude and protection he extended to Jews and other victims of political persecution, the Dean was tried some weeks ago before a law court. In his defence, he stood up vigorously for all he did, and is said to have impressed some of his judges deeply by his dauntless courage. His sentence was deportation to "Litznannstadt" (Lods, Poland). After the verdict, the Dean declared solemnly that this sentence made him very happy and that it was particularly suited to him, because it was not only his wish but his supreme vocation to extend comfort, edification, and hope to the terribly afflicted inmates of the Litzmannstadt concentration camps.

The Allied Attitude Towards the Austrians

Some considerable astonishment is expressed by informants at the fact that the Austrians are set apart from the Germans when the question of the German people's share in the guilt for what has occurred, and is daily occurring in its name, is under discussion by the Allies. For the sake of truth, it should be admitted that cruelties and inhuman atrocities have been perpetrated in Austria such as could hardly have occurred even in Germany. The population of Austria is reported to have taken part in excesses from which the German people have kept aloof. These facts stand out the more clearly when it is confirmed that Sudeten Germans and Austrians are given preference for the job of concentration camp guard, because they are known as particularly cruel. There has evolved a sort of classification by nationalities of guard personnel in descending order of frightfulness, according to which the Sudeten Germans top the list, the Austrians are second, the Bavarians third, with the rest of Germany following far behind. The classification is reported to be generally confirmed by the inmates of concentration camps and ghettos.

The Situation in the Occupied Territories

The situation in Greece, Yugoslavia, and Croatia is causing particular anxiety. Increasing partisan activity is anticipated as the opening of a second front draws nearer, and new measures for the rigorous suppression of irregulars have accordingly been taken last month. German casualties in Croatia owing to partisan activity from the occupation of the country to the end of June amounted to 27,000 officers and men. In Greece the dislocations of the transport system, particularly those caused by blown-up bridges and railroad sections, are reported to have repeatedly caused grave difficulties.

Respecting the "inner front" in France, it is stated that the intimidation caused by the terrorist measures enforced there so far is keeping the will of the French population to resist from expressing itself in more pronounced action. For the case of an invasion of the European continent and a closing-in of the fronts around the inner defensive ring of Greater Germany, it is planned by some accounts to exterminate ruthlessly, by Gestapo and SS measures, entire sections of the population, which might at such a junction engage in anti-German activity.

Commandant of Auschwitz: Testimony at Nuremberg, 1946

By Rudolf Hoess

Rudolf Hoess (1900–1947) lived a life of violence that was closely tied to the events of the early twentieth century in Germany. He entered the army at 14 years of age, seeing combat and becoming the youngest non-commissioned officer. After the war he joined the Freikorps, fighting in guerilla attacks against the French occupation force and ethnic Poles in Silesia. Hoess heard Hitler speak in Munich and joined the NAZI party in 1922. In 1923, under Martin Bormann's orders, he murdered a German communist. He served five years of his ten-year sentence before being amnestied. He joined the SS in 1933 and worked at the Dachau concentration camp from 1934 to 1938. Hoess took command of the Auschwitz camp in 1940, receiving orders from Himmler in June, 1941, to prepare it as a death camp. He experimented with different methods of killing, finally settling on hydrogen cyanide, produced from the pesticide Zyklon B. Hoess went into hiding after the war, evading arrest until British troops captured him in 1946. He was tried and executed in Poland in 1947.

I, RUDOLF FRANZ FERDINAND HOESS, being first duly sworn, depose and say as follows:

1. I am forty-six years old, and have been a member of the NSDAPI since 1922; a member of the SS since 1934; a member of the Waffen-SS since 1939. I was a member from 1 December 1934 of the SS Guard Unit, the so-called Deathshead Formation (Totenkopf Verband).

2. I have been constantly associated with the administration of concentration camps since 1934, serving at Dachau until 1938; then as Adjutant in Sachsenhausen

Rudolf Hoess, "Commandant of Auschwitz: Testimony at Nuremburg, 1946."

from 1938 to 1 May, 1940, when I was appointed Commandant of Auschwitz. I commanded Auschwitz until 1 December, 1943, and estimate that at least 2,500,000 victims were executed and exterminated there by gassing and burning, and at least another half million succumbed to starvation and disease, making a total dead of about 3,000,000. This figure represents about 70% or 80% of all persons sent to Auschwitz as prisoners, the remainder having been selected and used for slave labor in the concentration camp industries. Included among the executed and burnt were approximately 20,000 Russian prisoners of war (previously screened out of Prisoner of War cages by the Gestapo) who were delivered at Auschwitz in Wehrmacht transports operated by regular Wehrmacht officers and men. The remainder of the total number of victims included about 100,000 German Jews, and great numbers of citizens (*mostly* Jewish) from Holland, France, Belgium, Poland, Hungary, Czechoslovakia, Greece, or other countries. We executed about 400,000 Hungarian Jews alone at Auschwitz in the summer of 1944.

4. Mass executions by gassing commenced during the summer 1941 and continued until fall 1944. I personally supervised executions at Auschwitz until the first of December 1943 and know by reason of my continued duties in the Inspectorate of Concentration Camps WVHA2 that these mass executions continued as stated above. All mass executions by gassing took place under the direct order, supervision and responsibility of RSHA. I received all orders for carrying out these mass executions directly from RSHA.

6. The "final solution" of the Jewish question meant the complete extermination of all Jews in Europe. I was ordered to establish extermination facilities at Auschwitz in June 1941. At that time there were already in the general govemment three other extermination camps; BELZEK, TREBLINKA and WOLZEK. These camps were under the Einsatzkommando of the Security Police and SD. I visited Treblinka to find out how they carried out their exterminations. The Camp Commandant at Treblinka told me that he had liquidated 80,000 in the course of one half year. He was principally concerned with liquidating all the Jews from the Warsaw Ghetto. He used monoxide gas and I did not think that his methods were very efficient. So when I set up the extermination building at Auschwitz, I used Cyclon B, which was a crystallized Prussic Acid which we dropped into the death chamber from a small opening. It took from 3 to 15 minutes to kill the people in the death chamber depending upon climatic conditions. We knew when the people were dead because their screaming stopped. We usually waited about one half hour before we opened the doors and removed the bodies. After the bodies were removed our special commandos took off the rings and extracted the gold from the teeth of the corpses.

7. Another improvement we made over Treblinka was that we built our gas chambers to accommodate 2,000 people at one time, whereas at Treblinka their 10 gas chambers only accommodated 200 people each. The way we selected our victims was

as follows: we had two SS doctors on duty at Auschwitz to examine the incoming transports of prisoners. The prisoners would be marched by one of the doctors who would make spot decisions as they walked by. Those who were fit for work were sent into the Camp. Others were sent immediately to the extermination plants. Children of tender years were invariably exterminated since by reason of their youth they were unable to work. Still another improvement we made over Treblinka was that at Treblinka the victims almost always knew that they were to be exterminated and at Auschwitz we endeavored to fool the victims into thinking that they were to go through a delousing process. Of course, frequently they realized our true intentions and we sometimes had riots and difficulties due to that fact. Very frequently women would hide their children under the clothes but of course when we found them we would send the children in to be exterminated. We were required to carry out these exterminations in secrecy but of course the foul and nauseating stench from the continuous burning of bodies permeated the entire area and all of the people living in the surrounding communities knew that exterminations were going on at Auschwitz.

8. We received from time to time special prisoners from the local Gestapo office. The SS doctors killed such prisoners by injections of benzine. Doctors had orders to write ordinary death certificates and could put down any reason at all for the cause of death.

9. From time to time we conducted medical experiments on women inmates, including sterilization and experiments relating to cancer. Most of the people who died under these experiments had been already condemned to death by the Gestapo.

10. Rudolf Mildner was the chief of the Gestapo at Kattowicz and as such was head of the political department at Auschwitz which conducted third degree methods of interrogation from approximately March 1941 until September 1943. As such, he frequently sent prisoners to Auschwitz for incarceration or execution. He visited Auschwitz on several occasions. The Gestapo Court, the SS Standgericht, which tried persons accused of various crimes, such as escaping Prisoners of War, etc., frequently met within Auschwitz, and Mildner often attended the trial of such persons, who usually were executed in Auschwitz following their sentence. I showed Mildner throughout the extermination plant at Auschwitz and he was directly interested in it since he had to send the Jews from his territory for execution at Auschwitz.

I understand English as it is written above. The above statements are true; this declaration is made by me voluntarily and without compulsion; after reading over the statement, I have signed and executed the same at Nuremberg, Germany on the fifth day of April 1946.

My Political Testament

By Adolf Hitler

As the war progressed Hitler's mental state continued to deteriorate. As the army collapsed, he and his inner circle were confined to a bunker complex in Berlin. With the Soviet Red Army about to enter Berlin, Hitler married his longtime companion Eva Braun (1912–1945), wrote his last testament, had his dog Blondi killed, and then committed suicide with Braun on April 30, 1945.

Since 1914, when as a volunteer, I made my modest contribution in the World War which was forced upon the Reich, over thirty years have passed. In these three decades, only love for my people and loyalty to my people have guided me in all my thoughts, actions, and life. They gave me the strength to make the most difficult decisions, such as no mortal has yet had to face. I have exhausted my time, my working energy, and my health in these three decades.

It is untrue that I or anybody else in Germany wanted war in 1939. It was desired and instigated exclusively by those international statesmen who were either of Jewish origin or working for Jewish interests. I have made so many offers for the reduction and elimination of armaments, which posterity cannot explain away for all eternity, that the responsibility for the outbreak of this war cannot rest on me. Furthermore, I never desired that after the first terrible World War a second war should arise against England or even against America. Centuries may pass, but out of the ruins of our cities and monuments of art there will arise anew the hatred for the people who alone are ultimately responsible: International Jewry and its helpers!

As late as three days before the outbreak of the German-Polish War, I proposed to the British Ambassador in Berlin a solution for the German-Polish problem—similar to the problem of the Saar area, under international control. This offer cannot be explained away, either. It was only rejected because the responsible circles in English

Adolf Hitler, "My Political Testament." Copyright © 1945 by Humanitas International.

politics wanted the war, partly in the expectation of business advantages, partly driven by propaganda promoted by international Jewry.

But I left no doubt about the fact that if the peoples of Europe were again only regarded as so many packages of stock shares by these international money and finance conspirators, then that race, too, which is the truly guilty party in this murderous struggle would also have to be held to account: the Jews! I further left no doubt that this time we would not permit millions of European children of Aryan descent to die of hunger, nor millions of grown-up men to suffer death, nor hundreds of thousands of women and children to be burned and bombed to death in their cities, without the truly guilty party having to atone for its guilt, even if through more humane means.

After six years of struggle, which in spite of all reverses will go down in history as the most glorious and most courageous manifestation of a people's will to live. I cannot separate myself from the city which is the capital of this Reich. Because our forces are too few to permit any further resistance against the enemy's assaults, and because individual resistance is rendered valueless by blinded and characterless scoundrels, I desire to share the fate that millions of others have taken upon themselves, in that I shall remain in this city. Furthermore, I do not want to fall into the hands of enemies who for the delectation of the hate-riddled masses require a new spectacle promoted by the Jews.

I have therefore resolved to remain in Berlin and there to choose death of my own will at the very moment when, as I believe, the seat of the Fuehrer and Chancellor can no longer be defended. I die with a joyful heart in the awareness the immeasurable deeds and achievements of our soldiers at the front, of our women at home, the achievements of our peasants and workers, and the contribution, unique in history, of our youth, which bears my name.

It goes without saying that I thank them all from the bottom of my heart and that it is also my desire that in spite of everything they should not give up the struggle, but continue fighting wherever they may be, faithful to the great Clausewitz, against the enemies of the Fatherland. From the sacrifices of our soldiers and from my own comradeship with them, there will come in one way or another into German history the seed of a brilliant renaissance of the National Socialist movement and thus the realization of a true national community.

Many very brave men and women have resolved to link their lives to mine to the very end. I have requested them, and finally ordered them, not to do so, but instead to take part in the continuing struggle of the nation. I ask the commanders of the army, navy, and air force to strengthen by all possible means the spirit of resistance of our soldiers in the spirit of National Socialism, emphasizing especially that I too, as founder and creator of this movement, have preferred death to cowardly flight or even capitulation.

May it be one day a part of the code of honor; as it is already in the navy, that the surrender of an area or of a town is impossible, and above all in this respect the leaders should give a shining example of faithful devotion to duty unto death. Before my death I expel the former Reichsmarschall Hermann Goering and deprive him of all the rights he may enjoy by virtue of the decree of June 29, 1941, and also by virtue of my statement in the Reichstag on September 1, 1939. I appoint in his place Grossadmiral Doenitz as President of the Reich and Supreme Commander of the Armed Forces.

Before my death I expel the former Reichsfuehrer-SS and Minister of the Interior Heinrich Himmler from the Party and all offices of state. In his place I appoint Gauleiter Karl Hanke as Reichsfuehrer-SS and Chief of the German Police and Gauleiter Paul Giesler as Reich Minister of the Interior.

Goering and Himmler, by their secret negotiations with the enemy, without my knowledge or approval, and by their illegal attempts to seize power in the state, quite apart from their treachery to my person, have brought irreparable shame to the country and the whole people.

In order to give the German people a government composed of honorable men, who will fulfill their duty of continuing the war by all available means, I, as the Fuehrer of the nation, nominate the following members of the new Cabinet:

President of the Reich: Doenitz; Chancellor of the Reich: Dr. Goebbels; Party Minister: Bormann; Foreign Minister: Seyss-Inquart; Minister of the Interior: Gauleiter Giesler; Minister for War: Doenitz; C.-in-C. of the Army: Schoerner; C.-in-C. of the Navy: Doenitz; C.-in-C. of the Air Force: Greim; Reichsfuehrer-SS and Chief of the German Police: Gauleiter Hanke; Economics: Funk; Agriculture: Backe; Justice: Thierack; Culture: Dr. Scheel; Propaganda: Dr. Naumann; Finance: Schwerin-Krossigk; Labor: Dr. Hupfater; Munitions: Saur; Leader of the German Labor Front and Member of the Reich Cabinet: Reichminister Dr. Ley.

Several of these men such as Martin Bormann, Dr. Goebbels, etc., together with their wives, have joined me by their own free will and do not wish to leave the capital of the Reich under any circumstances, but on the contrary are willing to perish with me here. Yet I must ask them to obey my request, and in this instance place the interests of the nation above their own feelings.

Through their work and loyalty they will remain just as close to me as companions after my death, just as I hope that my spirit will remain amongst them and will always accompany them. Let them be hard, but never unjust; above all, let them never allow fear to counsel their actions, but may they place the honor of the nation above everything on this earth. Finally, may they be conscious of the fact that our task of building a National Socialist state represents the labor of the coming centuries, and this places every single person under an obligation always to serve the common interest and to subordinate his own interests. I demand of all Germans, all National Socialists, men and women and all soldiers of the Armed Forces, that they remain faithful and obedient to the new government and to their President unto death.

Above all, I charge the leadership of the nation and their followers with the strict observance of the racial laws and with merciless resistance against the universal poisoners of all peoples, international Jewry.

Given at Berlin, 29 April 1945, 4 AM.

ADOLF HITLER

As witnesses:
Dr. JOSEPH GOEBBELS
WILHELM BURGDORF
MARTIN BORMANN
HANS KREBS

Yalta Conference

By Stalin, F.D. Roosevelt, and Churchill

As the famous saying goes, politics makes strange bedfellows. Indeed, it could only be in the context of the struggle against Hitler that these three leaders could work together. Churchill was one of the last great imperialists, Roosevelt wanted a world open to free trade and trans-national capital, and Stalin sought to keep his totalitarian control over the Soviet Union and a protective buffer zone. During the war, the Big Three worked together with the Yalta Conference being a high point n their cooperation. Unfortunately, a few months after Hitler's death differences arose and the Cold War began.

February, 1945

Washington, March 24—The text of the agreements reached at the Crimea (Yalta) Conference between President Roosevelt, Prime Minister Churchill and Generalissimo Stalin, as released by the State Department today, follows:

PROTOCOL OF PROCEEDINGS OF CRIMEA CONFERENCE

The Crimea Conference of the heads of the Governments of the United States of America, the United Kingdom, and the Union of Soviet Socialist Republics, which took place from Feb. 4 to 11, came to the following conclusions:

Joseph Stalin, Franklin D. Roosevelt, Winston S. Churchill, "The Yalta Conference."

I. WORLD ORGANIZATION

It was decided:

1. That a United Nations conference on the proposed world organization should be summoned for Wednesday, 25 April, 1945, and should be held in the United States of America.

2. The nations to be invited to this conference should be:

(a) the United Nations as they existed on 8 Feb., 1945; and

(b) Such of the Associated Nations as have declared war on the common enemy by 1 March, 1945. (For this purpose, by the term "Associated Nations" was meant the eight Associated Nations and Turkey.) When the conference on world organization is held, the delegates of the United Kingdom and United State of America will support a proposal to admit to original membership two Soviet Socialist Republics, i.e., the Ukraine and White Russia.

3. That the United States Government, on behalf of the three powers, should consult the Government of China and the French Provisional Government in regard to decisions taken at the present conference concerning the proposed world organization.

4. That the text of the invitation to be issued to all the nations which would take part in the United Nations conference should be as follows:

The Government of the United States of America, on behalf of itself and of the Governments of the United Kingdom, the Union of Soviet Socialistic Republics and the Republic of China and of the Provisional Government of the French Republic invite the Government of -------- to send representatives to a conference to be held on 25 April, 1945, or soon thereafter , at San Francisco, in the United States of America, to prepare a charter for a general international organization for the maintenance of international peace and security.

The above-named Governments suggest that the conference consider as affording a basis for such a Charter the proposals for the establishment of a general international organization which were made public last October as a result of the Dumbarton Oaks conference and which have now been supplemented by the following provisions for Section C of Chapter VI:

C. Voting

1. Each member of the Security Council should have one vote.

2. Decisions of the Security Council on procedural matters should be made by an affirmative vote of seven members.

3. Decisions of the Security Council on all matters should be made by an affirmative vote of seven members, including the concurring votes of the permanent members; provided that, in decisions under Chapter VIII, Section A and under the second sentence of Paragraph 1 of Chapter VIII, Section C, a party to a dispute should abstain from voting.'

Further information as to arrangements will be transmitted subsequently.

In the event that the Government of ------- desires in advance of the conference to present views or comments concerning the proposals, the Government of the United States of America will be pleased to transmit such views and comments to the other participating Governments.

Territorial trusteeship:

It was agreed that the five nations which will have permanent seats on the Security Council should consult each other prior to the United Nations conference on the question of territorial trusteeship.

The acceptance of this recommendation is subject to its being made clear that territorial trusteeship will only apply to

(a) existing mandates of the League of Nations;

(b) territories detached from the enemy as a result of the present war;

(c) any other territory which might voluntarily be placed under trusteeship; and

(d) no discussion of actual territories is contemplated at the forthcoming United Nations conference or in the preliminary consultations, and it will be a matter for subsequent agreement which territories within the above categories will be place under trusteeship.

II. DECLARATION OF LIBERATED EUROPE

The following declaration has been approved:

The Premier of the Union of Soviet Socialist Republics, the Prime Minister of the United Kingdom and the President of the United States of America have consulted with each other in the common interests of the people of their countries and those of liberated Europe. They jointly declare their mutual agreement to concert during the temporary period of instability in liberated Europe the policies of their three Governments in assisting the peoples liberated from the domination of Nazi Germany and the peoples of the former Axis satellite states of Europe to solve by democratic means their pressing political and economic problems.

The establishment of order in Europe and the rebuilding of national economic life must be achieved by processes which will enable the liberated peoples to destroy the last vestiges of Nazism and fascism and to create democratic institutions of their own choice. This is a principle of the Atlantic Charter—the right of all people to choose the form of government under which they will live—the restoration of sovereign rights and self-government to those peoples who have been forcibly deprived to them by the aggressor nations.

To foster the conditions in which the liberated people may exercise these rights, the three governments will jointly assist the people in any European liberated state or former Axis state in Europe where, in their judgment conditions require,

(a) to establish conditions of internal peace;

(b) to carry out emergency relief measures for the relief of distressed peoples;

(c) to form interim governmental authorities broadly representative of all democratic elements in the population and pledged to the earliest possible establishment through free elections of Governments responsive to the will of the people; and

(d) to facilitate where necessary the holding of such elections.

The three Governments will consult the other United Nations and provisional authorities or other Governments in Europe when matters of direct interest to them are under consideration.

When, in the opinion of the three Governments, conditions in any European liberated state or former Axis satellite in Europe make such action necessary, they will immediately consult together on the measure necessary to discharge the joint responsibilities set forth in this declaration.

By this declaration we reaffirm our faith in the principles of the Atlantic Charter, our pledge in the Declaration by the United Nations and our determination to build in cooperation with other peace-loving nations world order, under law, dedicated to peace, security, freedom and general well-being of all mankind.

In issuing this declaration, the three powers express the hope that the Provisional Government of the French Republic may be associated with them in the procedure suggested.

III. DISMEMBERMENT OF GERMANY

It was agreed that Article 12 (a) of the Surrender terms for Germany should be amended to read as follows:

"The United Kingdom, the United States of America and the Union of Soviet Socialist Republics shall possess supreme authority with respect to Germany. In the exercise of such authority they will take such steps, including the complete dismemberment of Germany as they deem requisite for future peace and security."

The study of the procedure of the dismemberment of Germany was referred to a committee consisting of Mr. Anthony Eden, Mr. John Winant, and Mr. Fedor T. Gusev. This body would consider the desirability of associating with it a French representative.

IV. ZONE OF OCCUPATION FOR THE FRENCH AND CONTROL COUNCIL FOR GERMANY

It was agreed that a zone in Germany, to be occupied by the French forces, should be allocated France. This zone would be formed out of the British and American zones and its extent would be settled by the British and Americans in consultation with the French Provisional Government.

It was also agreed that the French Provisional Government should be invited to become a member of the Allied Control Council for Germany.

V. REPARATION

The following protocol has been approved:

Protocol

On the Talks Between the Heads of Three Governments at the Crimean Conference on the Question of the German Reparations in Kind:

1. Germany must pay in kind for the losses caused by her to the Allied nations in the course of the war. Reparations are to be received in the first instance by those countries which have borne the main burden of the war, have suffered the heaviest losses and have organized victory over the enemy.

2. Reparation in kind is to be exacted from Germany in three following forms:

(a) Removals within two years from the surrender of Germany or the cessation of organized resistance from the national wealth of Germany located on the territory of Germany herself as well as outside her territory (equipment, machine tools, ships, rolling stock, German investments abroad, shares of industrial, transport and other enterprises in Germany, etc.), these removals to be carried out chiefly for the purpose of destroying the war potential of Germany.

(b) Annual deliveries of goods from current production for a period to be fixed.

(c) Use of German labor.

3. For the working out on the above principles of a detailed plan for exaction of reparation from Germany an Allied reparation commission will be set up in Moscow. It will consist of three representatives—one from the Union of Soviet Socialist Republics, one from the United Kingdom and one from the United States of America.

4. With regard to the fixing of the total sum of the reparation as well as the distribution of it among the countries which suffered from the German aggression, the Soviet and American delegations agreed as follows:

The Moscow reparation commission should take in its initial studies as a basis for discussion the suggestion of the Soviet Government that the total sum of the reparation in accordance with the points (a) and (b) of the Paragraph 2 should be 22 billion dollars and that 50 per cent should go to the Union of Soviet Socialist Republics.

The British delegation was of the opinion that, pending consideration of the reparation question by the Moscow reparation commission, no figures of reparation should be mentioned.

The above Soviet-American proposal has been passed to the Moscow reparation commission as one of the proposals to be considered by the commission.

VI. MAJOR WAR CRIMINALS

The conference agreed that the question of the major war criminals should be the subject of inquiry by the three Foreign Secretaries for report in due course after the close of the conference.

VII. POLAND

The following declaration on Poland was agreed by the conference:

A new situation has been created in Poland as a result of her complete liberation by the Red Army. This calls for the establishment of a Polish Provisional Government which can be more broadly based than was possible before the recent liberation of the western part of Poland. The Provisional Government which is now functioning in Poland should therefore be reorganized on a broader democratic basis with the inclusion of democratic leaders from Poland itself and from Poles abroad. This new Government should then be called the Polish Provisional Government of National Unity.

M. Molotov, Mr. Harriman and Sir A. Clark Kerr are authorized as a commission to consult in the first instance in Moscow with members of the present Provisional Government and with other Polish democratic leaders from within Poland and from abroad, with a view to the reorganization of the present Government along the above lines. This Polish Provisional Government of National Unity shall be pledged to the holding of free and unfettered elections as soon as possible on the basis of universal suffrage and secret ballot. In these elections all democratic and anti-Nazi parties shall have the right to take part and to put forward candidates.

When a Polish Provisional Government of National Unity has been properly formed in conformity with the above, the Government of the U.S.S.R., which now maintains diplomatic relations with the present Provisional Government of Poland,

and the Government of the United Kingdom and the Government of the United States of America will establish diplomatic relations with the new Polish Provisional Government of National Unity, and will exchange Ambassadors by whose reports the respective Governments will be kept informed about the situation in Poland.

"The three heads of Government consider that the eastern frontier of Poland should follow the Curzon Line with digressions from it in some regions of five to eight kilometers in favor of Poland. They recognize that Poland must receive substantial accessions in territory in the north and west. They feel that the opinion of the new Polish Provisional Government of National Unity should be sought in due course of the extent of these accessions and that the final delimitation of the western frontier of Poland should thereafter await the peace conference."

VIII. YUGOSLAVIA

It was agreed to recommend to Marshal Tito and to Dr. Ivan Subasitch:

(a) That the Tito-Subasitch agreement should immediately be put into effect and a new government formed on the basis of the agreement.

(b) That as soon as the new Government has been formed it should declare:

(I) That the Anti-Fascist Assembly of the National Liberation (AVNOJ) will be extended to include members of the last Yugoslav Skupstina who have not compromised themselves by collaboration with the enemy, thus forming a body to be known as a temporary Parliament and

(II) That legislative acts passed by the Anti-Fascist Assembly of the National Liberation (AVNOJ) will be subject to subsequent ratification by a Constituent Assembly; and that this statement should be published in the communiqué of the conference.

IX. ITALO-YOGOSLAV FRONTIER—ITALO-AUSTRIAN FRONTIER

Notes on these subjects were put in by the British delegation and the American and Soviet delegations agreed to consider them and give their views later.

X. YUGOSLAV-BULGARIAN RELATIONS

There was an exchange of views between the Foreign Secretaries on the question of the desirability of a Yugoslav-Bulgarian pact of alliance. The question at issue was whether a state still under an armistice regime could be allowed to enter into a treaty with another state. Mr. Eden suggested that the Bulgarian and Yugoslav Governments should be informed that this could not be approved. Mr. Stettinius suggested that the British and American Ambassadors should discuss the matter further with Mr. Molotov in Moscow. Mr. Molotov agreed with the proposal of Mr. Stettinius.

XI. SOUTHEASTERN EUROPE

The British delegation put in notes for the consideration of their colleagues on the following subjects:

(a) The Control Commission in Bulgaria.
(b) Greek claims upon Bulgaria, more particularly with reference to reparations.
(c) Oil equipment in Rumania.

XII. IRAN

Mr. Eden, Mr. Stettinius and Mr. Molotov exchanged views on the situation in Iran. It was agreed that this matter should be pursued through the diplomatic channel.

XIII. MEETINGS OF THE THREE FOREIGN SECRETARIES

The conference agreed that permanent machinery should be set up for consultation between the three Foreign Secretaries; they should meet as often as necessary, probably about every three or four months.

These meetings will be held in rotation in the three capitals, the first meeting being held in London.

XIV. THE MONTREAUX CONVENTION AND THE STRAITS

It was agreed that at the next meeting of the three Foreign Secretaries to be held in London, they should consider proposals which it was understood the Soviet

Government would put forward in relation to the Montreaux Convention, and report to their Governments. The Turkish Government should be informed at the appropriate moment.

The forgoing protocol was approved and signed by the three Foreign Secretaries at the Crimean Conference Feb. 11, 1945.

E. R. Stettinius Jr.
M. Molotov
Anthony Eden

AGREEMENT REGARDING JAPAN

The leaders of the three great powers—the Soviet Union, the United States of America and Great Britain—have agreed that in two or three months after Germany has surrendered and the war in Europe is terminated, the Soviet Union shall enter into war against Japan on the side of the Allies on condition that:

1. The status quo in Outer Mongolia (the Mongolian People's Republic) shall be preserved.

2. The former rights of Russia violated by the treacherous attack of Japan in 1904 shall be restored, viz.:

(a) The southern part of Sakhalin as well as the islands adjacent to it shall be returned to the Soviet Union;

(b) The commercial port of Dairen shall be internationalized, the pre-eminent interests of the Soviet Union in this port being safeguarded, and the lease of Port Arthur as a naval base of the U.S.S.R. restored;

(c) The Chinese-Eastern Railroad and the South Manchurian Railroad, which provide an outlet to Dairen, shall be jointly operated by the establishment of a joint Soviet-Chinese company, it being understood that the pre-eminent interests of the Soviet Union shall be safeguarded and that China shall retain sovereignty in Manchuria.

3. The Kurile Islands shall be handed over to the Soviet Union.

It is understood that the agreement concerning Outer Mongolia and the ports and railroads referred to above will require concurrence of Generalissimo Chiang Kai-shek. The President will take measures in order to maintain this concurrence on advice from Marshal Stalin.

The heads of the three great powers have agreed that these claims of the Soviet Union shall be unquestionably fulfilled after Japan has been defeated.

For its part, the Soviet Union expresses it readiness to conclude with the National Government of China a pact of friendship and alliance between the U.S.S.R. and China in order to render assistance to China with its armed forces for the purpose of liberating China from the Japanese yoke.

Joseph Stalin
Franklin D. Roosevelt
Winston S. Churchill
February 11, 1945

Chapter 7

Hot Rhetoric of the Cold War

Introduction

The crisis of the NAZI war of conquest was so intense that it brought together leaders as different as Comrade Stalin, a Communist dictator, Prime Minister Churchill, a British imperialist, and President F.D. Roosevelt, a proponent of democracy and national self-determination. Yet with the death of Hitler (and the subsequent death of Roosevelt and Churchill's electoral defeat) the Grand Alliance quickly fell apart. Almost immediately, President Truman and Stalin began to quarrel over the fate of Eastern Europe. Not privy to the various wartime conferences, Truman viewed Stalin with suspicion and concluded that the U.S.S.R. was bent on the global expansion of its totalitarian system (not unlike the recently defeated NAZI state). While Churchill had been able to work with Stalin as late as 1945, the British statesman openly condemned the Communist leader in 1946. Thus the quarrelling victors divided Europe in two, with competing zones of occupation becoming the basis for ideologically opposed blocs. With the advent of atomic weapons and the adoption of a policy of Mutually Assured Destruction, open conflict between the U.S.A. and the U.S.S.R. became unthinkable. Tensions between the super-powers manifested themselves as proxy-wars in what became known as the Third World, the recently independent states and developing economies of Asia, Africa, and Latin America. However, some leaders such as Sukarno of Indonesia and Nehru of India, refused to choose sides in this bi-polar world. Business interests also influenced American foreign policy, leading to the overthrow of regimes that threatened American corporations and the support of dictators who would provide a safe environment for investment. In the end, open fighting between the super-powers was avoided, but the Cold War took a heavy human toll in Asia, Africa, and Latin America, leading the novelist Nadeem Aslam to write that "the Cold War was cold only for the rich and privileged places of the planet." These selections guide the reader through various perspectives on the global Cold War.

This chapter relates to sections 10.9 and 10.10 of the History-Social Science Content Standards for California Public Schools.

The Sinews of Peace (Iron Curtain Speech)

By Winston Churchill

In 1946, when Winston Churchill coined the phrase "iron curtain" in a speech at Westminster College, in Fulton, Missouri, after receiving an honorary degree, he acknowledged the end of the wartime cooperation and the onset of the Cold War. He paints the picture of Europe divided into two hostile and mutually suspicious camps.

A shadow has fallen upon the scenes so lately lighted by the Allied victory. Nobody knows what Soviet Russia and its Communist international organization intends to do in the immediate future, or what are the limits, if any, to their expansive and proselytizing tendencies. I have a strong admiration and regard for the valiant Russian people and for my wartime comrade, Marshal Stalin. There is deep sympathy and goodwill in Britain—and I doubt not here also—towards the peoples of all the Russias and a resolve to persevere through many differences and rebuffs in establishing lasting friendships. We understand the Russian need to be secure on her western frontiers by the removal of all possibility of German aggression. We welcome Russia to her rightful place among the leading nations of the world. We welcome her flag upon the seas. Above all, we welcome constant, frequent and growing contacts between the Russian people and our own people on both sides of the Atlantic. It is my duty, however, for I am sure you would wish me to state the facts as I see them to you, to place before you certain facts about the present position in Europe.

From Stettin in the Baltic to Trieste in the Adriatic, an iron curtain has descended across the Continent. Behind that line lie all the capitals of the ancient states of Central and Eastern Europe. Warsaw, Berlin, Prague, Vienna, Budapest, Belgrade, Bucharest and Sofia, all these famous cities and the populations around them lie in what I must call the Soviet sphere, and all are subject in one form or another, not only to Soviet influence but to a very high and, in many cases, increasing measure of control from

Winston Churchill, "The Sinews of Peace (Iron Curtain speech)," Speech Delivered on March 5, 1946.

Moscow. Athens alone—Greece with its immortal glories—is free to decide its future at an election under British, American and French observation. The Russian-dominated Polish Government has been encouraged to make enormous and wrongful inroads upon Germany, and mass expulsions of millions of Germans on a scale grievous and undreamed-of are now taking place. The Communist parties, which were very small in all these Eastern states of Europe, have been raised to pre-eminence and power far beyond their numbers and are seeking everywhere to obtain totalitarian control. Police governments are prevailing in nearly every case, and so far, except in Czechoslovakia, there is no true democracy.

Turkey and Persia [Iran] are both profoundly alarmed and disturbed at the claims which are being made upon them and at the pressure being exerted by the Moscow Government. An attempt is being made by the Russians in Berlin to build up a quasi-Communist party in their zone of Occupied Germany by showing special favours to groups of left-wing German leaders. At the end of the fighting last June, the American and British Armies withdrew westwards, in accordance with an earlier agreement, to a depth at some points of one hundred and fifty miles upon a front of nearly four hundred miles, in order to allow our Russian allies to occupy this vast expanse of territory which the Western Democracies had conquered.

If now the Soviet Government tries, by separate action, to build up a pro-Communist Germany in their areas, this will cause new serious difficulties in the British and American zones, and will give the defeated Germans the power of putting themselves up to auction between the Soviets and the Western Democracies. Whatever conclusions may be drawn from these facts—and facts they are—this is certainly not the Liberated Europe we fought to build up. Nor is it one which contains the essentials of permanent peace.

The safety of the world requires a new unity in Europe, from which no nation should be permanently outcast. It is from the quarrels of the strong parent races in Europe that the world wars we have witnessed, or which occurred in former times, have sprung. Twice in our own lifetime we have seen the United States, against their wishes and their traditions, against arguments, the force of which it is impossible not to comprehend, drawn by irresistible forces, into these wars in time to secure the victory of the good cause, but only after frightful slaughter and devastation had occurred. Twice the United States has had to send several millions of its young men across the Atlantic to find the war; but now war can find any nation, wherever it may dwell between dusk and dawn. Surely we should work with conscious purpose for a grand pacification of Europe, within the structure of the United Nations and in accordance with its Charter. That I feel is an open cause of policy of very great importance.

The Long Telegram

By George Kennan

George Kennan (1904–2005) was one of the first Cold Warriors. Diplomat, political advisor, historian, and political scientist, he demonstrated informed and sophisticated thinking in his analysis. Since in 1946 he saw the Soviet Union as inherently expansionistic, he advocated a policy of "Containment," stopping the spread of Communist wherever it should arise. The Truman administration used his work for an increasingly confrontational policy with the Soviet Union. Yet, within a few years, Kennan held that his analysis was being misinterpreted and misused. He left the State Department in 1950, becoming a critical voice of American Cold War foreign policy.

861.00/2—2246: Telegram
The Charge in the Soviet Union (Kennan) to the Secretary of State
SECRET
Moscow, February 22, 1946—9 p.m. [Received February 22—3: 52 p.m.]
511. Answer to Dept's 284, Feb 3 [13] involves questions so intricate, so delicate, so strange to our form of thought, and so important to analysis of our international environment that I cannot compress answers into single brief message without yielding to what I feel would be dangerous degree of over-simplification. I hope, therefore, Dept will bear with me if I submit in answer to this question five parts, subjects of which will be roughly as follows:

(1) Basic features of post-war Soviet outlook.
(2) Background of this outlook.
(3) Its projection in practical policy on official level.
(4) Its projection on unofficial level.
(5) Practical deductions from standpoint of US policy.

George Kennan, "The Long Telegram," *Origins of the Cold War: The Novikov, Kennan, and Roberts 'Long Telegrams' of 1946*, pp. 17–32.

I apologize in advance for this burdening of telegraphic channel; but questions involved are of such urgent importance, particularly in view of recent events, that our answers to them, if they deserve attention at all, seem to me to deserve it at once. There follows

Part 1: Basic Features of Post War Soviet Outlook, as Put Forward by Official Propaganda Machine

Are as Follows:

(a) USSR still lives in antagonistic "capitalist encirclement" with which in the long run there can be no permanent peaceful coexistence. As stated by Stalin in 1927 to a delegation of American workers:

> In course of further development of international revolution there will emerge two centers of world significance: a socialist center, drawing to itself the countries which tend toward socialism, and a capitalist center, drawing to itself the countries that incline toward capitalism. Battle between these two centers for command of world economy will decide fate of capitalism and of communism in entire world.

(b) Capitalist world is beset with internal conflicts, inherent in nature of capitalist society. These conflicts are insoluble by means of peaceful compromise. Greatest of them is that between England and US.

(c) Internal conflicts of capitalism inevitably generate wars. Wars thus generated may be of two kinds: intra-capitalist wars between two capitalist states, and wars of intervention against socialist world. Smart capitalists, vainly seeking escape from inner conflicts of capitalism, incline toward latter.

(d) Intervention against USSR, while it would be disastrous to those who undertook it, would cause renewed delay in progress of Soviet socialism and must therefore be forestalled at all costs.

(e) Conflicts between capitalist states, though likewise fraught with danger for USSR, nevertheless hold out great possibilities for advancement of socialist cause, particularly if USSR remains militarily powerful, ideologically monolithic and faithful to its present brilliant leadership.

(f) It must be borne in mind that capitalist world is not all bad. In addition to hopelessly reactionary and bourgeois elements, it includes (1) certain wholly enlightened and positive elements united in acceptable communistic parties and (2) certain other elements (now described for tactical reasons as progressive or democratic) whose reactions, aspirations and activities happen to be "objectively" favorable to interests of USSR. These last must be encouraged and utilized for Soviet purposes.

(g) Among negative elements of bourgeois-capitalist society, most dangerous of all are those whom Lenin called false friends of the people, namely moderate-socialist or social-democratic leaders (in other words, non-Communist left-wing). These are more dangerous than out-and-out reactionaries, for latter at least march under their true colors, whereas moderate left-wing leaders confuse people by employing devices of socialism to seine interests of reactionary capital.

So much for premises. To what deductions do they lead from standpoint of Soviet policy? To following:

(a) Everything must be done to advance relative strength of USSR as factor in international society. Conversely, no opportunity most be missed to reduce strength and influence, collectively as well as individually, of capitalist powers.

(b) Soviet efforts, and those of Russia's friends abroad, must be directed toward deepening and exploiting of differences and conflicts between capitalist powers. If these eventually deepen into an "imperialist" war, this war must be turned into revolutionary upheavals within the various capitalist countries.

(c) "Democratic-progressive" elements abroad are to be utilized to maximum to bring pressure to bear on capitalist governments along lines agreeable to Soviet interests.

(d) Relentless battle must be waged against socialist and social-democratic leaders abroad.

Part 2: Background of Outlook

Before examining ramifications of this party line in practice there are certain aspects of it to which I wish to draw attention.

First, it does not represent natural outlook of Russian people. Latter are, by and large, friendly to outside world, eager for experience of it, eager to measure against it talents they are conscious of possessing, eager above all to live in peace and enjoy fruits of their own labor. Party line only represents thesis which official propaganda machine puts forward with great skill and persistence to a public often remarkably resistant in the stronghold of its innermost thoughts. But party line is binding for outlook and conduct of people who make up apparatus of power—party, secret police and Government—and it is exclusively with these that we have to deal.

Second, please note that premises on which this party line is based are for most part simply not true. Experience has shown that peaceful and mutually profitable coexistence of capitalist and socialist states is entirely possible. Basic internal conflicts in advanced countries are no longer primarily those arising out of capitalist ownership of means of production, but are ones arising from advanced urbanism and industrialism as such, which Russia has thus far been spared not by socialism but only by her own backwardness. Internal rivalries of capitalism do not always generate wars; and not all wars are attributable to this cause. To speak of possibility of intervention against USSR today, after elimination of Germany and Japan and after example of recent war, is sheerest nonsense. If not provoked by forces of intolerance and subversion "capitalist" world of today is quite capable of living at peace with itself and with Russia. Finally, no sane person has reason to doubt sincerity of moderate socialist leaders in Western countries. Nor is it fair to deny success of their efforts to improve conditions for working population whenever, as in Scandinavia, they have been given chance to show what they could do.

Falseness of those premises, every one of which predates recent war, was amply demonstrated by that conflict itself Anglo-American differences did not turn out to be major differences of Western World. Capitalist countries, other than those of Axis, showed no disposition to solve their differences by joining in crusade against USSR. Instead of imperialist war turning into civil wars and revolution, USSR found itself obliged to fight side by side with capitalist powers for an avowed community of aim.

Nevertheless, all these theses, however baseless and disproven, are being boldly put forward again today. What does this indicate? It indicates that Soviet party line is not based on any objective analysis of situation beyond Russia's borders; that it has, indeed, little to do with conditions outside of Russia; that it arises mainly from basic inner-Russian necessities which existed before recent war and exist today.

At bottom of Kremlin's neurotic view of world affairs is traditional and instinctive Russian sense of insecurity. Originally, this was insecurity of a peaceful agricultural people trying to live on vast exposed plain in neighborhood of fierce nomadic peoples. To this was added, as Russia came into contact with economically advanced West, fear of more competent, more powerful, more highly organized societies in that area. But this latter type of insecurity was one which afflicted rather Russian rulers than Russian people; for Russian rulers have invariably sensed that their rule was relatively archaic in form fragile and artificial in its psychological foundation, unable to stand comparison or contact with political systems of Western countries. For this reason they have always feared foreign penetration, feared direct contact between Western world and their own, feared what would happen if Russians learned truth about world without or if foreigners learned truth about world within. And they have learned to seek security only in patient but deadly struggle for total destruction of rival power, never in compacts and compromises with it.

It was no coincidence that Marxism, which had smoldered ineffectively for half a century in Western Europe, caught hold and blazed for first time in Russia. Only in this land which had never known a friendly neighbor or indeed any tolerant equilibrium of separate powers, either internal or international, could a doctrine thrive which viewed economic conflicts of society as insoluble by peaceful means. After establishment of Bolshevist regime, Marxist dogma, rendered even more truculent and intolerant by

Lenin's interpretation, became a perfect vehicle for sense of insecurity with which Bolsheviks, even more than previous Russian rulers, were afflicted. In this dogma, with its basic altruism of purpose, they found justification for their instinctive fear of outside world, for the dictatorship without which they did not know how to rule, for cruelties they did not dare not to inflict, for sacrifice they felt bound to demand. In the name of Marxism they sacrificed every single ethical value in their methods and tactics. Today they cannot dispense with it. It is fig leaf of their moral and intellectual respectability. Without it they would stand before history, at best, as only the last of that long succession of cruel and wasteful Russian rulers who have relentlessly forced country on to ever new heights of military power in order to guarantee external security of their internally weak regimes. This is why Soviet purposes most always be solemnly clothed in trappings of Marxism, and why no one should underrate importance of dogma in Soviet affairs. Thus Soviet leaders are driven [by?] necessities of their own past and present position to put forward which [apparent omission] outside world as evil, hostile and menacing, but as bearing within itself germs of creeping disease and destined to be wracked with growing internal convulsions until it is given final *Coup de grace* by rising power of socialism and yields to new and better world. This thesis provides justification for that increase of military and police power of Russian state, for that isolation of Russian population from outside world, and for that fluid and constant pressure to extend limits of Russian police power which are together the natural and instinctive urges of Russian rulers. Basically this is only the steady advance of uneasy Russian nationalism, a centuries old movement in which conceptions of offense and defense are inextricably confused. But in new guise of international Marxism, with its honeyed promises to a desperate and war torn outside world, it is more dangerous and insidious than ever before.

It should not be thought from above that Soviet party line is necessarily disingenuous and insincere on part of all those who put it forward. Many of them are too ignorant of outside world and mentally too dependent to question [apparent omission] self-hypnotism, and who have no difficulty making themselves believe what they find it comforting and convenient to believe. Finally we have the unsolved mystery as to who, if anyone, in this great land actually receives accurate and unbiased information about outside world. In atmosphere of oriental secretiveness and conspiracy which pervades this Government, possibilities for distorting or poisoning sources and currents of information are infinite. The very disrespect of Russians for objective truth—indeed, their disbelief in its existence—leads them to view all stated facts as instruments for furtherance of one ulterior purpose or another. There is good reason to suspect that this Government is actually a conspiracy within a conspiracy; and I for one am reluctant to believe that Stalin himself receives anything like an objective picture of outside world. Here there is ample scope for the type of subtle intrigue at which Russians are past masters. Inability of foreign governments to place their case squarely before Russian policy makers—extent to which they are delivered up in their relations with Russia to good graces of obscure and unknown advisors whom they never see and cannot influence—this to my mind is most disquieting feature of diplomacy in Moscow, and one which Western statesmen would do well to keep in mind if they would understand nature of difficulties encountered here.

Part 3: Projection of Soviet Outlook in Practical Policy on Official Level

We have now seen nature and background of Soviet program. What may we expect by way of its practical implementation?

Soviet policy, as Department implies in its query under reference, is conducted on two planes: (1) official plane represented by actions undertaken officially in name of Soviet Government; and (2) subterranean plane of actions undertaken by agencies for which Soviet Government does not admit responsibility.

Policy promulgated on both planes will be calculated to serve basic policies (a) to (d) outlined in part 1. Actions taken on different planes will differ considerably, but will dovetail into each other in purpose, timing and effect.

On official plane we must look for following:

(a) Internal policy devoted to increasing in every way strength and prestige of Soviet state: intensive military-industrialization; maximum development of armed forces; great displays to impress outsiders; continued secretiveness about internal matters, designed to conceal weaknesses and to keep opponents in dark.

(b) Wherever it is considered timely and promising, efforts will be made to advance official limits of Soviet power. For the moment, these efforts are restricted to certain neighboring points conceived of here as being of immediate strategic necessity, such as Northern Iran, Turkey, possibly Bornholm. However, other points may at any time come into question, if and as, concealed Soviet political power is extended to new areas. Thus a "friendly Persian Government might be asked to grant Russia a port on Persian Gulf. Should Spain fall under Communist control, question of Soviet base at Gibraltar Strait might be activated. But such claims will appear on official level only when unofficial preparation is complete.

(c) Russians will participate officially in international organizations where they see opportunity of extending Soviet power or of inhibiting or diluting power of others. Moscow sees in UNO not the mechanism for a permanent and stable world society founded on mutual interest and aims of all nations, but an arena in which aims just mentioned can be favorably pursued. As long as UNO is considered here to serve this purpose, Soviets will remain with it. But if at any time they come to conclusion that it is serving to embarrass or frustrate their aims for power expansion and if they see better prospects for pursuit of these aims along other lines, they will not hesitate to abandon UNO. This would imply, however, that they felt themselves strong enough to split unity of other nations by their withdrawal to render UNO ineffective as a threat to their aims or security, replace it with an international weapon more effective from their viewpoint. Thus Soviet attitude toward UNO will depend largely on loyalty of other nations to it, and on degree of vigor, decisiveness and cohesion with which those nations defend in UNO the peaceful and hopeful concept of international life, which that organization represents to our way of thinking. I reiterate, Moscow has no abstract devotion to UNO ideals. Its attitude to that organization will remain essentially pragmatic and tactical.

(d) Toward colonial areas and backward or dependent peoples, Soviet policy, even on official plane, will be directed toward weakening of power and influence and contacts of advanced Western nations, on theory that in so far as this policy is successful, there will be created a vacuum which will favor Communist-Soviet penetration. Soviet pressure for participation in trusteeship arrangements thus represents, in my opinion, a desire to be in a position to complicate and inhibit exertion of Western influence at such points rather than to provide major channel for exerting of Soviet power. Latter motive is not lacking, but for this Soviets prefer to rely on other channels than official trusteeship arrangements. Thus we may expect to find Soviets asking for admission everywhere to trusteeship or similar arrangements and using levers thus acquired to weaken Western influence among such peoples.

(e) Russians will strive energetically to develop Soviet representation in, and official ties with, countries in which they sense Strong possibilities of opposition to Western centers of power. This applies to such widely separated points as Germany, Argentina, Middle Eastern countries, etc.

(f) In international economic matters, Soviet policy will really be dominated by pursuit of autarchy for Soviet Union and Soviet-dominated adjacent areas taken together. That, however, will be underlying policy. As far as official line is concerned, position is not yet clear. Soviet Government has shown strange reticence since termination hostilities on subject foreign trade. If large scale long term credits should be forthcoming, I believe Soviet Government may eventually again do lip service, as it did in 1930's to desirability of building up international economic exchanges in general. Otherwise I think it possible Soviet foreign trade may be restricted largely to Soviet's own security sphere, including occupied areas in Germany, and that a cold official shoulder may be turned to principle of general economic collaboration among nations.

(g) With respect to cultural collaboration, lip service will likewise be rendered to desirability of deepening cultural contacts between peoples, but this will not in practice be interpreted in any way which could weaken security position of Soviet peoples. Actual manifestations of Soviet policy in this respect will be restricted to arid channels of closely shepherded official visits and functions, with superabundance of vodka and speeches and dearth of permanent effects.

(h) Beyond this, Soviet official relations will take what might be called "correct" course with individual foreign governments, with great stress being laid on prestige of Soviet Union and its representatives and with punctilious attention to protocol as distinct from good manners.

Part 4: Following May Be Said as to What We May Expect by Way of Implementation of Basic Soviet Policies on Unofficial, or Subterranean Plane, i.e. on Plane for Which Soviet Government Accepts no Responsibility

Agencies utilized for promulgation of policies on this plane are following:

1. Inner central core of Communist Parties in other countries. While many of persons who compose this category may also appear and act in unrelated public capacities, they are in reality working closely together as an underground operating directorate of world communism, a concealed Comintern tightly coordinated and directed by Moscow. It is important to remember that this inner core is actually working on underground lines, despite legality of parties with which it is associated.

2. Rank and file of Communist Parties. Note distinction is drawn between those and persons defined in paragraph 1. This distinction has become much sharper in recent years. Whereas formerly foreign Communist Parties represented a curious (and from Moscow's standpoint often inconvenient) mixture of conspiracy and legitimate activity, now the conspiratorial element has been neatly concentrated in inner circle and ordered underground, while rank and file—no longer even taken into confidence about realities of movement—are thrust forward as bona fide internal partisans of certain political tendencies within their respective countries, genuinely innocent of conspiratorial connection with foreign states. Only in certain countries where communists are numerically strong do they now regularly appear and act as a body. As a rule they are used to penetrate, and to influence or dominate, as case may be, other organizations less likely to be suspected of being tools of Soviet Government, with a view to accomplishing their purposes through [apparent omission] organizations, rather than by direct action as a separate political party.

3. A wide variety of national associations or bodies which can be dominated or influenced by such penetration. These include: labor unions, youth leagues, women's organizations, racial societies, religious societies, social organizations, cultural groups, liberal magazines, publishing houses, etc.

4. International organizations which can be similarly penetrated through influence over various national components. Labor, youth and women's organizations are prominent among them. Particular, almost vital importance is attached in this connection to international labor movement. In this, Moscow sees possibility of sidetracking western governments in world affairs and building up international lobby capable of

compelling governments to take actions favorable to Soviet interests in various countries and of paralyzing actions disagreeable to USSR

5. Russian Orthodox Church, with its foreign branches, and through it the Eastern Orthodox Church in general.

6. Pan-Slav movement and other movements (Azerbaijan, Armenian, Turcoman, etc.) based on racial groups within Soviet Union.

7. Governments or governing groups willing to lend themselves to Soviet purposes in one degree or another, such as present Bulgarian and Yugoslav Governments, North Persian regime, Chinese Communists, etc. Not only propaganda machines but actual policies of these regimes can be placed extensively at disposal of USSR.

It may be expected that component parts of this far-flung apparatus will be utilized in accordance with their individual suitability, as follows:

(a) To undermine general political and strategic potential of major western powers. Efforts will be made in such countries to disrupt national self confidence, to hamstring measures of national defense, to increase social and industrial unrest, to stimulate all forms of disunity. All persons with grievances, whether economic or racial, will be urged to spelt redress not in mediation and compromise, but in defiant violent struggle for destruction of other elements of society. Here poor will be set against rich, black against white, young against old, newcomers against established residents, etc.

(b) On unofficial plane particularly violent efforts will be made to weaken power and influence of Western Powers of [on] colonial backward, or dependent peoples. On this level, no holds will be barred. Mistakes and weaknesses of western colonial administration will be mercilessly exposed and exploited. Liberal opinion in Western countries will be mobilized to weaken colonial policies. Resentment among dependent peoples will be stimulated. And while latter are being encouraged to seek independence of Western Powers, Soviet dominated puppet political machines will be undergoing preparation to take over domestic power in respective colonial areas when independence is achieved.

(c) Where individual governments stand in path of Soviet purposes pressure will be brought for their removal from office. This can happen where governments directly oppose Soviet foreign policy aims (Turkey, Iran), where they seal their territories off against Communist penetration (Switzerland, Portugal), or where they compete too strongly, like Labor Government in England, for moral domination among elements which it is important for Communists to dominate. (Sometimes, two of these elements are present in a single case. Then Communist opposition becomes particularly shrill and savage.[)]

(d) In foreign countries Communists will, as a rule, work toward destruction of all forms of personal independence, economic, political or moral. Their system can handle only individuals who have been brought into complete dependence on higher power. Thus, persons who are financially independent—such as individual businessmen, estate owners, successful farmers, artisans and all those who exercise local leadership or have local prestige, such as popular local clergymen or political figures, are anathema. It is not by chance that even in USSR local officials are kept constantly on move from one job to another, to prevent their taking root.

(e) Everything possible will be done to set major Western Powers against each other. Anti-British talk will be plugged among Americans, anti-American talk among British. Continentals, including Germans, will be taught to abhor both Anglo-Saxon powers. Where suspicions exist, they will be fanned; where not, ignited. No effort will be spared to discredit and combat all efforts which threaten to lead to any sort of unity or cohesion among other [apparent omission] from which Russia might be excluded. Thus, all forms of international organization not amenable to Communist penetration and control, whether it be the Catholic [apparent omission] international economic concerns, or the international fraternity of royalty and aristocracy, must expect to find themselves under fire from many, and often [apparent omission].

(f) In general, all Soviet efforts on unofficial international plane will be negative and destructive in character, designed to tear down sources of strength beyond reach of Soviet control. This is only in line with basic Soviet instinct that there can be no compromise with rival power and that constructive work can start only when Communist power is dominating. But behind all this will be applied insistent, unceasing pressure for penetration and command of key positions in administration and especially in police apparatus of foreign countries. The Soviet regime is a police regime par excellence, reared in the dim half world of Tsarist police intrigue, accustomed to think primarily in terms of police power. This should never be lost sight of in gauging Soviet motives.

Part 5: [Practical Deductions from Standpoint of US Policy]

In summary, we have here a political force committed fanatically to the belief that with US there can be no permanent *modus vivendi* that it is desirable and necessary that the internal harmony of our society be disrupted, our traditional way of life be destroyed, the international authority of our state be broken, if Soviet power is to be secure. This political force has complete power of disposition over energies of one of world's greatest peoples and resources of world's richest national territory, and is borne along by deep and powerful currents of Russian nationalism. In addition, it has an elaborate and far flung apparatus for exertion of its influence in other countries, an apparatus of amazing flexibility and versatility, managed by people whose experience and skill in underground methods are presumably without parallel in history. Finally, it is seemingly inaccessible to considerations of reality in its basic reactions. For it, the vast fund of objective fact about human society is not, as with us, the measure against which outlook is constantly being tested and re-formed, but a grab bag from which individual items are selected arbitrarily and tendenciously to bolster an outlook already preconceived. This is admittedly not a pleasant picture. Problem of how to cope with this force in [is] undoubtedly greatest task our diplomacy has ever faced and probably greatest it will ever have to face. It should be point of departure from which our political general staff work at present juncture should proceed. It should be approached with same thoroughness and care as solution of major strategic problem in war, and if necessary, with no smaller outlay in planning effort. I cannot attempt to suggest all answers here. But I would like to record my conviction that problem is within our power to solve—and that without recourse to any general military conflict. And in support of this conviction there are certain observations of a more encouraging nature I should like to make:

(1) Soviet power, unlike that of Hitlerite Germany, is neither schematic nor adventunstic. It does not work by fixed plans. It does not take unnecessary risks. Impervious to logic of reason, and it is highly sensitive to logic of force. For this reason it can easily withdraw—and usually does when strong resistance is encountered at any point. Thus, if the adversary has sufficient force and makes clear his readiness to use it, he rarely has to do so. If situations are properly handled there need be no prestige-engaging showdowns.

(2) Gauged against Western World as a whole, Soviets are still by far the weaker force. Thus, their success will really depend on degree of cohesion, firmness and vigor which Western World can muster. And this is factor which it is within our power to influence.

(3) Success of Soviet system, as form of internal power, is not yet finally proven. It has yet to be demonstrated that it can survive supreme test of successive transfer of power from one individual or group to another. Lenin's death was first such transfer, and its effects wracked Soviet state for 15 years. After Stalin's death or retirement will be second. But even this will not be final test. Soviet internal system will now be subjected, by virtue of recent territorial expansions, to series of additional strains which once proved severe tax on Tsardom. We here are convinced that never since termination of civil war have mass of Russian people been emotionally farther removed from doctrines of Communist Party than they are today. In Russia, party has now become a great and—for the moment—highly successful apparatus of dictatorial administration, but it has ceased to be a source of emotional inspiration. Thus, internal soundness and permanence of movement need not yet be regarded as assured.

(4) All Soviet propaganda beyond Soviet security sphere is basically negative and destructive. It should therefore be relatively easy to combat it by any intelligent and really constructive program.

For those reasons I think we may approach calmly and with good heart problem of how to deal with Russia. As to how this approach should be made, I only wish to advance, by way of conclusion, following comments:

(1) Our first step must be to apprehend, and recognize for what it is, the nature of the movement with which we are dealing. We must study it with same courage, detachment, objectivity, and same determination not to be emotionally provoked or unseated by it, with which doctor studies unruly and unreasonable individual.

(2) We must see that our public is educated to realities of Russian situation. I cannot over-emphasize importance of this. Press cannot do this alone. It must be done mainly by Government, which is necessarily more experienced and better informed on practical problems involved. In this we need not be deterred by [ugliness?] of picture. I am convinced that there would be far less hysterical anti-Sovietism in our country today if realities of this situation were better understood by our people. There is nothing as dangerous or as terrifying as the unknown. It may also be argued that to reveal more information on our difficulties with Russia would reflect unfavorably on Russian-American relations. I feel that if there is any real risk here involved, it is one which we should have courage to face, and sooner the better. But I cannot see what we would be risking. Our stake in this country, even coming on heels of tremendous demonstrations of our friendship for Russian people, is remarkably small. We have here no investments to guard, no actual trade to lose, virtually no citizens to protect, few cultural contacts to preserve. Our only stake lies in what we hope rather than what we have; and I am convinced we have better chance of realizing those hopes if our public is enlightened and if our dealings with Russians are placed entirely on realistic and matter-of-fact basis.

(3) Much depends on health and vigor of our own society. World communism is like malignant parasite which feeds only on diseased tissue. This is point at which domestic and foreign policies meets Every courageous and incisive measure to solve internal problems of our own society, to improve self-confidence, discipline, morale and community spirit of our own people, is a diplomatic victory over Moscow worth a thousand diplomatic notes and joint communiqués. If we cannot abandon fatalism and indifference in face of deficiencies of our own society, Moscow will profit—Moscow cannot help profiting by them in its foreign policies.

(4) We must formulate and put forward for other nations a much more positive and constructive picture of sort of world we would like to see than we have put forward in past. It is not enough to urge people to develop political processes similar to our own. Many foreign peoples, in Europe at least, are tired and frightened by experiences of past, and are less interested in abstract freedom than in security. They are seeking guidance rather than responsibilities. We should be better able than Russians to give them this. And unless we do, Russians certainly will.

(5) Finally we must have courage and self-confidence to cling to our own methods and conceptions of human society. After Al, the greatest danger that can befall us in coping with this problem of Soviet communism, is that we shall allow ourselves to become like those with whom we are coping.

A Report to the National Security Council—NSC 68

By Paul Nitze

For four decades Paul Nitze (1907–2004) was a chief architect of American policy towards the Soviet Union. In "NSC 68," 1950, he provided the rationale for dramatically expanding the American military. Seeing the Soviet Union as "fanatical," he argued that the United States had to meet what he deemed as a threat not just to the American government but "civilization itself."

Analyses

I. BACKGROUNDS OF THE PRESENT WORLD CRISIS

Within the past thirty-five years the world has experience two global wars of tremendous violence. It has witnessed two revolutions—the Russian and the Chinese—of extreme scope and intensity. It has also seen the collapse of five empires—the Ottoman, the Austro-Hungarian, German, Italian and Japanese—and the drastic decline of two major imperial systems, the British and the French. During the span of one generation the international distribution of power has been fundamentally altered. For several centuries it had proved impossible for any one nation to gain such preponderant strength that a coalition of other nations could not in time face it with greater strength. The international scene was marked by recurring periods of violence and war, but a system of sovereign and independent states was maintained, over which no state was able to achieve hegemony.

Two complex sets of factors have now basically altered this historical distribution of power. First, the defeat of Germany and Japan and the decline of the British and

Paul Nitze, "A Report to the National Security Council—NSC 68," pp. 4–6.

French Empires have interacted with the development of the United States and the Soviet Union in such a way that power has increasingly gravitated to these two centers. Second, the Soviet Union, unlike previous aspirants to hegemony, is animated by a new fanatic faith, antithetical to our own, and seeks to impose its absolute authority over the rest of the world. Conflict has, therefore, become endemic and is waged, on the part of the Soviet Union, by violent or non-violent methods in accordance with the dictates of expediency. With the development of increasingly terrifying weapons of mass destruction, every individual faces the ever-present possibility of annihilation should the conflict enter the phase of total war.

On the one hand, the people of the world yearn for relief from the anxiety arising from the risk of atomic war. On the other hand, any substantial further extension of the area under the domination of the Kremlin would raise the possibility that no coalition adequate to confront the Kremlin with greater strength could be assembled, It is in this context that this Republic and its citizens in the ascendancy of their strength stand in their deepest peril.

The issues that face us are momentous, involving the fulfillment or destruction not only of this Republic but of civilization itself. They are issues which will not await our deliberations. With conscience and resolution this Government and the people it represents must now take new and fateful decisions.

II. FUNDAMENTAL PURPOSE OF THE UNITED STATES

The fundamental purpose of the United States is laid down in the Preamble to the constitution: "...to form a more perfect Union, establish Justice, insure domestic Tranquility, provide for the common defence, promote the general Welfare, and secure the Blessings of Liberty to ourselves and our Posterity." In essence, the fundamental purpose is to assure the integrity and vitality of our free society, which is founded upon the dignity and worth of the individual.

Three realities emerge as a consequence of this purpose: Our determination to maintain the essential elements of individual freedom, as set forth in the Constitution and Bill of Rights; our determination to create conditions under which our free and democratic system can live and prosper; and our determination to fight if necessary to defend our way of life, for which as in the Declaration of Independence, "with a firm reliance on the protection of Divine Providence, we mutually pledge to each other our lives, our Fortunes and our sacred Honor."

III. FUNDAMENTAL DESIGN OF THE KREMLIN

The fundamental design of those who control the Soviet Union and the international communist movement is to retain and solidify their absolute power, first in the Soviet

Union and second in the areas now under their control. In the minds of the Soviet leaders, however, achievement of this design requires the dynamic extension of their authority and the ultimate elimination of any effective opposition to their authority.

The design, therefore, calls for the complete subversion or forcible destruction of the machinery of government and structure of society in the countries of the non-Soviet world and their replacement by an apparatus and structure subservient to and controlled from the Kremlin. To that end soviet efforts are now directed toward the domination of the Eurasian land mass. The United States, as the principal center of power in the non-Soviet world and the bulwark of opposition to Soviet expansion, is the principal enemy whose integrity and vitality must be subverted or destroyed by one means or another if the Kremlin is to achieve its fundamental design.

CIA and Guatemala Assassination Proposals 1952–1954—CIA History Staff Analysis

By Gerald K. Haines

Colonel Jacobo Árbenz Guzmán (1913–1971) was a Guatemalan military officer and politician who served as Defense Minister from 1944–1951 and as President from 1951 to 1954. He had personal and professional ties to Marxists and Communists and was elected in 1950 on a platform based on land reform. While not a Communist himself, his promised reforms would take land from the United Fruit Company (now Chiquita) and give it to poor peasants. United Fruit had numerous connections to the Eisenhower administration, including Secretary of State John Foster Dulles, whose law firm had represented United Fruit, and his brother Allen Dulles, who headed the CIA and sat on United Fruit's board of directors. In order to oust Arbenz and protect the company's interests, the CIA engineered a coup d'etat and installed a military junta, creating a classic "banana republic." Civil war and genocidal massacres of the impoverished indigenous population plagued Guatemala into the early 1990s.

Introduction

In the early 1950s, the Central Intelligence Agency directed covert operations aimed at removing the government of Jacobo Arbenz Guzman from power in Guatemala. Included in these efforts were various suggestions for the disposal of key Arbenz government officials and Guatemalan Communists. The Agency drew up lists

Gerald K. Haines, "CIA and Guatemala Assassination Proposals: 1952–1954—CIA History Staff Analysis."

of individuals for assassination, discussed training Guatemalan exiles for assassination teams, and conducted intimidation programs against prominent Guatemalan officials.

This brief study traces, in a chronological manner, the injection of assassination planning and proposals into the PBFORTUNE covert operation against the Arbenz government in 1952 and into the PBSUCCESS operation in 1954. It attempts to illustrate the depth of such planning and the level of involvement of Agency officials. It also attempts to detail where the proposals originated, who approved them, and how advanced the preparations for such actions were. Finally, the study examines the implementation of such planning and the results—i.e., in the end, the plans were abandoned and no Arbenz officials or Guatemalan Communists were killed. The study is based almost exclusively on Directorate of Operations records relating to PBFORTUNE and PBSUCCESS.

Background

As early as 1952 US policy makers viewed the government of President Arbenz with some alarm. Although he had been popularly elected in 1950, growing Communist influence within his government gave rise to concern in the United States that Arbenz had established an effective working alliance with the Communists. Moreover, Arbenz' policies had damaged US business interests in Guatemala; a sweeping agrarian reform called for the expropriation and redistribution of much of the United Fruit Company's land. Although most high-level US officials recognized that a hostile government in Guatemala by itself did not constitute a direct security threat to the United States, they viewed events there in the context of the growing global Cold War struggle with the Soviet Union and feared that Guatemala could become a client state from which the Soviets could project power and influence throughout the Western Hemisphere.

CIA and Intelligence Community reports tended to support the view that Guatemala and the Arbenz regime were rapidly falling under the sway of the Communists. Director of Central Intelligence (DCI) Walter Bedell Smith and other Agency officials believed the situation called for action. Their assessment was, that without help, the Guatemalan opposition would remain inept, disorganized and ineffective. The anti-Communist elements—the Catholic hierarchy, landowners, business interests, the railway workers union, university students, and the Army—were prepared to prevent a Communist accession to power, but they had little outside support.

Other US officials, especially in the Department of State, urged a more cautious approach. The Bureau of Inter-American Affairs, for example, did not want to present "the spectacle of the elephant shaking with alarm before the mouse." It wanted a policy of firm persuasion with the withholding of virtually all cooperative assistance, and the concluding of military defense assistance pacts with El Salvador, Nicaragua, and Honduras. Although the Department of State position became the official public US policy, the CIA assessment of the situation had support within the Truman administration as well. This led to the development of a covert action program designed to topple the Arbenz government—PBFORTUNE.

PBFORTUNE

Following a visit to Washington by Nicaraguan President Anastasio Somoza in April 1952, in which Somoza boasted that if provided arms he and Guatemalan exile Carlos Castillo Armas could overthrow Arbenz, President Harry Truman asked DCI Smith, to investigate the possibility. Smith sent an agent, code named SEEKFORD, to contact Guatemalan dissidents about armed action against the Arbenz regime. After seeing his report, [ ] Chief of the [ ] Division of the Directorate of Plans (DP), proposed to Deputy Director of Central Intelligence Allen Dulles that the Agency supply Castillo Armas with arms and $225,000 and that Nicaragua and Honduras furnish the Guatemalans with air support. Gaining Department of State support, Smith, on 9 September 1952, officially approved [ ]'s request to initiate operation PBFORTUNE to aid Guatemalan exiles in overthrowing Arbenz. Planning for PBFORTUNE lasted barely a month, however, when Smith terminated it after he learned in October that it had been blow.

Throughout planning for PBFORTUNE there were proposals for assassination. Even months before the official approval of PBFORTUNE, Directorate of Plans (DP) officers compiled a "hit list." Working from an old 1949 Guatemalan Army list of Communists and information supplied by the Directorate of Intelligence, in January 1952 DP officers compiled a list of "top flight Communists whom the new government would desire to eliminate immediately in event of successful anti-Communist coup." Headquarters asked [ ] to verify the list and recommend any additions or deletions. Headquarters also requested [ ] to verify a list of an additional 16 Communists and/or sympathizers whom the new government would desire to incarcerate immediately if the coup succeeded. [ ] in Guatemala City added three names to the list in his reply. Nine months later, SEEKFORD, the CIA agent in touch with Castillo Armas, forwarded to Headquarters a disposal list compiled by Castillo Armas. That list called for the execution through executive action of 58 Guatemalans (Category I) and the imprisonment or exile of 74 additional Guatemalans (Category II). SEEKFORD also reported at the same time, 18 September 1952, that General Rafael Trujillo, the dictator of the Dominican Republic, had agreed to aid Castillo Armas in return for the "killing of four Santo Dominicans at present residing in Guatemala a few days prior to D-Day." According to SEEKFORD, Castillo Armas readily agreed, but cautioned that it could not be done prior to D-day because of security reasons. Castillo Armas further added that his own plans included similar action and that special squads were already being trained. There is no record that Headquarters took any action regarding Castillo Armas' list.

After the PBFORTUNE operation was officially terminated, the Agency continued to pick up reports of assassination planning on the part of the Guatemalan opposition. In late November 1952, for example, an opposition Guatemalan leader, in a conversation with SEEKFORD, confirmed that Castillo Armas had special "K" groups whose mission was to kill all leading political and military leaders, and that the hit list with the location of the homes and offices of all targets had already been drawn up. On 12 December SEEKFORD reported further that Castillo Armas planned to make maximum use of the "K" groups. Another source subsequently reported that Nicaraguan, Honduran, and Salvadoran soldiers in civilian clothes would infiltrate Guatemala and assassinate unnamed Communist leaders.

In addition to monitoring events in Guatemala, the Agency continued to try to influence developments and to float ideas for disposing of key figures in the [ ] government. [ ] in 1953 proposed not only to focus on sabotage, defection, penetration, and propaganda efforts with regard to Guatemala, but to eliminate [ ]. According to [ ]'s draft memorandum, after creating a story that [ ] was preparing to oust the Communists, he could be eliminated. His assassination would be "laid to the Commies" and used to bring about a mass defection of the Guatemalan army. A Western Hemisphere Division memo of 28 August 1953 also suggested possibly assassinating key Guatemalan military officers if they refused to be converted to the rebel cause. In September 1953 [ ] also sent [ ] an updated plan of action which included a reference to "neutralizing" key Guatemalan military leaders.

In the psychological warfare area, Guatemala City Station sent [ ] all leading Communists in Guatemala, "death notice" cards for 30 straight days beginning 15 April 1953. The Station repeated the operation beginning 15 June 1953 but reported no reaction from the targeted leaders.

PBSUCCESS

By the fall of 1953, US policy makers, including CIA officials, were searching for a new overall program for dealing with Arbenz. The Guatemalan leader had moved even closer to the Communists. He had expropriated additional United Fruit Company holdings, legalized the Guatemalan Communist Party, the PGT, and suppressed anti-Communist opposition following an abortive uprising at Salmá. In response, the National Security Council authorized a covert action operation against Arbenz and gave the CIA primary responsibility.

The CIA plan, as drawn up by [ ]s Western Hemisphere Division, combined psychological warfare, economic, diplomatic, and paramilitary actions against Guatemala. Named PBSUCCESS, and coordinated with the Department of State, the plan's stated objective was "to remove covertly, and without bloodshed if possible, the menace of the present Communist-controlled government of Guatemala." In the outline of the operation the sixth stage called for the "roll-up" of Communists and collaborators after a successful coup.

Dulles placed [ ] in charge of PBSUCCESS and sent a senior DDP officer, [ ] to establish a temporary station (LINCOLN), to coordinate the planning and execution of PBSUCCESS. Other key Agency figures involved were [ ] and [ ] Chief of the [ ] Staff. Department of State [ ] Assistant Secretary of State for [ ] from the office of [ ] Affairs, and [ ] State liaison to the agency, also played major roles.

Training

Although assassination was not mentioned specifically in the overall plan, the Chief of [ ] at [ ] requested a special paper on the liquidation of personnel on 5 January 1954. This paper, according to the [ ] chief, was to be utilized to brief the training chief for PBSUCCESS before he left to begin training Castillo Armas' forces in Honduras on 10 January 1954. A cable from [ ] the following day requested 20 silencers (converters) for .22 caliber rifles. Headquarters sent the rifles. The [ ] chief also discussed the training plan with the agent SEEKFORD on 13 January 1954, indicating that he wanted Castillo Armas and the PBSUCCESS [ ] offices to train two assassins. In addition, he discussed these "assassination specialists" with Castillo Armas on 3 February 1954.

The idea of forming assassination teams ("K" groups) apparently originated with Castillo Armas in 1952. Adapting Castillo Armas' concept, the [ ] chief routinely included two assassination specialists in his training plans.

CIA planning for sabotage teams in early 1954 also included creating a "K" group trained to perform assassinations. The main mission of the sabotage teams or harassment teams, however, was to attack local Communists and Communist property and to avoid attacks on the army. A chart depicting the [ ] chief's plan for the CALLIGERIS (Castillo Armas) organization showed the "K" Group. It was distributed in various paramilitary planning packets as late as the spring of 1954. In a briefing for [ ] in June 1954, [ ] also mentioned that sabotage teams would assassinate known Communists once the invasion operation began.

Psychological Warfare

As in PBFORTUNE, an intensive psychological warfare program paralleled the planning for paramilitary action. Utilizing the anti-Communist network established by a Guatemalan dissident, the Chief of Political and Psychological Operations at LINCOLN developed a major propaganda campaign against the Arbenz government. Part of this program included the sending of new mourning cards to top Communist leaders. These cards mourned the imminent purge or execution of various Communists throughout the world and hinted of the forthcoming doom of the addressee. Death letters were also sent to top Guatemalan Communists such as [ ] Guatemala City Station, [ ] prepared these letters for the dissident leader. The "Nerve War Against Individuals," as it was called, also included sending wooden coffins, hangman's nooses, and phony bombs to selected individuals. Such slogans as "Here Lives a Spy" and "You have Only 5 Days" were painted on their houses.

Wanting to go beyond mere threats, the dissident leader suggested that the "violent disposal" of one of the top Guatemalan Communists would have a positive effect on the resistance movement and undermine Communist morale. The dissident leader's recommendations called for the formulation of a covert action group to perform violent, illegal acts against the government. LINCOLN cautioned the dissident leader, however, that such techniques were designed only to destroy a person's usefulness. By destroy "we do not mean to kill the man," LINCOLN cabled the dissident leader. Responding to the proposal that a top Communist leader be killed, [ ] Guatemala City told [ ] he could not recommend assassinating any "death letter" recipients at this time because it might touch off "wholesale reprisals." Reiterating that the plan was "to scare not kill" he nevertheless suggested that [ ] might wish to "study the suggestion for utility now or in the future."

While Agency paramilitary and psychological warfare planning both included suggestions which implied assassination proposals, these proposals appear never to have been implemented. The [ ] chief had sought to use Castillo Armas' "K" group scheme but there was no State Department or White House support. Such was also the case when the subject of assassination emerged in high-level Agency and inter-agency planning discussions.

Target Lists

A weekly PBSUCCESS meeting at Headquarters on 9 March 1954 considered the elimination of 15–20 of Guatemala's top leaders with "Trujillo's trained pistoleros." Those attending the meeting were [ ], DP Operations, along with State Department representatives [ ]. Addressing the group, [ ] while stating clearly that "such elimination was part of the plan and could be done," objected to the proposal at that time. [ ] however, expressed the view that "knocking off" the leaders might make it possible for the Army to take over."

Following this meeting, [ ] appears to be the Agency official who revived discussion of assassination as an option. On 25 March he broached the subject with [ ] who had just returned from the Organization of American States meeting in Caracas, Venezuela, that voted 17 to 1 to condemn communism in Guatemala. With [ ] and [ ] again present, [ ] asked [ ] if he had changed his thinking since the conference on the possible methods to get rid of the Arbenz government. [ ] replied that in his opinion "the elimination of those in high positions of the government would bring about its collapse." He then qualified his statement, according to [ ]'s bebo, by saying that perhaps "even a smaller number, say 20, would be sufficient."

Less than a week later, [ ] visited [ ] on 31 March. The records do not indicate why [ ] flew to [ ], but on that date the [ ] officers were asked to draw up an up-dated target list. Criteria for inclusion on the disposal list required that individuals be (1) high government and organizational leaders "irrevocably implicated in Communist doctrine and policy," (2) "out and out proven Communist leaders," or (3) those few individuals in key government and military positions of tactical importance "whose removal for psychological, organizational or other reasons is mandatory for the success of military action."

The [ ] chief took the new list with him when he consulted Castillo Armas on 7 April 1954. [ ] also borrowed a copy of the list on the same day. The [ ] chief and Castillo Armas apparently discussed the list and at least tentatively agreed that any assassination would take place during the actual invasion of Guatemala by Castillo Armas' forces. There was still no time date for the actual beginning of hostilities, however.

Agency contacts with conservative Guatemalan exile leader [ ] at the same time also produced an assassination list. [ ] provided a CIA cutout with a list of Communist leaders he would like to see executed. [ ] saw [ ] as a loose cannon, however. They did not want him to become involved in PBSUCCESS.

CIA received further Department of State encouragement for assassination plotting in April 1954. Fueling the fire for action, [ ], in a meeting with [ ] and another CIA officer, concluded that "more drastic and definitive stops to overthrow the government [in Guatemala] must be taken." In response to a question of whether Guatemalan [ ] was "salvageable," [ ] replied in the negative and suggested "he be eliminated."

On 16 May 1954 the [ ] Officer at [ ] proposed in a memorandum to [ ] the new Chief of [ ] and [ ] now serving as [ ] that assassination be incorporated into the psychological part of PBSUCCESS. The [ ] Officer laid out a specific assassination schedule leading up to D-Day, the actual invasion by Castillo Armas. He proposed a raid on [ ] on D12. This was to be a show of force, no one was to be harmed and the attack was to take place when [ ] was absent [ ]. The [ ] Officer, however, proposed the disposal of [ ], on D-10 as a means of paralyzing the [ ]. The [ ] Officer suggested that [ ] be killed on D-8. This would, according to the [ ] Officer, eliminate the [ ] character of the Arbenz regime. The [ ] Officer called for the disposal on D-6 of [ ] in the Guatemalan Communist Party (PGT) [ ]. This would leave Guatemala's [ ] believed. On D-4 [ ] would be eliminated. [ ] was to be eliminated so that the rebel forces would not have to worry about him or deal with him after the Victory. The [ ] Officer considered the possibility of reprisals as a weakness in his scheme, but decided that "such actions were expected anyway." The [ ] Officer argued that his proposal, if adopted, would not only be physically impressive but psychologically significant by providing a show of strength for the opposition. It would also "soften-up" the enemy. He added his first three suggestions had the previous approval of [ ].

On 21 May [ ] asked Headquarters for permission to implement the Officer's proposal and asked for suggestions about the specific individuals to be targeted. No reply from Headquarters to [ ] has been found. On 29 May 1954, however, the [ ] chief requested the names of the "four men" he and the [ ] Officer discussed assassinating. More than likely, the [ ] chief wanted to take up the issue again with Castillo Armas. Again, no cable reply from Headquarters or [ ] has been found. At the same time, [ ] continued compiling information on [ ] and lists of home addresses for individuals named on the "disposal list" drafted in April. [ ] believed [ ] was a "worthy target."

Meanwhile, [ ] traveled to Washington and submitted a proposal on 1 June 1954 that suggested that as an alternative approach to the paramilitary action program "specific sabotage and possibly political assassination should be carefully worked out and effected." [ ] took up [ ]'s suggestion in discussions with [ ] on 1 and 2 June. According to [ ] considered the proposal and then ruled it out, "at least for the immediate future," on the ground that it would prove counter-productive. [ ] wanted more specific plans concerning the individual targets, timing, and statement of purpose. Both [ ] and [ ] agreed that the advantages gained by this type of activity needed to be clearly spelled out. This appears to be the end of serious planning in Washington for the inclusion of selective assassination proposals in PBSUCCESS. Returning from Washington to [ ], on 2 June 1954, [ ] however, reported to his staff that the consensus in Washington was that "Arbenz must go; how does not matter."

The Paramilitary Operation

On 16 June 1954 Castillo Armas' CIA-supported force of armed exiles entered Guatemala. While these forces advanced tentatively in the hinterland, [ ] Guatemala City on 16 and 17 June met with a leading Guatemalan military commander, in the hopes of convincing him to lead a coup against Arbenz. In these discussions, the military commander hinted he would like to see [ ] killed. The [ ], frustrated by the continued inaction of the Guatemalan military commander, told him that if he wanted them killed he should do it himself. Despite the Guatemalan military commander's vacillation, a [ ] cable indicated that he remained convinced that [ ] had to be eliminated.

With the Guatemala Army's position uncertain and the outcome still in doubt, a few days later, the [ ] chief, in [ ], requested permission to bomb the [ ] and [ ]. LINCOLN responded on 22 June that it did not want to waste air strikes on [ ] or [ ] while a battle was raging at Zacapa. The [ ] and [ ] also supported the [ ] chief's request to bomb [ ] with a dramatic cable which ended "Bomb Repeat Bomb." LINCOLN and Headquarters held fast and [ ] was never bombed. "We do not take action with grave foreign policy implications except as agent for the policy makers," Dulles cabled LINCOLN.

President Arbenz, on 27 June 1954, in a bitterly anti-American speech, resigned his office and sought asylum in the Mexican embassy in Guatemala City. [ ]. After Castillo Armas assumed the presidency, however, Arbenz was allowed to leave the country for Mexico, which granted him political asylum. In addition, 120 other Arbenz government officials or Communists departed Guatemala under a safe passage agreement with the Castillo Armas government. There is no evidence that any Guatemalans were executed.

CONCLUSION

CIA officers responsible for planning and implementing covert action against the Arbenz government engaged in extensive discussions over a two-and-a-half year period about the possibility of assassinating Guatemalan officials [ ]. Consideration of using assassination to [ ] purge Guatemala of Communist influence was born of the extreme international tensions in the early Cold War years. The Agency did not act unilaterally, but consulted with State Department officials with responsibility for policy toward Latin America. In the end, no assassinations of Guatemalan officials were carried out, according to all available evidence.

Proposals for assassination pervaded both PBFORTUNE and PBSUCCESS, rather than being confined to an early stage of these programs. Even before official approval of PBFORTUNE, CIA officers compiled elimination lists and discussed the concept of assassination with Guatemalan opposition leaders. Until the day that Arbenz resigned in June 1954 the option of assassination was still being considered.

Discussions of assassination reached a high level within the Agency. Among those involved were [ ]. [ ] is known to have been present at one meeting where the subject of assassination came up. It is likely that [ ] was also aware in general terms that assassination was under discussion. Beyond planning, some actual preparations were made. Some assassins were selected, training began, and tentative "hit lists" were drawn up.

Yet no covert action plan involving assassinations of Guatemalans was ever approved or implemented. The official objective of PBSUCCESS was to remove the Guatemalan government covertly "without bloodshed if possible." Elimination lists were never finalized, assassination proposals remained controversial within the Agency, and it appears that no Guatemalans associated with Arbenz were assassinated. Both CIA and State Department officers were divided (and undecided) about using assassination.

Discussion of whether to assassinate Guatemalan Communists and leaders sympathetic to Communist programs took place in a historical era quite different from the present. Soviet Communism had earned a reputation of using whatever means were expedient to advance Moscow's interests internationally. Considering Moscow's machinations in Eastern Europe, role in the Korean War, sponsorship of subversion through Communist surrogates in the Third World, and espousal of an ideology that seemed to have global hegemony as the ultimate objective, American officials and the American public alike regarded foreign Communist Parties as Soviet pawns and as threatening to vital US security interests.

Cold War realities and perceptions conditioned American attitudes toward what political weapons were legitimate to use in the struggle against Communism. It would be over two decades after the events in Guatemala before DCI William Colby prohibited any CIA involvement in assassination and a subsequent Executive Order banned any US government involvement in assassination.

Speech at the Opening of the Bandung Conference

By Sukarno

Sukarno (1901–1970) many Indonesians use only one name) was the most prominent leader of the nationalist movement against Dutch rule in the East Indies. He became the first president of Indonesia after independence. As the Cold War spread into the developing world of newly independent nations, Sukarno refused to be part of a bi-polar world dived between the Americans and the Soviets. In 1955 he hosted the Bandung Conference to create the Non-Aligned Movement. He argued that Cold War politics were a new form of colonialism.

President Sukarno of Indonesia: Speech at the Opening of the Bandung Conference, April 18 1955;—This twentieth century has been a period of terrific dynamism. Perhaps the last fifty years have seen more developments and more material progress than the previous five hundred years. Man has learned to control many of the scourges which once threatened him.

He has learned to consume distance. He has learned to project his voice and his picture across oceans and continents. He has probed deep into the secrets of nature and learned how to make the desert bloom and the plants of the earth increase their bounty. He has learned how to release the immense forces locked in the smallest particles of matter. But has man's political skill marched hand-in-hand with his technical and scientific skill? Man can chain lightning to his command—can he control the society in which be lives? The answer is No! The political skill of man has been far outstripped by technical skill, and what lie has made he cannot be sure of controlling.

The result of this is fear. And man gasps for safety and morality.

Sukarno, "Sukarno's speech at the Bandung Conference, 1955," *Africa-Asia Speaks from Bandong*, pp. 19-29. Copyright © 1955 by Ministry of Foreign Affairs of the Republic of Indonesia. Reprinted with permission.

Perhaps now more than at any other moment in the history of the world, society, government and statesmanship need to be based upon the highest code of morality and ethics. And in political terms, what is the highest code of morality? It is the subordination of everything to the well-being of mankind. But today we are faced with a situation where the well-being of mankind is not always the primary consideration. Many who are in places of high power think, rather, of controlling the world.

Yes, we are living in a world of fear. The life of man today is corroded and made bitter by fear. Fear of the future, fear of the hydrogen bomb, fear of ideologies. Perhaps this fear is a greater danger than the danger itself, because it is fear which drives men to act foolishly, to act thoughtlessly, to act dangerously. …

All of us, I am certain, are united by more important things than those which superficially divide us. We are united, for instance, by a common detestation of colonialism in whatever form it appears. We are united by a common detestation of racialism. And we are united by a common determination to preserve and stabilise peace in the world. …

We are often told "Colonialism is dead." Let us not be deceived or even soothed by that. 1 say to you, colonialism is not yet dead. How can we say it is dead, so long as vast areas of Asia and Africa are unfree.

And, I beg of you, do not think of colonialism only in the classic form which we of Indonesia, and our brothers in different parts of Asia and Africa, knew. Colonialism has also its modern dress, in the form of economic control, intellectual control, actual physical control by a small but alien community within a nation. It is a skilful and determined enemy, and it appears in many guises. It does not give up its loot easily. Wherever, whenever and however it appears, colonialism is an evil thing, and one which must be eradicated from the earth. …

Not so very long ago we argued that peace was necessary for us because an outbreak of fighting in our part of the world would imperil our precious independence, so recently won at such great cost.

Today, the picture is more black. War would not only mean a threat to our independence, it may mean the end of civilisation and even of human life. There is a force loose in the world whose potentiality for evil no man truly knows. Even in practice and rehearsal for war the effects may well be building up into something of unknown horror.

Not so long ago it was possible to take some little comfort from the idea that the clash, if it came, could perhaps be settled by what were called "conventional weapons"—bombs, tanks, cannon and men. Today that little grain of comfort is denied us for it has been made clear that the weapons of ultimate horror will certainly be used, and the military planning of nations is on that basis. The unconventional has become the conventional, and who knows what other examples of misguided and diabolical scientific skill have been discovered as a plague on humanity.

And do not think that the oceans and the seas will protect us. The food that we eat, the water that we drink, yes, even the very air that we breathe can be contaminated by poisons originating from thousands of miles away. And it could be that, even if we ourselves escaped lightly, the unborn generations of our children would bear on their distorted bodies the marks of our failure to control the forces which have been released on the world.

No task is more urgent than that of preserving peace. Without peace our independence means little. The rehabilitation and upbuilding of our countries will have little meaning. Our revolutions will not be allowed to run their course. ...

What can we do? We can do much! We can inject the voice of reason into world affairs. We can mobilise all the spiritual, all the moral, all the political strength of Asia and Africa on the side of peace. Yes, we! We, the peoples of Asia and Africa, 1,400,000,000 strong, far more than half the human population of the world, we can mobilise what I have called the Moral Violence of Nations in favour of peace. We can demonstrate to the minority of the world which lives on the other continents that we, the majority are for peace, not for war, and that whatever strength we have will always be thrown on to the side of peace.

In this struggle, some success has already been scored. I think it is generally recognised that the activity of the Prime Ministers of the Sponsoring Countries which invited you here had a not unimportant role to play in ending the fighting in Indo-China.

Look, the peoples of Asia raised their voices, and the world listened. It was no small victory and no negligible precedent! The five Prime Ministers did not make threats. They issued no ultimatum, they mobilised no troops. Instead they consulted together, discussed the issues, pooled their ideas, added together their individual political skills and came forward with sound and reasoned suggestions which formed the basis for a settlement of the long struggle in Indo-China.

I have often since then asked myself why these five were successful when others, with long records of diplomacy, were unsuccessful, and, in fact, had allowed a bad situation to get worse, so that there was a danger of the conflict spreading. ... I think that the answer really lies in the fact that those five Prime Ministers brought a fresh approach to bear on the problem. They were not seeking advantage for their own countries. They had no axe of power-politics to grind. They had but one interest—how to end the fighting in such a way that the chances of continuing peace and stability were enhanced. ...

So, let this Asian-African Conference be a great success! Make the "Live and let live" principle and the "Unity in Diversity" motto the unifying force which brings us all together—to seek in friendly, uninhibited discussion, ways and means by which each of us can live his own life, and let others live their own lives, in their own way, in harmony, and in peace.

If we succeed in doing so, the effect of it for the freedom, independence and the welfare of man will be great on the world at large. The Light of Understanding has again been lit, the Pillar of Cooperation again erected. The likelihood of success of this Conference is proved already by the very presence of you all here today. It is for us to give it strength, to give it the power of inspiration—to spread its message all over the World.

U.S. Imperialism Is the Most Ferocious Enemy of the World's People

By Mao Zedong

This 1964 statement by Mao specifically condemns various American foreign policy moves as imperialism. While some might view it as hyperbole and propaganda, his heated rhetoric is supported by direct references to specific actions by the United States.

The heroic struggle now being waged by the people of Panama against U.S. aggression and in defence of their national sovereignty is a great patriotic struggle. The Chinese people stand firmly on the side of the Panamanian people and fully support their just action in opposing the U.S. aggressors and seeking to regain sovereignty over the Panama Canal Zone.

U.S. imperialism is the most ferocious enemy of the people of the entire world.

It has not only committed the grave crime of aggression against the Panamanian people, and painstakingly and stubbornly plotted against socialist Cuba, but has continuously been plundering and oppressing the people of the Latin American countries and suppressing the national-democratic revolutionary struggles there.

In Asia, U.S. imperialism has forcibly occupied China's Taiwan, turned the southern part of Korea and the southern part of Vietnam into its colonies, kept Japan under its control and semi-military occupation, sabotaged the peace, neutrality and independence of Laos, plotted to subvert the Royal Government of Cambodia, and committed intervention and aggression against other Asian countries. More recently, it has decided to send a U.S. fleet to the Indian Ocean, menacing the security of all the countries of South-east Asia.

Mao Tse-Tung, "Full Text of Comrade Mao's statement of 12 January, 1964 in support of the Panamanian people," Peking Review, no. 2. Copyright © 1964 by Foreign Languages Press.

In Africa, U.S. imperialism is feverishly pursuing its neocolonialist policies, seeking vigorously to take the place of the old colonialists, to plunder and enslave the peoples of Africa, and to undermine and stamp out the national liberation movements.

The policies of aggression and war of U.S. imperialism also seriously threaten the Soviet Union, China, and the other socialist countries. Moreover, it is vigorously seeking to push its policy of 'peaceful evolution' in the socialist countries, in order to bring about the restoration of capitalism there and disintegrate the socialist camp.

Even toward its allies in Western Europe, North America, and Oceania, U.S. imperialism is pursuing a policy of the law of the jungle, trying hard to trample them underfoot.

The aggressive plans of U.S. imperialism to dominate the whole world run in a continuous line from Truman through Eisenhower and Kennedy to Johnson.

The people of the countries in the socialist camp should unite, the people of all the countries of Asia, Africa, and Latin America should unite, the people of all the continents of the world should unite, all peace-loving countries and all countries that are subject to U.S. aggression, control, interference and bullying should unite, and so form the broadest united front to oppose the U.S. imperialist policies of aggression and war and to safeguard world peace.

Riding roughshod everywhere, U.S. imperialism has placed itself in the position of the enemy of the people the world over, and has increasingly isolated itself. The atom bombs and hydrogen bombs in the hands of the U.S. imperialists can never cow people not willing to be enslaved. The raging tide of the people of the world in opposition to the U.S. aggressors is irresistible. The struggle of the people the world over against U.S. imperialism and its running dogs will assuredly win still greater victories.

The (First) Declaration of Havana, 1960

By Fidel Castro

Fidel Castro (1926–) came to power in Cuba in 1959 at head of a broad based and popular revolution against the brutal dictator Batista. After the revolution he created a Communist state. He quickly became the most prominent critics of American intervention in Latin America, condemning the United States as an imperialist power in the region.

Close to the monument and to the memory of José Martí in Cuba, free territory of America, the people, in the full exercise of the inalienable powers that proceed from the true exercise of the sovereignty expressed in the direct, universal and public suffrage, has constituted itself into a National General Assembly.

Acting on its own behalf and echoing the true sentiments of the people of our America, the National General Assembly of the People of Cuba:

1. Condemns in all its terms the so-called **"Declaration of San José,"** a document dictated by North American imperialism that is detrimental to the national self-determination, the sovereignty and the dignity of the sister nations of the Continent.

2. The National General Assembly of the People of Cuba energetically condemns the overt and criminal intervention exerted by North American imperialism for more than a century over all the nations of Latin America, which have seen their lands invaded more than once in Mexico, Nicaragua, Haiti, Santo Domingo and Cuba; have lost, through the voracity of Yankee imperialism, huge and rich areas, whole countries, such as Puerto Rico, which has been converted into an occupied territory; and have suffered, moreover, the outrageous treatment dealt by the Marines to our wives and daughters, as well as to the most exalted symbols of our history, such as the statue of José Martí.

Fidel Castro, "The Declaration of Havana."

This intervention, based upon military superiority, inequitable treaties and the miserable submission of treacherous rulers throughout one hundred years has converted our America—the America that Bolivar, Hidalgo, Juarez, San Martin, O'Higgens, Sucre and Martí wanted free—into an area of exploitation, the backyard of the political and financial Yankee empire, a reserve of votes for the international organization in which the Latin America countries have figured only as the herds driven by the "restless and brutal North that despises us."

The National General Assembly of the People declares that the acceptance by the governments that officially represent the countries of Latin America of that continued and historically irrefutable intervention betrays the ideals of independence of its peoples, negates its sovereignty and prevents true solidarity among our nations, all of which obliges this assembly to repudiate it in the name of the people of Cuba with a voice that echoes the hope and determination of the Latin American people and liberating accent of immortal patriots of our America.

3. The National General Assembly of the People of Cuba rejects likewise the intention of preserving the Monroe Doctrine, used until now , as forseen [sic] by José Martí, "to extend the dominance in America" of the voracious imperialists, to better inject the poison also denounced in his time by José Martí, "the poison of the loans, the canals, the railroads…" Therefore, in the presents of the hypocritical Pan-Americanism which is only the dominance of Yankee monopolies over the interests of people and Yankee manipulation of governments prostrated before Washington, the Assembly of the People of Cuba proclaims the liberating Latin-Americanism that throbs in Martí and Benito Juarez. And, upon extending its friendship to the North American people—a country where Negroes are lynched, intellectuals are persecuted and workers are forced to accept the leadership of gangsters—reaffirms its will to march "with all the worlds and not with just a part of it."

4. The National General Assembly of the People declares that the help spontaneously offered by the Soviet Union to Cuba in the event our country is attacked by the military forces of the imperialists could never be considered as an act of intrusion, but that it constitutes an evident act of solidarity, and that such help, offered to Cuba in the face of an imminent attack by the Pentagon, honors the Government of the Soviet Union that offered it, as much as the cowardly and criminal aggressions against Cuba dishonor the Government of the United States.

Nixon and Kissinger Escalate the Bombing of Cambodia (Declassified Transcripts of Telephone Conversations)

By Nixon and Kissinger

President Richard Milhous Nixon (1913–1994) and Secretary of State Henry Alfred Kissinger (1923–) were inheritors of the policy of Containment. They also subscribed to the Domino Theory, which simplistically argued that Communism would spread from country to country like dominos knocking each other over. The logic of Containment drew the United States into the civil war in Vietnam and the Vietnamese supply line through Cambodia seemed to confirm the Domino Theory. To break the supply line, the famous Ho Chi Minh Trail, Nixon and Kissinger secretly and illegally bombed neutral Cambodia causing mass devastation to the Cambodian civilian population but failing to break the trail. Ironically, the bombing did increase Cambodian support for the Khmer Rouge, the local Communist insurgency against the US-backed regime.

Mr. Kissinger/The President (tape)
December 9, 1970 8:45 p.m.
jlj

    K: Mr. President

    P: The thing that concerns me about this thing you sent over on Cambodia was Moorer's, it seems to me, lame excuse that they did not have any intelligence because the weather has been bad. I don't think they are trying to do a good enough job in trying to get the intelligence over there. You understand what I mean?

    K: Yes I do.

    P: There are other methods of getting intelligence than simply flying. They've got the methods of the Cambodians to talk to and a hell of a lot of other people

Richard Milhous Nixon and Henry Alfred Kissinger, "Nixon and Kissinger Escalate the Bombing of Cambodia, Dec. 9, 1970 (declassified transcripts of telephone conversations): Document 1: Nixon and Kissinger."

and I don't think they have done enough there. The second thing is as I have put on here now I want you to get ahold of Moorer tonight and I want a plan where every goddamn thing that can fly goes into Cambodia and hits every target that is open.

K: Right

P: That's to be done tomorrow. Tomorrow. Is that clear?

K: That is right.

P: I want this done. Now that is one thing that can turn this around some. They are running these goddamn milk runs in order to get the air medal. You know what they are doing Henry. It's horrible what the Air Force is doing. They aren't doing anything at all worth a damn.

K: They are not imaginative.

P: Well, their not only not imaginative but they are just running these things—bombing jungles. You know that. They have got to go in there and I mean really go in. I don't want the gunships, I want the helicopter ships. I want everything that can fly to go in there and crack the hell out of them. There is no limitation on mileage and there is no limitation on budget. Is that clear?

K: Right, Mr. President.

P: Now that he's got to understand. Now the second thing on this drill and I want you to tell both Bill and Mel that this is what I have decided to do. We will go forward on it on the basis, and we will do it—we're not going to do it on the basis of an open end commitment but on the basis that you are going to fly in supplies—airlift supplies to a place and so you airlift a hell of a lot of troops with it too. Now there must be absolute security on it. It should be supplies. In other words the troops go in with their supplies—so what? The South Vietnamese have to—the troops have to unload them don't they?

K: Right.

P: And I think that should be …

K: No, that is a very ingeneous formula.

P: The point is that Bill understands that. We have been airlifting supplies into Phnom Penh haven't we?

K: Yes. No, Bill actually—That's right—Bill made that point and actually …

P: Airlifting supplies to me is the thing. We are airlifting supplies and sure there are some troops but I don't want any numbers out. I don't want anything like that. I don't want any plan out and I don't want the air force bragging about it and I don't want a goddamn thing said.

K: Well, Mr. President. Actually with this airlift we don't have to do anything for 48 hours on the troops. They have to go ahead—the whole thing wasn't really planned to go before the 11th or 12th.

P: All right.

K: They just felt that if there was no chance of it going we shouldn't get the Vietnamese all cranked up.

P: Get 'em ready. Get 'em ready and do it. And I think the main thing is if the Vietnamese are ready to go in there and they think they are going to have—Can they give them a real bloody nose and …

K: That's what they think and that's what Abrams seems to think.

P: If Abrams strongly recommends it we will do it.

K: Right.

P: We will take the heat on it. I'll do it, but it is on the basis of the airlift thing and that's all and they have got to remember that there is absolute security on this, having in mind that we have a situation here which is political, which is going to be with us until about the 23rd and then that is over. Then we either have the damn supplemental or we don't have it.

K: Exactly.

P: So we don't want them to screw that up. And if they can delay it a week then fine but the point is that I see no objection to it if it doesn't screw up the supplemental. We've got to do the things that are necessary to see that this doesn't … But there is absolutely—they are not even"to submit to me any plan that requires the use of American ground forces. Under any circumstances whatever!!!! Is that clear?

K: Absolutely, Right.

P: It is not going to be done.

K: No, there is no …

P: And I am not going to keep it open at the press conference. There is not going to be done. It isn't what we want to do at this point. Don't expect to have to answer it but if I do I am not going to keep anything open. I am simply going to say that we don't have any such plans.

K: Well that …

P: Don't even—Understand. It isn't the question we can't play these Mickey Mouse games right now. We have got …

K: No, No. I agree with it!

P: We have got to get down to the real thing that matters and the thing that matters is not to have a big debate about whether—If we don't get this supplemental through—See we have got to make a commitment on that Henry or there is no chance on the supplemental. You don't understand what it means unless we make an absolute commitment that no American ground forces are going to be used in Cambodia you will never get the supplemental. That's why …

K: I have no problem with that.

P: That's the problem. Well, I have left it open up to this point, but I can't now because the supplemental's up there, see? So we will nail it and say the purpose of the supplemental is only to help the Cambodians defend themselves.

K: Right.

P: That's all.

K: No, I was certain that we were not going to use any American ground forces …

P: I know. We have always been certain of that but we were keeping it open in order to keep the enemy off balance over it. But right now we have another enemy here to fight. And that is a group of legislators who will not support us unless they have an absolute commitment.

K: Well, your instinct on those things has always been right.

P: We have to do what is necessary to go it and it is a long shot and that's the way it is. The point of the matter is—oh Goddammit Abrams can do more and that damned Air Force can do more about hitting Cambodia with their bombing attacks. There is something wrong here. I don't know what it is.

K: I'll get that laid on.

P: What the hell are they doing?

K: I'll get that laid on immediately.

P: The whole goddamn Air Force over there farting around doing nothing and I have watched that stuff and they aren't doing a thing. I mean they get one or two trucks a day and fly 800 sorties and get 1500 air medals. You know that's all it is. It's awful.

K: Yep, Yep.

P: It is a disgraceful performance and they are going to get off their ass and start doing something on it. I want gunships in there. That means armed helicopters, DC-3s, anything else that will destroy personnel that can fly. I want it done!! Get them off their ass and get them to work now.

K: Well we will get it done immediately Mr. President.

P: What is needed here is they need a little drive out there. I don't know what the hell is the matter with them. What are they doing?

K: The problem Mr. President …

P: You know we talk about this Cambodia thing and I am not going to have another crisis on Cambodia hit us in the face like it did last year. That again was a case of them not being on top of things. By God we are not going to let this happen this time.

K: The problem is Mr. President the Air Force is designed to fight an air battle again the Soviet Union. They are not designed for this war and that is the—in fact they are not designed for any war we are likely to have to fight.

P: That's right. There isn't going to be any air battle against the Soviet Union as you well know.

K: Exactly, I agree completely.

P: The difficulty is that they need some TBFs and a hell of a lot of SBDs and things like that could go in and knock the hell out of them. Bazookas—anything. That's what they need. A world war II Air Force would definitely make the North Vietnamese …

K: That is unfortunately true.

P: And we do not have a World War II Air Force.

K: That is unfortunately …

P: And they should be told this. Now goddamit maybe they have some stuff over here than can do that. I want that examined tomorrow and I mean on an urgency basis. I am disappointed in the fact that their jets and the rest—and get those goddamned jet pilots the hell over to Taiwan and get somebody else out there that can fight them. You understand?

K: Of course and I will move on that immediately.

P: Look. Get some conventional prop airplanes over there fast. And those prop airplanes whatever they are. We've got a lot of prop airplanes left. I have seen them on the runways. The National Guard's got them. I want them to give me a report by tomorrow—not tomorrow but Saturday morning every prop plane that could be made air worthy for the purpose of fighting the kind of battle we need to fight there. I want the goddamn planes over there. You understand?

K: I will get that report …

P: Get it out of there. Get it out of the Air National Guard and everything else. Shake up this air force and tell them exactly that I have reached the conclusion that they are designed to fight only the Soviets and they are not doing worth a damn here and it's time we are going to start doing different.

K: I will get that report for you by first thing Saturday.

P: But tomorrow …

K: And I will get the bombing campaign laid on for tomorrow.

P: I want them to hit everything. I want them to use the big planes, the small planes, everything/that will help out here and let's start giving them a little shock. There must be something we can do. Let L. Abrams, he's to take personal charge and dismiss the Air Force commander if necessary over there. And I want Haig to look into this when he is over there.

K: Absolutely.

P: We have got to do a better job because we are just coming to the crunch. Right now there is a chance to win this goddamn war and that's probably what we are going to have to do because we are not going to do anything at the conference table. But we aren't going to win it with the people—the kind of assholes come in here like today saying well now there is a crisis in Cambodia. Hell, I have been asking about it for the last two weeks you know and you said no there isn't one.

K: Well, because …

P: So we learn it today, right?

K: That's what they told me. I asked them every day. I sent back channels for three months. I have been bugging them about that column that is now being attacked. And so has Haig, Mr. President, On Houdek, I think the best answer to give is I am satisfied that the relevant information was not given to the White House and I have set up procedures that this cannot happen again. Because the relevant information was not given to the White House.

P: The relevant information was not given. Okay, I will just say that. The relevant information was not given to the White House. And I am satisfied.

K: I am satisfied that the relevant information was not given to the White House and I have ordered—set up procedures—that this cannot happen again. And that is exactly the fact, as it is.

P: You can't blame him. I don't blame Houdek at all. You don't fire a person . .

K: Hell, he didn't even understand what he was being told.

P: He just tried to piss off on us and he ought to take the responsibility himself.

K: They shouldn't have put it in their report. That was outrageous.

P: Well, why don't we put something—as I say, the report should be hitting them for what they did on … let me ask you this. Have we ordered a court marshall?

K: Volpe promised us a report tonight or tomorrow morning.

P: Is there going to be one, or not?

K: He said he was moving towards a court marshall. But I will get you a report on that …

P: I don't want to have a long report Henry. I don't want … one sentence.

K: Yes or no? That's right.

P: Is there going to be one, or not. If there is one then I can, after all, defer all questions. I have to. If there is not going to be one, then I'll have to go into some detail on the damn thing. I want a court marshall. I think the Commandant up there should be court marshalled. Let's find out what the hell he did.

K: You will have the answer on that by noon.

P: That's right. Just say there is, or there isn't. And no fooling around. But let me tell you on this business on Cambodia—I want something done tonight. I don't want any screwing around and I want that Air Force to make its study immediately of anything in conventional World War II type craft that can be used over there. I am disappointed in what they have been doing. I want a new plan. I want it fast and let's get going. Also, the program for the South Vietnamese to make the ground attack is laid on, it's approved as of today. Have it go the first time it gets dry enough to go. Now get going on these things and don't let them delay so long. I think that the trouble is we are so busy over here—we got so many things. We worry about the Chilean elections and we worry about whether or not there is going to be a vote on Guinea and all that bull and the only thing that really matters at this point is this and I just want everybody to clear their minds of all this other crap. Let the State Department handle that. I don't give a goddamn what happens in those other places now—there is nothing we can do about it anyway. But this does matter and I just think that we have made a mistake here. We haven't put enough emphasis on it and let's start putting the emphasis in there where it matters.

K: Exactly.

P: Forget all that other crap.

K: Right. And I will get after Moorer this minute.

P: And those are the only reports I want to see from now on. For the next two months I don't want to see anything about Chile, I don't want to see anything about Biafra. I don't want to see anything about Guinea. I don't want to see anything about all the other crap. Doesn't make any difference right now. The Pakistan elections; there's not a goddamn thing we can do about any of those things. You understand?

K: Right.

P: Right now Henry we have got to concentrate on what can make or break us and none of those things will. And that's what we have got to … We've got to get more of a sense of direction here. A direction and urgency and priority or otherwise the whole thing will go down the drain. Some of these other things just don't matter.

K: Right.

P: They don't matter. You put it right to them. I really want some action now. Okay?

K: Right, Mr. President. I will get it done immediately.

Memorandum of Conversation Between Kissinger and Anaconda Copper Executives Regarding President Allende of Chile (Confidential)

In 1970, Salvador Allende (1908–1973) was elected president of Chile. A moderate Marxist, friend of Fidel Castro, and a member of the socialist party, his politics were a concern in Washington. His policies, like Arbenz in Guatemala, threatened American business interests, specifically Anaconda Copper. Nixon and Kissinger supported a faction of the military led by General Augusto Pinochet (1915–2006) that overthrew Allende in a violent coup d'etat. Allende died in the presidential palace and Pinochet ordered the arrest of thousands of socialists, communists, union members, students, and other activists. Many of those arrested were detained and tortured in two soccer stadiums in the capital, Santiago. Among those tortured and killed was Victor Jara, a popular folk singer. Pinochet remained in power until 1990, presiding over an oppressive but pro-business regime. The free market fundamentalist economist Milton Friedman and the University of Chicago maintained close ties to Pinochet despite his egregious human rights abuses

Dr. Henry Kissinger, "Chile," Memorandum of Conversation with Anaconda Copper Executives, 17 August 1971, White House, memoranda and letters attached, Confidential.

David Rockefeller to Dr. Henry Kissinger, The White House
Washington, D. C., August 10, 1971 (On Chase Manhattan stationery)

Dr. Henry Kissinger
The White House
Washington, D. C.

Dear Henry:

As you may know, John Place, who was Vice Chairman of the Chase Manhattan Bank, left us a couple of months ago to become President and Chief Executive Officer of the Anaconda Company. I need not tell you that the assignment he took on is not an easy one. Nevertheless, John is a very able citizen, and does not shrink from a challenge. If anyone can handle the job, I am sure he can.

John tells me that the situation in Chile appears to be deteriorating and that there are now rumors that the government is talking of defaulting on and payment to Anaconda for the 51% they expropriated only a year or two ago. Up until now, these payments at least have been coming in although there has been no settlement on the remaining 49% which they have now expropriated as well. John would very much appreciate having an opportunity to discuss this situation with you so that you might have a full understanding of Anaconda's position and the background of the negotiations. He would be happy to go to Washington any time you could arrange to see him, and will be in touch with your office to find out when you might be able to make an appointment. Both he and I would be grateful if you could take the time to meet with him at your convenience.

I am in Seal Harbor on vacation which I must say I am thoroughly enjoying. I wish you could get up. Best regards.
Sincerely,

David Rockefeller

National Security Confidential Memorandum, August 17, 1971

Memorandum of Conversation with Anaconda Copper Executives

PARTICIPANTS: John Place, President of Anaconda Company William. Quigley, Vice Chairman of the Board of the Anaconda Company Henry A. Kissinger, Assistant to the President for National Security Affairs Arnold Nachmanoff, National Security Council Staff

SUBJECT: Chile

Held August 17, 1971 at 12:00 noon in Dr. Kissinger's Office

Mr. Place and Mr. Quigley expressed concern over the deteriorating situation in Chile. They noted that the radical left within the UP coalition was gaining power and restricting Allende's maneuverability. They also commented that President Allende apparently does not believe that the US intends to do anything drastic if he doesn't reach fair settlements with the copper companies. Mr. Quigley suggested that the US might send an envoy, perhaps someone like Robert Anderson or Tom Mann to indicate that we are aware that the GOC's procedures will not not result in fair compensation, and to reiterate our position that if they do not reach fair settlements, we will make every effort to cut off their access to international credit, but if they do reach fair settlements, and live up to their international obligations, we would be willing to have normal relations.

Dr. Kissinger asked what they meant by normal relations. Mr. Quigley replied that this meant that we would not object to Export-Import Bank loans on a justifiable commercial basis, or World Bank and IDB lending for legitimate projects.

Dr. Kissinger suggested that this meant in other words that the US would finance the compensation for the companies. Mr. Place and Mr. Quigley objected, and indicated they would not want to put it in that light since it would set a bad precedent.

Dr. Kissinger stated that we are, of course, interested in seeing Anaconda receive fair compensation and that we will take a strong stand on this question. However, he suggested that if we agree to open up international credits, we may just be speeding up the process of establishing a communist regime in Chile, and that in the end Allende might still find a way out of paying compensation. He indicated that Ambassador Korry had been authorized to explore this possibility in a non-committal way, and that we would look carefully at any concrete proposals he submits. He noted that this was a very difficult problem: we cannot buy Allende off, and in any event, the balance of forces in Chile would not permit that any way. He noted that it seemed improbable to him that Allende would be a normal debtor.

Mr. Place expressed his approval of Henry Kearns' position on the Boeing loan. He suggested that we should take a tough line and not "give away" the planes.

Dr. Kissinger noted that there is a real question of whether we should keep the pressures on Allende now, while there is still a chance that Allende might be overthrown before he consolidates his position, or whether we should go slow and avoid a confrontation. There is some question about whether the latter course does not serve Allende's purposes rather than ours. He noted that he favored a tough line. Mr. Place and Mr. Quigley reiterated their approval of a tough line.

Mr. Nachmanoff suggested that there might be some misunderstanding of the term "tough line." Mr. Place and Mr. Quigley apparently meant that the US should keep the economic pressures on Chile until compensation was paid, but that credits might be opened up after that. He noted that another interpretation of "tough line" was that we should not open up credits at all in order to maximize the pressure on Allende.

Dr. Kissinger stated that he leaned toward the position that we not open up credits no matter what Allende does with regard to Anaconda. Mr. Place said he could understand that position but thought that if Allende agrees to reasonable settlements with the copper companies, we might be willing to see certain commercial transactions by say the European banks and the World Bank. Mr. Place suggested that perhaps there was still some possibility that Allende would not inevitably consolidate a communist regime in Chile. Mr. Quigley commented that the only hope for democratic elections is closer cooperation between the PDC and the Nationalist Party. He suggested that the US Government might promote a more unified approach by the two parties. Dr. Kissinger assured them that we would give careful consideration to their proposal.

Personal Letter from Kissinger to Rockefeller, September 2, 1971

Dear David:

Thank you for your letter of August 10 suggesting that I meet with John Place of Anaconda. I met with him and one of his colleagues Tuesday, August 17, and appreciated the opportunity to hear their views. We will do whatever we can to help Anaconda receive fair compensation for its properties, though as Mr. Place recognizes, this is a very difficult problem in which broader U.S. Government interests are involved.

I hope you have had a pleasant vacation. I will look forward to seeing you before long.

Warm regards,

Henry

U.S. Embassy Jakarta Telegram 1579 to Secretary State, December 6, 1975 (Text of Ford-Kissinger-Suharto Discussion)

In 1965, President Sukarno was losing control over Indonesia. Despite his nationalist speeches and his aggressive foreign policy, the nation's economy was failing. As the Indonesian Communist Party (PKI) grew in power and membership, Sukarno began to openly support it. Meanwhile, a clique of American trained Indonesian generals formed an anti-communist conspiracy. With CIA support, they overthrew Sukarno and installed General Suharto (1921–2008) as the new president. As part of Sukarno's fall, Suharto purged the nation of communism. He encouraged popular attacks on the PKI that quickly escalated into mass murder. Soon, regiments from the Indonesian army began to move across the islands of Java and Bali, killing thousands of PKI members and supporters. In the space of a year, between five hundred thousand and one million people were murdered. Debate continues as to whether or not this politicide should be considered as genocide. With the PKI gone, Suharto became a staunch American ally. Arguing that there was a communist threat in the newly independent East Timor, Suharto received President Ford (1913–2006) and Kissinger's support to invade on December 7, 1975.

"U.S. Embassy Jakarta Telegram 1579 to Secretary State, December 6, 1975 (Text of Ford-Kissinger-Suharto Discussion)," Gerald R. Ford Library, Kissinger-Scowcroft Temporary Parallel File, Box A3, Country File, Far East-Indonesia, State Department Telegram.

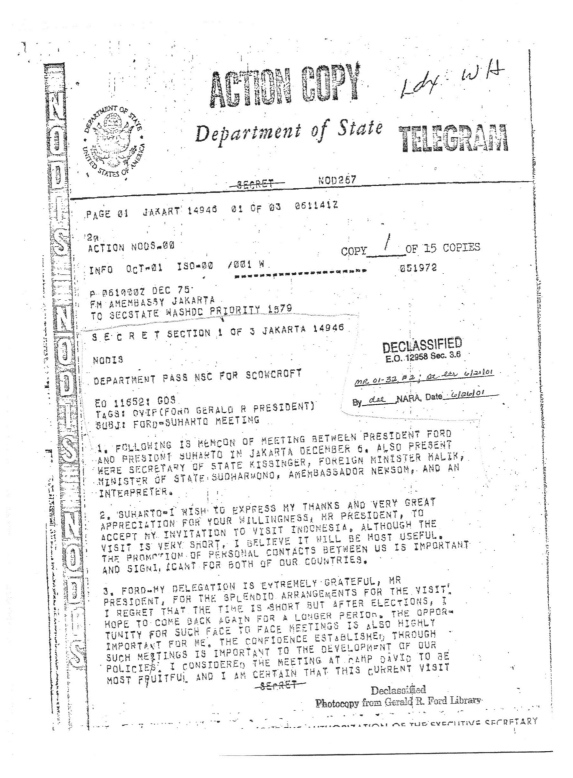

ACTION COPY

Department of State **TELEGRAM**

Ldr WH

~~SECRET~~   NOD267

PAGE 01   JAKART 14946   01 OF 03   061141Z

2a
ACTION NODS-00   COPY 1 OF 15 COPIES

INFO OCT-01 ISO-00 /001 W   051972

P 061920Z DEC 75
FM AMEMBASSY JAKARTA
TO SECSTATE WASHDC PRIORITY 1879

S E C R E T SECTION 1 OF 3 JAKARTA 14946

NODIS

DEPARTMENT PASS NSC FOR SCOWCROFT

DECLASSIFIED
E.O. 12958 Sec. 3.6

MR 01-32 #2; or ltr 6/21/01

By dee NARA, Date 6/26/01

EO 11652: GDS
TAGS: OVIP(FORD GERALD R PRESIDENT)
SUBJ: FORD-SUHARTO MEETING

1. FOLLOWING IS MEMCON OF MEETING BETWEEN PRESIDENT FORD
AND PRESIDENT SUHARTO IN JAKARTA DECEMBER 6. ALSO PRESENT
WERE SECRETARY OF STATE KISSINGER, FOREIGN MINISTER MALIK,
MINISTER OF STATE SUDHARMONO, AMEMBASSADOR NEWSOM, AND AN
INTERPRETER.

2. SUHARTO-I WISH TO EXPRESS MY THANKS AND VERY GREAT
APPRECIATION FOR YOUR WILLINGNESS, MR PRESIDENT, TO
ACCEPT MY INVITATION TO VISIT INDONESIA, ALTHOUGH THE
VISIT IS VERY SHORT, I BELIEVE IT WILL BE MOST USEFUL.
THE PROMOTION OF PERSONAL CONTACTS BETWEEN US IS IMPORTANT
AND SIGNIFICANT FOR BOTH OF OUR COUNTRIES.

3. FORD-MY DELEGATION IS EXTREMELY GRATEFUL, MR
PRESIDENT, FOR THE SPLENDID ARRANGEMENTS FOR THE VISIT.
I REGRET THAT THE TIME IS SHORT BUT AFTER ELECTIONS, I
HOPE TO COME BACK AGAIN FOR A LONGER PERIOD. THE OPPOR-
TUNITY FOR SUCH FACE TO FACE MEETINGS IS ALSO HIGHLY
IMPORTANT FOR ME. THE CONFIDENCE ESTABLISHED THROUGH
SUCH MEETINGS IS IMPORTANT TO THE DEVELOPMENT OF OUR
POLICIES. I CONSIDERED THE MEETING AT CAMP DAVID TO BE
MOST FRUITFUL AND I AM CERTAIN THAT THIS CURRENT VISIT

~~SECRET~~

Declassified
Photocopy from Gerald R. Ford Library

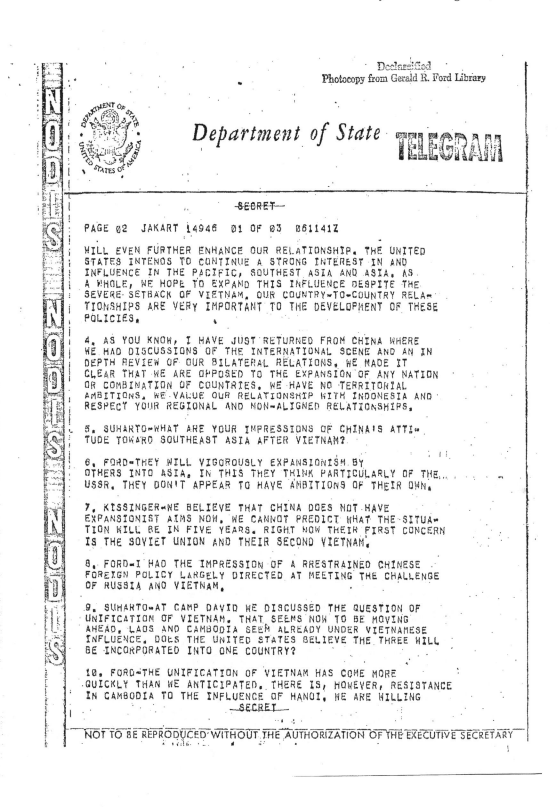

Declassified
Photocopy from Gerald R. Ford Library

Department of State TELEGRAM

SECRET

PAGE 02   JAKART 14946   01 OF 03   061141Z

WILL EVEN FURTHER ENHANCE OUR RELATIONSHIP. THE UNITED
STATES INTENDS TO CONTINUE A STRONG INTEREST IN AND
INFLUENCE IN THE PACIFIC, SOUTHEST ASIA AND ASIA. AS
A WHOLE, WE HOPE TO EXPAND THIS INFLUENCE DESPITE THE
SEVERE SETBACK OF VIETNAM. OUR COUNTRY-TO-COUNTRY RELA-
TIONSHIPS ARE VERY IMPORTANT TO THE DEVELOPMENT OF THESE
POLICIES.

4. AS YOU KNOW, I HAVE JUST RETURNED FROM CHINA WHERE
WE HAD DISCUSSIONS OF THE INTERNATIONAL SCENE AND AN IN
DEPTH REVIEW OF OUR BILATERAL RELATIONS. WE MADE IT
CLEAR THAT WE ARE OPPOSED TO THE EXPANSION OF ANY NATION
OR COMBINATION OF COUNTRIES. WE HAVE NO TERRITORIAL
AMBITIONS. WE VALUE OUR RELATIONSHIP WITH INDONESIA AND
RESPECT YOUR REGIONAL AND NON-ALIGNED RELATIONSHIPS.

5. SUHARTO-WHAT ARE YOUR IMPRESSIONS OF CHINA'S ATTI-
TUDE TOWARD SOUTHEAST ASIA AFTER VIETNAM?

6. FORD-THEY WILL VIGOROUSLY EXPANSIONISM BY
OTHERS INTO ASIA. IN THIS THEY THINK PARTICULARLY OF THE
USSR. THEY DON'T APPEAR TO HAVE AMBITIONS OF THEIR OWN.

7. KISSINGER-WE BELIEVE THAT CHINA DOES NOT HAVE
EXPANSIONIST AIMS NOW. WE CANNOT PREDICT WHAT THE SITUA-
TION WILL BE IN FIVE YEARS. RIGHT NOW THEIR FIRST CONCERN
IS THE SOVIET UNION AND THEIR SECOND VIETNAM.

8. FORD-I HAD THE IMPRESSION OF A RRESTRAINED CHINESE
FOREIGN POLICY LARGELY DIRECTED AT MEETING THE CHALLENGE
OF RUSSIA AND VIETNAM.

9. SUHARTO-AT CAMP DAVID WE DISCUSSED THE QUESTION OF
UNIFICATION OF VIETNAM. THAT SEEMS NOW TO BE MOVING
AHEAD. LAOS AND CAMBODIA SEEM ALREADY UNDER VIETNAMESE
INFLUENCE. DOES THE UNITED STATES BELIEVE THE THREE WILL
BE INCORPORATED INTO ONE COUNTRY?

10. FORD-THE UNIFICATION OF VIETNAM HAS COME MORE
QUICKLY THAN WE ANTICIPATED. THERE IS, HOWEVER, RESISTANCE
IN CAMBODIA TO THE INFLUENCE OF HANOI. WE ARE WILLING
SECRET

NOT TO BE REPRODUCED WITHOUT THE AUTHORIZATION OF THE EXECUTIVE SECRETARY

386 | Twentieth-Century World History

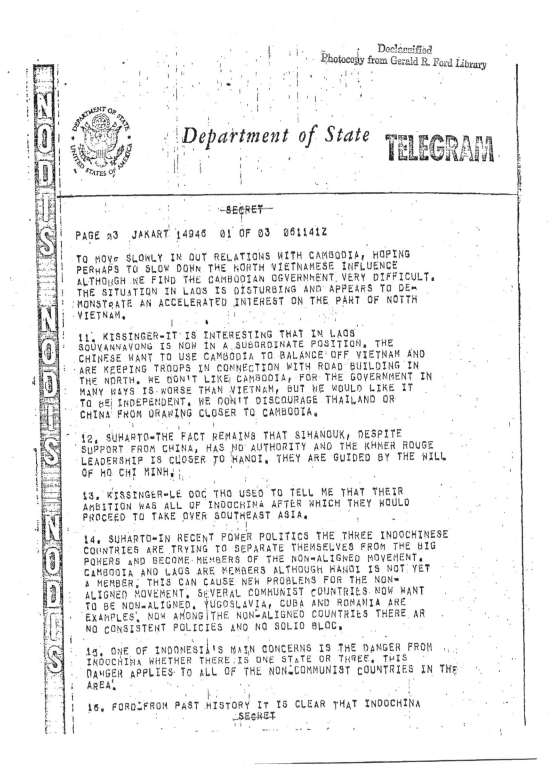

Department of State TELEGRAM

SECRET

PAGE 03 JAKART 14946 01 OF 03 061141Z

TO MOVE SLOWLY IN OUR RELATIONS WITH CAMBODIA, HOPING
PERHAPS TO SLOW DOWN THE NORTH VIETNAMESE INFLUENCE
ALTHOUGH WE FIND THE CAMBODIAN OGVERNMENT VERY DIFFICULT.
THE SITUATION IN LAOS IS DISTURBING AND APPEARS TO DE-
MONSTRATE AN ACCELERATED INTEREST ON THE PART OF NOTTH
VIETNAM.

11. KISSINGER-IT IS INTERESTING THAT IN LAOS
SOUVANNAVONG IS NOW IN A SUBORDINATE POSITION. THE
CHINESE WANT TO USE CAMBODIA TO BALANCE OFF VIETNAM AND
ARE KEEPING TROOPS IN CONNECTION WITH ROAD BUILDING IN
THE NORTH. WE DON'T LIKE CAMBODIA, FOR THE GOVERNMENT IN
MANY WAYS IS WORSE THAN VIETNAM, BUT WE WOULD LIKE IT
TO BE INDEPENDENT. WE DON'T DISCOURAGE THAILAND OR
CHINA FROM DRAWING CLOSER TO CAMBODIA.

12. SUHARTO-THE FACT REMAINS THAT SIHANOUK, DESPITE
SUPPORT FROM CHINA, HAS NO AUTHORITY AND THE KHMER ROUGE
LEADERSHIP IS CLOSER TO HANOI. THEY ARE GUIDED BY THE WILL
OF HO CHI MINH.

13. KISSINGER-LE DOC THO USED TO TELL ME THAT THEIR
AMBITION WAS ALL OF INDOCHINA AFTER WHICH THEY WOULD
PROCEED TO TAKE OVER SOUTHEAST ASIA.

14. SUHARTO-IN RECENT POWER POLITICS THE THREE INDOCHINESE
COUNTRIES ARE TRYING TO SEPARATE THEMSELVES FROM THE BIG
POWERS AND BECOME MEMBERS OF THE NON-ALIGNED MOVEMENT.
CAMBODIA AND LAOS ARE MEMBERS ALTHOUGH HANOI IS NOT YET
A MEMBER. THIS CAN CAUSE NEW PROBLEMS FOR THE NON-
ALIGNED MOVEMENT. SEVERAL COMMUNIST COUNTRIES NOW WANT
TO BE NON-ALIGNED. YUGOSLAVIA, CUBA AND ROMANIA ARE
EXAMPLES. NOW AMONG THE NON-ALIGNED COUNTRIES THERE AR
NO CONSISTENT POLICIES AND NO SOLID BLOC.

15. ONE OF INDONESIA'S MAIN CONCERNS IS THE DANGER FROM
INDOCHINA WHETHER THERE IS ONE STATE OR THREE. THIS
DANGER APPLIES TO ALL OF THE NON-COMMUNIST COUNTRIES IN THE
AREA.

16. FORD-FROM PAST HISTORY IT IS CLEAR THAT INDOCHINA

SECRET

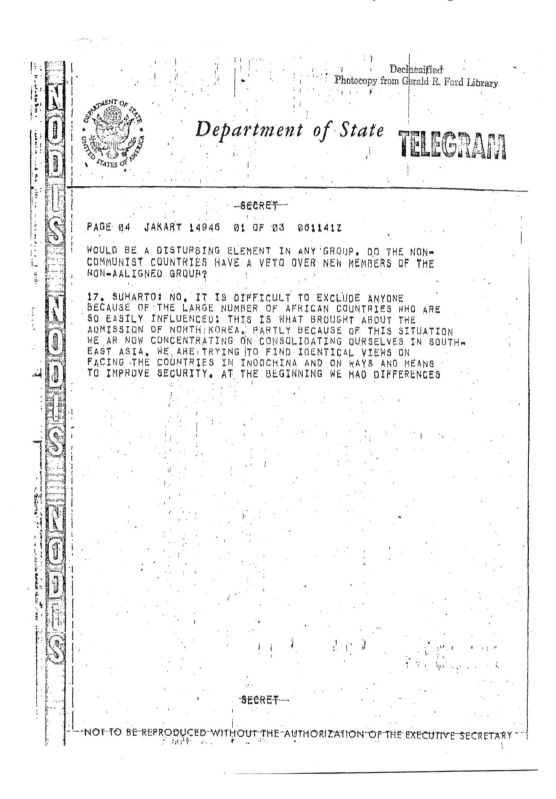

Declassified
Photocopy from Gerald R. Ford Library

Department of State TELEGRAM

—SECRET—

PAGE 04   JAKART 14946   01 OF 03   061141Z

WOULD BE A DISTURBING ELEMENT IN ANY GROUP. DO THE NON-
COMMUNIST COUNTRIES HAVE A VETO OVER NEW MEMBERS OF THE
NON-AALIGNED GROUP?

17. SUHARTO: NO. IT IS DIFFICULT TO EXCLUDE ANYONE
BECAUSE OF THE LARGE NUMBER OF AFRICAN COUNTRIES WHO ARE
SO EASILY INFLUENCED: THIS IS WHAT BROUGHT ABOUT THE
ADMISSION OF NORTH KOREA. PARTLY BECAUSE OF THIS SITUATION
WE AR NOW CONCENTRATING ON CONSOLIDATING OURSELVES IN SOUTH-
EAST ASIA. WE ARE TRYING TO FIND IDENTICAL VIEWS ON
FACING THE COUNTRIES IN INDOCHINA AND ON WAYS AND MEANS
TO IMPROVE SECURITY. AT THE BEGINNING WE HAD DIFFERENCES

—SECRET—

NOT TO BE REPRODUCED WITHOUT THE AUTHORIZATION OF THE EXECUTIVE SECRETARY

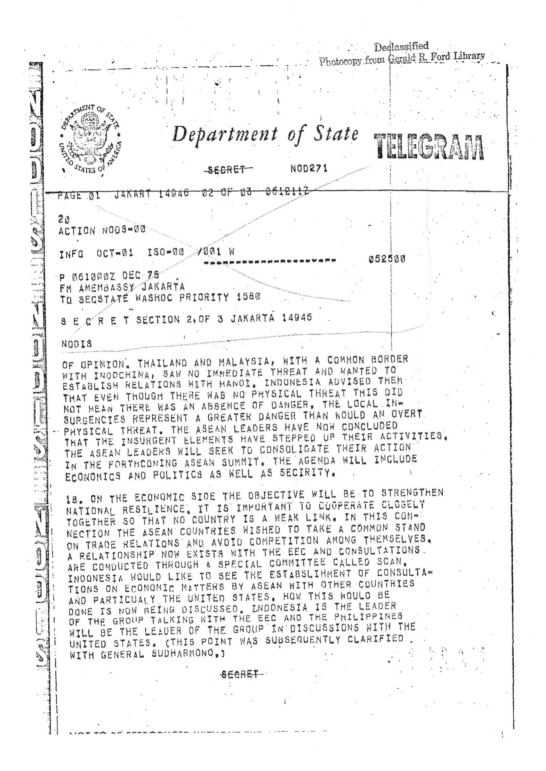

Department of State TELEGRAM

SECRET   NOD271

PAGE 01   JAKART 14946 02 OF 03 0610112

20
ACTION NODS-00

INFO OCT-01 ISO-00 /001 W   052500

P 061080Z DEC 75
FM AMEMBASSY JAKARTA
TO SECSTATE WASHDC PRIORITY 1580

S E C R E T SECTION 2 OF 3 JAKARTA 14946

NODIS

OF OPINION. THAILAND AND MALAYSIA, WITH A COMMON BORDER
WITH INDOCHINA, SAW NO IMMEDIATE THREAT AND WANTED TO
ESTABLISH RELATIONS WITH HANOI. INDONESIA ADVISED THEM
THAT EVEN THOUGH THERE WAS NO PHYSICAL THREAT THIS DID
NOT MEAN THERE WAS AN ABSENCE OF DANGER. THE LOCAL IN-
SURGENCIES REPRESENT A GREATER DANGER THAN WOULD AN OVERT
PHYSICAL THREAT. THE ASEAN LEADERS HAVE NOW CONCLUDED
THAT THE INSURGENT ELEMENTS HAVE STEPPED UP THEIR ACTIVITIES.
THE ASEAN LEADERS WILL SEEK TO CONSOLIDATE THEIR ACTION
IN THE FORTHCOMING ASEAN SUMMIT. THE AGENDA WILL INCLUDE
ECONOMICS AND POLITICS AS WELL AS SECURITY.

18. ON THE ECONOMIC SIDE THE OBJECTIVE WILL BE TO STRENGTHEN
NATIONAL RESILIENCE. IT IS IMPORTANT TO COOPERATE CLOSELY
TOGETHER SO THAT NO COUNTRY IS A WEAK LINK. IN THIS CON-
NECTION THE ASEAN COUNTRIES WISHED TO TAKE A COMMON STAND
ON TRADE RELATIONS AND AVOID COMPETITION AMONG THEMSELVES.
A RELATIONSHIP NOW EXISTS WITH THE EEC AND CONSULTATIONS
ARE CONDUCTED THROUGH A SPECIAL COMMITTEE CALLED SCAN.
INDONESIA WOULD LIKE TO SEE THE ESTABSLIHMENT OF CONSULTA-
TIONS ON ECONOMIC MATTERS BY ASEAN WITH OTHER COUNTRIES
AND PARTICUALY THE UNITED STATES. HOW THIS WOULD BE
DONE IS NOW BEING DISCUSSED. INDONESIA IS THE LEADER
OF THE GROUP TALKING WITH THE EEC AND THE PHILIPPINES
WILL BE THE LEADER OF THE GROUP IN DISCUSSIONS WITH THE
UNITED STATES. (THIS POINT WAS SUBSEQUENTLY CLARIFIED
WITH GENERAL SUDHARMONO.)

SECRET

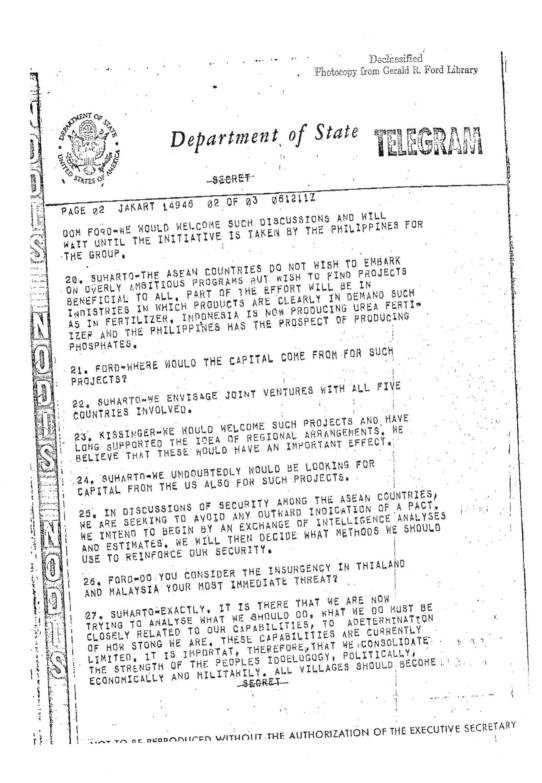

Declassified
Photocopy from Gerald R. Ford Library

Department of State TELEGRAM

-SECRET-

PAGE 02 JAKART 14946 02 OF 03 061211Z

OON FORD—WE WOULD WELCOME SUCH DISCUSSIONS AND WILL
WAIT UNTIL THE INITIATIVE IS TAKEN BY THE PHILIPPINES FOR
THE GROUP.

20. SUHARTO—THE ASEAN COUNTRIES DO NOT WISH TO EMBARK
ON OVERLY AMBITIOUS PROGRAMS BUT WISH TO FIND PROJECTS
BENEFICIAL TO ALL. PART OF THE EFFORT WILL BE IN
INDISTRIES IN WHICH PRODUCTS ARE CLEARLY IN DEMAND SUCH
AS IN FERTILIZER. INDONESIA IS NOW PRODUCING UREA FERTI-
IZER AND THE PHILIPPINES HAS THE PROSPECT OF PRODUCING
PHOSPHATES.

21. FORD—WHERE WOULD THE CAPITAL COME FROM FOR SUCH
PROJECTS?

22. SUHARTO—WE ENVISAGE JOINT VENTURES WITH ALL FIVE
COUNTRIES INVOLVED.

23. KISSINGER—WE WOULD WELCOME SUCH PROJECTS AND HAVE
LONG SUPPORTED THE IDEA OF REGIONAL ARRANGEMENTS. WE
BELIEVE THAT THESE WOULD HAVE AN IMPORTANT EFFECT.

24. SUHARTO—WE UNDOUBTEDLY WOULD BE LOOKING FOR
CAPITAL FROM THE US ALSO FOR SUCH PROJECTS.

25. IN DISCUSSIONS OF SECURITY AMONG THE ASEAN COUNTRIES,
WE ARE SEEKING TO AVOID ANY OUTWARD INDICATION OF A PACT.
WE INTEND TO BEGIN BY AN EXCHANGE OF INTELLIGENCE ANALYSES
AND ESTIMATES. WE WILL THEN DECIDE WHAT METHODS WE SHOULD
USE TO REINFORCE OUR SECURITY.

26. FORD—DO YOU CONSIDER THE INSURGENCY IN THIALAND
AND MALAYSIA YOUR MOST IMMEDIATE THREAT?

27. SUHARTO—EXACTLY. IT IS THERE THAT WE ARE NOW
TRYING TO ANALYSE WHAT WE SHOULD DO. WHAT WE DO MUST BE
CLOSELY RELATED TO OUR CAPABILITIES, TO ADETERMINATION
OF HOW STONG WE ARE. THESE CAPABILITIES ARE CURRENTLY
LIMITED. IT IS IMPORTAT, THEREFORE, THAT WE CONSOLIDATE
THE STRENGTH OF THE PEOPLES IDOELUGOGY, POLITICALLY,
ECONOMICALLY AND MILITARILY. ALL VILLAGES SHOULD BECOME
-SECRET-

NOT TO BE REPRODUCED WITHOUT THE AUTHORIZATION OF THE EXECUTIVE SECRETARY

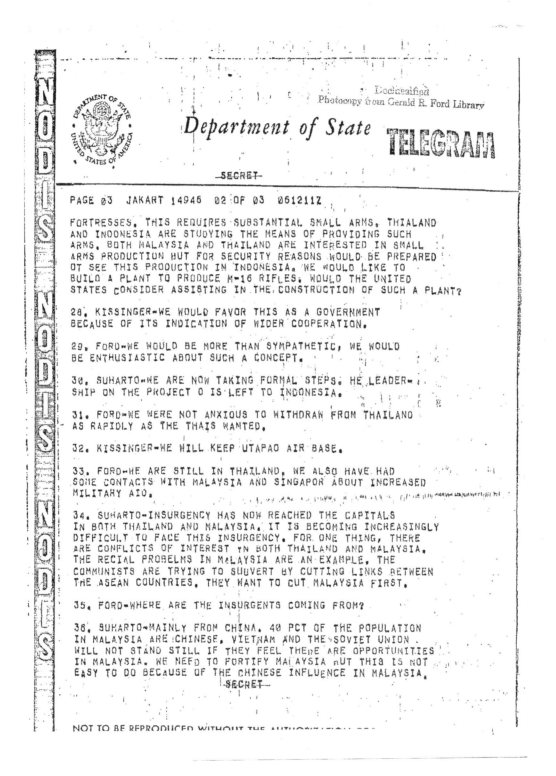

Declassified
Photocopy from Gerald R. Ford Library

Department of State TELEGRAM

SECRET

PAGE 03   JAKART 14946   02 OF 03   061211Z

FORTRESSES, THIS REQUIRES SUBSTANTIAL SMALL ARMS, THIALAND
AND INDONESIA ARE STUDYING THE MEANS OF PROVIDING SUCH
ARMS, BOTH MALAYSIA AND THAILAND ARE INTERESTED IN SMALL
ARMS PRODUCTION BUT FOR SECURITY REASONS WOULD BE PREPARED
OT SEE THIS PRODUCTION IN INDONESIA, WE WOULD LIKE TO
BUILD A PLANT TO PRODUCE M-16 RIFLES, WOULD THE UNITED
STATES CONSIDER ASSISTING IN THE CONSTRUCTION OF SUCH A PLANT?

28. KISSINGER-WE WOULD FAVOR THIS AS A GOVERNMENT
BECAUSE OF ITS INDICATION OF WIDER COOPERATION.

29. FORD-WE WOULD BE MORE THAN SYMPATHETIC, WE WOULD
BE ENTHUSIASTIC ABOUT SUCH A CONCEPT.

30. SUHARTO-WE ARE NOW TAKING FORMAL STEPS, HE LEADER-
SHIP ON THE PROJECT O IS LEFT TO INDONESIA.

31. FORD-WE WERE NOT ANXIOUS TO WITHDRAW FROM THAILAND
AS RAPIDLY AS THE THAIS WANTED.

32. KISSINGER-WE WILL KEEP UTAPAO AIR BASE.

33. FORD-WE ARE STILL IN THAILAND, WE ALSO HAVE HAD
SOME CONTACTS WITH MALAYSIA AND SINGAPOR ABOUT INCREASED
MILITARY AID.

34. SUHARTO-INSURGENCY HAS NOW REACHED THE CAPITALS
IN BOTH THAILAND AND MALAYSIA, IT IS BECOMING INCREASINGLY
DIFFICULT TO FACE THIS INSURGENCY, FOR ONE THING, THERE
ARE CONFLICTS OF INTEREST IN BOTH THAILAND AND MALAYSIA,
THE RECIAL PROBELMS IN MALAYSIA ARE AN EXAMPLE, THE
COMMUNISTS ARE TRYING TO SUBVERT BY CUTTING LINKS BETWEEN
THE ASEAN COUNTRIES, THEY WANT TO CUT MALAYSIA FIRST.

35. FORD-WHERE ARE THE INSURGENTS COMING FROM?

36. SUHARTO-MAINLY FROM CHINA, 40 PCT OF THE POPULATION
IN MALAYSIA ARE CHINESE, VIETNAM AND THE SOVIET UNION
WILL NOT STAND STILL IF THEY FEEL THERE ARE OPPORTUNITIES
IN MALAYSIA, WE NEED TO FORTIFY MALAYSIA BUT THIS IS NOT
EASY TO DO BECAUSE OF THE CHINESE INFLUENCE IN MALAYSIA.

SECRET

NOT TO BE REPRODUCED WITHOUT THE AUTHORIZATION OF

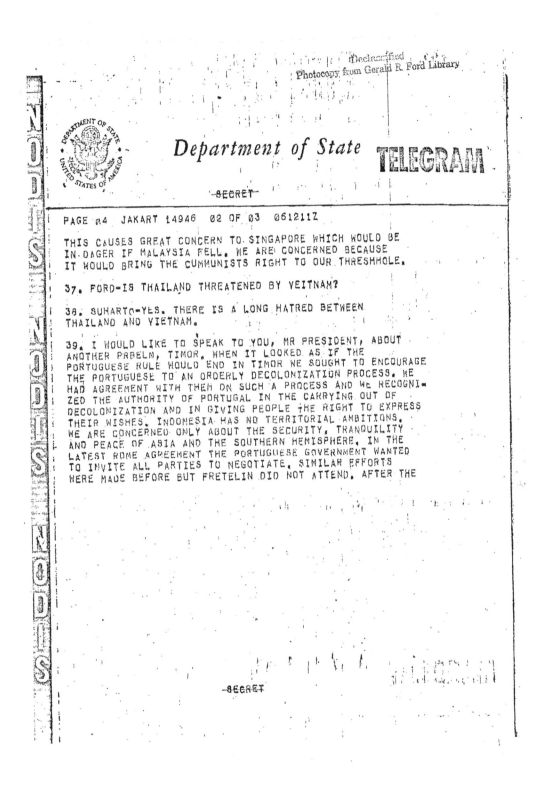

Declassified
Photocopy from Gerald R. Ford Library

Department of State TELEGRAM

SECRET

PAGE 04   JAKART 14946   02 OF 03   061211Z

THIS CAUSES GREAT CONCERN TO SINGAPORE WHICH WOULD BE
IN DAGER IF MALAYSIA FELL. WE ARE CONCERNED BECAUSE
IT WOULD BRING THE CUMMUNISTS RIGHT TO OUR THRESHHOLE.

37. FORD-IS THAILAND THREATENED BY VEITNAM?

38. SUHARTO-YES. THERE IS A LONG HATRED BETWEEN
THAILAND AND VIETNAM.

39. I WOULD LIKE TO SPEAK TO YOU, MR PRESIDENT, ABOUT
ANOTHER PRBELM, TIMOR. WHEN IT LOOKED AS IF THE
PORTUGUESE RULE WOULD END IN TIMOR WE SOUGHT TO ENCOURAGE
THE PORTUGUESE TO AN ORDERLY DECOLONIZATION PROCESS. WE
HAD AGREEMENT WITH THEM ON SUCH A PROCESS AND WE RECOGNI-
ZED THE AUTHORITY OF PORTUGAL IN THE CARRYING OUT OF
DECOLONIZATION AND IN GIVING PEOPLE THE RIGHT TO EXPRESS
THEIR WISHES. INDONESIA HAS NO TERRITORIAL AMBITIONS.
WE ARE CONCERNED ONLY ABOUT THE SECURITY, TRANQUILITY
AND PEACE OF ASIA AND THE SOUTHERN HEMISPHERE. IN THE
LATEST ROME AGREEMENT THE PORTUGUESE GOVERNMENT WANTED
TO INVITE ALL PARTIES TO NEGOTIATE. SIMILAR EFFORTS
WERE MADE BEFORE BUT FRETELIN DID NOT ATTEND. AFTER THE

SECRET

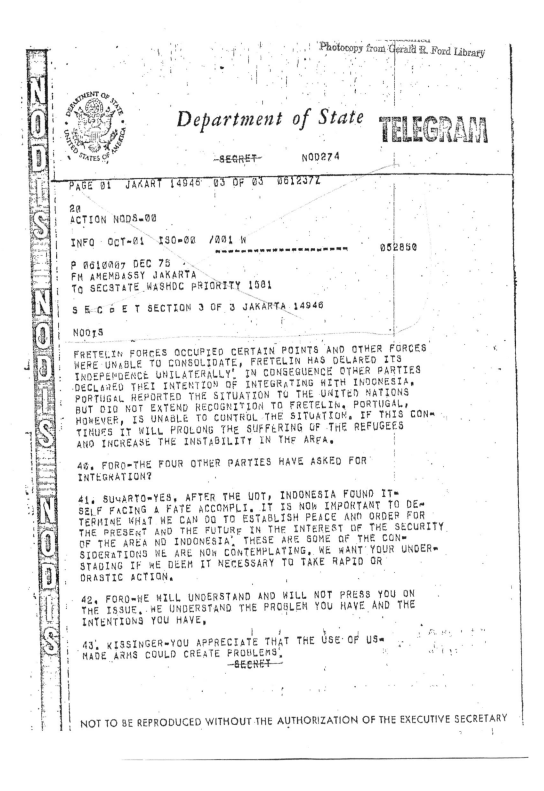

Department of State TELEGRAM

SECRET   NOD274

PAGE 01 JAKART 14946 03 OF 03 0612372

20
ACTION NODS-00

INFO OCT-01 ISO-00 /001 W
                                              052850

P 0610007 DEC 75
FM AMEMBASSY JAKARTA
TO SECSTATE WASHDC PRIORITY 1581

S E C R E T SECTION 3 OF 3 JAKARTA 14946

NODIS

FRETELIN FORCES OCCUPIED CERTAIN POINTS AND OTHER FORCES
WERE UNABLE TO CONSOLIDATE, FRETELIN HAS DELARED ITS
INDEPENDENCE UNILATERALLY. IN CONSEGUENCE OTHER PARTIES
DECLARED THEI INTENTION OF INTEGRATING WITH INDONESIA,
PORTUGAL REPORTED THE SITUATION TO THE UNITED NATIONS
BUT DID NOT EXTEND RECOGNITION TO FRETELIN, PORTUGAL,
HOWEVER, IS UNABLE TO CONTROL THE SITUATION. IF THIS CON-
TINUES IT WILL PROLONG THE SUFFERING OF THE REFUGEES
AND INCREASE THE INSTABILITY IN THE AREA.

40. FORD-THE FOUR OTHER PARTIES HAVE ASKED FOR
INTEGRATION?

41. SUHARTO-YES. AFTER THE UDT, INDONESIA FOUND IT-
SELF FACING A FATE ACCOMPLI. IT IS NOW IMPORTANT TO DE-
TERMINE WHAT WE CAN DO TO ESTABLISH PEACE AND ORDER FOR
THE PRESENT AND THE FUTURE IN THE INTEREST OF THE SECURITY
OF THE AREA ND INDONESIA. THESE ARE SOME OF THE CON-
SIDERATIONS WE ARE NOW CONTEMPLATING, WE WANT YOUR UNDER-
STADING IF WE DEEM IT NECESSARY TO TAKE RAPID OR
DRASTIC ACTION.

42. FORD-WE WILL UNDERSTAND AND WILL NOT PRESS YOU ON
THE ISSUE. WE UNDERSTAND THE PROBLEM YOU HAVE AND THE
INTENTIONS YOU HAVE,

43. KISSINGER-YOU APPRECIATE THAT THE USE OF US-
MADE ARMS COULD CREATE PROBLEMS.
                    SECRET

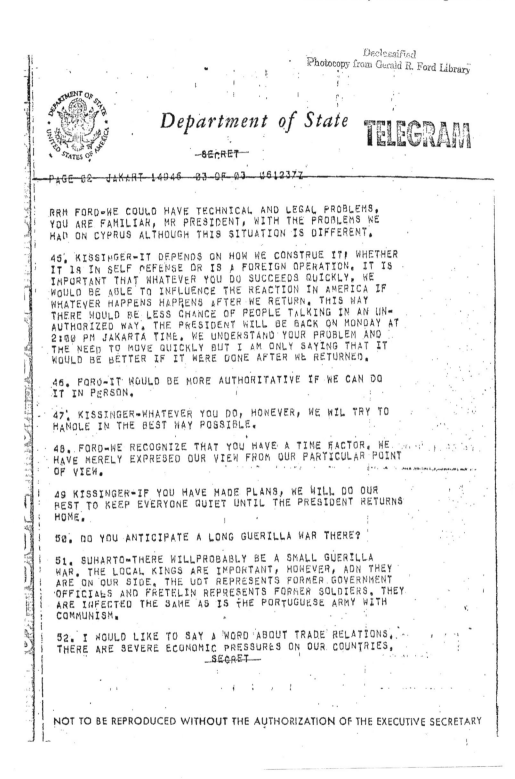

Declassified
Photocopy from Gerald R. Ford Library

Department of State TELEGRAM

—SECRET—

PAGE 02   JAKART 14946   03 OF 03   0612377

RRM FORD—WE COULD HAVE TECHNICAL AND LEGAL PROBLEMS.
YOU ARE FAMILIAR, MR PRESIDENT, WITH THE PROBLEMS WE
HAD ON CYPRUS ALTHOUGH THIS SITUATION IS DIFFERENT.

45. KISSINGER—IT DEPENDS ON HOW WE CONSTRUE IT; WHETHER
IT IS IN SELF DEFENSE OR IS A FOREIGN OPERATION. IT IS
IMPORTANT THAT WHATEVER YOU DO SUCCEEDS QUICKLY. WE
WOULD BE ABLE TO INFLUENCE THE REACTION IN AMERICA IF
WHATEVER HAPPENS HAPPENS AFTER WE RETURN. THIS WAY
THERE WOULD BE LESS CHANCE OF PEOPLE TALKING IN AN UN-
AUTHORIZED WAY. THE PRESIDENT WILL BE BACK ON MONDAY AT
2:00 PM JAKARTA TIME. WE UNDERSTAND YOUR PROBLEM AND
THE NEED TO MOVE QUICKLY BUT I AM ONLY SAYING THAT IT
WOULD BE BETTER IF IT WERE DONE AFTER WE RETURNED.

46. FORD—IT WOULD BE MORE AUTHORITATIVE IF WE CAN DO
IT IN PERSON.

47. KISSINGER—WHATEVER YOU DO, HOWEVER, WE WIL TRY TO
HANDLE IN THE BEST WAY POSSIBLE.

48. FORD—WE RECOGNIZE THAT YOU HAVE A TIME FACTOR. WE
HAVE MERELY EXPRESED OUR VIEW FROM OUR PARTICULAR POINT
OF VIEW.

49 KISSINGER—IF YOU HAVE MADE PLANS, WE WILL DO OUR
BEST TO KEEP EVERYONE QUIET UNTIL THE PRESIDENT RETURNS
HOME.

50. DO YOU ANTICIPATE A LONG GUERILLA WAR THERE?

51. SUHARTO—THERE WILLPROBABLY BE A SMALL GUERILLA
WAR. THE LOCAL KINGS ARE IMPORTANT, HOWEVER, ADN THEY
ARE ON OUR SIDE. THE UDT REPRESENTS FORMER GOVERNMENT
OFFICIALS AND FRETELIN REPRESENTS FORMER SOLDIERS. THEY
ARE INFECTED THE SAME AS IS THE PORTUGUESE ARMY WITH
COMMUNISM.

52. I WOULD LIKE TO SAY A WORD ABOUT TRADE RELATIONS.
THERE ARE SEVERE ECONOMIC PRESSURES ON OUR COUNTRIES.

—SECRET—

NOT TO BE REPRODUCED WITHOUT THE AUTHORIZATION OF THE EXECUTIVE SECRETARY

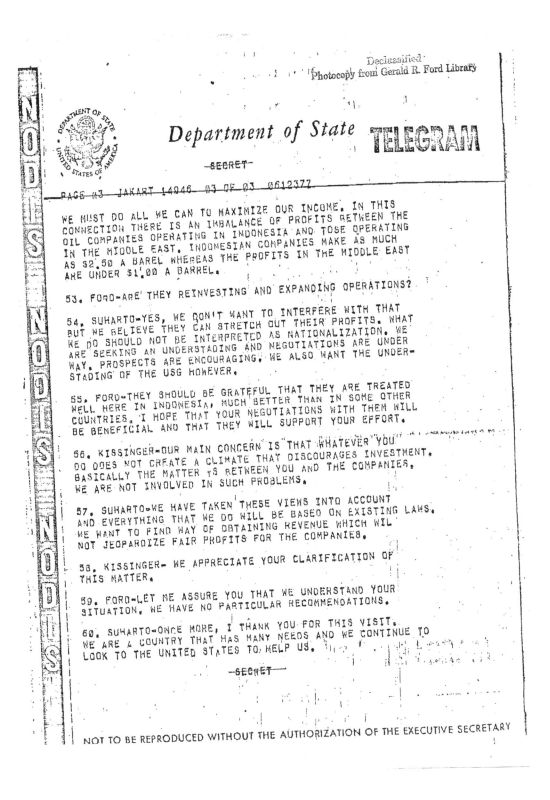

Declassified
Photocopy from Gerald R. Ford Library

Department of State TELEGRAM

SECRET

PAGE 03 JAKART 14046 03 OF 03 0612377

WE MUST DO ALL WE CAN TO MAXIMIZE OUR INCOME. IN THIS
CONNECTION THERE IS AN IMBALANCE OF PROFITS BETWEEN THE
OIL COMPANIES OPERATING IN INDONESIA AND TOSE OPERATING
IN THE MIDDLE EAST. INDONESIAN COMPANIES MAKE AS MUCH
AS $2.50 A BARREL WHEREAS THE PROFITS IN THE MIDDLE EAST
ARE UNDER $1.00 A BARREL.

53. FORD-ARE THEY REINVESTING AND EXPANDING OPERATIONS?

54. SUHARTO-YES, WE DON'T WANT TO INTERFERE WITH THAT
BUT WE BELIEVE THEY CAN STRETCH OUT THEIR PROFITS. WHAT
WE DO SHOULD NOT BE INTERPRETED AS NATIONALIZATION. WE
ARE SEEKING AN UNDERSTADING AND NEGOTIATIONS ARE UNDER
WAY. PROSPECTS ARE ENCOURAGING. WE ALSO WANT THE UNDER-
STADING OF THE USG HOWEVER.

55. FORD-THEY SHOULD BE GRATEFUL THAT THEY ARE TREATED
WELL HERE IN INDONESIA, MUCH BETTER THAN IN SOME OTHER
COUNTRIES. I HOPE THAT YOUR NEGOTIATIONS WITH THEM WILL
BE BENEFICIAL AND THAT THEY WILL SUPPORT YOUR EFFORT.

56. KISSINGER-OUR MAIN CONCERN IS THAT WHATEVER YOU
DO DOES NOT CREATE A CLIMATE THAT DISCOURAGES INVESTMENT.
BASICALLY THE MATTER IS BETWEEN YOU AND THE COMPANIES.
WE ARE NOT INVOLVED IN SUCH PROBLEMS.

57. SUHARTO-WE HAVE TAKEN THESE VIEWS INTO ACCOUNT
AND EVERYTHING THAT WE DO WILL BE BASED ON EXISTING LAWS.
WE WANT TO FIND WAY OF OBTAINING REVENUE WHICH WIL
NOT JEOPARDIZE FAIR PROFITS FOR THE COMPANIES.

58. KISSINGER- WE APPRECIATE YOUR CLARIFICATION OF
THIS MATTER.

59. FORD-LET ME ASSURE YOU THAT WE UNDERSTAND YOUR
SITUATION. WE HAVE NO PARTICULAR RECOMMENDATIONS.

60. SUHARTO-ONCE MORE, I THANK YOU FOR THIS VISIT.
WE ARE A COUNTRY THAT HAS MANY NEEDS AND WE CONTINUE TO
LOOK TO THE UNITED STATES TO HELP US.

SECRET

NOT TO BE REPRODUCED WITHOUT THE AUTHORIZATION OF THE EXECUTIVE SECRETARY

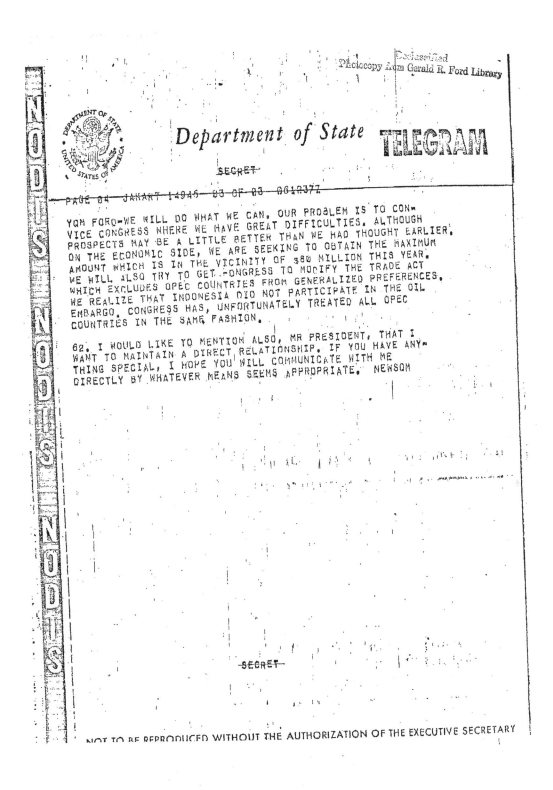

Declassified
Photocopy from Gerald R. Ford Library

Department of State TELEGRAM

SECRET

PAGE 04   JAKART 14946   03 OF 03   061237Z

YOM FORD—WE WILL DO WHAT WE CAN. OUR PROBLEM IS TO CON-
VINCE CONGRESS WHERE WE HAVE GREAT DIFFICULTIES. ALTHOUGH
PROSPECTS MAY BE A LITTLE BETTER THAN WE HAD THOUGHT EARLIER,
ON THE ECONOMIC SIDE, WE ARE SEEKING TO OBTAIN THE MAXIMUM
AMOUNT WHICH IS IN THE VICINITY OF $80 MILLION THIS YEAR.
WE WILL ALSO TRY TO GET CONGRESS TO MODIFY THE TRADE ACT
WHICH EXCLUDES OPEC COUNTRIES FROM GENERALIZED PREFERENCES.
WE REALIZE THAT INDONESIA DID NOT PARTICIPATE IN THE OIL
EMBARGO. CONGRESS HAS, UNFORTUNATELY TREATED ALL OPEC
COUNTRIES IN THE SAME FASHION.

62. I WOULD LIKE TO MENTION ALSO, MR PRESIDENT, THAT I
WANT TO MAINTAIN A DIRECT RELATIONSHIP. IF YOU HAVE ANY-
THING SPECIAL, I HOPE YOU WILL COMMUNICATE WITH ME
DIRECTLY BY WHATEVER MEANS SEEMS APPROPRIATE. NEWSOM

SECRET

NOT TO BE REPRODUCED WITHOUT THE AUTHORIZATION OF THE EXECUTIVE SECRETARY

Khmer Rouge Biographical Questionnaire

On April 17, 1975, the Khmer Rouge came out of the jungles of eastern Cambodia and seized Phnom Penh, the capital. Led by Pol Pot, the Khmer Rouge enacted a revolution based upon an extreme and idiosyncratic interpretation of Marxism and an equally extreme form of Khmer nationalism. Using excess violence the regime engaged in a murderous reign of terror from 1975 to December, 1978, with over a million Cambodians killed or dying from starvation, neglect, and maltreatment. Deeply paranoid and xenophobic, the regime obsessively sought out traitors, real or (far more commonly) imagined. The Khmer Rouge forced its members to present biographies in order to ensure their political correctness.

A Khmer Rouge Personal Life History Questionnaire Examining the Revolutionary Biography of Comrade _____

I. About Yourself

   1. Original name: Revolutionary name:

   2. Place, day, month and year of birth:

   3. Sex female or male? Ethnicity:

   4. Married or single?

   5. Occupation and original class before joining the revolution:

   6. Occupation and class after joining the revolution:

   7. Had you joined any political organizations prior to joining the revolution? Reason for joining these organizations…

   8. When did you join the revolution? Where? Who brought you to join? Reason for joining the revolution…

9. When did you join the Kampuchean Communist Youth League (SYK), the Kampuchean Peasants Association (SKK), the Union (SHC), Democratic Workers and Laborers Association (SKPP) ? Where? Who brought you to join? Reason for joining these organizations…

10. When did you join the Party? Where? Who authorized you to join? Reason for joining the Party…

11. What position have you obtained since joining the revolution?

12. What was your educational level during the old regime? In the new regime? What diplomas do you have?

13. What kinds of people did you live and work among? workers, farmers, intellectuals, capitalists, women, monks? What is your understanding of these groups?

14. Have you studied about the revolution at a seminar or school? What did you study?

15. How many times did Angkar examine and discuss your personal biography and revolutionary lifestyle? How long did it take to both prepare and present it?

16. How clearly do you know your character? To what level? How well do you know your strengths and weaknesses? How have you changed your non-revolutionary character and weaknesses? What is the result?

II. About Your Husband or Wife, if you have one

1. Original name: Revolutionary Name:

2. Ethnicity:

3. Place, day, month and year of birth:

4. Occupation and original class before marriage:

5. Occupation and class after marriage:

6. Did [he/she] used to join a political organization? What is [his/her] political attitude toward the revolution?

7. Has [she/he] joined the revolution, yet? When did [she/he] join? Which organization? Currently has what position in the revolution?

8. Does [your spouse] have any political, economic or emotional influence or power over comrade [you]? To what level [extent]?

9. Do you, comrade, have any political, economic, emotional influence or power over your spouse?

10. What is your worldview about love, hatred and marriage? What kind of attachments do these have over you, comrade?

III. About Your Biological Children

1. How many children do you have? How many girls? How many boys? How old are they?

2. How many of them are working or married? What work do they do? What class are they? Have they joined any political organizations? Have they joined the revolution, yet? What is their attitude toward the revolution?

3. How many are dependent [on you] and not yet married? What do they do? Have they joined any political organizations? Have they joined the revolution, yet? What is their attitude toward the revolution?

4. What is your standpoint concerning revolutionary worldview in relation to love, hatred, and raising of children?

5. What kind of influence, power and attachment do the children have over you, comrade?

IV. About Your Biological Parents

1. Original name: father/mother Revolutionary name: father/mother

2. Ethnicity: father mother

3. Place, day, month, year of birth, age, living or deceased

father:

mother:

4. Occupation and class:

father:

mother:

5. Political involvement: Have they joined any political organizations? What is their attitude toward the revolution?

6. What kind of political, economic, material, emotional influence, power and attachment do they have over you, comrade?

7. What influence or power do you, comrade, have on your parents?

V. About Your Parents-in-Law

1. Original name: father-in-law/mother-in-law

Revolutionary name: father-in-law/mother-in-law

2. Place, day, month, year of birth, age, living or deceased

father-in-law:

mother-in-law:

3. Occupation and class:

father-in-law:

mother-in-law:

4. Political involvement: Have they joined any political organizations? What is their attitude toward the revolution?

5. What kind of political, economic, material, emotional influence, power and attachment do they have over you, comrade?

6. What influence or power do you, comrade, have on your parents-in-law?

VI. About Your Biological Siblings

1. How many siblings do you have? How many sisters? How many brothers? How old are they?

2. Occupation and class of each:

3. Political involvement: Which political organizations have they joined? Have they joined the revolution, yet? What is their attitude toward the revolution?

4. What influence or attachment do they have over you, comrade?

5. What influence do you, comrade, have over each of your biological siblings?

VII. Close Friends and Social Environment You Enjoy Outside of Revolutionary Organizations

1. What very close friends do you have? How many?

2. Occupation and social class of each:

3. Political involvement: What is the political attitude of each toward the revolution?

4. What influence do they have over you, comrade?

5. Which social setting do you most enjoy being part of: workers, farmers, intellectuals, petty bourgeoisie, capitalists, aristocrats, feudalists, foreigners? What political, economic, emotional influence do these groups have over you, comrade?

Surviving Indonesia's Gulag (excerpts)

By Carmel Budiardjo

Carmel Budiardjo (1925–) is a British woman who married an Indonesian leftist. They were living in Jakarta when Suharto came to power and unleashed the anti-PKI massacres of 1965–1966. They were both arrested and sent into Suharto's growing system of prison camps. She spent three years in jail and her husband was detained for thirteen. She became a human rights activist upon her release. Here she details the brutal treatment suffered by those accused of PKI affiliation under the Suharto dictatorship, known as the New Order, 1966–1998.

There was a great deal of mutual suspicion among the prisoners, especially during these first days, which made it difficult, with few exceptions, to establish any companionship with others who were suffering the same fate. Much of the time, I felt lonely and defenceless against a system of evil that had me in its grip. Each of us with our own fears had few emotions left to sympathize with others.

The only woman in our room I drew close to was Nuriah. She had a very practical approach to life and was always ready with advice. She was a tower of strength in moments of crisis. When people came back to the room in pain or physically damaged in any way, she was the one best able to comfort them or treat their injuries. She had what I can only describe as a sixth sense and always seemed to know before anyone else what was going on. I valued this greatly because I am not very perceptive and often failed to pick up signals or notice remarks made by officers during the course of the day. A few days after we first met, arrangements were made for her baby to be taken home and be cared for by a relative; and this was the only time I can recollect when she broke down. She was occasionally asked to help with chores outside our room, particularly in the kitchen, and this gave her access to all kinds of stories and rumours about the camp.

She told me that there were regular showings of pornographic films for officers so as to encourage them to be unrestrained in their use of sexual abuse and gross indecency when interrogating women.

Shortly before I was transferred from Satgas-Pusat, a row of cages was constructed inside the shed, to the left of our room. These cages were not yet in use by the time I left, but I later heard that they were used to isolate and humiliate detainees. Alone and in the eye of the guards at every moment of the day, some of these men and women went insane, some attempted suicide even though their tormentors deprived them of the means of inflicting physical harm on themselves. The only way of telling whether a person had succumbed was to see whether they remained in the cages and whether they were restricted to a punitive diet of unpalatable rice.

The night after my brief visit home, I slept even more fitfully. To add to our discomfort, one of the guards on duty had a transistor radio on full blast all night and walked past our windows a number of times, with his radio under his arm.

When I awoke the next morning, I was horrified to see a man stripped to the waist, dangling by his wrists from a tree near the well. His wrists were pulled just high enough to keep him touching the ground with his toes. His body was covered with swollen, red weals and his head hung down on his chest. Occasionally, a guard would walk across the courtyard or along the corridor past our room, ignoring him. To see other people moving around normally, unconcerned about the sufferings of this man, made the scene even more horrific. It was more than I could do to go to the well or cross the yard to the toilet while he was still hanging there and I avoided looking out of the window. Later, when we were escorted on our morning visit to the toilet, it was a relief to see that he had been taken away. I never discovered his name but we later heard that he was a low-ranking army officer who, until his arrest, had worked at the army's recruitment office and was accused of having helped young communists to join the army. Many thousands of soldiers and officers were arrested after 1965 and accused of being PKI agents or Sukarnoists.

As the day wore on, I tried to get the tortured man out of my mind as I sat answering the inquisitor's questionnaire. But, that afternoon, there was another incident that shook me profoundly. I had just finished writing and was lying on my mat, trying to rest when we heard angry shouts in the courtyard. I looked out and saw a detainee standing outside one of the toilets, being harangued by Bonar.

'How dare you answer me back? You're a prisoner here, don't forget.' He screeched the words over and over again, *kamu tahanan*, using *katnu* for you.' Officers were always addressing us as *kamu*. This is an acceptable form of address among friends but is very offensive when used between adults who have no grounds for familiarity with each other. Bonar lost no opportunity to remind us that we were prisoners, unworthy of respect and utterly at his mercy.

The man refused to be silenced by Bonar, insisting that he wanted to go to the toilet. Then Bonar started pummelling him with his fists but the man refused to budge. By now Bonar was livid. He barked an order to the guard on duty to summon others to help him deal with this infraction. Five or six soldiers turned up, all carrying rifles. They seized the man by the arms, dragged him along the ground to the centre of the courtyard and started laying into him with their fists, rifle butts and boots, as Bonar stood a short distance away, shouting at them to 'give him a good thrashing.' I sank to the floor unable to watch the scene, but there was no way I could avoid hearing the sound of beating, the words of abuse and the groans of the victim. After several minutes of this, the noise and the voices receded towards the shed as they dragged the defenceless man back to his room.

Then things went quiet again . . .

A few days after my arrest, two more women joined us in our room. The first to arrive had been a member of the MPRS, the upper House of parliament. Like all left-wing members of both Houses, she was expelled from parliament immediately after the Suharto takeover; her husband, a member of the lower House, had also been arrested. During Bud's first and second arrests, I had often met her outside Salemba Prison in Jakarta when I used to take food to him three times a week.

Although these were called *hari bezoek* or 'visiting days,' they were not visiting days at all. We were permitted to bring food parcels but were not allowed to meet the detainees. Visits were permitted only once a year on special days like Christmas or Lebaran, the end of the Muslim fasting month. Sometimes even annual visits were cancelled for selected prisoners.

The hardship and sufferings of the wives and children of detainees are a story in themselves. The vast majority of these women had no means of support or regular income and were cold-shouldered even by close relatives, who were afraid of being tainted by contact with prisoners and their families. Some women managed to survive by setting up food stalls and selling home-made cakes. Others turned to dressmaking, but few were able to earn enough to keep hunger from the door. Some, in desperation, handed their children over to relatives or neighbours. In many cases, the children were hounded from their schools—as Tari had been—and were unable to get places in other schools.

Prison 'visiting days' were occasions for chatting to other wives or relatives, exchanging gossip, and gleaning what we could about the prospects for release.

'Is your husband still in Salemba?' I asked our new room-mate after she had had time to settle in.

'Yes, and what about Mas Bud? He was released, wasn't he?'

'Yes, but they picked him up again, together with me. He's here now, somewhere upstairs.' Little had changed, I thought, except that we were meeting now as fellow detainees rather than detainees' wives.

A day or so after she arrived, something very unusual happened. After we had returned from our early morning toilet, we were suddenly ordered to lie down flat on the floor and keep still for a few minutes. We had to do this again several times during the next few days. At first, we could not understand what was going on, then realized that each time we had to lie down, someone was taken across the courtyard who, for some reason, was not allowed to see us in the room.

After three days of this, another woman joined us. Her left eye was black with bruises and, as soon as the guard had gone, she sank to the floor, obviously relieved.

'They told me there weren't any other women here. They said all the women here had been killed and their bodies had been buried under a heap of sand in the shed.'

For three days, she told us, she had been held in strict isolation in a tiny room upstairs. She slept at night on a table with a guard sleeping on the floor underneath. Enormous pressure was used to force her into submission. She was stripped naked by torturers who deliberately started punching her breasts, knowing that she had recently given birth and had been unable to suckle her baby for days so that her breasts were full of milk and particularly painful and sensitive. She got a black eye when one of the thugs punched her hard in the face with his fist, striking her eye with a huge ring on one of his fingers. This had broken a blood vessel in her left eyeball. She was in a state of shock when she joined us, though she gradually calmed down, greatly relieved to be with other women.

But her problems were not at an end. They arrested a cousin of hers whose address they had forced out of her. She was summoned for a confrontation with him in the room next to ours. They stripped her naked in front of him while he, also stripped naked, was beaten by another woman detainee, the former member of the upper House of parliament, who was ordered to beat him by one of the torturers. As this frightful atrocity proceeded, I sat cowed in my corner trying to drive the sounds out of my head. But there was no closing my ears to the orders being yelled, the sound of the rattan stick being lashed against bare flesh, and the screams of pain. When things like this happened within earshot, a deathly silence fell in our room.

As for my own 'case,' nothing more happened after I handed in my answers to the questions I had been asked. There were no further interrogations, except for a rather unexpected brief encounter with Atjep. He appeared one day in the courtyard and I was summoned to go and talk to him.

'Did you have anything to do with the Gilchrist Letter? It wasn't you who wrote it, was it?' he asked.

'What on earth makes you think that? I did no such thing,' I replied.

This was a confidential cable dispatched in March 1965 by the British ambassador in Jakarta, Sir Andrew Gilchrist, to the Foreign Office about 'our local army friends,' hinting that the British were informed about an army plot to eliminate Sukarno. The document fell into the hands of the BPI, the state intelligence agency headed by Dr

Subandrio, concurrently Foreign Minister. It was drawn to Sukarno's attention in May that year and was widely commented on. The Gilchrist Letter helped to stir up speculations in Jakarta, reinforcing the rumours of a council of generals that was plotting to depose Sukarno. Britain had reasons of its own to despise Sukarno, who had initiated a campaign of *konfrontasi* with Malaysia in 1964, after the British colonies in northern Borneo were united with Peninsular Malaysia against strong opposition from Jakarta. The crucial sentence read: 'It would be as well to emphasise once more to our local friends in the army that the strictest caution, discipline and co-ordination are essential to the success of the enterprise.'

Army intelligence insisted that the document was a forgery produced by the BPI, part of a series of pre-October 1965 events that, according to them, had been designed to create an atmosphere of tension. Many years later, Sir Andrew Gilchrist wrote to an Indian academic, confirming that the letter was not a forgery and confirming that it was 'one found by the Indonesians in the wreckage of the British Embassy.' But here was Atjep, trying to pin this one on me because I had worked closely with Dr Subandrio for many months before October 1965. This was the first and last I heard of the Gilchrist Letter during my detention.

One evening, when things at the camp had not yet heated up, we were sitting bracing ourselves for whatever horror would occur next when Bonar suddenly appeared at one of the windows. He stood leaning on the ledge and looked at each of us in turn, leering. What kind of mood was he in now? Had he come to bully, to intimidate or threaten, or to ridicule and gloat?

'Well, well. How are you all feeling this evening? Quite well and happy, I hope?'

Happy! His taunts were sometimes more cutting than his tempers.

'We'll only be happy when you release us and let us go home to our children,' one of the women said.

The leer did not leave his face but he nodded slowly—a habit of his when he wanted to impress us.

'There's no going home for any of you lot, you dirty communists. This isn't like any other place. Once here, you'll never get out alive.'

Had I thought about it calmly, I would have realized that he was playing on our vulnerability. But any sense of calm and rationality had by now been destroyed. None of us said anything.

After a pause to let his words sink in, he said 'Hey, you,' pointing at me, 'how old is Tari?'

'Seventeen.'

'That's a nice age for a girl to be left alone at home, isn't it? What's going to become of her?'

'I don't know,' I replied, 'but I'm sure she'll be able to look after herself.'

'Ugh, rubbish! She'll be out on the streets soon enough, selling herself to make a living. And what about your daughters,' he said, turning to the other women. 'Two years old? Four years old? In fifteen years, they'll be grown up, all of them, and out on the streets. Prostitutes. And you lot won't be there to look after them, will you?'

I felt so vulnerable that his words hit me like a knife. Would we really be here for ever? And what would happen to the children?

'Ever heard of Eichmann?' he asked, looking at me.

'Yes, he was the man who planned the annihilation of the Jews in the German concentration camps,' I replied. 'Of course, I've heard of him.'

'Eichmann, that's me, commander of this camp. I've read all about him. A great fellow. He's my model.'

I stared at him, hardly believing my ears. After a few moments, he swaggered off chuckling something to himself about Eichmann and concentration camps.

By now it was already more than a week since I had last seen Tari and Anto and the separation was getting me down. It was unbearable to be cut off from any news of home, and I could well imagine how hard it was for them, knowing nothing about the two of us. I spent much of the time worrying about how they were coping.

His words were senseless but I find it difficult to describe the mood of desolation that overcame me. And I was not alone. Nobody in the room spoke after he left and the atmosphere was laden with gloom. I spent the night dozing off occasionally, unable to dispel the fear that I would never leave this place alive, never see the children again. I woke next morning in a fit of sobbing. I managed to calm myself but broke down every time anyone said anything to me. I could not lift myself out of this depression for the whole day.

Late that afternoon, I saw Bud crossing the courtyard. He glanced in my direction as he always did and noticed that I was utterly miserable. On his way back across the yard, I saw him speak to one of the guards. Then, quite unexpectedly, the guard came over and entered the room.

'He wants to tell you something. I'll let you out but please be quick.'

I went out and stood just near enough to hear Bud's words.

'Please don't cry. Don't worry about the children. They'll learn a lot through all these experiences. They'll grow up much more quickly and grow wiser in the process.'

I could say nothing in reply. I only nodded and tried to smile through my tears. The guard escorted me back to the room, whispering as we went: 'Cheer up, Ibu. Things aren't all that bad. Why don't you try singing, to keep your mind off things?'

It had been foolish of me to let Bonar get the better of me like this. I took their advice to heart. Never again during all the years of my detention did I suffer the fears and heartaches of that dreadful night and day.

The Kalong Torture Chamber

Most of the people transferred to Likdam came from an interrogation centre in Gunung Sahari, Jakarta, the headquarters of a special unit established by the Jakarta military command in 1966 to smash the underground movement. The exploits of this unit—though not the methods it used—were widely reported in the press. Its most spectacular achievements were the arrest of Sudisman, the only member of the PKI politbureau not to be caught and murdered in 1965, and Brigadier-General Supardjo, the most senior army officer in the Untung Group that planned and carried out the kidnappings of the generals. Both men were later tried by Suharto's extraordinary military tribunal, Mahmilub, sentenced to death and executed.

This was the place where Tari had spent a few dreadful hours. From my own brief visit there when I was summoned by Atjep, I remembered it as a derelict house with nothing outside to distinguish it from the other houses in the quiet side street. It still bore the name-board of the social services union for becak-drivers which had occupied the building until it was requisitioned by the army. But the oppressive feel of an intel unit hit you the moment you entered the front door, the detached, sullen attitude of the soldiers on guard and the swagger of the officers in charge of operations.

The operation conducted from Gunung Sahari was called *Operasi Kalong* or 'Operation of the Bats.' As the name suggested, it functioned mainly at night. I knew from Tari's experience that this was a torture centre, but it was not until I met the detainees who came to Likdam that I got a true sense of what went on there. Every time new tapols arrived, we would hear more accounts of horrific torture sessions. Sometimes, a prisoner at Likdam would be summoned back to Kalong for further interrogation. A burly lieutenant whom we knew only as Bob would turn up and 'borrow' the person for a few days. The word in Indonesian is *dibon*, which means 'being exchanged for a voucher,' a word I heard many times in detention. Whenever Bob appeared, a shudder would go through the camp.

When a new detainee arrived at Kalong, he or she would be kept in the interrogation room for days, sleeping on one of the tables and not allowed to mix with the other people. The unit was geared for rapid action and reaction, and the turnover of prisoners would sometimes be very high. Newcomers had to be isolated, shocked and demoralized and were forced to watch others being interrogated and tortured, a form of torment in itself.

During its first years of operation, Kalong was run by Atjep and Major Suroso, an officer who won rapid promotion in recognition for his successes in rounding up communist activists. The two of them had recruited and trained a team of tough, dedicated and ruthless torturers and had also been able to recruit a number of communist activists to assist in the interrogation of their comrades. By late 1968, when I began to hear first-hand accounts about the centre, two senior communists were playing a crucial role on the Kalong operations; they were widely despised because of their active participation in the torture of detainees.

One was S. who, until October 1965, had been the personal bodyguard of D. N. Aidit; the other was B. from South Sumatra, who had been made a member of the party's international department only a short while before his arrest.

The commonest form of torture was the electric shock, first applied on the thumbs, then on other parts of the body, including the genitals. Another favourite was beating the victim with the long, spiked tail of the mammoth pari (stingray) fish. Several of the men arriving at Likdam bore the scars of newly healed wounds on their arms and backs. The physical state of one young man particularly horrified me. He was very handsome and had a lithe body and thick black hair; his skin was darker than usual for an Indonesian. When I first set eyes on him, he reminded me of a proud young Indian sitting astride an elephant. But one day, when he was stripped to the waist, I saw fresh scars all over his body, hideous thin, white streaks across his dark skin where the tail had torn through his flesh. He was the younger brother of a PKI leader and had been beaten mercilessly to make him divulge information about his brother's whereabouts.

Some tapols who joined us from Kalong bore psychological rather than physical scars. One man who slept just outside our room always had an empty stare on his face. He could have been taken for a simpleton. He spent the whole time cooking and doing chores for his food group. He only ever spoke when spoken to and responded like an automaton to whatever people asked him to do. The torturers had used electric shock on his genitals to devastating effect. He was a victim of mistaken identity; they mistook him for a communist member of the upper House of parliament, the MPRS. Although the confusion was cleared up, he remained in detention because he happened to be a member of the banned peasants' union, the BTI.

I heard exactly the same stories from everyone who arrived from Kalong. Even after the initial interrogation sessions were over and the newcomer could now join the others being held in the compound, conditions were intolerable. The detainees were segregated into groups and were forbidden to talk to anyone in another group. There were plenty of informers spying on the detainees, most of them former comrades, who were constantly on the lookout for breaches of camp discipline. Torture went on all day and night. There was a term for the shrieks of the torture victims—*lagu wajib* or 'obligatory song.' In the evenings, the inmates were required to watch television, except for the news bulletins when the set was turned off. Perhaps this kind of regime was maintained to prevent the tapols from spending the evenings in discussions with each other. It is really frustrating watching people on television living normal lives when you yourself are held behind barbed wire in a detention camp. When I later had the chance to watch, I sometimes felt like screaming at the people inside the box and wanted to tell them things they would never read in the Indonesian press.

What was particularly disturbing about Kalong was the number of communist cadres who were now working for the army. But there were plenty more whose courage defies belief. One who stands out for me is Sri Ambar, a member of SOBSI and one of its leading women activists. She had succeeded in escaping arrest for about nine months after October 1965 but her husband was caught and their home was mobbed and destroyed by a gang of young men. I first heard about Sri when I moved to Likdam. She had come there from Kalong about a year earlier. Stories about Sri were legendary. Even the guards spoke about her with awe. One soldier told me she was so distraught when she came to Likdam that the mere sight of a uniformed soldier would cause her to scream 'Get away from me, you brute!'

Later, when we met in Bukit Duri Prison, she told me about everything that had happened to her.

After her home was destroyed, she and her two daughters moved in with her mother. One day she met a former comrade in the street. In the course of a chat, the man asked her where she was living. She took the precaution of not giving him her address, mentioning only the district where she was staying. As it turns out, that was more than enough. Little did she know that he was working for army intelligence. He went to the local government office and scanned the photos of local residents handed in when applying for identity cards. He found hers and was able to direct the army to her mother's home. Other activists had just been arrested during an operation against the underground and, under torture, one told the army that she was helping to distribute illegal pamphlets. While she was certainly a victim of betrayal, she agreed that her own lack of vigilance was partly to blame.

As soon as she arrived in Kalong, she was interrogated but denied everything. They brought in the man who had betrayed her and ordered him to repeat his allegations in her presence. Still she refused to confess. They were both stripped naked and flogged in an attempt to find out who was lying. By now it was late in the evening. They were both taken to a yard in the middle of the camp, tied to a tree by their wrists and left dangling with their toes just touching the ground till morning. As she hung there in great agony, an elderly civilian employee at the camp crept up to her while the guards were out of sight. He held a cup of hot, sweet tea to her lips for her to sip. Then he took a jar of balsam from his pocket.

'Excuse me for touching you,' he said, as he rubbed her body with the ointment.

After this, the torture sessions continued daily, till one night, things came to a head. Atjep who took personal charge of her interrogation was enraged by her stubborn refusal to talk. On this occasion, she had been stripped naked as usual and was being beaten in the presence of some of her male colleagues, when Atjep suddenly shouted 'Let her have it.'

One of the torturers pulled out a knife and plunged it into her left thigh, causing a long, deep gash. One of the other prisoners in the room who saw this fell unconscious at the sight of so much blood, but she herself could hardly feel the pain.

'You sadists,' she yelled, then bent down and, scarcely conscious of what she was doing, she pushed the two sides of the gash together, to try to stop the bleeding. But Atjep would not let things rest and nodded in her direction to the man who had knifed her. He made another plunge at her with his knife, this time in the right buttock. By now, she was so weak from loss of blood that she fainted.

When she came to, she was lying in a military hospital and was told that she had been brought in two days earlier. The first doctor to examine her said she had only herself to blame. But other medical staff were more sympathetic and told her that the doctors on duty had been shocked to see how badly injured she was. Apart from the deep knife wounds, there were many other injuries and bruises on her back and neck. Two days after the gashes on her legs had been stitched up, a doctor came to say he would have to remove the stitches. When she protested, he told her that the doctors on duty when she arrived had complained to army headquarters about her condition. An investigation had been ordered and the doctors had been instructed to remove the stitches so that they could measure the length and depth of the gashes.

'The removal of the stitches was more painful than anything I had suffered,' she told me.

She heard later that Atjep was suspended from duty while the inquiry was under way and spent some time in detention.

Long before she had fully recovered, she was discharged from hospital and ordered to return to Kalong so that the interrogations could continue. When she next turned up for questioning, her two daughters were in the room and were being beaten. They had recently been taken into custody and had been asked to give information about people who used to visit their mother at home. When they refused, the decision was made to confront them with their mother. As she stood and watched, the girls shouted 'Mother, don't say anything. Never mind if we have to go through this.'

Sri kept quiet as the girls were beaten. The two of them were taken away and she heard nothing more about them for several months. Later she was told that one of her daughters was being held at another camp run by Kalong. The younger daughter, who was under ten years of age, was taken away by an army officer who said he would look after her. Sri was never able to discover what happened to this child or where she was taken. Up to the time I last saw Sri, the quest to find her daughter had led nowhere.

The loss of her child was the worst tragedy of all for Sri. She told me that whenever she was brought before interrogators or army officers, the first thing she always did was to ask them where her daughter was.

There was to be yet another confrontation, this time with her mother. The elderly woman had been detained and was accused of helping her daughter. The army had no respect for her parental bond with Sri. She was quite fearless and made no secret of her views when interrogated in Sri's presence:

'Did you help your daughter and give her shelter after the coup?'

'Yes, of course I did. Why shouldn't I?'

'Didn't you know the security forces were after her because she was scheming against the Government?'

'That's nothing to do with me. She's my only daughter and it's my duty to help her in every way I can when she's in trouble.'

'But didn't you realize you would get yourself into trouble by helping her?'

'I don't care about that. I'm her mother and that's all that matters to me.'

While all this was going on, the soldiers were slapping her face, punching and beating her. Undeterred she turned to Sri and shouted 'Don't take any notice of what they are doing. You must do what you have to do. All this doesn't matter.'

Sri's mother remained in detention for several months together with her grand-daughter, the older of Sri's two daughters.

Some years later, when I was being held in the same prison as Sri, she heard that her mother had died of a brain tumor. Together with her, we mourned the passing of a courageous woman. She may have known little about politics but would not allow anyone to shake her faith in her daughter.

Sri was kept in the interrogation room at Kalong for so long that she witnessed a great deal of torture. She told me she saw a soldier bite off the ear lobe of Tari's friend.

'How could he possibly do such a thing?' I asked her.

'One of Atjep's most brutal thugs held the boy's head in his hands, dug his teeth into the fleshy part of the ear and bit it off. Then he spat it onto the floor. That's how he did it,' she said.

Another scene had shaken her profoundly. As she was sitting in the interrogation room one day, a young boy was brought in. He had been caught carrying messages which the interrogators had reason to believe were intended for Sudisman, the PKI politburo member who was still at large, in hiding somewhere in Jakarta. They beat him mercilessly, to force him to say where Sudisman was hiding, but he said nothing. Sri was struck by the dignity of the boy as they flogged him without respite.

'It was remarkable. He stood there, his head held high, defying these sadists.'

Then they tried to undermine his confidence by telling him they had obtained plenty of information from people in the party leadership so he might as well tell them all he knew. They mentioned a name, Sujono Pratiknjo, a PKI central committee member who had just been captured. He held a key position in the clandestine movement and had worked closely with Sudisman. The boy could not believe someone so high up would betray Sudisman and was convinced that they were bluffing. Sujono was brought in, but still the boy showed no sign of weakening.

'Now,' said one of the interrogators to Sujono, 'tell us about the underground organization you've set up in Jakarta.'

Sujono walked to a blackboard, picked up a piece of chalk and began to draw a diagram of the underground network, indicating the cells that had been created and writing down the names of people in the cells. He also described the ways each of the cells kept contact with Sudisman.

As Sujono was busy scribbling, Sri looked at the boy. She saw him quiver. All his poise had gone; he was limp with horror. Torture he could stand but not the sight of such treachery. Sudisman was captured the very next day and the underground network crumbled to pieces.

Later I found out more about this incident and the tragic consequences for the underground movement. Immediately after Sujono's betrayal, one of the young couriers escaped from the detention centre with the help of his close comrades and rushed to Sudisman's hideout to warn him to flee. Sudisman refused to believe that Sujono had betrayed him and thought this was a ploy to force him to leave his hideout. But within hours Sudisman was arrested.

For Sri, the worst of her memories was witnessing the treatment of another courageous young activist caught carrying messages from Central Java to Jakarta. She had seen him in the prisoners' compound and he had whispered words of admiration for all her courage.

She was in the room when they started flogging him. They aimed at his back and neck, the most vulnerable parts of the body. I was told by prisoners who had gone through such beating that the only way to protect yourself is to bend the head back as far as possible against the top of the spine. The flogging grew in intensity and Sri tried not to watch. She stared at a piece of paper in front of her, trying to concentrate on anything but the atrocity going on in her presence. But when she heard him fall, she turned round to see what had happened. He was lying prostrate on the floor; thick white foam was oozing out of his mouth. When she rushed over to him, the torturers did nothing to hold her back. They seemed stunned by what they had done.

She bent down and just managed to hear him whisper a girl's name, probably the name of his sweetheart. A few moments later, the boy was dead.

Not long after all these experiences, Sri was summoned to appear as a witness at Sudisman's trial but she refused to testify. She held her hand cupped behind her ear to indicate to the judge that she could not hear properly and told the court that her hearing had been impaired by torture.

Many years later, in 1975, Sri was tried and sentenced to fifteen years. After being released in the early 1980s, she lived in Bogor, West Java, with her husband who had spent fourteen years in detention without trial. They managed to survive from the proceeds of a small stall which they set up with the help of Amnesty members in Austria, but after her husband died she stopped writing to the group. Now a widow, she lives somewhere on the outskirts of Jakarta and has begun to lose her mind, hardly surprising for someone who has lived through such a terrible ordeal. But the legend of Sri Ambar's unshakable courage is still spoken of with awe by all those who knew her in prison.

Washington Bullets

By The Clash

The Clash was perhaps the most prominent and influential band in the British punk rock scene of the late 1970s and early 1980s. Known for their left-wing politics, this song is unsurprisingly critical of American foreign policy in Latin America. The lyrics call attention to US involvement in the cocaine trade, the overthrow of Allende (including Victor Jara's torture and murder in a soccer stadium), and attempts to kill Fidel Castro, as well as celebrate the Sandinista victory in Nicaragua. Yet the lyrics also note human rights abuses committed by Communist China in Tibet and the Soviet Union in Afghanistan as well as British support for mercenaries fighting in various conflicts around the world. This song is off the album Sandinista! *from 1980.*

Oh! Mama, Mama look there!
Your children are playing in that street again
Don't you know what happened down there?
A youth of fourteen got shot down there
The Kokane guns of Jamdown Town
The killing clowns, the blood money men
Are shooting those Washington bullets again

As every cell in Chile will tell
The cries of the tortured men
Remember Allende, and the days before,
Before the army came.
Please remember Victor Jara,
In the Santiago Stadium,
Es verdad—those Washington Bullets again.

Joe Strummer and Mick Jones, "Washington Bullets," *Sandinista*. Copyright © 1992 by Nineden Ltd.

And in the Bay of Pigs in 1961,
Havana fought the playboy in the Cuban sun,
For Castro is a colour,
Is a redder than red,
Those Washington bullets want Castro dead.
For Castro is the colour...
...That will earn you a spray of lead.

For the very first time ever,
When they had a revolution in Nicaragua,
There was no interference from America.
Human rights in America.

Well the people fought the leader,
And up he flew...
With no Washington bullets what else could he do?

'N' if you can find a Afghan rebel
That the Moscow bullets missed
Ask him what he thinks of voting Communist...
...Ask the Dalai Lama in the hills of Tibet,
How many monks did the Chinese get?
In a war-torn swamp stop any mercenary,
'N' check the British bullets in his armoury.
Que?
Sandinista!

Chapter 8

Decolonization and Nation Building

Introduction

If the late nineteenth- and early twentieth-century conquest of so much of Africa, Asia, and Oceania was a crucial world historical event, so was the sudden decolonization of the post-war era. Starting in 1947 with India and Pakistan's independence, what British Prime Minister Harold Macmillan would call "the winds of change" would sweep away British Malaya, the Dutch East Indies, and French Indochina in Southeast Asia, as well as the massive French, British, Belgian, and Portuguese holdings in Africa. When seventeen nations became independent in a year, 1960 became known as "the year of Africa." While the dissolution of these empires was welcome with rejoicing in the streets, the new nation-states of Asia and Africa were plagued with a number of problems. In Indonesia for example, the old colonial boundaries brought some 350 ethnic and language groups together. In parts of Africa, the colonial-era borders divided ethnic and religious groups and placed them in separate countries. In South Asia, the end of the British Raj allocated separate states for Hindus and Muslims in India and Pakistan, respectively. In this tragic event, known as Partition, millions of people found themselves on the wrong side of the line, creating widespread inter-communal violence and a massive refugee crisis. To make matters worse, many of the colonial economic relationships survived the formal political process of decolonization. As most empires were little more than systems of exploitation created for the benefit of Europeans, there was little in the way of preparing independent and sustainable post-colonial economies. While some political leaders called for local control over development and others condemned various forms of "neo-colonialism," millions of Africans, Asians, and Afro-Carribeans immigrated to Europe and North America in search of a better life. Thus, in the last decades of the twentieth century the cities of the former colonizing nations saw the advent of communities of formerly colonized subjects. Curry shops appeared in London, as did mosques in Paris. If some celebrated this new multi-culturalism, others reacted with xenophobia and racism.

To complicate things even further, decolonization occurred during the height of the Cold War. Many new states found themselves trapped in a bi-polar world where the super-powers sought to influence, if not control, these young governments. These documents show how the process of decolonization and the subsequent nation-building created opportunities and crises throughout the world.

This chapter relates to sections 10.4, 10.9, and 10.10 of the History-Social Science Content Standards for California Public Schools.

Vietnamese Declaration of Independence

By Ho Chi Minh

In 1941 Ho Chi Minh officially dissolved the Indochinese Communist Party and created the Viet Minh, a coalition of anti-colonial groups that was secretly controlled by the communists. After the Japanese occupation, the Viet Minh resisted both the French and the Japanese. As the war ended, the Japanese did not want to see a return to European colonial control of Southeast Asia, so Ho Chi Minh in Vietnam and Sukarno in Indonesia were allowed to declare independence before the French and Dutch could take control of their respective colonies. Citing the American and French Revolutions as precedents and noting the wartime commitment of the Allied Powers to national self-determination, Ho declared Vietnam's independence in September 1945. As the French were unwilling to give up on their colony, the Viet Minh fought a guerilla war for national liberation from 1946 to 1954.

"All men are created equal. They are endowed by their Creator with certain inalienable rights, among these are Life, Liberty, and the pursuit of Happiness." This immortal statement was made in the Declaration of Independence of the United States of America in 1776. In a broader sense, this means: All the peoples on the earth are equal from birth, all the peoples have a right to live, to be happy and free. The Declaration of the French Revolution made in 1791 on the Rights of Man and the Citizen also states: "All men are born free and with equal rights, and must always remain free and have equal rights." Those are undeniable truths. Nevertheless, for more than eighty years, the French imperialists, abusing the standard of Liberty, Equality, and Fraternity, have violated our Fatherland and oppressed our fellow-citizens. They have acted contrary to the ideals of humanity and justice. In the field of politics, they have deprived our people of every democratic liberty. They have enforced inhuman laws; they have set

Ho Chi Minh, "Vietnamese Declaration of Independence," Ho Chi Minh, Selected Works. Copyright © 1960. Reprinted with permission.

up three distinct political regimes in the North, the Center and the South of Vietnam in order to wreck our national unity and prevent our people from being united. They have built more prisons than schools. They have mercilessly slain our patriots—they have drowned our uprisings in rivers of blood. They have fettered public opinion; they have practised obscurantism against our people. To weaken our race they have forced us to use opium and alcohol. In the fields of economics, they have fleeced us to the backbone, impoverished our people, and devastated our land. They have robbed us of our rice fields, our mines, our forests, and our raw materials. They have monopolised the issuing of bank-notes and the export trade. They have invented numerous unjustifiable taxes and reduced our people, especially our peasantry, to a state of extreme poverty. They have hampered the prospering of our national bourgeoisie; they have mercilessly exploited our workers. In the autumn of 1940, when the Japanese Fascists violated Indochina's territory to establish new bases in their fight against the Allies, the French imperialists went down on their bended knees and handed over our country to them. Thus, from that date, our people were subjected to the double yoke of the French and the Japanese. Their sufferings and miseries increased. The result was that from the end of last year to the beginning of this year, from Quang Tri province to the North of Vietnam, more than two million of our fellow-citizens died from starvation. On March 9, the French troops were disarmed by the Japanese. The French colonialists either fled or surrendered, showing that not only were they incapable of "protecting" us, but that, in the span of five years, they had twice sold our country to the Japanese. On several occasions before March 9, the Vietminh League urged the French to ally themselves with it against the Japanese. Instead of agreeing to this proposal, the French colonialists so intensified their terrorist activities against the Vietminh members that before fleeing they massacred a great number of our political prisoners detained at Yen Bay and Cao Bang. Not withstanding all this, our fellow-citizens have always manifested toward the French a tolerant and humane attitude. Even after the Japanese putsch of March 1945, the Vietminh League helped many Frenchmen to cross the frontier, rescued some of them from Japanese jails, and protected French lives and property. From the autumn of 1940, our country had in fact ceased to be a French colony and had become a Japanese possession. After the Japanese had surrendered to the Allies, our whole people rose to regain our national sovereignty and to found the Democratic Republic of Vietnam. The truth is that we have wrested our independence from the Japanese and not from the French The French have fled, the Japanese have capitulated, Emperor Bao Dai has abdicated. Our people have broken the chains which for nearly a century have fettered them and have won independence for the Fatherland. Our people at the same time have overthrown the monarchic regime that has reigned supreme for dozens of centuries. In its place has been established the present Democratic Republic. For these reasons, we, members of the Provisional Government, representing the whole Vietnamese people, declare that from now on we break off all relations of a colonial character with France;

we repeal all the international obligation that France has so far subscribed to on behalf of Vietnam and we abolish all the special rights the French have unlawfully acquired in our Fatherland. The whole Vietnamese people, animated by a common purpose, are determined to fight to the bitter end against any attempt by the French colonialists to reconquer their country. We are convinced that the Allied nations which at Tehran and San Francisco have acknowledged the principles of self-determination and equality of nations, will not refuse to acknowledge the independence of Vietnam. A people who have courageously opposed French domination for more than eighty years, a people who have fought side by side with the Allies against the Fascists during these last years, such a people must be free and independent. For these reasons, we, members of the Provisional Government of the Democratic Republic of Vietnam, solemnly declare to the world that Vietnam has the right to be a free and independent country and in fact it is so already. The entire Vietnamese people are determined to mobilise all their physical and mental strength, to sacrifice their lives and property in order to safeguard their independence and liberty.

Tryst with Destiny

By Jawaharlal Nehru

Jawaharlal Nehru (1889–1964) and Gandhi were the most prominent figures of the Indian National Congress in its struggle for swaraj, or "home-rule." Their goal was a united, democratic, and secular India. Unfortunately, many Indian Muslims were suspicious of the Congress' Hindu rhetoric and feared that they would be a suppressed minority in a Hindu dominated democracy. Muhammad Ali Jinnah (1876–1948) headed the All India Muslim League which worked with the Congress for independence but wanted a separate state for Muslim South Asians. Hindu-Muslims tensions had ebbed and flowed for centuries, but British colonial rule aggravated conflicts between the communities. In a cynical, if not hypocritical, manner, the British argued that they needed to remain in India to keep the peace. After World War Two, the British realized that they could not hold on to their empire and quickly drew a line separating the Raj into a Hindu majority India and a Muslim majority West and East Pakistan (now Pakistan and Bangladesh, respectively). This 1947 division, known as Partition, divided some communities, such as Kashmir, in half, and left many Hindus, Sikhs, and Muslims on the "wrong side." In the resulting (and foreseeable) confusion, over twelve million refugees fled either east or west. Rioting broke out in many cities and there were numerous reports of massacres and counter-massacres. As many as a million people may have lost their lives in the year of Partition. The India-Pakistan border became one of the most dangerous and contested international boundaries in the world, seeing several wars, regular small-scale skirmishes, state sponsored terrorist attacks, and an alarming nuclear arms race. Thus, Nehru's speech at the moment of independence, the stroke of midnight on the 15th of August, rings with a bittersweet tone. A few months later, a Hindu fanatic would assassinate Gandhi as a traitor to the faith. Nehru served as India's first and longest Prime Minister from 1947 to 1964.

Jawaharlal Nehru, "Tryst with Destiny," Speech Delivered on August 14, 1947.

Long years ago we made a tryst with destiny, and now the time comes when we shall redeem our pledge, not wholly or in full measure, but very substantially. At the stroke of the midnight hour, when the world sleeps, India will awake to life and freedom. A moment comes, which comes but rarely in history, when we step out from the old to the new, when an age ends, and when the soul of a nation, long suppressed, finds utterance. It is fitting that at this solemn moment we take the pledge of dedication to the service of India and her people and to the still larger cause of humanity.

At the dawn of history India started on her unending quest, and trackless centuries are filled with her striving and the grandeur of her success and her failures. Through good and ill fortune alike she has never lost sight of that quest or forgotten the ideals which gave her strength. We end today a period of ill fortune and India discovers herself again. The achievement we celebrate today is but a step, an opening of opportunity, to the greater triumphs and achievements that await us. Are we brave enough and wise enough to grasp this opportunity and accept the challenge of the future?

Freedom and power bring responsibility. The responsibility rests upon this Assembly, a sovereign body representing the sovereign people of India. Before the birth of freedom we have endured all the pains of labour and our hearts are heavy with the memory of this sorrow. Some of those pains continue even now. Nevertheless, the past is over and it is the future that beckons to us now.

That future is not one of ease or resting but of incessant striving so that we may fulfil the pledges we have so often taken and the one we shall take today. The service of India means the service of the millions who suffer. It means the ending of poverty and ignorance and disease and inequality of opportunity. The ambition of the greatest man of our generation has been to wipe every tear from every eye. That may be beyond us, but as long as there are tears and suffering, so long our work will not be over.

And so we have to labour and to work, and work hard, to give reality to our dreams. Those dreams are for India, but they are also for the world, for all the nations and peoples are too closely knit together today for any one of them to imagine that it can live apart. Peace has been said to be indivisible; so is freedom, so is prosperity now, and so also is disaster in this One World that can no longer be split into isolated fragments.

To the people of India, whose representatives we are, we make an appeal to join us with faith and confidence in this great adventure. This is no time for petty and destructive criticism, no time for ill-will or blaming others. We have to build the noble mansion of free India where all her children may dwell.

II

The appointed day has come—the day appointed by destiny—and India stands forth again, after long slumber and struggle, awake, vital, free and independent. The past clings on to us still in some measure and we have to do much before we redeem the pledges we have so often taken. Yet the turning-point is past, and history begins anew for us, the history which we shall live and act and others will write about.

It is a fateful moment for us in India, for all Asia and for the world. A new star rises, the star of freedom in the East, a new hope comes into being, a vision long cherished materializes. May the star never set and that hope never be betrayed!

We rejoice in that freedom, even though clouds surround us, and many of our people are sorrow-stricken and difficult problems encompass us. But freedom brings responsibilities and burdens and we have to face them in the spirit of a free and disciplined people.

On this day our first thoughts go to the architect of this freedom, the Father of our Nation [Gandhi], who, embodying the old spirit of India, held aloft the torch of freedom and lighted up the darkness that surrounded us. We have often been unworthy followers of his and have strayed from his message, but not only we but succeeding generations will remember this message and bear the imprint in their hearts of this great son of India, magnificent in his faith and strength and courage and humility. We shall never allow that torch of freedom to be blown out, however high the wind or stormy the tempest.

Our next thoughts must be of the unknown volunteers and soldiers of freedom who, without praise or reward, have served India even unto death.

We think also of our brothers and sisters who have been cut off from us by political boundaries and who unhappily cannot share at present in the freedom that has come. They are of us and will remain of us whatever may happen, and we shall be sharers in their good [or] ill fortune alike.

The future beckons to us. Whither do we go and what shall be our endeavour? To bring freedom and opportunity to the common man, to the peasants and workers of India; to fight and end poverty and ignorance and disease; to build up a prosperous, democratic and progressive nation, and to create social, economic and political institutions which will ensure justice and fullness of life to every man and woman.

We have hard work ahead. There is no resting for any one of us till we redeem our pledge in full, till we make all the people of India what destiny intended them to be. We are citizens of a great country, on the verge of bold advance, and we have to live up to that high standard. All of us, to whatever religion we may belong, are equally the children of India with equal rights, privileges and obligations. We cannot encourage communalism or narrow-mindedness, for no nation can be great whose people are narrow in thought or in action.

To the nations and peoples of the world we send greetings and pledge ourselves to cooperate with them in furthering peace, freedom and democracy.

And to India, our much-loved motherland, the ancient, the eternal and the ever-new, we pay our reverent homage and we bind ourselves to her service. Jai Hind.

Speech at the Ceremony of the Proclamation of the Congo's Independence

By Patrice Lumumba

Patrice Émery Lumumba (1925–1961) was a leader in the Congo's struggle for independence from Belgium. At the turn of the century, the Congo experienced one of the most brutal and repressive colonial occupations with perhaps ten million deaths in twenty years. Lumumba was elected as the first prime minister but overthrown in an American and Belgian backed coup d'etat. CIA chief Allen Dulles may have ordered his assassination because of his pursuit of ties with the Soviet Union. In this 1960 speech, he makes it clear that the Congolese suffered from the racism of colonial rule.

Men and women of the Congo,
Victorious independence fighters,

I salute you in the name of the Congolese Government.

I ask all of you, my friends, who tirelessly fought in our ranks, to mark this June 30, 1960, as an illustrious date that will be ever engraved in your hearts, a date whose meaning you will proudly explain to your children, so that they in turn might relate to their grandchildren and great-grandchildren the glorious history of our struggle for freedom.

Although this independence of the Congo is being proclaimed today by agreement with Belgium, an amicable country, with which we are on equal terms, no Congolese will ever forget that independence was won in struggle, a persevering and inspired struggle carried on from day to day, a struggle, in which we were undaunted by privation or suffering and stinted neither strength nor blood.

It was filled with tears, fire and blood. We are deeply proud of our struggle, because it was just and noble and indispensable in putting an end to the humiliating bondage forced upon us.

Patrice Lumumba, "Speech at the Ceremony of the Proclamation of the Congo's Independence, June 30, 1960," *The Truth About a Monstrous Crime of the Colonialists*, pp. 44–47. Copyright © 1961 by Foreign Languages Publishing House. Reprinted with permission.

That was our lot for the eighty years of colonial rule and our wounds are too fresh and much too painful to be forgotten.

We have experienced forced labour in exchange for pay that did not allow us to satisfy our hunger, to clothe ourselves, to have decent lodgings or to bring up our children as dearly loved ones.

Morning, noon and night we were subjected to jeers, insults and blows because we were "Negroes." Who will ever forget that the black was addressed as *"tu,"* not because he was a friend, but because the polite *"vous"* was reserved for the white man?

We have seen our lands seized in the name of ostensibly just laws, which gave recognition only to the right of might.

We have not forgotten that the law was never the same for the white and the black, that it was lenient to the ones, and cruel and inhuman to the others.

We have experienced the atrocious sufferings, being persecuted for political convictions and religious beliefs, and exiled from our native land: our lot was worse than death itself.

We have not forgotten that in the cities the mansions were for the whites and the tumbledown huts for the blacks; that a black was not admitted to the cinemas, restaurants and shops set aside for "Europeans"; that a black travelled in the holds, under the feet of the whites in their luxury cabins.

Who will ever forget the shootings which killed so many of our brothers, or the cells into which were mercilessly thrown those who no longer wished to submit to the regime of injustice, oppression and exploitation used by the colonialists as a tool of their domination?

All that, my brothers, brought us untold suffering.

But we, who were elected by the votes of your representatives, representatives of the people, to guide our native land, we, who have suffered in body and soul from the colonial oppression, we tell you that henceforth all that is finished with.

The Republic of the Congo has been proclaimed and our beloved country's future is now in the hands of its own people.

Brothers, let us commence together a new struggle, a sublime struggle that will lead our country to peace, prosperity and greatness.

Together we shall establish social justice and ensure for every man a fair remuneration for his labour.

We shall show the world what the black man can do when working in liberty, and we shall make the Congo the pride of Africa.

We shall see to it that the lands of our native country truly benefit its children.

We shall revise all the old laws and make them into new ones that will be just and noble.

We shall stop the persecution of free thought. We shall see to it that all citizens enjoy to the fullest extent the basic freedoms provided for by the Declaration of Human Rights.

We shall eradicate all discrimination, whatever its origin, and we shall ensure for everyone a station in life befitting his human dignity and worthy of his labour and his loyalty to the country.

We shall institute in the country a peace resting not on guns and bayonets but on concord and goodwill.

And in all this, my dear compatriots, we can rely not only on our own enormous forces and immense wealth, but also on the assistance of the numerous foreign states, whose co-operation we shall accept when it is not aimed at imposing upon us an alien policy, but is given in a spirit of friendship.

Even Belgium, which has finally learned the lesson of history and need no longer try to oppose our independence, is prepared to give us its aid and friendship; for that end an agreement has just been signed between our two equal and independent countries. I am sure that this co-operation will benefit both countries. For our part, we shall, while remaining vigilant, try to observe the engagements we have freely made.

Thus, both in the internal and the external spheres, the new Congo being created by my government will be rich, free and prosperous. But to attain our goal without delay, I ask all of you, legislators and citizens of the Congo, to give us all the help you can.

I ask you all to sink your tribal quarrels: they weaken us and may cause us to be despised abroad.

I ask you all not to shrink from any sacrifice for the sake of ensuring the success of our grand undertaking.

Finally, I ask you unconditionally to respect the life and property of fellow-citizens and foreigners who have settled in our country; if the conduct of these foreigners leaves much to be desired, our Justice will promptly expel them from the territory of the republic; if, on the contrary, their conduct is good, they must be left in peace, for they, too, are working for our country's prosperity.

The Congo's independence is a decisive step towards the liberation of the whole African continent.

Our government, a government of national and popular unity, will serve its country.

I call on all Congolese citizens, men, women and children, to set themselves resolutely to the task of creating a national economy and ensuring our economic independence.

Eternal glory to the fighters for national liberation!

Long live independence and African unity!

Long live the independent and sovereign Congo!

I Have a Dream

By Martin Luther King

Martin Luther King, Jr., (1929–1968) was the most prominent civil rights activist in the United States. His strategy of non-violent protests drew from Gandhi's examples of satyagraha and the principle of ahimsa. His struggle coincided with the global struggle for decolonization and the end of racist regimes of white supremacy in Algeria, South Africa, and Rhodesia.

Delivered on the Steps at the Lincoln Memorial in Washington D.C. on August 28, 1963

Five score years ago, a great American, in whose symbolic shadow we stand signed the Emancipation Proclamation. This momentous decree came as a great beacon light of hope to millions of Negro slaves who had been seared in the flames of withering injustice. It came as a joyous daybreak to end the long night of captivity.

But one hundred years later, we must face the tragic fact that the Negro is still not free. One hundred years later, the life of the Negro is still sadly crippled by the manacles of segregation and the chains of discrimination. One hundred years later, the Negro lives on a lonely island of poverty in the midst of a vast ocean of material prosperity. One hundred years later, the Negro is still languishing in the corners of American society and finds himself an exile in his own land. So we have come here today to dramatize an appalling condition.

In a sense we have come to our nation's capital to cash a check. When the architects of our republic wrote the magnificent words of the Constitution and the declaration of Independence, they were signing a promissory note to which every American was to fall heir. This note was a promise that all men would be guaranteed the inalienable rights of life, liberty, and the pursuit of happiness.

It is obvious today that America has defaulted on this promissory note insofar as her citizens of color are concerned. Instead of honoring this sacred obligation, America has given the Negro people a bad check which has come back marked "insufficient funds." But we refuse to believe that the bank of justice is bankrupt. We refuse to believe that there are insufficient funds in the great vaults of opportunity of this nation. So we have come to cash this check—a check that will give us upon demand the riches of freedom and the security of justice. We have also come to this hallowed spot to remind America of the fierce urgency of now. This is no time to engage in the luxury of cooling off or to take the tranquilizing drug of gradualism. Now is the time to rise from the dark and desolate valley of segregation to the sunlit path of racial justice. Now is the time to open the doors of opportunity to all of God's children. Now is the time to lift our nation from the quicksands of racial injustice to the solid rock of brotherhood.

It would be fatal for the nation to overlook the urgency of the moment and to underestimate the determination of the Negro. This sweltering summer of the Negro's legitimate discontent will not pass until there is an invigorating autumn of freedom and equality. Nineteen sixty-three is not an end, but a beginning. Those who hope that the Negro needed to blow off steam and will now be content will have a rude awakening if the nation returns to business as usual. There will be neither rest nor tranquility in America until the Negro is granted his citizenship rights. The whirlwinds of revolt will continue to shake the foundations of our nation until the bright day of justice emerges.

But there is something that I must say to my people who stand on the warm threshold which leads into the palace of justice. In the process of gaining our rightful place we must not be guilty of wrongful deeds. Let us not seek to satisfy our thirst for freedom by drinking from the cup of bitterness and hatred.

We must forever conduct our struggle on the high plane of dignity and discipline. We must not allow our creative protest to degenerate into physical violence. Again and again we must rise to the majestic heights of meeting physical force with soul force. The marvelous new militancy which has engulfed the Negro community must not lead us to distrust of all white people, for many of our white brothers, as evidenced by their presence here today, have come to realize that their destiny is tied up with our destiny and their freedom is inextricably bound to our freedom. We cannot walk alone.

And as we walk, we must make the pledge that we shall march ahead. We cannot turn back. There are those who are asking the devotees of civil rights, "When will you be satisfied?" We can never be satisfied as long as our bodies, heavy with the fatigue of travel, cannot gain lodging in the motels of the highways and the hotels of the cities. We cannot be satisfied as long as the Negro's basic mobility is from a smaller ghetto to a larger one. We can never be satisfied as long as a Negro in Mississippi cannot vote and a Negro in New York believes he has nothing for which to vote. No, no, we are not satisfied, and we will not be satisfied until justice rolls down like waters and righteousness like a mighty stream.

I am not unmindful that some of you have come here out of great trials and tribulations. Some of you have come fresh from narrow cells. Some of you have come from areas where your quest for freedom left you battered by the storms of persecution and staggered by the winds of police brutality. You have been the veterans of creative suffering. Continue to work with the faith that unearned suffering is redemptive.

Go back to Mississippi, go back to Alabama, go back to Georgia, go back to Louisiana, go back to the slums and ghettos of our northern cities, knowing that somehow this situation can and will be changed. Let us not wallow in the valley of despair.

I say to you today, my friends, that in spite of the difficulties and frustrations of the moment, I still have a dream. It is a dream deeply rooted in the American dream.

I have a dream that one day this nation will rise up and live out the true meaning of its creed: "We hold these truths to be self-evident: that all men are created equal."

I have a dream that one day on the red hills of Georgia the sons of former slaves and the sons of former slave owners will be able to sit down together at a table of brotherhood.

I have a dream that one day even the state of Mississippi, a desert state, sweltering with the heat of injustice and oppression, will be transformed into an oasis of freedom and justice.

I have a dream that my four children will one day live in a nation where they will not be judged by the color of their skin but by the content of their character.

I have a dream today.

I have a dream that one day the state of Alabama, whose governor's lips are presently dripping with the words of interposition and nullification, will be transformed into a situation where little black boys and black girls will be able to join hands with little white boys and white girls and walk together as sisters and brothers.

I have a dream today.

I have a dream that one day every valley shall be exalted, every hill and mountain shall be made low, the rough places will be made plain, and the crooked places will be made straight, and the glory of the Lord shall be revealed, and all flesh shall see it together.

This is our hope. This is the faith with which I return to the South. With this faith we will be able to hew out of the mountain of despair a stone of hope. With this faith we will be able to transform the jangling discords of our nation into a beautiful symphony of brotherhood. With this faith we will be able to work together, to pray together, to struggle together, to go to jail together, to stand up for freedom together, knowing that we will be free one day.

This will be the day when all of God's children will be able to sing with a new meaning, "My country, 'tis of thee, sweet land of liberty, of thee I sing. Land where my fathers died, land of the pilgrim's pride, from every mountainside, let freedom ring."

And if America is to be a great nation this must become true. So let freedom ring from the prodigious hilltops of New Hampshire. Let freedom ring from the mighty mountains of New York. Let freedom ring from the heightening Alleghenies of Pennsylvania!

Let freedom ring from the snow-capped Rockies of Colorado!

Let freedom ring from the curvaceous peaks of California!

But not only that; let freedom ring from Stone Mountain of Georgia!

Let freedom ring from Lookout Mountain of Tennessee!

Let freedom ring from every hill and every molehill of Mississippi. From every mountainside, let freedom ring.

When we let freedom ring, when we let it ring from every village and every hamlet, from every state and every city, we will be able to speed up that day when all of God's children, black men and white men, Jews and Gentiles, Protestants and Catholics, will be able to join hands and sing in the words of the old Negro spiritual, "Free at last! free at last! Thank God Almighty, we are free at last!"

Neo-Colonialism, the Last Stage of Imperialism (1965) (Conclusion)

By Kwame Nkrumah

Throughout the 1960s and 1970s, Nkrumah continued to warn of various forms of European and American control of the developing world. Like Sukarno, Castro, and others, he theorized such influence as neocolonialism, a new stage of imperialism unforeseen by Lenin.

In the Introduction I attempted to set out the dilemma now facing the world. The conflict between rich and poor in the second half of the nineteenth century and the first half of the twentieth, which was fought out between the rich and the poor in the developed nations of the world ended in a compromise. Capitalism as a system disappeared from large areas of the world, but where socialism was established it was in its less-developed rather than its more-developed parts and, in fact, the revolt against capitalism had its greatest successes in those areas where early neocolonialism had been most actively practised. In the industrially more developed countries, capitalism, far from disappearing, became infinitely stronger. This strength was only achieved by the sacrifice of two principles which had inspired early capitalism, namely the subjugation of the working classes within each individual country and the exclusion of the State from any say in the control of capitalist enterprise.

By abandoning these two principles and substituting for them 'welfare states' based on high working-class living standards and on a State-regulated capitalism at home, the developed countries succeeded in exporting their internal problem and transferring the conflict between rich and poor from the national to the international stage.

Marx had argued that the development of capitalism would produce a crisis within each individual capitalist State because within each State the gap between the 'haves' and the 'have nots' would widen to a point where a conflict was inevitable and that it would be the capitalists who would be defeated. The basis of his argument is not invalidated by the fact that the conflict, which he had predicted as a national one, did not everywhere take place on a national scale but has been transferred instead to the world stage. World capitalism has postponed its crisis but only at the cost of transforming it into an international crisis. The danger is now not civil war within individual States provoked by intolerable conditions within those States, but international war provoked ultimately by the misery of the majority of mankind who daily grow poorer and poorer.

When Africa becomes economically free and politically united, the monopolists will come face to face with their own working class in their own countries, and a new struggle will arise within which the liquidation and collapse of imperialism will be complete.

As this book has attempted to show, in the same way as the internal crisis of capitalism within the developed world arose through the uncontrolled action of national capital, so a greater crisis is being provoked today by similar uncontrolled action of international capitalism in the developing parts of the world. Before the problem can be solved it must at least be understood. It cannot be resolved merely by pretending that neocolonialism does not exist. It must be realised that the methods at present employed to solve the problem of world poverty are not likely to yield any result other than to extend the crisis.

Speaking in 1951, the then President of the United States, Mr Truman, said, 'The only kind of war we seek is the good old fight against man's ancient enemies… poverty, disease, hunger and illiteracy.' Sentiments of a similar nature have been re-echoed by all political leaders in the developed world but the stark fact remains: whatever wars may have been won since 1951, none of them is the war against poverty, disease, hunger and illiteracy. However little other types of war have been deliberately sought, they are the only ones which have been waged. Nothing is gained by assuming that those who express such views are insincere. The position of the leaders of the developed capitalist countries of the world are, in relation to the great neo-colonialist international combines, very similar to that which Lord Macaulay described as existing between the directors of the East India Company and their agent, Warren Hastings, who, in the eighteenth century, engaged in the wholesale plunder of India. Macaulay wrote:

'The Directors, it is true, never enjoined or applauded any crime. Far from it. Whoever examines their letters written at the time will find there are many just and humane sentiments, many excellent precepts, in short, an admirable code of political ethics. But each exultation is modified or nullified by a demand for money. … We by no means accuse or suspect those who framed these dispatches of hypocrisy. It is probable that, written 15,000 miles from the place where their orders were to be carried into effect, they never perceived the gross inconsistency of which they were guilty. But the inconsistency was at once manifest to their lieutenant in Calcutta.

'… Hastings saw that it was absolutely necessary for him to disregard either the moral discourses or the pecuniary requisitions of his employers. Being forced to disobey them in something, he had to consider what kind of disobedience they would most readily pardon; and he correctly judged that the safest course would be to neglect the sermons and to find the rupees.'

Today the need both to maintain a welfare state, i.e. a parasite State at home, and to support a huge and ever-growing burden of armament costs makes it absolutely essential for developed capitalist countries to secure the maximum return in profit from such parts of the international financial complex as they control. However much private capitalism is exhorted to bring about rapid development and a rising standard of living in the less developed areas of the world, those who manipulate the system realise the inconsistency between doing this and producing at the same time the funds necessary to maintain the sinews of war and the welfare state at home. They know when it comes to the issue they will be excused if they fail to provide for a world-wide rise in the standard of living. They know they will never be forgiven it they betray the system and produce a crisis at home which either destroys the affluent State or interferes with its military preparedness.

Appeals to capitalism to work out a cure for the division of the world into rich and poor are likely to have no better result than the appeals of the Directors of the East India Company to Warren Hastings to ensure social justice in India. Faced with a choice, capitalism, like Hastings, will come down on the side of exploitation.

Is there then no method of avoiding the inevitable world conflict occasioned by an international class war? To accept that world conflict is inevitable is to reject any belief in co-existence or in the policy of non-alignment as practised at present by many of the countries attempting to escape from neocolonialism. A way out is possible.

To start with, for the first time in human history the potential material resources of the world are so great that there is no need for there to be rich and poor. It is only the organisation to deploy these potential resources that is lacking. Effective world pressure can force such a redeployment, but world pressure is not exercised by appeals, however eloquent, or by arguments, however convincing. It is only achieved by deeds. It is necessary to secure a world realignment so that those who are at the moment the helpless victims of a system will be able in the future to exert a counter pressure. Such counter pressures do not lead to war. On the contrary, it is often their absence which constitutes the threat to peace.

A parallel can be drawn with the methods by which direct colonialism was ended. No imperial power has ever granted independence to a colony unless the forces were such that no other course was possible, and there are many instances where independence was only achieved by a war of liberation, but there are many other instances when no such war occurred. The very organisation of the forces of independence within the colony was sufficient to convince the imperial power that resistance to independence would be impossible or that the political and economic consequences of a colonial war outweighed any advantage to be gained by retaining the colony.

In the earlier chapters of this book I have set out the argument for African unity and have explained how this unity would destroy neocolonialism in Africa. In later chapters I have explained how strong is the world position of those who *profit* from neocolonialism. Nevertheless, African unity is something which is within the grasp of the African people. The foreign firms who exploit our resources long ago saw the strength to be gained from acting on a Pan-African scale. By means of interlocking directorships, cross-shareholdings and other devices, groups of apparently different companies have formed, in fact, one enormous capitalist monopoly. The only effective *way* to challenge this economic empire and to recover possession of our heritage, is for us also to act on a Pan-African basis, through a Union Government.

No one would suggest that if all the peoples of Africa combined to establish their unity their decision could be revoked by the forces of neocolonialism. On the contrary, faced with a new situation, those who practise neocolonialism would adjust themselves to this new balance of world forces in exactly the same way as the capitalist world has in the past adjusted itself to any other change in the balance of power.

The danger to world peace springs not from the action of those who seek to end neocolonialism but from the inaction of those who allow it to continue. To argue that a third world war is not inevitable is one thing, to suppose that it can be avoided by shutting our eyes to the development of a situation likely to produce it is quite another matter.

If world war is not to occur it must be prevented by positive action. This positive action is within the power of the peoples of those areas of the world which now suffer under neocolonialism but it is only within their power if they act at once, with resolution and in unity.

Supplement, Kwame Nkrumah, President of Ghana

By Federal Bureau of Investigations

Concerned about Nkrumah's public condemnations of American "neocolonialism," the United States government investigated the President and published this secret intelligence report.

ALL FBI INFORMATION CONTAINED HEREIN IS UNCLASSIFIED DATE 04-21-2006 BY 60309 AUC TAM/DCG/EHL

This is the 28th of a series of analyses of key government leaders around the world whose demise or ouster could have far-reaching implications for US military plans and policies.

Ghana's President Kwame Nkrumah is the undisputed ruler of that country, which he in effect created and which he has pushed to a position on the world scene far out of proportion to its size, population, or strategic importance. No real challenge to his leadership is now apparent and he seems likely to continue in office indefinitely. Nevertheless, his dictatorial rule, his suppression of political opposition, his disastrous financial policies, and his pro-Communist sympathies and policies have inevitably led to dissatisfaction among various elements in Ghana and could eventually force a change.

Federal Bureau of Investigations, "Supplement, Kwame Nkrumah, President of Ghana," pp. 1–9.

The military might instigate his overthrow, although this is not now considered likely unless popular discontent deriving from economic unrest should result in widespread instability. Should Nkrumah die or be assassinated, a power struggle is likely, and chaos could ensue. At that time, the armed forces, heretofore largely aloof from political activity, would probably determine the outcome by imposing direct military rule or by assuring that Nkrumah was followed by a man of more conservative policies. Such a successor government would probably be more truly nonaligned than the present regime.

Early Years and Rise to Power

Nkrumah was born in the primitive coastal village of Nkroful in what was then the Gold Coast, a British Colony. His father was a goldsmith, and his mother—one of several wives—a petty trader. Originally named Francis Nwia Kofi Nkrumah, he later took the name Kwame, which in his Nzima tribal dialect means "Saturday's child" since he knows only the day of the week on which he was born. He has accepted the estimated birthdate, 21 Sep 09, given him by the Roman Catholic priest who baptized him, but he may have been born in 1906.

NOT RECORDED

Nkrumah spent eight years in elementary school and became a student teacher at Half Assini for a year. He then enrolled in Achimota College, Ghana's leading secondary school, and after graduating in 1930 taught for several years in local elementary mission schools and then at a Roman Catholic seminary. During this period, he seriously considered becoming a Jesuit priest.

In 1935, aided financially by his uncle, Nkrumah came to the US to study at Lincoln University, a Negro institution in Pennsylvania. After four years of unexceptional academic work, he earned a BA degree. In the next five years, he received a BD from the Lincoln Theological Seminary, and an MA and an MS from the University of Pennsylvania. During his ten years in the US, Nkrumah suffered great financial hardship and held a variety of menial jobs. Although never a top student, he was active in African student organizations and read widely in political theory and philosophy.

Nkrumah went to England in 1945 and enrolled at the London School of Economics and Political Science. He undertook the study of law but failed the course, probably as a result of his many outside activities in student organizations, He helped set up the fifth Pan-African Congress, held in Manchester in 1945, which endorsed a program of revolutionary rather than evolutionary African nationalism. During his stay in the UK, he was sought out by leftists and Communists and learned much from them about organization and agitation. He has, however, vigorously denied ever having been a member of the Communist Party, although he attended meetings in London.

At the invitation of Dr. J. B. Danquah, Nkrumah returned to the Gold Coast in November 1947 to serve as general secretary of the newly formed Nationalist Party, the United Gold Coast Convention (UGCC). His fiery oratory, charm, and organizational ability quickly established for him a large personal following. A trade boycott and demonstrations in 1948 resulted in riots, and Nkrumah was arrested along with other UGCC leaders who blamed him for their detention. When he was released, he was demoted from his position as secretary general of the party but continued to organize mass support and, when the UGCC refused to reinstate him as secretary general, Nkrumah and his followers broke away and founded the Convention People's Party (CPP) on 12 Jun 49.

The more radical CPP quickly eclipsed the UGCC and embarked on a program of "Positive Action"—strikes, boycotts and noncooperation—which in 1950 led to Nkrumah's conviction on three counts of sedition, for which he was sentenced to three years in jail. Imprisonment increased his popularity, however, and the general elections of 1951 brought the CPP to power. He was elected to Parliament and, on 12 Feb 51, was freed to become Leader of Government Business.

Once in a position of political power, Nkrumah realized the necessity for convincing the British that an independent Gold Coast would be viable and moderate. With this in mind, he made an about-face under the slogan of "Tactical Action" and began a campaign of close cooperation with the authorities, expelled Communists from the ranks of the CPP, and forced the Trades Union Congress to affiliate with the Western-oriented International Confederation of Free Trade Unions. By March 1952, he had so impressed the British as a responsible and moderate leader that he was given the formal title of Prime Minister.

For the next several years, Nkrumah generally continued to exhibit a moderate pro-Western posture, while at the same time building the CPP into a national mass party by the use of repressive tactics against the opposition and by gaining control of labor and farmers' organizations. By 6 Mar 57, when the UK granted independence to Ghana, the CPP was in unquestioned control of the government and Nkrumah in unquestioned control of the CPP. On 1 Jul 60, Nkrumah became the first president of Ghana, which became a republic but retained membership in the British Commonwealth. He began a second five-year term on 11 Jun 65 when he was proclaimed President, by Parliament after it had been decided to dispense with the formalities of the electoral process since no opposition candidates to the CPP's nominees had filed for election.

Nkrumah the Man

Nkrumah is an extremely complex man whose most marked characteristic is his egocentricity. His usually friendly, easy-going manner belies the resolute determination with which he has accomplished so much. His charm, personal magnetism, and sense of humor have favorably impressed most observers, but he has a tendency to be less than frank and to tell his listeners what he thinks they want to hear; the resulting inconsistencies between what Nkrumah says and does have over the years considerably lessened his impact on those he wishes to impress. He is an effective public speaker, a quick thinker, and adroit at parrying questions.

Nkrumah is enormously energetic and resilient but suffers from periods of depression during which he is apt to become distracted and to indulge in fits of crying. He is increasingly concerned about his health and almost obsessively fearful for his safety, particularly since the assassination attempts of the past few years. His rather vague Christianity does not preclude his superstitious use of fetishes and oracles. He is bored by economics and frequently refuses to accept unpleasant facts, traits which in part explain his seeming lack of serious concern about the state of Ghana's economy.

Nkrumah is of medium height, has a comb of frizzy hair on his balding head, and has big soul-eyes and a manner that has been described as messianic. He normally wears Western clothes, but frequently dons the toga-like native dress for ceremonial occasions. Until December 1957, Nkrumah flatly asserted that he intended to remain a bachelor; thus, his marriage at the end of that month to a 26-year old Coptic Christian Egyptian woman whom he had never met, and who spoke no English, came as a stunning surprise. Mrs. Nkrumah does not play a prominent social role, and their marriage has apparently not been a great success. The couple have three children, however, and Nkrumah also recognizes an illegitimate son, Francis Nkrumah, a doctor born about 1935 who is reportedly opposed to his father's regime.

Pro-Communist Policies

Nkrumah began in 1960 to display openly his pro-Communist, anti-Western beliefs. Under his influence and with his encouragement, Ghana negotiated a number of economic agreements with Communist nations, waged increasingly strident campaigns against "capitalism, imperialism, and neocolonialism," and generally championed positions and policies in world affairs which support and further Communist aims. Moderates within the government were eliminated or lost their influence, while radicals and leftists assumed positions of importance and leadership and became increasingly influential in guiding Ghana further to the left.

Despite all of this, however, Ghana today is not as far into the Communist camp as would seem probable. That Nkrumah and his like-minded followers have not succeeded in more closely identifying Ghana with the Communist world is due to a number of factors—the Western culture and tradition ingrained over the years of British rule; the fact that Ghana's economy is still closely tied to Western markets; the fact that the governing party is far from being a monolithic organization and has never fully exercised the powers it theoretically possesses; the opposition of the armed forces to closer military ties with the Communists; and the fact that the Communist nations have been increasingly reluctant to shore up the deteriorating economy, thus forcing Nkrumah not to alienate completely, possible sources of Western assistance.

Attitude Toward the US

Ghana, at Nkrumah's direction or at least with his approbation, carries on a continuing propaganda campaign against the leading Western nations, but the US has been by far the favorite target of leftist venom. The US is regularly attacked by the press and radio as the leading imperialist power, for its alleged subversive activities in Africa, and for its policies throughout the world. Nkrumah's latest book, Neo-Colonialism: The Last Stage of Imperialism, contained such scathing charges against the US as to provoke an official protest from Washington. Despite Nkrumah's apparently sincere conviction that the US is bent on bringing about his downfall, however, his personal relations with many US Embassy and other official personnel have often been marked, by apparently warm friendliness and, despite public charges that the Peace Corps is engaged in subversion in Ghana, Nkrumah has shown no desire to dispense with its services.

Aspirations for African and World Leadership

Nkrumah, who is driven by ambition to be far more than Ghana's leader, aspires to be recognized not only as the predominant African political personality but as a man to be reckoned with on the international stage. His dreams of grandeur have led to a number of attempts to make Ghana the focal point of wider African political entities—the abortive Ghana-Guinea-Mali Union, the defunct Joint African High Command, and his current project of a united Africa—all of which have foundered in the face of reality and because of the refusal of other African leaders to accord Nkrumah the position of predominance implicit in all of his schemes. Instead, Ghana has become increasingly isolated, and Nkrumah has earned the distrust of most African leaders and has even alienated his erstwhile radical cronies in Guinea, Mali, and the UAR.

On the international scene, Nkrumah's conception of himself as a world leader has led him to make contacts with other leaders whose real or fancied friendship he values highly. His self-created role has also resulted in frequent offers of gratuitous advice in resolving non-African problems, the details and complexities of which he is largely ignorant. He has thus attempted to insert himself in the Cuban missile crisis, the Sino-Indian border conflict, the Arab-Israeli dispute, the nuclear-disarmament question, and the Vietnamese situation. Nothing has come of any of these efforts.

Although he has succeeded in projecting himself into the African and international scene to a greater extent than most African leaders, Nkrumah is considered by most world leaders to be more of a nuisance and a figure of ridicule than a statesman. These rebuffs, and Nkrumah's consequent sense of extreme frustration, are in part responsible for his policy of encouraging and abetting subversion in Africa, activity which he also rationalizes on the grounds that many African nations—including all of his close neighbors—do not support the radical policies which he advocates and are followed by his government.

Nkrumah's Position in Ghana

Although he has suffered reverses abroad, Nkrumah still reigns supreme in Ghana; he is the personification and living symbol of his nation and its people, he has achieved this position in part through his genuinely charismatic quality and the manner in which his considerable vanity has exploited every means of keeping his name before the public. His official title is "Osagyefo" (The Redeemer), and there are overtones of deification in the adulation which he sanctions and probably encourages. Nkrumah's name and likeness are everywhere in Ghana—on its currency, postage stamps, street names, statues, and schools, and in "Nkrumahism," the murky and confused embodiment of his Marxist-Leninist African socialist-religious philosophies.

Despite Nkrumah's encouragement of the cult of personality and his genuine popularity with many of his people, his position has been frequently challenged and he has been the object of several assassination attempts. Overt political opposition has been suppressed over the years since Nkrumah came to power, however, and there is at present no known organized group within the country which is soon likely to have the capability to overthrow him. There is some resentment of Nkrumah's pro-Communist policies within the military and several coup plots have been under consideration in the past two years, but the armed forces have so far been unwilling to take a step which is not in character with their apolitical position. Popular dissatisfaction is on the rise, however, due to the growing impact of Ghana's disastrous financial policies, and the greatest potential threat to Nkrumah's continued rule lies in the country's deteriorating economy.

Nkrumah is well aware, despite his egocentric nature and the fact that he is surrounded by sycophants, that he is not universally loved. As a result of a number of assassination attempts—at least two of which were almost successful—he has an obsessive fear for his personal safety and has surrounded himself with a number of safeguards, including the President's Own Guard Regiment (POGR). The POGR, although nominally part of the army, is directly responsible to Nkrumah, and its commander and personnel of its battalion (now being expanded to two) have been chosen for their loyalty to him. The POGR is equipped in part with Soviet materiel—the only army unit to be so provided—and several Soviet security officers are on hand. Because of his own anti-Western, anti-Capitalist beliefs, Nkrumah tends to attribute any and all opposition to the intrigues of imperialists and neocolonialists, and he is apparently convinced that the US is actively attempting to bring about his downfall.

He is also extremely distrustful of the security forces and suspects—with some reason—that certain of their leaders have contemplated removing him. To forestall such attempts, the police were disarmed following the January 1964 assassination attempt, and in mid-1965 Nkrumah abruptly dismissed the two top army officers, replacing them with men in whom he has more confidence—although it remains to be seen how long they will retain their positions in view of Nkrumah's highly suspicious nature. In September 1965, he was presented with the Supreme Commander's Baton of Office, a gesture intended to emphasize that he is the operational commander of the armed forces. His latest move to curtail the power of the military was the creation in December of a "people's militia," supposedly formed to prepare for armed action against Rhodesia but apparently intended to provide a counter force to the army. Whether this new organization will ever be one, however, seems highly questionable.

When Nkrumah Goes

Like many other rulers who have concentrated political power in their persons, Nkrumah has made no provision for a successor. Should he leave the scene, a scramble for control would be likely to ensue among the several factions of the government party, and a period of instability would be probable. In such an event, the military might play an important—and perhaps decisive—role. If a strong successor of moderate leaning were to emerge, the military would probably follow and support him. If, however, a leftist were to succeed, or should dissension and chaos result as political figures vie for control, the army would probably set up an interim government pending the selection or emergence of a president it would be willing to accept.

Thus, it seems likely that a successor government would probably be more moderate and adopt more truly neutralist policies than those followed by Nkrumah. It would probably still feel the compulsion to be no less nationalistic than the present government, however, and probably be less stable since any successor would lack Nkrumah's popularity and his identification not only with the people but with Ghana itself. Further, the existence within the governmental hierarchy of moderate and leftist factions would probably continue to engender conflict as contending groups struggled for control.

I Seem to See the River Tiber Foaming with Much Blood

By Enoch Powell

Enoch Powell (1912–1998) was a Classics professor before he entered the British Parliament as a Conservative MP. He is most famous for this 1968 speech in which he warned that post-colonial immigration would create racial and cultural conflicts in England. While proponents of a multi-cultural society point to this speech as a fundamental text in the history of European racism, xenophobic nationalists hail Powell as a prophet. The speech ignores the history of British and European colonial exploitation.

The supreme function of statesmanship is to provide against preventable evils. In seeking to do so, it encounters obstacles which are deeply rooted in human nature. One is that by the very order of things such evils are not demonstrable until they have occurred: at each stage in their onset there is room for doubt and for dispute whether they be real or imaginary. By the same token, they attract little attention in comparison with current troubles, which are both indisputable and pressing. Hence the besetting temptation of all politics to concern itself with the immediate present at the expense of the future. Above all, people are disposed to mistake predicting troubles for causing troubles and even for desiring troubles: 'if only,' they love to think, 'if only people wouldn't talk about it, it probably wouldn't happen.' Perhaps this habit goes back to the primitive belief that the word and the thing, the name and the object, are identical. At all events, the discussion of future grave but, with effort now, avoidable evils is the most unpopular and at the same time the most necessary occupation for the politician. Those who knowingly shirk it, deserve, and not infrequently receive, the curses of those who come after.

A week or two ago I fell into conversation with a constituent, a middle-aged, quite ordinary working man employed in one of our nationalized industries. After a sentence

Enoch Powell; Brian MacArthur, ed., "I Seem to See the River Tiber Flowing with Much Blood," *The Penguin Book of Twentieth-Century Speeches*, pp. 383–392. Copyright © 1999 by Penguin Group (USA) Inc. Reprinted with permission.

or two about the weather, he suddenly said: 'If I had the money to go, I wouldn't stay in this country.' I made some deprecatory reply, to the effect that even this government wouldn't last for ever; but he took no notice, and continued: 'I have three children, all of them been through grammar school and two of them married now, with family. I shan't be satisfied till I have seen them all settled overseas. In this country in fifteen or twenty years' time the black man will have the whip hand over the white man.'

I can already hear the chorus of execration. How dare I say such a horrible thing? How dare I stir up trouble and inflame feelings by repeating such a conversation? The answer is that I do not have the right not to do so. Here is a decent, ordinary fellow-Englishman, who in broad daylight in my own town says to me, his Member of Parliament, that this country will not be worth living in for his children. I simply do not have the right to shrug my shoulders and think about something else. What he is saying, thousands and hundreds of thousands are saying and thinking—not throughout Great Britain, perhaps, but in the areas that are already undergoing the total transformation to which there is no parallel in a thousand years of English history.

In fifteen or twenty years, on present trends, there will be in this country three and a half million Commonwealth immigrants and their descendants. That is not my figure. That is the official figure given to Parliament by the spokesman of the Registrar-General's office. There is no comparable official figure for the year 2000; but it must be in the region of five to seven million, approximately one-tenth of the whole population, and approaching that of Greater London. Of course, it will not be evenly distributed from Margate to Aberystwyth and from Penzance to Aberdeen. Whole areas, towns and parts of towns across England will be occupied by different sections of the immigrant and immigrant-descended population.

As time goes on, the proportion of this total who are immigrant descendants, those born in England, who arrived here by exactly the same route as the rest of us, will rapidly increase. Already by 1985 those born here would constitute the majority. It is this fact above all which creates the extreme urgency of action now, of just that kind of action which is hardest for politicians to take, action where the difficulties lie in the present but evils to be prevented or minimized lie several parliaments ahead.

The natural and rational first question for a nation confronted by such a prospect is to ask: 'How can its dimensions be reduced?' Granted it be not wholly preventable, can it be limited, bearing in mind that numbers are of the essence. The significance and consequences of an alien element introduced into a country or population are profoundly different according to whether that element is one per cent or ten per cent. The answers to the simple and rational question are equally simple and rational: by stopping, or virtually stopping, further inflow, and by promoting the maximum outflow. Both answers are part of the official policy of the Conservative Party.

It almost passes belief that at this moment twenty or thirty additional immigrant children are arriving from overseas in Wolverhampton alone every week—and that means fifteen or twenty additional families a decade or two hence. Those whom the gods wish to destroy, they first make mad. We must be mad, literally mad, as a nation to be permitting the annual inflow of some fifty thousand dependants, who are for the most part the material of the future growth of the immigrant-descended population. It is like watching a nation busily engaged in heaping up its own funeral pyre. So insane are we that we actually permit unmarried persons to immigrate for the purpose of founding a family with spouses and fiancés whom they have never seen. Let no one suppose that the flow of dependants will automatically tail off. On the contrary, even at the present admission rate of only five thousand a year by voucher, there is sufficient for a further twenty-five thousand dependants per annum *ad infinitum*, without taking into account the huge reservoir of existing relations in this country—and I am making no allowance at all for fraudulent entry. In these circumstances nothing will suffice but that the total inflow for settlement be reduced at once to negligible proportions, and that the necessary legislative and administrative measures be taken without delay. I stress the words 'for settlement.' This has nothing to do with the entry of Commonwealth citizens, any more than of aliens, into this country, for the purposes of study or of improving their qualifications, like (for instance) the Commonwealth doctors who, to the advantage of their own countries, have enabled our hospital service to be expanded faster than would otherwise have been possible. These are not, and never have been, immigrants.

I turn to re-emigration. If all immigration ended tomorrow, the rate of growth of the immigrant-descended population would be substantially reduced, but the prospective size of this element in the population would still leave the basic character of the national danger unaffected. This can only be tackled while a considerable proportion of the total still comprises persons who entered this country during the last ten years or so. Hence the urgency of implementing now the second element of the Conservative Party's policy: the encouragement of re-emigration. Nobody can make an estimate of the numbers which, with generous grants and assistance would choose either to return to their countries of origin or go to other countries anxious to receive the manpower and the skills they represent. Nobody knows, because no such policy has yet been attempted. I can only say that, even at present, immigrants in my own constituency from time to time come to me, asking if I can find them assistance to return home. If such a policy were adopted and pursued, with the determination which the gravity of the alternative justifies, the resultant outflow could appreciably alter the prospects for the future.

It can be no part of any policy that existing families should be kept divided; but there are two directions in which families can be reunited, and if our former and present immigration laws have brought about the division of families, albeit voluntary or semi-voluntary, we ought to be prepared to arrange for them to be reunited in their countries of origin. In short, suspension of immigration and encouragement of re-emigration belong together, logically and humanly, as two aspects of the same approach.

The third element of the Conservative Party's policy is that all who are in this country as citizens should be equal before the law and that there shall be no discrimination or difference made between them by public authority. As Mr Heath has put it, we will have no 'first-class citizens' and 'second-class citizens.' This does not mean that the immigrant and his descendants should be elevated into a privileged or special class or that the citizen should be denied his right to discriminate in the management of his own affairs between one fellow-citizen and another or that he should be subjected to inquisition as to his reasons and motives for behaving in one lawful manner rather than another.

There could be no grosser misconception of the realities than is entertained by those who vociferously demand legislation as they call it 'against discrimination,' whether they be leaderwriters of the same kidney and sometimes on the same newspapers which year after year in the 1930s tried to blind this country to the rising peril which confronted it, or archbishops who live in palaces, faring delicately, with the bedclothes pulled right over their heads. They have got it exactly and diametrically wrong. The discrimination and the deprivation, the sense of alarm and of resentment, lies not with the immigrant population but with those among whom they have come and are still coming. This is why to enact legislation of the land before Parliament at this moment is to risk throwing a match on to gunpowder. The kindest thing that can be said about those who propose and support it is that they know not what they do.

Nothing is more misleading than comparison between the Commonwealth immigrant in Britain and the American Negro. The Negro population of the United States, which was already in existence before the United States became a nation, started literally as slaves and were later given the franchise and other rights of citizenship, to the exercise of which they have only gradually and still incompletely come. The Commonwealth immigrant came to Britain as a full citizen, to a country which knew no discrimination between one citizen and another, and he entered instantly into the possession of the rights of every citizen, from the vote to free treatment under the National Health Service. Whatever drawbacks attended the immigrants—and they were drawbacks which did not, and do not, make admission into Britain by hook or by crook appear less than desirable—arose not from the law or from public policy or from administration but from those personal circumstances and accidents which cause, and always will cause, the fortunes and experience of one man to be different from another's.

But while to the immigrant entry to this country was admission to privileges and opportunities eagerly sought, the impact upon the existing population was very different. For reasons which they could not comprehend, and in pursuance of a decision by default, on which they were never consulted, they found themselves made strangers in their own country. They found their wives unable to obtain hospital beds in child-birth, their children unable to obtain school places, their homes and neighbourhoods changed beyond recognition, their plans and prospects for the future defeated; at work they found that employers hesitated to apply to the immigrant worker the standards of discipline and competence required of the native-born worker; they began to hear, as time went by, more and more voices which told them that they were now the unwanted. On top of this, they now learn that a one-way privilege is to be established by Act of Parliament: a law, which cannot, and is not intended, to operate to protect them or redress their grievances, is to be enacted to give the stranger, the disgruntled and the *agent provocateur* the power to pillory them for their private actions.

In the hundreds upon hundreds of letters I received when I last spoke on this subject two or three months ago, there was one striking feature which was largely new and which I find ominous. All Members of Parliament are used to the typical anony-mous correspondent; but what surprised and alarmed me was the high proportion of ordinary, decent, sensible people, writing a rational and often well-educated letter, who believed that they had to omit their address because it was dangerous to have committed themselves to paper to a Member of Parliament agreeing with the views I had expressed, and that they would risk either penalties or reprisals if they were known to have done so. The sense of being a persecuted minority which is growing among ordinary English people in the areas of the country which are affected is something that those without direct experience can hardly imagine. I am going to allow just one of those hundreds of people to speak for me. She did give her name and address, which I have detached from the letter which I am about to read. She was writing from Northumberland about something which is happening at this moment in my own constituency:

Eight years ago in a respectable street in Wolverhampton a house was sold to a Negro. Now only one white (a woman old-age pensioner) lives there. This is her story. She lost her husband and both her sons in the war. So she turned her seven-roomed house, her only asset, into a boarding house. She worked hard and did well, paid off her mortgage and began to put something by for her old age. Then the immigrants moved in. With growing fear, she saw one house after another taken over. The quiet street became a place of noise and confusion. Regretfully, her white tenants moved out.

The day after the last one left, she was awakened at 7 a.m. by two Negroes who wanted to use her phone to contact their employer. When she refused, as she would have refused any stranger at such an hour, she was abused and feared she would have been attacked but for the chain on her door. Immigrant families have tried to rent rooms in her house, but she always refused. Her little store of money went, and after paying her rates, she has less than £2 per week. She went to apply for a rate reduction and was seen by a young girl, who on hearing she had a seven-roomed house, suggested she should let part of it. When she said the only people she could get were Negroes, the girl said 'racial prejudice won't get you anywhere in this country.' So she went home.

The telephone is her lifeline. Her family pay the bill, and help her out as best they can. Immigrants have offered to buy her house—at a price which the prospective landlord would be able to recover from his tenants in weeks, or at most a few months. She is becoming afraid to go out. Windows are broken. She finds excreta pushed through her letterbox. When she goes to the shops, she is followed by children, charming, wide-grinning piccaninnies. They cannot speak English, but one word they know. 'Racialist,' they chant. When the new Race Relations Bill is passed, this woman is convinced she will go to prison. And is she so wrong? I begin to wonder.

The other dangerous delusion from which those who are wilfully or otherwise blind to realities suffer, is summed up in the word "integration." To be integrated into a population means to become for all practical purposes indistinguishable from its other members. Now, at all times, where there are marked physical differences, especially of colour, integration is difficult, though over a period, not impossible. There are among the Commonwealth, immigrants who have come to live here in the last fifteen years or so, many thousands whose wish and purpose is to be integrated and whose every thought and endeavour is bent in that direction. But to imagine that such a thing enters the heads of a great and growing majority of immigrants and their descendants is a ludicrous misconception, and a dangerous one to boot.

We are on the verge of a change. Hitherto, it has been force of circumstance and of background which has rendered the very idea of integration inaccessible to the greater part of the immigrant population—that they never conceived or intended such a thing, and that their numbers and physical concentration meant the pressures towards integration which normally bear upon any small minority did not operate. Now we are seeing the growth of positive forces acting against integration, of vested interests in the preservation and sharpening of racial and religious differences, with a view to the exercise of actual domination, first over fellow-immigrants and then over the rest of the population. The cloud no bigger than a man's hand, that can so rapidly overcast the sky, has been visible recently in Wolverhampton and has shown signs of spreading quickly. The words I am about to use, verbatim as they appeared in the local press of 17 February [1968] , are not mine, but those of a Labour Member of Parliament who is a Minister in the Government. 'The Sikh community's campaign to maintain customs inappropriate in Britain is much to be regretted. Working in Britain, particularly in the public services, they should be prepared to accept the terms and conditions of their employment. To claim special communal rights (or should one say rites?) leads to a dangerous fragmentation within society. This communalism is a canker; whether practised by one colour or another it is to be strongly condemned.' All credit to John Stonehouse for having had the insight to perceive that, and the courage to say it.

For these dangerous and divisive elements the legislation proposed in the Race Relations Bill is the very pabulum they need to flourish. Here is the means of showing that the immigrant communities can organize to consolidate their members, to agitate and campaign against their fellow-citizens, and to overawe and dominate the rest with legal weapons which the ignorant and the ill-informed have provided. As I look ahead, I am filled with foreboding. Like the Roman, I seem to see 'the River Tiber foaming with much blood.' The tragic and intractable phenomenon which we watch with horror on the other side of the Atlantic but which there is interwoven with the history and existence of the States itself, is coming upon us here by our own volition and our own neglect. Indeed, it has all but come. In numerical terms, it will be of American proportions long before the end of the century. Only resolute and urgent action will avert it even now. Whether there will be the public will to demand and obtain that action, I do not know. All I know is that to see, and not to speak, would be the great betrayal.

The New Empire Within Britain

By Salman Rushdie

Salman Rushdie, was born to a Muslim family in Bombay, India, and came to the United Kingdom and pursued a career as a writer. Having crossed boundaries his entire life, many of his novels explore and celebrate cultural diversity in India, the United Kingdom, and the United States of America. In this 1982 piece he criticizes the racism and xenophobia of post-colonial England.

Britain isn't South Africa. I am reliably informed of this. Nor is it Nazi Germany. I've got that on the best authority as well. You may feel that these two statements are not exactly the most dramatic of revelations. But it's remarkable how often they, or similar statements, are used to counter the arguments of anti-racist campaigners. Things aren't as bad as all that, we are told, 'you exaggerate, you're indulging in special pleading, you must be paranoid.' So let me concede at once that, as far as I know, there are no pass laws here. Inter-racial marriages are permitted. And Auschwitz hasn't been rebuilt in the Home Counties. I find it odd, however, that those who use such absences as defences rarely perceive that their own statements indicate how serious things have become. Because if the defence for Britain is that mass extermination of racially impure persons hasn't yet begun, or that the principle of white supremacy hasn't actually been enshrined in the constitution, then something must have gone very wrong indeed.

I want to suggest that racism is not a side-issue in contemporary Britain; that it's not a peripheral minority affair. I believe that Britain is undergoing a critical phase of its post-colonial period, and this crisis is not simply economic or political. It's a crisis of the whole culture, of the society's entire sense of itself. And racism is only the most clearly visible part of this crisis, the tip of the kind of iceberg that sinks ships.

Salman Rushdie, "The New Empire Within Britain," *Imaginary Homelands: Essays and Criticism, 1981–1991*, pp. 129–138. Copyright © 1982 by Penguin Group (USA) Inc. Reprinted with permission.

Now I don't suppose many of you think of the British Empire as a subject worth losing much sleep over. After all, surely the one thing one can confidently say about that roseate age of England's precedence, when the map of half the world blushed with pleasure as it squirmed beneath the Pax Britannica, is that it's over, isn't it? Give or take a Falkland Island, the imperial sun has set. And how fine was the manner of its setting; in what good order the British withdrew. Union Jacks fluttered down their poles all round the world, to be replaced by other flags, in all manner of outlandish colours. The pink conquerors crept home, the boxwallahs and memsahibs and bwanas, leaving behind them parliaments, schools, Grand Trunk Roads and the rules of cricket. How gracefully they shrank back into their cold island, abandoning their lives as the dashing people of their dreams, diminishing from the endless steaming landscapes of India and Africa into the narrow horizons of their pallid, drizzled streets. The British have got other things to worry about now; no point, you may say, in exhuming this particular dead horse in order to flog the poor, decomposed creature all over again.

But the connection I want to make is this: that those same attitudes are in operation right here as well, here in what E. P. Thompson has described as the last colony of the British Empire. It sometimes seems that the British authorities, no longer capable of exporting governments, have chosen instead to import a new Empire, a new community of subject peoples of whom they think, and with whom they can deal, in very much the same way as their predecessors thought of and dealt with 'the fluttered folk and wild,' the 'new-caught, sullen peoples, half-devil and half-child,' who made up, for Rudyard Kipling, the White Man's Burden. In short, if we want to understand British racism—and without understanding no improvement is possible—it's impossible even to begin to grasp the nature of the beast unless we accept its historical roots. Four hundred years of conquest and looting, four centuries of being told that you are superior to the Fuzzy-Wuzzies and the wogs, leave their stain. This stain has seeped into every part of the culture, the language and daily life; and nothing much has been done to wash it out.

For proof of the existence of this stain, we can look, for instance, at the huge, undiminished appetite of white Britons for television series, films, plays and books all filled with nostalgia for the Great Pink Age. Or think about the ease with which the English language allows the terms of racial abuse to be coined: wog, frog, kraut, dago, spic, yid, coon, nigger, Argie. Can there be another language with so wide-ranging a vocabulary of racist denigration? And, since I've mentioned Argies, let me quote from Margaret Thatcher's speech at Cheltenham on the third of July, her famous victory address: 'We have learned something about ourselves,' she said then, 'a lesson which we desperately need to learn. When we started out, there were the waverers and the fainthearts. ... The people who thought we could no longer do the great things which we once did ... that we could never again be what we were. There were those who would not admit it... but—in their heart of hearts—they too had their secret fears that it was true: that Britain was no longer the nation that had built an Empire and ruled a quarter of the world. Well, they were wrong.'

There are several interesting aspects to this speech. Remember that it was made by a triumphant Prime Minister at the peak of her popularity; a Prime Minister who could claim with complete credibility to be speaking for an overwhelming majority of the electorate, and who, as even her detractors must admit, has a considerable gift for assessing the national mood. Now if such a leader at such a time felt able to invoke the spirit of imperialism, it was because she knew how central that spirit is to the self-image of white Britons of all classes. I say white Britons because it's clear that Mrs Thatcher wasn't addressing the two million or so blacks, who don't feel quite like that about the Empire. So even her use of the word 'we' was an act of racial exclusion, like her other well-known speech about the fear of being 'swamped' by immigrants. With such leaders, it's not surprising that the British are slow to learn the real lessons of their past.

Let me repeat what I said at the beginning: Britain isn't Nazi Germany. The British Empire isn't the Third Reich. But in Germany, after the fall of Hitler, heroic attempts were made by many people to purify German thought and the German language of the pollution of Nazism. Such acts of cleansing are occasionally necessary in every society. But British thought, British society, has never been cleansed of the filth of imperialism. It's still there, breeding lice and vermin, waiting for unscrupulous people to exploit it for their own ends. One of the key concepts of imperialism was that military superiority implied cultural superiority, and this enabled the British to condescend to and repress cultures far older than their own; and it still does. For the citizens of the new, imported Empire, for the colonized Asians and blacks of Britain, the police force represents that colonizing army, those regiments of occupation and control.

Now the peoples whom I've characterized as members of a new colony would probably be described by most of you as 'immigrants.' (You'll notice, by the way, that I've pinched one of Mrs. Thatcher's strategies and the You to whom I'm talking is a white You.) So now I'd like to ask you to think about this word 'immigrant,' because it seems to me to demonstrate the extent to which racist concepts have been allowed to seize the central ground, and to shape the whole nature of the debate. The facts are that for many years now there has been a sizeable amount of white immigration as well as black, that the annual number of emigrants leaving these shores is now larger than the number of immigrants coming in; and that, of the black communities, over forty per cent are not immigrants, but black Britons, born and bred, speaking in the many voices and accents of Britain, and with no homeland but this one. And still the word 'immigrant' means 'black immigrant'; the myth of 'swamping' lingers on; and even British-born blacks and Asians are thought of as people whose real 'home' is elsewhere. Immigration is only a problem if you are worried about blacks; that is, if your whole approach to the question is one of racial prejudice.

But perhaps the worst thing about the so-called 'numbers game' is its assumption that less black immigration is self-evidently desirable. The effect of this assumption is that governments of both parties have eagerly passed off gross injustice as success. Let me explain. The immigration laws of this country have established a quota system for migration of UK passport holders from various countries. But after Idi Amin drove out the Ugandan Asians, and Britain did her best to prevent those British citizens from entering this country, that African quota was never increased; and, as a result, the total number of black immigrants to Britain has fallen. Now you might think that natural justice would demand that the already lamentably low quotas for British citizens from Africa would be made available to those same citizens, many of whom are now living as refugees in India, a desperately poor country which can ill-afford to care for them. But natural justice has never been much in evidence in this field. In fact, the British tax system now intends to withhold tax relief from wage-earners here whose dependants are trapped abroad. So first you keep people's families away from them and then you alter your laws to make it twice as hard for those people to keep their families fed. They're only 'immigrants,' after all.

A couple of years ago the British press made a huge stink about a family of African Asians who arrived at Heathrow airport and were housed by the very reluctant local authority. It became a classic media witch hunt: 'They come over here, sponge off the State and jump the housing queue.' But that same week, another family also landed at Heathrow, also needing, and getting, housing from the same local authority. This second family barely made the papers. It was a family of white Rhodesians running away from the prospect of a free Zimbabwe. One of the more curious aspects of British immigration law is that many Rhodesians, South Africans and other white non-Britons have automatic right of entry and residence here, by virtue of having one British-born grandparent; whereas many British citizens are denied these rights, because they happen to be black.

One last point about the 'immigrants.' It's a pretty obvious point, but it keeps getting forgotten. It's this: they came because they were invited. The Macmillan government embarked on a large-scale advertising campaign to attract them. They were extraordinary advertisements, full of hope and optimism, which made Britain out to be a land of plenty, a golden opportunity not to be missed. And they worked. People travelled here in good faith, believing themselves wanted. This is how the new Empire was imported. This country was named 'perfidious Albion' long ago; and that shaming nickname is now being earned all over again.

So what's it like, this country to which the immigrants came and in which their children are growing up? You wouldn't recognize it. Because this isn't the England of fair play, tolerance, decency and equality—maybe that place never existed anyway, except in fairy-tales. In the streets of the new Empire, black women are abused and black children are beaten up on their way home from school. In the rundown housing estates of the new Empire, black families have their windows broken, they are afraid to go out after dark, and human and animal excrement arrives through their letter-boxes. The police offer threats instead of protection, and the courts offer small hope of redress. Britain is now two entirely different worlds, and the one you inhabit is determined by the colour of your skin. Now in my experience, very few white people, except for those active in fighting racism, are willing to believe the descriptions of contemporary reality offered by blacks. And black people, faced with what Professor Michael Dummett has called 'the will not to know—a chosen ignorance, not the ignorance of innocence,' grow increasingly suspicious and angry.

A gulf in reality has been created. White and black perceptions of everyday life have moved so far apart as to be incompatible. And the rift isn't narrowing; it's getting wider. We stand on opposite sides of the abyss, yelling at each other and sometimes hurling stones, while the ground crumbles beneath our feet. I make no apology for taking an uncompromising view of the reasons for the existence of this chasm. The will to ignorance of which Professor Dummett speaks arises out of the desire not to face the consequences of what is going on.

The fact remains that every major institution in this country is permeated by racial prejudice to some degree, and the unwillingness of the white majority to recognize this is the main reason why it can remain the case. Let's take the Law. We have, in Britain today, judges like McKinnon who can say in court that the word 'nigger' cannot be considered an epithet of racial abuse because he was nicknamed 'Nigger' at his public school; or like the great Lord Denning, who can publish a book claiming that black people aren't as fit as whites to serve on juries, because they come from cultures with less stringent moral codes. We've got a police force that harasses blacks every day of their lives. There was a policeman who sat in an unmarked car on Railton Road in Brixton last year, shouting abuse at passing black kids and arresting the first youngsters who made the mistake of answering back. There were policemen at a Southall demonstration who sat in their vans, writing the letters NF in the steam of their breath on the windows. The British police have even refused to make racial discrimination an offence in their code of conduct, in spite of Lord Scarman's recommendations. Now it is precisely because the law courts and the police are not doing their jobs that the activities of racist hooligans are on the increase. It's just not good enough to deplore the existence of neo-Fascists in society. They exist because they are permitted to exist. (I said every major institution, so let's consider the government itself. When the Race Relations Act was passed, the government of Britain specifically exempted itself and all its actions from the jurisdiction of the Act.)

A friend of mine, an Indian, was deported recently for the technical offence known as 'overstaying.' This means that after a dozen or so years of living here, he was found to be a couple of days late sending in the forms applying for an extension to his stay. Now neither he nor his family had ever claimed a penny in welfare, or, I suppose I should say, been in trouble with the police. He and his wife financed themselves by running a clothes stall, and gave all their spare time and effort to voluntary work helping their community. My friend was chairman of his local traders' association. So when the deportation order was made, this association, all three of his borough MPs and about fifty other MPs of all parties pleaded with the Home Office for clemency. None was forthcoming. My friend's son had a rare disease, and a doctor's report was produced stating that the child's health would be endangered if he was sent to India. The Home Office replied that it considered there were no compassionate grounds for reversing its decision. In the end, my friend offered to leave voluntarily—he had been offered sanctuary in Germany—and he asked to be allowed to go freely, to avoid the stigma of having a deportation order stamped into his passport. The Home Office refused him this last scrap of his self-respect, and threw him out. As the Fascist John Kingsley Read once said, one down, a million to go.

The combination of this sort of institutional racism and the willed ignorance of the public was clearly in evidence during the passage through Parliament of the Nationality Act of 1981. This already notorious piece of legislation, expressly designed to deprive black and Asian Britons of their citizenship rights, went through in spite of some, mainly non-white, protests. And because it didn't really affect the position of the whites, you probably didn't even realize that one of your most ancient rights, a right you had possessed for nine hundred years, was being stolen from you. This was the right to citizenship by virtue of birth, the *ius soli*, or right of the soil. For nine centuries any child born on British soil was British. Automatically. By right. Not by permission of the State. The Nationality Act abolished the *ius soli*. From now on citizenship is the gift of government. You were blind, because you believed the Act was aimed at the blacks; and so you sat back and did nothing as Mrs. Thatcher stole the birthright of every one of us, black and white, and of our children and grandchildren for ever.

Now it's possible that this blindness is incurable. One of the SDP's better-known candidates told me recently that while he found the idea of working-class racism easy to accept, the parallel notion of widespread prejudice in the middle classes was unconvincing to him. Yet, after many years of voluntary work in this field, I know that the management levels of British industry and business are just as shot through by the threads of prejudice as are many unions. It is believed for instance, that as many as fifty per cent of all telephone calls made by employers to employment agencies specify no blacks. Black unemployment is much, much higher than white; and such anomalies don't arise by accident.

Let me illustrate my point by talking about television. I once earned my living by writing commercials, and I found the prejudice of senior executives in British industry quite appalling. I could tell you the name of the chairman of a leading building society who rejected a jingle on the grounds that the off-screen singer sounded as if he had a black voice. The irony was that the singer was actually white, but the previous year's jingle *had* been sung by a black man who obviously had the good fortune not to sound like one. I know the marketing director of a leading confectionery firm who turned down all requests to cast a black child—as one of an otherwise white group of children—in his commercial. He said his research showed such casting would be counterproductive. I know an airline advertising manager who refused to permit the use, in his TV ads, of a genuine air stewardess employed by his own airline, because she was black. She was good enough to serve his customers their drinks, but not good enough to be shown doing so on television.

A language reveals the attitudes of the people who use and shape it. And a whole declension of patronizing terminology can be found in the language in which inter-racial relations have been described inside Britain. At first, we were told, the goal was 'integration.' Now this word rapidly came to mean 'assimilation': a black man could only become integrated when he started behaving like a white one. After 'integration' came the concept of 'racial harmony.' Now once again, this sounded virtuous and desirable, but what it meant in practice was that blacks should be persuaded to live peaceably with whites, in spite of all the injustices done to them every day. The call for 'racial harmony' was simply an invitation to shut up and smile while nothing was done about our grievances. And now there's a new catchword: 'multiculturalism.' In our schools, this means little more than teaching the kids a few bongo rhythms, how to tie a sari and so forth. In the police training programme, it means telling cadets that black people are so 'culturally different' that they can't help making trouble. Multiculturalism is the latest token gesture towards Britain's blacks, and it ought to be exposed, like 'integration' and 'racial harmony,' for the sham it is.

Meanwhile, the stereotyping goes on. Blacks have rhythm, Asians work hard. I've been told by Tory politicians that the Conservative Party seriously discusses the idea of wooing the Asians and leaving the Afro-Caribbeans to the Labour Party, because Asians are such good capitalists. In the new Empire, as in the old one, it seems our masters are willing to use the tried and trusted strategies of divide-and-rule.

But I've saved the worst and most insidious stereotype for last. It is the characterization of black people as a Problem. You talk about the Race Problem, the Immigration Problem, all sorts of problems. If you are liberal, you say that black people have problems. If you aren't, you say they are the problem. But the members of the new colony have only one real problem, and that problem is white people. British racism, of course, is not our problem. It's yours. We simply suffer from the effects of your problem.

And until you, the whites, see that the issue is not integration, or harmony, or multiculturalism, or immigration, but simply the business of facing up to and eradicating the prejudices within almost all of you, the citizens of your new, and last, Empire will be obliged to struggle against you. You could say that we are required to embark on a new freedom movement.

And so it's interesting to remember that when Mahatma Gandhi, the father of an earlier freedom movement, came to England and was asked what he thought of English civilization, he replied: 'I think it would be a good idea.'

1982

Chapter 9

New World (Dis)Order

Introduction

The year 1989 was a dramatic one. Some might argue that the twentieth century ended in 1989. Pointing to the fall of the Berlin Wall and the collapse of Communism in Eastern Europe and eventually the Soviet Union in 1991, American political scientist Francis Fukuyama argued that 1989 was the start of "the end of history." Yet 1989 also witnessed other key events. The Chinese Communist Party brutally suppressed the student-led democracy movement in Tiananmen Square in June and in December President George H. W. Bush invaded Panama in Operation Just Cause. Bush would later deploy troops to Kuwait and Saudi Arabia to stop Iraq's occupation of Kuwait and support a failed peace-keeping mission in Somalia. Bush began to openly speak of creating a "New World Order" in which America would be the lone super-power. Despite China's poor record on human rights, the regime pursued economic reforms and liberalization. With the goal of expanding trade relations between the United States and the People's Republic of China, Bush's successor President Clinton was willing to overlook China's policies of ethnic, religious, and political repression. In 1989 the 14th Dalai Lama won the Nobel Prize for his activism on behalf of Tibet but also as a statement against China's repressive policies. Meanwhile, when Soviet forces withdrew from Afghanistan on February 15, 1989, Islamic militants known as Mujahideen could claim a great victory in their defeat of the Communist super-power. Amongst the celebrants was the young radicalized Saudi, Osama bin Laden. He would later vent his anger at the United States for sending troops into the Arabian Peninsula, which he viewed as a sacred land. 1989 also was the year of the Ayatollah Khomeini's *fatwa* calling for the death of Salman Rushdie for his allegedly offensive novel *The Satanic Verses*. The documents in this section are designed to guide the reader through the last decade of the century, showing how the end of the Cold War and the process of decolonization created the crises of the early twenty-first century.

This chapter relates to sections 10.9, 10.10, and 10.11 of the History-Social Science Content Standards for California Public Schools.

Nobel Peace Prize Lecture, 1989

By Dalai Lama

The 14th Dalai Lama, Tenzin Gyatso (1935–), is both the head of state and the spiritual leader of Tibet. Born to a farming family in a small hamlet located in northeastern Tibet, the child, named Lhamo Dhondup, at the age of two, was recognized as the reincarnation of the previous Dalai Lama. Tibetans believe the Dalai Lamas to be Bodhisattvas, enlightened beings who have postponed their own nirvana and chosen to take rebirth in order to serve humanity. In 1950 he assumed full political power after Communist China's invasion of Tibet in 1949. In 1954, the Dalai Lama went to Beijing for peace talks with Mao Zedong, Deng Xiaoping, and Chou Enlai, but after the brutal suppression of the Tibetan national uprising in Lhasa by Chinese troops, he was forced to escape into exile. Since 1959 he has been living in Dharamsala, northern India, the seat of the Tibetan political administration in exile. The Dalai Lama has frequently appealed to the United Nations on the question of Tibet. He was the 1989 Nobel Peace Prize winner for his non-violent struggle for the liberation of Tibet and for his concern for global environmental problems. He continues to maintain that he is a simple Buddhist monk.

Brothers and Sisters:

It is an honour and pleasure to be among you today. I am really happy to see so many old friends who have come from different corners of the world, and to make new friends, whom I hope to meet again in the future. When I meet people in different parts of the world, I am always reminded that we are all basically alike: we are all human beings. Maybe we have different clothes, our skin is of a different colour, or we speak different languages. That is on the surface. But basically, we are the same human beings. That is what binds us to each other. That is what makes it possible for us to understand each other and to develop friendship and closeness.

Thinking over what I might say today, I decided to share with you some of my thoughts concerning the common problems all of us face as members of the human family. Because we all share this small planet earth, we have to learn to live in harmony and peace with each other and with nature. That is not just a dream, but a necessity. We are dependent on each other in so many ways, that we can no longer live in isolated communities and ignore what is happening outside those communities, and we must share the good fortune that we enjoy. I speak to you as just another human being; as a simple monk. If you find what I say useful, then I hope you will try to practise it.

I also wish to share with you today my feelings concerning the plight and aspirations of the people of Tibet. The Nobel Prize is a prize they well deserve for their courage and unfailing determination during the past forty years of foreign occupation. As a free spokesman for my captive countrymen and -women, I feel it is my duty to speak out on their behalf. I speak not with a feeling of anger or hatred towards those who are responsible for the immense suffering of our people and the destruction of our land, homes and culture. They too are human beings who struggle to find happiness and deserve our compassion. I speak to inform you of the sad situation in my country today and of the aspirations of my people, because in our struggle for freedom, truth is the only weapon we possess.

The realisation that we are all basically the same human beings, who seek happiness and try to avoid suffering, is very helpful in developing a sense of brotherhood and sisterhood; a warm feeling of love and compassion for others. This, in turn, is essential if we are to survive in this ever shrinking world we live in. For if we each selfishly pursue only what we believe to be in our own interest, without caring about the needs of others, we not only may end up harming others but also ourselves. This fact has become very clear during the course of this century. We know that to wage a nuclear war today, for example, would be a form of suicide; or that by polluting the air or the oceans, in order to achieve some short-term benefit, we are destroying the very basis for our survival. As interdependents, therefore, we have no other choice than to develop what I call a sense of universal responsibility.

Today, we are truly a global family. What happens in one part of the world may affect us all. This, of course, is not only true of the negative things that happen, but is equally valid for the positive developments. We not only know what happens elsewhere, thanks to the extraordinary modern communications technology. We are also directly affected by events that occur far away. We feel a sense of sadness when children are starving in Eastern Africa. Similarly, we feel a sense of joy when a family is reunited after decades of separation by the Berlin Wall. Our crops and livestock are contaminated and our health and livelihood threatened when a nuclear accident happens miles away in another country. Our own security is enhanced when peace breaks out between warring parties in other continents.

But war or peace; the destruction or the protection of nature; the violation or promotion of human rights and democratic freedoms; poverty or material well-being; the lack of moral and spiritual values or their existence and development; and the breakdown or development of human understanding, are not isolated phenomena that can be analysed and tackled independently of one another. In fact, they are very much interrelated at all levels and need to be approached with that understanding.

Peace, in the sense of the absence of war, is of little value to someone who is dying of hunger or cold. It will not remove the pain of torture inflicted on a prisoner of conscience. It does not comfort those who have lost their loved ones in floods caused by senseless deforestation in a neighbouring country. Peace can only last where human rights are respected, where the people are fed, and where individuals and nations are free. True peace with oneself and with the world around us can only be achieved through the development of mental peace. The other phenomena mentioned above are similarly interrelated. Thus, for example, we see that a clean environment, wealth or democracy mean little in the face of war, especially nuclear war, and that material development is not sufficient to ensure human happiness.

Material progress is of course important for human advancement. In Tibet, we paid much too little attention to technological and economic development, and today we realise that this was a mistake. At the same time, material development without spiritual development can also cause serious problems, In some countries too much attention is paid to external things and very little importance is given to inner development. I believe both are important and must be developed side by side so as to achieve a good balance between them. Tibetans are always described by foreign visitors as being a happy, jovial people. This is part of our national character, formed by cultural and religious values that stress the importance of mental peace through the generation of love and kindness to all other living sentient beings, both human and animal. Inner peace is the key: if you have inner peace, the external problems do not affect your deep sense of peace and tranquility. In that state of mind you can deal with situations with calmness and reason, while keeping your inner happiness. That is very important. Without this inner peace, no matter how comfortable your life is materially, you may still be worried, disturbed or unhappy because of circumstances.

Clearly, it is of great importance, therefore, to understand the interrelationship among these and other phenomena, and to approach and attempt to solve problems in a balanced way that takes these different aspects into consideration. Of course it is not easy. But it is of little benefit to try to solve one problem if doing so creates an equally serious new one. So really we have no alternative: we must develop a sense of universal responsibility not only in the geographic sense, but also in respect to the different issues that confront our planet.

Responsibility does not only lie with the leaders of our countries or with those who have been appointed or elected to do a particular job. It lies with each one of us individually. Peace, for example, starts with each one of us. When we have inner peace, we can be at peace with those around us. When our community is in a state of peace, it can share that peace with neighbouring communities, and so on. When we feel love and kindness towards others, it not only makes others feel loved and cared for, but it helps us also to develop inner happiness and peace. And there are ways in which we can consciously work to develop feelings of love and kindness. For some of us, the most effective way to do so is through religious practice. For others it may be non-religious practices. What is important is that we each make a sincere effort to take our responsibility for each other and for the natural environment we live in seriously.

I am very encouraged by the developments which are taking place around us. After the young people of many countries, particularly in northern Europe, have repeatedly called for an end to the dangerous destruction of the environment which was being conducted in the name of economic development, the world's political leaders are now starting to take meaningful steps to address this problem. The report to the United Nations Secretary-General by the World Commission on the Environment and Development (the Brundtland Report) was an important step in educating governments on the urgency of the issue. Serious efforts to bring peace to war-torn zones and to implement the right to self-determination of some people have resulted in the withdrawal of Soviet troops from Afghanistan and the establishment of independent Namibia. Through persistent nonviolent popular efforts dramatic changes, bringing many countries closer to real democracy, have occurred in many places, from Manila in the Philippines to Berlin in East Germany. With the Cold War era apparently drawing to a close, people everywhere live with renewed hope. Sadly, the courageous efforts of the Chinese people to bring similar change to their country was brutally crushed last June. But their efforts too are a source of hope. The military might has not extinguished the desire for freedom and the determination of the Chinese people to achieve it. I particularly admire the fact that these young people who have been taught that "power grows from the barrel of the gun," chose, instead, to use nonviolence as their weapon.

What these positive changes indicate, is that reason, courage, determination, and the inextinguishable desire for freedom can ultimately win. In the struggle between forces of war, violence and oppression on the one hand, and peace, reason and freedom on the other, the latter are gaining the upper hand. This realisation fills us Tibetans with hope that some day we too will once again be free.

The awarding of the Nobel Prize to me, a simple monk from faraway Tibet, here in Norway, also fills us Tibetans with hope. It means, despite the fact that we have not drawn attention to our plight by means of violence, we have not been forgotten. It also means that the values we cherish, in particular our respect for all forms of life and the belief in the power of truth, are today recognised and encouraged. It is also a tribute to my mentor, Mahatma Gandhi, whose example is an inspiration to so many of us. This year's award is an indication that this sense of universal responsibility is developing. I am deeply touched by the sincere concern shown by so many people in this part of the world for the suffering of the people of Tibet. That is a source of hope not only for us Tibetans, but for all oppressed people.

As you know, Tibet has, for forty years, been under foreign occupation. Today, more than a quarter of a million Chinese troops are stationed in Tibet. Some sources estimate the occupation army to be twice this strength. During this time, Tibetans have been deprived of their most basic human rights, including the right to life, movement, speech, worship, only to mention a few. More than one sixth of Tibet's population of six million died as a direct result of the Chinese invasion and occupation. Even before the Cultural Revolution started, many of Tibet's monasteries, temples and historic buildings were destroyed. Almost everything that remained was destroyed during the Cultural Revolution. I do not wish to dwell on this point, which is well documented. What is important to realise, however, is that despite the limited freedom granted after 1979, to rebuild parts of some monasteries and other such tokens of liberalisation, the fundamental human rights of the Tibetan people are still today being systematically violated. In recent months this bad situation has become even worse.

If it were not for our community in exile, so generously sheltered and supported by the government and people of India and helped by organisations and individuals from many parts of the world, our nation would today be little more than a shattered remnant of a people. Our culture, religion and national identity would have been effectively eliminated. As it is, we have built schools and monasteries in exile and have created democratic institutions to serve our people and preserve the seeds of our civilisation. With this experience, we intend to implement full democracy in a future free Tibet. Thus, as we develop our community in exile on modern lines, we also cherish and preserve our own identity and culture and bring hope to millions of our countrymen and -women in Tibet.

The issue of most urgent concern at this time is the massive influx of Chinese settlers into Tibet. Although in the first decades of occupation a considerable number of Chinese were transferred into the eastern parts of Tibet—in the Tibetan provinces of Amdo (Chinghai) and Kham (most of which has been annexed by neighboring Chinese provinces)—since 1983 an unprecedented number of Chinese have been encouraged by their government to migrate to all parts of Tibet, including central and western Tibet (which the People's Republic of China refers to as the so-called Tibet Autonomous Region). Tibetans are rapidly being reduced to an insignificant minority in their own country. This development, which threatens the very survival of the Tibetan nation, its culture and spiritual heritage, can still be stopped and reversed. But this must be done now, before it is too late.

The new cycle of protest and violent repression, which started in Tibet in September of 1987 and culminated in the imposition of martial law in the capital, Lhasa, in

March of this year, was in large part a reaction to this tremendous Chinese influx. Information reaching us in exile indicates that the protest marches and other peaceful forms of protest are continuing in Lhasa and a number of other places in Tibet, despite the severe punishment and inhumane treatment given to Tibetans detained for expressing their grievances. The number of Tibetans killed by security forces during the protest in March and of those who died in detention afterwards is not known but is believed to be more than two hundred. Thousands have been detained or arrested and imprisoned, and torture is commonplace.

It was against the background of this worsening situation and in order to prevent further bloodshed, that I proposed what is generally referred to as the Five-Point Peace Plan for the restoration of peace and human rights in Tibet. I elaborated on the plan in a speech in Strasbourg last year. I believe the plan provides a reasonable and realistic framework for negotiations with the People's Republic of China. So far, however, China's leaders have been unwilling to respond constructively. The brutal suppression of the Chinese democracy movement in June of this year, however, reinforced my view that any settlement of the Tibetan question will only be meaningful if it is supported by adequate international guarantees.

The Five-Point Peace Plan addresses the principal and interrelated issues, which I referred to in the first part of this lecture. It calls for (1) Transformation of the whole of Tibet, including the eastern provinces of Kham and Amdo, into a zone of Ahimsa (nonviolence); (2) Abandonment of China's population transfer policy; (3) Respect for the Tibetan people's fundamental rights and democratic freedoms; (4) Restoration and protection of Tibet's natural environment; and (5) Commencement of earnest negotiations on the future status of Tibet and of relations between the Tibetan and Chinese people. In the Strasbourg address I proposed that Tibet become a fully self-governing democratic political entity.

I would like to take this opportunity to explain the Zone of Ahimsa or peace sanctuary concept, which is the central element of the Five-Point Peace Plan. I am convinced that it is of great importance not only for Tibet, but for peace and stability in Asia.

It is my dream that the entire Tibetan plateau should become a free refuge where humanity and nature can live in peace and in harmonious balance. It would be a place where people from all over the world could come to seek the true meaning of peace within themselves, away from the tensions and pressures of much of the rest of the world. Tibet could indeed become a creative center for the promotion and development of peace.

The following are key elements of the proposed Zone of Ahimsa:

• the entire Tibetan plateau would be demilitarised;

- the manufacture, testing, and stockpiling of nuclear weapons and other armaments on the Tibetan plateau would be prohibited;
- the Tibetan plateau would be transformed into the world's largest natural park or biosphere. Strict laws would be enforced to protect wildlife and plant life; the exploitation of natural resources would be carefully regulated so as not to damage relevant ecosystems; and a policy of sustainable development would be adopted in populated areas;
- the manufacture and use of nuclear power and other technologies which produce hazardous waste would be prohibited;
- national resources and policy would be directed towards the active promotion of peace and environmental protection. Organisations dedicated to the furtherance of peace and to the protection of all forms of life would find a hospitable home in Tibet;
- the establishment of international and regional organisations for the promotion and protection of human rights would be encouraged in Tibet.

Tibet's height and size (the size of the European Community), as well as its unique history and profound spiritual heritage makes it ideally suited to fulfill the role of a sanctuary of peace in the strategic heart of Asia. It would also be in keeping with Tibet's historical role as a peaceful Buddhist nation and buffer region separating the Asian continent's great and often rival powers.

In order to reduce existing tensions in Asia, the President of the Soviet Union, Mr. Gorbachev, proposed the demilitarisation of Soviet-Chinese borders and their transformation into "a frontier of peace and good-neighborliness." The Nepal government had earlier proposed that the Himalayan country of Nepal, bordering on Tibet, should become a zone of peace, although that proposal did not include demilitarisation of the country.

For the stability and peace of Asia, it is essential to create peace zones to separate the continent's biggest powers and potential adversaries. President Gorbachev's proposal, which also included a complete Soviet troop withdrawal from Mongolia, would help to reduce tension and the potential for confrontation between the Soviet Union and China. A true peace zone must, clearly, also be created to separate the world's two most populous states, China and India.

The establishment of the Zone of Ahimsa would require the withdrawal of troops and military installations from Tibet, which would enable India and Nepal also to withdraw troops and military installations from the Himalayan regions bordering Tibet. This would have to be achieved by international agreements. It would be in the best interest of all states in Asia, particularly China and India, as it would enhance their security, while reducing the economic burden of maintaining high troop concentrations in remote areas.

Tibet would not be the first strategic area to be demilitarised. Parts of the Sinai peninsula, the Egyptian territory separating Israel and Egypt, have been demilitarised for some time. Of course, Costa Rica is the best example of an entirely demilitarised country. Tibet would also not be the first area to be turned into a natural preserve or biosphere. Many parks have been created throughout the world. Some very strategic areas have been turned into natural "peace parks." Two examples are the La Amistad Park, on the Costa Rica-Panama border and the Si A Paz project on the Costa Rica-Nicaragua border.

When I visited Costa Rica earlier this year, I saw how a country can develop successfully without an army, to become a stable democracy committed to peace and the protection of the natural environment. This confirmed my belief that my vision of Tibet in the future is a realistic plan, not merely a dream.

Let me end with a personal note of thanks to all of you and our friends who are not here today. The concern and support which you have expressed for the plight of the Tibetans have touched us all greatly, and continue to give us courage to struggle for freedom and justice: not through the use of arms, but with the powerful weapons of truth and determination. I know that I speak on behalf of all the people of Tibet when I thank you and ask you not to forget Tibet at this critical time in our country's history. We too hope to contribute to the development of a more peaceful, more humane and more beautiful world. A future free Tibet will seek to help those in need throughout the world, to protect nature, and to promote peace. I believe that our Tibetan ability to combine spiritual qualities with a realistic and practical attitude enables us to make a special contribution, in however modest a way. This is my hope and prayer.

In conclusion, let me share with you a short prayer which gives me great inspiration and determination:

> For as long as space endures,
> And for as long as living beings remain,
> Until then may I, too, abide
> To dispel the misery of the world.
> Thank you.

Remarks by President Clinton During the Announcement of the Renewal of MFN Trade Status for China

By William Jefferson Clinton

President William Jefferson Clinton (1948–) was the first post–Cold War American president. Coming into office after the 1989 fall of the Berlin Wall and the 1991 collapse of the Soviet Union, he saw Russia's transition from Communism to democracy and capitalism. In the People's Republic of China, however, the Communist Party refused to share power but it did adopt an increasingly tolerant attitude towards the free market. Clinton worked to strengthen economic ties between the two nations, regardless of China's poor track record on human rights (in 1989 the regime brutally suppressed a pro-democracy protest in Tiananmen Square). One of the themes of the last decade of the twentieth century was capital's ability to cross political and ideological boundaries, best seen in the way in which the People's Republic of China became the United States' most significant trading partner. In this May 1994 speech, he advocated delinking human rights issues from Sino-American trade agreements.

O ur relationship with China is important to all Americans. We have significant interests in what happens there and what happens between us.

China has an atomic arsenal and a vote and a veto in the U.N. Security Council. It is a major factor in Asian and global security. We share important interests, such as in a nuclear-free Korean peninsula and in sustaining the global environment.

William Jefferson Clinton, "Remarks by President Clinton during the Announcement of the Renewal of MFN Trade Status for China."

China is also the world's fastest-growing economy. Over $8 billion of United States exports to China last year supported over 150,000 American jobs.

I have received Secretary Christopher's letter recommending, as required by last year's executive order—reporting to me on the conditions in that executive order. He has reached a conclusion with which I agree, that the Chinese did not achieve overall significant progress in all the areas outlined in the executive order relating to human rights, even though clearly there was progress made in important areas, including the resolution of all emigration cases, the establishment of a memorandum of understanding with regard to how prison labor issues would be resolved, the adherence to the Universal Declaration of Human Rights, and other issues.

Nevertheless, serious human rights abuses continue in China, including the arrest and detention of those who peacefully voice their opinions and the repression of Tibet's religious and cultural traditions.

The question for us now is, given the fact that there has been some progress but that not all the requirements of the executive order were met, how can we best advance the cause of human rights and the other profound interests the United States has in our relationship with China?

I have decided that the United States should renew Most Favored Nation trading status toward China. This decision, I believe, offers us the best opportunity to lay the basis for long-term sustainable progress in human rights, and for the advancement of our other interests with China.

Extending M.F.N. will avoid isolating China and instead will permit us to engage the Chinese with not only economic contacts but with cultural, educational and other contacts, and with a continuing aggressive effort in human rights—an approach that I believe will make it more likely that China will play a responsible role, both at home and abroad.

I am moving, therefore, to delink human rights from the annual extension of Most Favored Nation trading status for China. That linkage has been constructive during the past year, but I believe, based on our aggressive contacts with the Chinese in the past several months, that we have reached the end of the usefulness of that policy, and it is time to take a new path toward the achievement of our constant objectives. We need to place our relationship into a larger and more productive framework.

In view of the continuing human rights abuses, I am extending the sanctions imposed by the United States as a result of the events in Tiananmen Square. And I am also banning the import of munitions, principally guns and ammunition, from China.

I am also pursuing a new and vigorous American program to support those in China working to advance the cause of human rights and democracy. This program will include increased broadcasts for Radio-Free Asia and the Voice of America, increased support for nongovernmental organizations working on human rights in China, and the development, with American business leaders, of a voluntary set of principles for business activity in China.

I don't want to be misunderstood about this. China continues to commit very serious human rights abuses. Even as we engage the Chinese on military, political and economic issues, we intend to stay engaged with those in China who suffer from human rights abuses.

The United States must remain a champion of their liberties.

I believe the question, therefore, is not whether we continue to support human rights in China but how we can best support human rights in China and advance our other very significant issues and interests. I believe we can do it by engaging the Chinese. …

The actions I have taken today to advance our security, to advance our prosperity, to advance our ideals, I believe are the important and appropriate ones. I believe, in other words, this is in the strategic economic and political interests of both the United States and China, and I am confident that over the long run this decision will prove to be the correct one.

Declaration of Jihad Against the Americans Occupying the Land of the Two Holiest Sites

By Osama Bin Laden

Osama bin Laden (1957–2011) was born into a wealthy Saudi family. Rather than pursue a career in the family construction business, he chose to volunteer with the Mujahideen, Islamic fighters, who were resisting the Soviet invasion of Afghanistan (1979–1989) in a prolonged guerilla war. The experience radicalized bin Laden. When, during and after George H. W. Bush's campaign against Iraq, the Saudi government allowed American troops to be stationed in the kingdom, bin Laden saw it as a Western incursion into the Holy Land. This 1996 fatwa is replete with citations of the Koran, historical references, and contemporary events.

Praise be to Allah, we seek His help and ask for his pardon, we take refuge in Allah from our wrongs and bad deeds. Who ever been guided by Allah will not be misled, and who ever has been misled, he will never be guided. I bear witness that there is no God except Allah-no associates with Him- and I bear witness that Muhammad is His slave and messenger.

{O you who believe! be careful of -your duty to- Allah with the proper care which is due to Him, and do not die unless you are Muslim} (Imraan; 3:102), {O people be careful of -your duty to- your Lord, Who created you from a single being and created its mate of the same -kind- and spread from these two, many men and women; and be careful of -your duty to- Allah , by whom you demand one of another -your rights-, and (be careful) to the ties of kinship; surely Allah ever watches over you} (An-Nisa; 4:1), {O you who believe! be careful- of your duty- to Allah and speak the right word;

Osama Bin Laden, "Declaration of Jihad Against the Americans Occupying the Land of the Two Holiest Sites."

He will put your deeds into a right state for you, and forgive you your faults; and who ever obeys Allah and his Apostle, he indeed achieve a mighty success} (Al-Ahzab; 33:70-71).

Praise be to Allah, reporting the saying of the prophet Shu'aib: {I desire nothing but reform so far as I am able, and with none but Allah is the direction of my affair to the right and successful path; On him do I rely and to him do I turn} (Hud; 11:88).

Praise be to Allah, saying: {You are the best of the nations raised up for -the benefit of- men; you enjoin what is right and forbid the wrong and believe in Allah} (Aal-Imraan; 3:110). Allah's blessing and salutations on His slave and messenger who said: (The people are close to an all encompassing-punishment from Allah if they see the oppressor and fail to restrain him.)

It should not be hidden from you that the people of Islam had suffered from aggression, iniquity and injustice imposed on them by the Zionist-Crusaders alliance and their collaborators; to the extent that the Muslims' blood became the cheapest and their wealth as loot in the hands of the enemies. Their blood was spilled in Palestine and Iraq. The horrifying pictures of the massacre of Qana, in Lebanon, are still fresh in our memory. Massacres in Tajakestan, Burma, Cashmere, Assam, Philippines, Fatani, Ogadin, Somalia, Erithria, Chechnia and in Bosnia-Herzegovina took place, massacres that send shivers in the body and shake the conscience. All of this and the world watch and hear, and not only didn't respond to these atrocities, but also with a clear conspiracy between the USA and its allies and under the cover of the iniquitous United Nations, the dispossessed people were even prevented from obtaining arms to defend themselves.

The people of Islam awakened and realised that they are the main target for the aggression of the Zionist-Crusaders alliance. All false claims and propaganda about "Human Rights" were hammered down and exposed by the massacres that took place against the Muslims in every part of the world.

The latest and the greatest of these aggressions, incurred by the Muslims since the death of the Prophet (ALLAH'S BLESSING AND SALUTATIONS ON HIM) is the occupation of the land of the two Holy Places -the foundation of the house of Islam, the place of the revelation, the source of the message and the place of the noble Ka'ba, the Qiblah of all Muslims- by the armies of the American Crusaders and their allies. (We bemoan this and can only say: "No power and power acquiring except through Allah").

Under the present circumstances, and under the banner of the blessed awakening which is sweeping the world in general and the Islamic world in particular, I meet with you today. And after a long absence, imposed on the scholars (Ulama) and callers (Da'ees) of Islam by the iniquitous crusaders movement under the leadership of the USA; who fears that they, the scholars and callers of Islam, will instigate the Ummah of Islam against its enemies as their ancestor scholars-may Allah be pleased with them- like

Ibn Taymiyyah and Al'iz Ibn Abdes-Salaam did. And therefore the Zionist-Crusader alliance resorted to killing and arresting the truthful Ulama and the working Da'ees (We are not praising or sanctifying them; Allah sanctify whom He pleased). They killed the Mujahid Sheikh Abdullah Azzaam, and they arrested the Mujahid Sheikh Ahmad Yaseen and the Mujahid Sheikh Omar Abdur Rahman (in America).

By orders from the USA they also arrested a large number of scholars, Da'ees and young people—in the land of the two Holy Places—among them the prominent Sheikh Salman Al-Oud'a and Sheikh Safar Al-Hawali and their brothers; (We bemoan this and can only say: "No power and power acquiring except through Allah"). We, myself and my group, have suffered some of this injustice ourselves; we have been prevented from addressing the Muslims. We have been pursued in Pakistan, Sudan and Afghanistan, hence this long absence on my part. But by the Grace of Allah, a safe base is now available in the high Hindukush mountains in Khurastan ; where—by the Grace of Allah-the largest infidel military force of the world was destroyed. And the myth of the super-power was withered in front of the Mujahideen cries of Allahu Akbar (God is greater). Today we work from the same mountains to lift the iniquity that had been imposed on the Ummah by the Zionist-Crusader alliance, particularly after they have occupied the blessed land around Jerusalem, route of the journey of the Prophet (ALLAH'S BLESSING AND SALUTATIONS ON HIM) and the land of the two Holy Places. We ask Allah to bestow us with victory, He is our Patron and He is the Most Capable.

From here, today we begin the work, talking and discussing the ways of correcting what had happened to the Islamic world in general, and the Land of the two Holy Places in particular. We wish to study the means that we could follow to return the situation to its normal path. And to return to the people their own rights, particularly after the large damages and the great aggression on the life and the religion of the people. An injustice that had affected every section and group of the people; the civilians, military and security men, government officials and merchants, the young and the old people as well as schools and university students. Hundred of thousands of the unemployed graduates, who became the widest section of the society, were also affected.

Injustice had affected the people of the industry and agriculture. It affected the people of the rural and urban areas. And almost every body complained about something. The situation at the land of the two Holy Places became like a huge volcano at the verge of eruption that would destroy the Kufr and the corruption and its sources. The explosion at Riyadh and Al-Khobar is a warning of this volcanic eruption emerging as a result of the severe oppression, suffering, excessive iniquity, humiliation and poverty.

People are fully concerned about their every day livings; everybody talks about the deterioration of the economy, inflation, ever increasing debts and jails full of prisoners.

Government employees with limited income talk about debts of ten thousands and hundred thousands of Saudi Riyals. They complain that the value of the Riyal is greatly and continuously deteriorating among most of the main currencies. Great merchants and contractors speak about hundreds and thousands of million Riyals are owed to them by the government. More than three hundred forty billions of Riyal owed by the government to the people in addition to the daily accumulated interest, let alone the foreign debt. People wonder whether we are the largest oil exporting country?! They even believe that this situation is a curse put on them by Allah for not objecting to the oppressive and illegitimate behaviour and measures of the ruling regime: Ignoring the divine Shari'ah law; depriving people of their legitimate rights; allowing the Americans to occupy the land of the two Holy Places; imprisonment, unjustly, of the sincere scholars. The honourable Ulamah and scholars as well as merchants, economists and eminent people of the country were all alerted by this disastrous situation.

Quick efforts were made by each group to contain and to correct the situation. All agreed that the country is heading toward a great catastrophe, the depth of which is not known except by Allah. One big merchant commented: "The king is leading the state into 'sixty-six' folded disaster," (We bemoan this and can only say: "No power and power acquiring except through Allah"). Numerous princes share with the people their feelings, privately expressing their concerns and objecting to the corruption, repression and the intimidation taking place in the country. But the competition between influential princes for personal gains and interest had destroyed the country. Through its course of actions the regime has torn off its legitimacy:

(1) Suspension of the Islamic Shari'ah law and exchanging it with man-made civil law. The regime entered into a bloody confrontation with the truthful Ulamah and the righteous youths (we sanctify nobody; Allah sanctify Whom He pleaseth).

(2) The inability of the regime to protect the country, and allowing the enemy of the Ummah—the American crusader forces—to occupy the land for the longest of years. The crusader forces became the main cause of our disastrous condition, particularly in the economical aspect of it due to the unjustified heavy spending on these forces. As a result of the policy imposed on the country, especially in the field of oil industry where production is restricted or expanded and prices are fixed to suit the American economy ignoring the economy of the country, expensive deals were imposed on the country to purchase arms. People asked what is the justification for the very existence of the regime, then?

Quick efforts were made by individuals and by different groups of the society to contain the situation and to prevent the danger. They advised the government both privately and openly; they sent letters and poems, reports after reports, reminders after reminders, they explored every avenue and enlisted every influential man in their movement of reform and correction. They wrote with style of passion, diplomacy and wisdom asking for corrective measures and repentance from the "great wrong doings and corruption that had engulfed even the basic principles of the religion and the legitimate rights of the people.

But—to our deepest regret—the regime refused to listen to the people accusing them of being ridiculous and imbecile. The matter got worse as previous wrong doings were followed by mischiefs of greater magnitudes. All of this taking place in the land of the Two Holy Places! It is no longer possible to be quiet. It is not acceptable to give a blind eye to this matter.

As the extent of these infringements reached the highest of levels and turned into demolishing forces threatening the very existence of the Islamic principles, a group of scholars-who can take no more- supported by hundreds of retired officials, merchants, prominent and educated people wrote to the King asking for implementation of the corrective measures. In 1411 A.H. (May 1991), at the time of the Gulf War, a letter, the famous letter of Shawwaal, with over four hundred signatures, was sent to the king demanding the lifting of oppression and the implementation of corrective actions. The king humiliated those people and choose to ignore the content of their letter, and the very bad situation of the country became even worse.

People, however, tried again and send more letters and petitions. One particular report, the glorious Memorandum Of Advice, was handed over to the king on Muharram, 1413 A.H. (July 1992), which tackled the problem, pointed out the illness, and prescribed the medicine in an original, righteous and scientific style. It described the gaps and the shortcoming in the philosophy of the regime and suggested the required course of action and remedy. The report gave a description of:

(1) The intimidation and harassment suffered by the leaders of the society, the scholars, heads of tribes, merchants, academic teachers and other eminent individuals;

(2) The situation of the law within the country and the arbitrary declaration of what is Halal and Haram (lawful and unlawful) regardless of the Shari'ah as instituted by Allah;

(3) The state of the press and the media which became a tool of truth-hiding and misinformation; the media carried out the plan of the enemy of idolising cult of certain personalities and spreading scandals among the believers to repel the people away from their religion, as Allah, the Exalted said:

{Surely-as for- those who love that scandal should circulate between the believers, they shall have a grievous chastisement in this world and in the hereafter} (An-Noor, 24:19);

(4) Abuse and confiscation of human rights;

(5) The financial and the economical situation of the country and the frightening future in the view of the enormous amount of debts and interest owed by the government; this is at the time when the wealth of the Ummah was being wasted to satisfy personal desires of certain individuals!! while imposing more custom duties and taxes

on the nation, (the prophet said about the woman who committed adultery: "She repented in such a way sufficient to bring forgiveness to a custom collector!!");

(6)   The miserable situation of the social services and infra-structure especially the water service and supply, the basic requirement of life;

(7)   The state of the ill-trained and ill-prepared army and the impotence of its commander-in-chief despite the incredible amount of money that has been spent on the army. The Gulf War clearly exposed the situation;

(8)   Shari'a law was suspended and man-made law was used instead;

(9)   And as far as the foreign policy is concerned the report exposed not only how this policy has disregarded the Islamic issues and ignored the Muslims, but also how help and support were provided to the enemy against the Muslims; the cases of Gaza-Ariha and the communists in the south of Yemen are still fresh in the memory, and more can be said.

As stated by the people of knowledge, it is not a secret that to use man-made law instead of the Shari'a and to support the infidels against the Muslims is one of the ten "voiders" that would strip a person from his Islamic status (turn a Muslim into a Mushrik, non-believer status). The All Mighty said: {and whoever did not judge by what Allah revealed, those are the unbelievers} (Al-Ma'ida; 5:44), and {but no! by your Lord! they do not believe (in reality) until they make you a judge of that which has become a matter of disagreement among them, and then do not find the slightest misgiving in their hearts as to what you have decided and submit with entire submission} (An-Nissa; 4:65).

In spite of the fact that the report was written with soft words and very diplomatic style, reminding of Allah, giving truthful sincere advice, and despite of the importance of advice in Islam—being absolutely essential for those in charge of the people—and the large number who signed this document as well as their supporters, all of that was not an intercession for the Memorandum. Its content was rejected and those who signed it and their sympathisers were ridiculed, prevented from travel, punished and even jailed.

Therefore it is very clear that the advocates of correction and reform movement were very keen on using peaceful means in order to protect the unity of the country and to prevent bloodshed. Why is it then the regime closed all peaceful routes and pushed the people toward armed actions?!! which is the only choice left for them to implement righteousness and justice. To whose benefit does prince Sultan and prince Nayeff push the country into a civil war that will destroy everything? And why consult those who ignite internal feuds, playing the people against each other and instigating the policemen, the sons of the nation, to abort the reform movement, while leaving in peace and security such traitors who implement the policy of the enemy in order to bleed the financial and the human resources of the Ummah, and leaving the main enemy in the area-the American Zionist alliance to enjoy peace and security?!

The advisor (Zaki Badr, the Egyptian ex-minister of the interior) to prince Nayeff, minister of interior, was not acceptable even to his own country; he was sacked from his position there due to the filthy attitude and the aggression he exercised on his own people, yet he was warmly welcomed by prince Nayeff to assist in sins and aggressions. He unjustly filled the prisons with the best sons of this Ummah and caused miseries to their mothers. Does the regime want to play the Civilians against their military personnel and vice versa, like what had happened in some of the neighbouring countries?!! No doubts this is the policy of the American-Israeli alliance as they are the first to benefit from this situation.

But with the grace of Allah, the majority of the nation, both Civilians and military individuals are aware of the wicked plan. They refused to be played against each other and to be used by the regime as a tool to carry out the policy of the American-Israeli alliance through their agent in our country: the Saudi regime.

Therefore everyone agreed that the situation can not be rectified (the shadow cannot be straightened when its' source, the rod, is not straight either) unless the root of the problem is tackled. Hence it is essential to hit the main enemy who divided the Ummah into small and little countries and pushed it, for the last few decades, into a state of confusion. The Zionist-Crusader alliance moves quickly to contain and abort any "corrective movement" appearing in the Islamic countries. Different means and methods are used to achieve their target; on occasion the "movement" is dragged into an armed struggle at a predetermined unfavourable time and place. Sometime officials from the Ministry of Interior, who are also graduates of the colleges of the Shari'ah, are leashed out to mislead and confuse the nation and the Ummah (by wrong Fatwas) and to circulate false information about the movement. At other occasions some righteous people were tricked into a war of words against the Ulama and the leaders of the movement, wasting the energy of the nation in discussing minor issues and ignoring the main one that is the unification of the people under the divine law of Allah.

In the shadow of these discussions and arguments truthfulness is covered by the falsehood, and personal feuds and partisanship created among the people increasing the division and the weakness of the Ummah; priorities of the Islamic work are lost while the blasphemy and polytheism continue its grip and control over the Ummah. We should be alert to these atrocious plans carried out by the Ministry of Interior. The right answer is to follow what have been decided by the people of knowledge, as was said by Ibn Taymiyyah (Allah's mercy upon him): "people of Islam should join forces and support each other to get rid of the main 'Kufr' who is controlling the countries of the Islamic world, even to bear the lesser damage to get rid of the major one, that is the great Kufr."

If there are more than one duty to be carried out, then the most important one should receive priority. Clearly after Belief (Imaan) there is no more important duty than pushing the American enemy out of the holy land. No other priority, except

Belief, could be considered before it; the people of knowledge, Ibn Taymiyyah, stated: "to fight in defence of religion and Belief is a collective duty; there is no other duty after Belief than fighting the enemy who is corrupting the life and the religion. There is no preconditions for this duty and the enemy should be fought with one's best abilities," (ref: supplement of Fatawa). If it is not possible to push back the enemy except by the collective movement of the Muslim people, then there is a duty on the Muslims to ignore the minor differences among themselves; the ill effect of ignoring these differences, at a given period of time, is much less than the ill effect of the occupation of the Muslims' land by the main Kufr. Ibn Taymiyyah had explained this issue and emphasised the importance of dealing with the major threat on the expense of the minor one. He described the situation of the Muslims and the Mujahideen and stated that even the military personnel who are not practising Islam are not exempted from the duty of Jihad against the enemy.

Ibn Taymiyyah, after mentioning the Moguls (Tatar) and their behaviour in changing the law of Allah, stated that: the ultimate aim of pleasing Allah, raising His word, instituting His religion and obeying His messenger (ALLAH'S BLESSING AND SALUTATIONS ON HIM) is to fight the enemy, in every aspect and in a complete manner; if the danger to the religion from not fighting is greater than that of fighting, then it is a duty to fight them even if the intention of some of the fighters is not pure i.e. fighting for the sake of leadership (personal gain) or if they do not observe some of the rules and commandments of Islam. To repel the greatest of the two dangers on the expense of the lesser one is an Islamic principle which should be observed. It was the tradition of the people of the Sunnah (Ahlul-Sunnah) to join and invade -fight- with the righteous and non-righteous men. Allah may support this religion by righteous and non-righteous people as told by the prophet (ALLAH'S BLESSING AND SALUTATIONS ON HIM). If it is not possible to fight except with the help of non-righteous military personnel and commanders, then there are two possibilities: either fighting will be ignored and the others, who are the great danger to this life and religion, will take control; or to fight with the help of non-righteous rulers and therefore repelling the greatest of the two dangers and implementing most, though not all of the Islamic laws. The latter option is the right duty to be carried out in these circumstances and in many other similar situation. In fact many of the fights and conquests that took place after the time of Rashidoon, the guided Imams, were of this type, (majmoo' al Fatawa, 26/506).

No one, not even a blind or a deaf person, can deny the presence of the widely spread mischiefs or the prevalence of the great sins that had reached the grievous iniquity of polytheism and to share with Allah in His sole right of sovereignty and making of the law. The All Mighty stated: {And when Luqman said to his son while he admonish him: O my son! do not associate ought with Allah; most surely polytheism is a grievous iniquity} (Luqman; 31:13). Man-fabricated laws were put forward permitting what has been forbidden by Allah such as usury (Riba) and other matters. Banks dealing in usury are competing, for lands, with the Two Holy Places and declaring war against Allah by disobeying His order {Allah has allowed trading and forbidden usury} (Baqarah; 2:275). All this taking place at the vicinity of the Holy Mosque in the Holy Land! Allah (SWT) stated in His Holy Book a unique promise (that had not been promised to any other sinner) to the Muslims who deals in usury: {O you who believe! Be careful of your duty to Allah and relinquish what remains (due) from usury, if you are believers. But if you do (it) not, then be appraised of WAR from Allah and His Apostle} (Baqarah; 2:278–279). This is for the "Muslim" who deals in usury (believing that it is a sin), what is it then to the person who make himself a partner and equal to Allah, legalising (usury and other sins) what has been forbidden by Allah. Despite of all of the above we see the government misled and dragged some of the righteous Ulamah and Da'ees away from the issue of objecting to the greatest of sins and Kufr. (We bemoan this and can only say: "No power and power acquiring except through Allah").

Under such circumstances, to push the enemy-the greatest Kufr- out of the country is a prime duty. No other duty after Belief is more important than the duty of had. Utmost effort should be made to prepare and instigate the Ummah against the enemy, the American-Israeli alliance occupying the country of the Two Holy Places and the route of the Apostle (Allah's Blessings and Salutations may be on him) to the Furthest Mosque (Al-Aqsa Mosque). Also to remind the Muslims not to be engaged in an internal war among themselves, as that will have grave consequences namely:

1-Consumption of the Muslims human resources as most casualties and fatalities will be among the Muslims people

2-Exhaustion of the economic and financial resources

3-Destruction of the country infrastructures

4-Dissociation of the society

5-Destruction of the oil industries. The presence of the USA Crusader military forces on land, sea and air of the states of the Islamic Gulf is the greatest danger threatening the largest oil reserve in the world. The existence of these forces in the area will provoke the people of the country and induces aggression on their religion, feelings and pride and pushes them to take up armed struggle against the invaders occupying the land; therefore spread of the fighting in the region will expose the oil wealth to the danger of being burned up. The economic interests of the States of the Gulf and the land of the Two Holy Places will be damaged and even a greater damage will be caused to the economy of the world. I would like here to alert my brothers, the Mujahideen, the sons of the nation, to protect this (oil) wealth and not to include it in the battle as it is a great Islamic wealth and a large economical power essential for the soon-to-be established Islamic state, by Allah's Permission and Grace. We also warn the aggressors, the USA, against burning this Islamic wealth (a crime which they may commit in order to prevent it, at the end of the war, from falling in the hands of its legitimate owners and to cause economic damages to the competitors of the USA in Europe or the Far East, particularly Japan which is the major consumer of the oil of the region).

6-Division of the land of the Two Holy Places, and annexing of the northerly part of it by Israel. Dividing the land of the Two Holy Places is an essential demand of the Zionist-Crusader alliance. The existence of such a large country with its huge resources under the leadership of the forthcoming Islamic State, by Allah's Grace, represent a serious danger to the very existence of the Zionist state in Palestine. The Nobel Ka'ba, -the Qiblah of all Muslims- makes the land of the Two Holy Places a symbol for the unity of the Islamic world. Moreover, the presence of the world's largest oil reserve makes the land of the Two Holy Places an important economical power in the Islamic world. The sons of the Two Holy Places are directly related to the lifestyle (Seerah) of their forefathers, the companions, may Allah be pleased with them. They consider the Seerah of their forefathers as a source and an example for reestablishing the greatness of this Ummah and to raise the word of Allah again. Furthermore the presence of a population of fighters in the south of Yemen, fighting in the cause of Allah, is a strategic threat to the Zionist-Crusader alliance in the area. The Prophet (ALLAH'S BLESSING AND SALUTATIONS ON HIM) said: (Around twelve thousands will emerge from Aden/Abian helping -the cause of- Allah and His messenger, they are the best, in the time, between me and them) narrated by Ahmad with a correct trustworthy reference.

7-An internal war is a great mistake, no matter what reasons are there for it. The presence of the occupier-the USA- forces will control the outcome of the battle for the benefit of the international Kufr.

I address now my brothers of the security and military forces and the national guards -may Allah preserve your hoard for Islam and the Muslim people:

O you protectors of unity and guardians of Faith; O you descendent of the ancestors who carried the light (torch) of guidance and spread it all over the world. O you grandsons of Sa'd Ibn Abi Waqqaas, Almothanna Ibn Haritha Ash-Sliaybani, Alga'ga' Ibn Amroo Al-Tameemi and those pious companions who fought Jihad alongside them; you competed to join the army and the guard forces with the intention to carry out Jihad in the cause of Allah -raising His word- and to defend the faith of Islam and the land of the Two Holy Places against the invaders and the occupying forces. That is the ultimate level of believing in this religion "Deen." But the regime had reversed these principles and their understanding, humiliating the Ummah and disobeying Allah. Half a century ago the rulers promised the Ummah to regain the first Qiblah, but fifty years later a new generation arrived and the promises have been changed; Al-Aqsa Mosque was handed over to the Zionists and the wounds of the IJmmah are still bleeding there. At the time when the Ummah has not regained the first Qiblah and the route of the journey of the Prophet (Allah's Blessings and Salutations may be on him), despite of all of the above, the Saudi regime had stunted the Ummah in the remaining sanctities, the Holy city of Makka and the mosque of the Prophet (Al-Masjid An-Nabawv), by calling the Christians' army to defend the regime. The crusaders were permitted to be in the land of the Two Holy Places. Not surprisingly though, the King himself wore the cross on his chest. The country was widely opened from the north to the south and from east to the west for the Crusaders. The land was filled with the military bases of the USA and the allies. The regime became unable to keep control without the help of these bases. You know more than anybody else about the size, intention and the danger of the presence of the USA military bases in the area. The regime betrayed the Ummah and joined the Kufr, assisting and helping them against the Muslims. It is well known that this is one of the ten "voiders" of Islam, deeds of de-Islamisation. By opening the Arab peninsula to the Crusaders the regime disobeyed and acted against what has been enjoined by the messenger of Allah (Allah's Blessings and Salutations may be on him), while he was at the bed of his death: (Expel the polytheists out of the Arab Peninsula); (narrated by Al-Bukhari) and: (If I survive, Allah willing, I'll expel the Jews and the Christians out of the Arab Peninsula); saheeh Aljame' As- Sagheer.

It is out of date and no longer acceptable to claim that the presence of the Crusaders is necessity and only a temporary measure to protect the land of the two Holy Places. Especially when the civil and the military infrastructures of Iraq were savagely destroyed showing the depth of the Zionist-Crusaders hatred to the Muslims and their children, and the rejection of the idea of replacing the Crusaders forces by an Islamic force composed of the sons of the country and other Muslim people, moreover the foundations of the claim and the claim itself were demolished and wiped out by the sequence of speeches given by the leaders of the Kuffar in America. The latest of these speeches was the one given by William Perry, the Defense Secretary, after the explosion in AI-Khobar saying that: the presence of the American solders there is to protect the interest of the USA. The imprisoned Sheikh Safar Al-Hawali, may Allah hasten his release, wrote a book of seventy pages; in it he presented evidence and proof that the presence of the Americans in the Arab Peninsula is a pre-planed military occupation. The regime want to deceive the Muslim people in the same manner when the Palestinian fighters, Mujahideen, were deceived causing the loss of Al-Aqsa Mosque. In 1304 A.H (1936 AD) the awakened Muslim nation of Palestine started their great struggle, Jihad, against the British occupying forces. Britain was impotent to stop the Mujahideen and their Jihad, but their devil inspired that there is no way to stop the armed struggle in Palestine unless through their agent King Abdul Azeez, who managed to deceives the Mujahideen. King Abdul Azeez earned out his duty to his British masters. He sent his two sons to meet the Mujahideen leaders and to inform them that King Abdul Azeez would guarantee the promises made by the British government in leaving the area and responding positively to the demands of the Mujahideen if the latter would stop their Jihad. And so King Abdul Azeez caused the loss of the first Qiblah of the Muslim people. The King joined the crusaders against the Muslims and instead of supporting the Mujahideen in the cause of Allah, to liberate the Al-Aqsa Mosque, he disappointed and humiliated them.

Today, his son, king Fahd, is trying to deceive the Muslims for the second time so as to lose what is left of the sanctities. When the Islamic world resented the arrival of the Crusader forces to the land of the Two Holy Places, the king told lies to the Ulamah (who issued Fatwas about the arrival of the Americans) and to the gathering of the Islamic leaders at the conference of Rabitah which was held in the Holy City of Makka. The King said that: "The issue is simple, the American and the alliance forces will leave the area in few months." Today it is seven years since their arrival and the regime is not able to move them out of the country. The regime made no confession about its inability and carried on lying to the people, claiming that the American will leave. But never-never again; a believer will not be bitten twice from the same hole or snake! Happy is the one who takes note of the sad experience of the others!!

Instead of motivating the army, the guards, and the security men to oppose the occupiers, the regime used these men to protect the invaders, and further deepened the humiliation and the betrayal. (We bemoan this and can only say: "No power and power acquiring except through Allah"). To those little group of men within the army, police and security forces, who have been tricked and pressured by the regime to attack the Muslims and spill their blood, we would like to remind them of the narration: (I promise war against those who take my friends as their enemy) narrated by Al–Bukhari. And his saying (Allah's Blessings and Salutations may be on him) saying of: (In the day of judgement a man conies holding another and complaining being slain by him. Allah, blessed be His Names, asks: Why did you slay him?! The accused replies: I did so that all exaltation may be Yours. Allah, blessed be His Names, says: All exaltation is indeed mine! Another man comes holding forth with a similar complaint. Allah, blessed be His Names, asks: Why did you kill him?! The accused replies: I did so that exaltation may be for Mr. X! Allah, blessed be His Names, says: Exaltation is mine, not for Mr. X, carry all the slain man's sins (and proceed to the Hell fire)!). In another wording of An-Nasa'i: "The accused says: for strengthening the rule or kingdom of Mr. X."

Today your brothers and sons, the sons of the two Holy Places, have started their Jihad in the cause of Allah, to expel the occupying enemy from the country of the Two Holy places. And there is no doubt you would like to carry out this mission too, in order to re-establish the greatness of this Ummah and to liberate its occupied sanctities. Nevertheless, it must be obvious to you that, due to the imbalance of power between our armed forces and the enemy forces, a suitable means of fighting must be adopted i.e. using fast moving light forces that work under complete secrecy. In other word to initiate a guerrilla warfare, were the sons of the nation, and not the military forces, to take part in it. And as you know, it is wise, in the present circumstances, for the armed military forces not to be engaged in conventional fighting with the forces of the Crusader enemy (the exceptions are the bold and the forceful operations carried out by the members of the armed forces individually, that is, without the movement of the formal forces in its conventional shape and hence the responses will not be directed, strongly, against the army) unless a big advantage is likely to be achieved; and great losses induced on the enemy side (that would shaken and destroy its foundations and infrastructures) that will help to expel the defeated enemy from the country.

The Mujahideen, your brothers and sons, request that you support them in every possible way by supplying them with the necessary information, materials and arms. Security men are especially asked to cover up for the Mujahideen and to assist them as much as possible against the occupying enemy; and to spread rumours, fear and discouragement among the members of the enemy forces.

We bring to your attention that the regime, in order to create a friction and feud between the Mujahideen and yourselves, might resort to take a deliberate action against personnel of the security, guards and military forces and blame the Mujahideen for these actions. The regime should not be allowed to have such opportunity.

The regime is fully responsible for what had been incurred by the country and the nation; however the occupying American enemy is the principle and the main cause of the situation. Therefore efforts should be concentrated on destroying, fighting and killing the enemy until, by the Grace of Allah, it is completely defeated. The time will come -by the Permission of Allah- when you'll perform your decisive role so that the word of Allah will be supreme and the word of the infidels (Kaferoon) will be the inferior. You will hit with iron fist against the aggressors. You'll re-establish the normal course and give the people their rights and carry out your truly Islamic duty. Allah willing, I'll have a separate talk about these issues.

My Muslim Brothers (particularly those of the Arab Peninsula): The money you pay to buy American goods will be transformed into bullets and used against our brothers in Palestine and tomorrow (future) against our sons in the land of the Two Holy places. By buying these goods we are strengthening their economy while our dispossession and poverty increases.

Muslim Brothers of land of the two Holy Places:

It is incredible that our country is the world's largest buyer of arms from the USA and the area's biggest commercial partner of the Americans who are assisting their Zionist brothers in occupying Palestine and in evicting and killing the Muslims there, by providing arms, men and financial supports.

To deny these occupiers from the enormous revenues of their trading with our country is a very important help for our Jihad against them. To express our anger and hate to them is a very important moral gesture. By doing so we would have taken part in (the process of) cleansing our sanctities from the Crusaders and the Zionists and forcing them, by the Permission of Allah, to leave disappointed and defeated.

We expect the woman of the land of the two Holy Places and other countries to carry out their role in boycotting the American goods.

If economical boycotting is intertwined with the military operations of the Mujahideen, then defeating the enemy will be even nearer, by the Permission of Allah. However if Muslims don't co-operate and support their Mujahideen brothers then, in effect, they are supplying the army of the enemy with financial help and extending the war and increasing the suffering of the Muslims.

The security and the intelligence services of the entire world can not force a single citizen to buy the goods of his/her enemy. Economical boycotting of the American goods is a very effective weapon of hitting and weakening the enemy, and it is not under the control of the security forces of the regime.

Before closing my talk, I have a very important message to the youths of Islam, men of the brilliant future of the Ummah of Muhammad (ALLAH'S BLESSING AND SALUTATIONS ON HIM). Our talk is with the youths about their duty in this difficult period in the history of our Ummah. A period in which the youths and no one else came forward to carry out the variable and different duties. While some of the well known individuals had hesitated in their duty of defending Islam and saving themselves and their wealth from the injustice, aggression and terror -exercised by the government- the youths (may Allah protect them) were forthcoming and raised the banner of Jihad against the American-Zionist alliance occupying the sanctities of Islam. Others who have been tricked into loving this materialistic world, and those who have been terrorised by the government choose to give legitimacy to the greatest betrayal, the occupation of the land of the Two Holy Places (We bemoan this and can only say: "No power and power acquiring except through Allah"). We are not surprised from the action of our youths. The youths were the companions of Muhammad (Allah's Blessings and Salutations may be on him), and was it not the youths themselves who killed Aba-Jahl, the Pharaoh of this Ummah? Our youths are the best descendent of the best ancestors.

Abdul-Rahman Ibn Awf -may Allah be pleased with him- said: (I was at Badr where I noticed two youths one to my right and the other to my left. One of them asked me quietly (so not to be heard by the other): O uncle point out Aba-Jahl to me. What do you want him for?, said Abdul Rahman. The boy answered: I have been informed that he—Aba-Jahl—abused the Messenger of Allah. O, I swear by Allah, who have my soul in His hand, that if I see Aba-Jahl I'll not let my shadow departs his shadow till one of us is dead. I was astonished, said Abdul Rahman; then the other youth said the same thing as the first one. Subsequently I saw Aba-Jahl among the people; I said to the boys do you see? this is the man you are asking me about. The two youths hit Aba-Jahl with their swords till he was dead. Allah is the greatest, Praise be to Him:

Two youths of young age but with great perseverance, enthusiasm, courage and pride for the religion of Allah's, each one of them asking about the most important act of killing that should be induced on the enemy. That is the killing of the pharaoh of this Ummah—Aba-Jahl—, the leader of the unbelievers (Mushrikeen) at the battle of Badr. The role of Abdul Rahman Ibn Awf, may Allah be pleased with him, was to direct the two youths toward Aba-Jahl. That was the perseverance and the enthusiasm of the youths of that time and that was the perseverance and the enthusiasm of their fathers. It is this role that is now required from the people who have the expertise and knowledge in fighting the enemy. They should guide their brothers and sons in this matter; once that has been done, then our youths will repeat what their forefathers had said before: "I swear by Allah if I see him I'll not let my shadow to departs from his shadow till one of us is dead."

And the story of Abdur-Rahman Ibn Awf about Ummayyah Ibn Klialaf shows the extent of Bilal's (may Allah be pleased with him) persistence in killing the head of the Kufr: "The head of Kufr is Ummayyah Ibn Khalaf… I shall live not if he survives" said Bilal.

Few days ago the news agencies had reported that the Defence Secretary of the Crusading Americans had said that "the explosion at Riyadh and Al-Kliobar had taught him one lesson: that is not to withdraw when attacked by coward terrorists."

We say to the Defence Secretary that his talk can induce a grieving mother to laughter! and shows the fears that had enshrined you all. Where was this false courage of yours when the explosion in Beirut took place on 1983 AD (1403 AH). You were turned into scattered pits and pieces at that time; 241 mainly marines solders were killed. And where was this courage of yours when two explosions made you to leave Aden in less than twenty four hours!

But your most disgraceful case was in Somalia; where- after vigorous propaganda about the power of the USA and its post-Cold War leadership of the new world order—you moved tens of thousands of international force, including twenty eight thousands American solders into Somalia. However, when tens of your solders were killed in minor battles and one American Pilot was dragged in the streets of Mogadishu you left the area earning disappointment, humiliation, defeat and your dead with you. Clinton appeared in front of the whole world threatening and promising revenge, but these threats were merely a preparation for withdrawal. You have been disgraced by Allah and you withdrew; the extent of your impotence and weaknesses became very clear. It was a pleasure for the "heart" of every Muslim and a remedy to the "chests" of believing nations to see you defeated in the three Islamic cities of Beirut, Aden and Mogadishu.

I say to Secretary of Defence: The sons of the land of the Two Holy Places had come out to fight against the Russian in Afghanistan, the Serb in Bosnia-Herzegovina and today they are fighting in Chechenia and -by the Permission of Allah- they have been made victorious over your partner, the Russians. By the command of Allah, they are also fighting in Tajakistan.

I say: Since the sons of the land of the two Holy Places feel and strongly believe that fighting (Jihad) against the Kuffar in every part of the world, is absolutely essential; then they would be even more enthusiastic, more powerful and larger in number upon fighting on their own land- the place of their births- defending the greatest of their sanctities, the noble Ka'ba (the Qiblah of all Muslims). They know that the Muslims of the world will assist and help them to victory. To liberate their sanctities is the greatest of issues concerning all Muslims; It is the duty of every Muslims in this world.

I say to you William (Defence Secretary) that: These youths love death as you loves life. They inherit dignity, pride, courage/generosity, truthfulness and sacrifice from father to father. They are most delivering and steadfast at war. They inherit these values from their ancestors (even from the time of the Jaheliyyah, before Islam). These values were approved and completed by the arriving Islam as stated by the messenger of Allah (Allah's Blessings and Salutations may be on him): "I have been sent to perfect the good values." (Saheeh Al-Jame' As-Sagheer).

When the pagan King Amroo Ibn Hind tried to humiliate the pagan Amroo Ibn Kulthoom, the latter cut the head of the King with his sword rejecting aggression, humiliation and indignation.

If the king oppresses the people excessively, we reject submitting to humiliation.

By which legitimacy (or command) O Amroo bin Hind you want us to be degraded?

By which legitimacy (or command) O Amroo bin Hind you listen to our foes and disrespect us?

Our toughness has, O Amroo, tired the enemies before you, never giving in!

Our youths believe in paradise after death. They believe that taking part in fighting will not bring their day nearer; and staying behind will not postpone their day either. Exalted be to Allah who said: {And a soul will not die but with the permission of Allah, the term is fixed} (Aal Imraan; 3:145). Our youths believe in the saving of the messenger of Allah (Allah's Blessings and Salutations may be on him): "O boy, I teach a few words; guard (guard the cause of, keep the commandments of) Allah, then He guards you, guard (the cause of) Allah, then He will be with you; if you ask (for your need) ask Allah, if you seek assistance, seek Allah's; and know definitely that if the Whole World gathered to (bestow) profit on you they will not profit you except with what was determined for you by Allah, and if they gathered to harm you they will not harm you except with what has been determined for you by Allah; Pen lifted, papers dried, it is fixed nothing in these truths can be changed" Saheeh Al-Jame' As-Sagheer. Our youths took note of the meaning of the poetic verse:

"If death is a predetermined must, then it is a shame to die cowardly" and the other poet saying:

"Who do not die by the sword will die by other reason; many causes are there but one death."

These youths believe in what has been told by Allah and His messenger (Allah's Blessings and Salutations may be on him) about the greatness of the reward for the Mujahideen and Martyrs; Allah, the most exalted said: {and -so far- those who are slain in the way of Allah, He will by no means allow their deeds to perish. He will guide them and improve their condition, and cause them to enter the garden -paradise- which He has made known to them}. (Muhammad; 47:4–6). Allah the Exalted also said: {and do not speak of those who are slain in Allah's way as dead; nay -they are- alive, but you do not perceive} (Bagarah; 2:154). His messenger (Allah's Blessings and Salutations may be on him) said: "for those who strive in His cause Allah prepared hundred degrees (levels) in paradise; in-between two degrees as the in-between heaven and earth." Saheeh Al-Jame' As-Sagheer. He (Allah's Blessings and Salutations may be on him) also said: "the best of the martyrs are those who do NOT turn their faces away from the battle till they are killed. They are in the high level of Jannah (paradise). Their Lord laughs to them (in pleasure) and when your Lord laughs to a slave of His, He will not hold him to an account," narrated by Ahmad with correct and trustworthy reference. And: "a martyr will not feel the pain of death except like how you feel when you are pinched." Saheeh Al-Jame' As-Sagheer. He also said: "a martyr privileges are guaranteed by Allah; forgiveness with the first gush of his blood, he will be shown his seat in paradise, he will be decorated with the jewels of belief (Imaan), married off to the beautiful ones, protected from the test in the grave, assured security in the day of judgement, crowned with the crown of dignity, a ruby of which is better than this whole world (Duniah) and its entire content, wedded to seventy two of the pure Houries (beautiful ones of Paradise) and his intercession on the behalf of seventy of his relatives will be accepted." Narrated by Ahmad and At-Tirmithi (with the correct and trustworthy reference).

Those youths know that their rewards in fighting you, the USA, is double than their rewards in fighting someone else not from the people of the book. They have no intention except to enter paradise by killing you. An infidel, and enemy of God like you, cannot be in the same hell with his righteous executioner.

Our youths chanting and reciting the word of Allah, the most exalted: {fight them; Allah will punish them by your hands and bring them to disgrace, and assist you against them and heal the heart of a believing people} (At-Taubah; 9:14) and the words of the prophet (ALLAH'S BLESSING AND SALUTATIONS ON HIM): "I swear by Him, who has my soul in His hand, that no man get killed fighting them today, patiently attacking and not retreating, surely Allah will let him into paradise." And his (Allah's Blessings and Salutations may be on him) saying to them: "get up to a paradise as wide as heaven and earth."

The youths also reciting the All Mighty words of: "so when you meat in battle those who disbelieve, then smite the necks…" (Muhammad; 47:19). Those youths will not ask you (William Perry) for explanations, they will tell you, singing, there is nothing between us need to be explained, there is only killing and neck smiting.

And they will say to you what their grandfather, Haroon Ar-Rasheed, Ameer-ul-Mu'meneen, replied to your grandfather, Nagfoor, the Byzantine emperor, when he threatened the Muslims: "from Haroon Ar-Rasheed, Ameer-ul-Mu'meneen, to Nagfoor, the dog of the Romans; the answer is what you will see not what you hear." Haroon El-Rasheed led the armies of Islam to the battle and handed Nagfoor a devastating defeat.

The youths you called cowards are competing among themselves for fighting and killing you reciting what one of them said:

The Crusader army became dust when we detonated al-Khobar.

With courageous youth of Islam fearing no danger.

If (they are) threatened: The tyrants will Mil you, they reply my death is a victory.

I did not betray that king, he did betray our Qiblah.

And he permitted in the holy country the most filthy sort of humans.

I have made an oath by Allah, the Great, to fight whoever rejected the faith.

For more than a decade, they carried arms on their shoulders in Afghanistan and they have made vows to Allah that as long as they are alive, they will continue to carry arms against you until you are -Allah willing- expelled, defeated and humiliated, they will carry on as long as they live saving:

O William, tomorrow you will know which young man is confronting your misguided brethren!

A youth fighting in smile, returning with the spear coloured red.

May Allah keep me close to knights, humans in peace, demons in war.

Lions in Jungle but their teeth are spears and Indian swords.

The horses witness that I push them hard forwarded in the fire of battle.

The dust of the battle bears witnesses for me, so also the fighting itself, the pens and the books!

So to abuse the grandsons of the companions, may Allah be pleased with them, by calling them cowards and challenging them by refusing to leave the land of the two Holy Places shows the insanity and the imbalance you are suffering from. Its appropriate "remedy," however, is in the hands of the youths of Islam, as the poet said:

I am willing to sacrifice self and wealth for knights who never disappointed me.

Knights who are never fed up or deterred by death, even if the mill of war turns.

In the heat of battle they do not care, and cure the insanity of the enemy by their 'insane' courage.

Terrorising you, while you are carrying arms on our land, is a legitimate and morally demanded duty. It is a legitimate right well known to all humans and other creatures.

Your example and our example is like a snake which entered into a house of a man and got killed by him. The coward is the one who lets you walk, while carrying arms, freely on his land and provides you with peace and security.

Those youths are different from your soldiers. Your problem will be how to convince your troops to fight, while our problem will be how to restrain our youths to wait for their turn in fighting and in operations. These youths are commendation and praiseworthy.

They stood up tall to defend the religion; at the time when the government misled the prominent scholars and tricked them into issuing Fatwas (that have no basis neither in the book of Allah, nor in the Sunnah of His prophet (Allah's Blessings and Salutations may be on him)) of opening the land of the Two Holy Places for the Christians' armies and handing the Al-Aqsa Mosque to the Zionists. Twisting the meanings of the holy text will not change this fact at all. They deserve the praise of the poet:

I rejected all the critics, who chose the wrong way;
I rejected those who enjoy fireplaces in clubs discussing eternally;
I rejected those, who inspite being lost, think they are at the goal;
I respect those who carried on not asking or bothering about the difficulties;
Never letting up from their goals, inspite all hardships of the road;
Whose blood is the oil for the flame guiding in the darkness of confusion;
I feel still the pain of (the loss) Al-Quds in my internal organs;
That loss is like a burning fire in my intestines;
I did not betray my covenant with God, when even states did betray it! As their grandfather Assim Bin Thabit said rejecting a surrender offer of the pagans:
What for an excuse I had to surrender, while I am still able, having arrows and my bow having a tough string?
Death is truth and ultimate destiny, and life will end anyway. If I do not fight you, then my mother must be insane!

The youths hold you responsible for all of the killings and evictions of the Muslims and the violation of the sanctities, carried out by your Zionist brothers in Lebanon; you openly supplied them with arms and finance. More than 600,000 Iraqi children have died due to lack of food and medicine and as a result of the unjustifiable aggression (sanction) imposed on Iraq and its nation. The children of Iraq are our children. You, the USA, together with the Saudi regime are responsible for the shedding of the blood of these innocent children. Due to all of that, whatever treaty you have with our country is now null and void.

The treaty of Hudaybiyyah was cancelled by the messenger of Allah (Allah's Blessings and Salutations may be on him) once Quraysh had assisted Bani Bakr against Khusa'ah, the allies of the prophet (Allah's Blessings and Salutations may be on him). The prophet (Allah's Blessings and Salutations may be on him) fought Quraysh and concurred Makka. He (Allah's Blessings and Salutations may be on him) considered the treaty with Bani Qainuqa' void because one of their Jews publicly hurt one Muslim woman, one single woman, at the market. Let alone then, the killing you caused to hundred of thousands Muslims and occupying their sanctities. It is now clear that those who claim that the blood of the American solders (the enemy occupying the land of the Muslims) should be protected are merely repeating what is imposed on them by the regime; fearing the aggression and interested in saving themselves. It is a duty now on every tribe in the Arab Peninsula to fight, Jihad, in the cause of Allah and to cleanse the land from those occupiers. Allah knows that their blood is permitted (to be spilled) and their wealth is a booty; their wealth is a booty to those who kill them. The most Exalted said in the verse of As-Sayef, The Sword: "so when the sacred months have passed away, then slay the idolaters wherever you find them, and take them captives and besiege them and lie in wait for them in every ambush" (At-Tauba; 9:5). Our youths knew that the humiliation suffered by the Muslims as a result of the occupation of their sanctities can not be kicked and removed except by explosions and Jihad. As the poet said:

The walls of oppression and humiliation cannot be demolished except in a rain of bullets.
The freeman does not surrender leadership to infidels and sinners.
Without shedding blood no degradation and branding can be removed from the forehead.

I remind the youths of the Islamic world, who fought in Afghanistan and Bosnia-Herzegovina with their wealth, pens, tongues and themselves that the battle had not finished yet. I remind them about the talk between Jibreel (Gabriel) and the messenger of Allah (Allah's Blessings and Salutations may be on both of them) after the battle of Ahzab when the messenger of Allah (Allah's Blessings and Salutations may be on him) returned to Medina and before putting his sword aside; when Jibreel (Allah's Blessings and Salutations may be on him) descend saying: "are you putting your sword aside? by Allah the angels haven't dropped their arms yet; march with your companions to Bani Quraydah, I am (going) ahead of you to throw fears in their hearts and to shake their fortresses on them." Jibreel marched with the angels (Allah's Blessings and Salutations may be on them all), followed by the messenger of Allah (Allah's Blessings and Salutations may be on him) marching with the immigrants, Muhajeroon, and supporters, Ansar. (narrated by Al-Bukhaiy).

These youths know that: if one is not to be killed one will die (any way) and the most honourable death is to be killed in the way of Allah. They are even more determined after the martyrdom of the four heroes who bombed the Americans in Riyadh. Those youths who raised high the head of the Ummah and humiliated the Americans-the occupier- by their operation in Riyadh. They remember the poetry of Ja'far, the second commander in the battle of Mu'tah, in which three thousand Muslims faced over a hundred thousand Romans:

How good is the Paradise and its nearness, good with cool drink But the Romans are promised punishment (in Hell), if I meet them.

I will fight them.

And the poetry of Abdullah Bin Rawaha, the third commander in the battle of Mu'tah, after the martyrdom of Ja'far, when he felt some hesitation:

O my soul if you do not get killed, you are going to die, anyway.

This is death pool in front of you!

You are getting what you have wished for (martyrdom) before, and you follow the example of the two previous commanders you are rightly guided!

As for our daughters, wives, sisters and mothers they should take prime example from the prophet (Allah's Blessings and Salutations may be on him) pious female companions, may Allah be pleased with them; they should adopt the lifestyle (Seerah) of the female companions of courage, sacrifice and generosity in the cause of the supremacy of Allah's religion.

They should remember the courage and the personality of Fatima, daughter of Khatab, when she accepted Islam and stood up in front of her brother, Omar Ibn Al-Khatab and challenged him (before he became a Muslim) saying: "O Omar, what will you do if the truth is not in your religion?!" And to remember the stand of Asma', daughter of Abu Bakr, on the day of Hijra, when she attended the Messenger and his companion in the cave and split her belt in two pieces for them. And to remember the stand of Naseeba Bent Ka'b striving to defend the messenger of Allah (Allah's Blessings and Salutations may be on him) on the day of Uhud, in which she suffered twelve injuries, one of which was so deep leaving a deep lifelong scar! They should remember the generosity of the early woman of Islam who raised finance for the Muslims army by selling their jewelery.

Our women had set a tremendous example of generosity in the cause of Allah; they motivated and encouraged their sons, brothers and husbands to fight- in the cause of Allah- in Afghanistan, Bosnia-Herzegovina, Chechenia and in other countries. We ask Allah to accept from them these deeds, and may He help their fathers, brothers, husbands and sons. May Allah strengthen the belief—Imaan—of our women in the way of generosity and sacrifice for the supremacy of the word of Allah. Our women weep not, except over men who fight in the cause of Allah; our women instigate their brothers to fight in the cause of Allah.

Our women bemoan only fighters in the cause of Allah, as said:

Do not moan on any one except a lion in the woods, courageous in the burning wars.

Let me die dignified in wars, honourable death is better than my current life.

Our women encourage Jihad saying:

Prepare yourself like a straggler, the matter is bigger than words!

Are you going to leave us else for the wolves of Kufr eating our wings?

The wolves of Kufr are mobilising all evil persons from everywhere!

Where are the freemen defending free women by the arms?!

Death is better than life in humiliation! Some scandals and shames will never be otherwise eradicated.

My Muslim Brothers of The World:

Your brothers in Palestine and in the land of the Two Holy Places are calling upon your help and asking you to take part in fighting against the enemy—your enemy and their enemy—the Americans and the Israelis, they are asking you to do whatever you can, with one's own means and ability, to expel the enemy, humiliated and defeated, out of the sanctities of Islam. Exalted be to Allah said in His book: {and if they ask your support, because they are oppressed in their faith, then support them!} (Anfaal; 8:72).

O you horses (soldiers) of Allah ride and march on. This is the time of hardship so be tough. And know that your gathering and co-operation in order to liberate the sanctities of Islam is the right step toward unifying the word of the Ummah under the banner of "No God but Allah").

From our place we raise our palms humbly to Allah asking Him to bestow on us His guide in every aspect of this issue.

Our Lord, we ask you to secure the release of the truthful scholars, Ulama, of Islam and pious youths of the Ummah from their imprisonment. O Allah, strengthen them and help their families.

Our Lord, the people of the cross had come with their horses (soldiers) and occupied the land of the Two Holy places. And the Zionist Jews fiddling as they wish with the Al-Aqsa Mosque, the route of the ascendance of the messenger of Allah (ALLAH'S BLESSING AND SALUTATIONS ON HIM). Our Lord, shatter their gathering, divide them among themselves, shaken the earth under their feet and give us control over them; Our Lord, we take refuge in you from their deeds and take you as a shield between us and them.

Our Lord, show us a black day in them!

Our Lord, show us the wonderment of your ability in them!

Our Lord, You are the Revealer of the book, Director of the clouds, You defeated the allies (Ahzab); defeat them and make us victorious over them.

Our Lord, You are the one who help us and You are the one who assist us, with Your Power we move and by Your Power we fight. On You we rely and You are our cause.

Our Lord, those youths got together to make Your religion victorious and raise Your banner.

Our Lord, send them Your help and strengthen their hearts. Our Lord, make the youths of Islam steadfast and descend patience on them and guide their shots! Our Lord, unify the Muslims and bestow love among their hearts!

O Lord pour down upon us patience, and make our steps firm and assist us against the unbelieving people!

Our Lord, do not lay on us a burden as Thou didst lay on those before us; Our Lord, do not impose upon us that which we have no strength to bear; and pardon us and grant us protection and have mercy on us. Thou art our patron, so help us against the unbelieving people.

Our Lord, guide this Ummah, and make the right conditions (by which) the people of your obedience will be in dignity and the people of disobedience in humiliation, and by which the good deeds are enjoined and the bad deeds are forebode.

Our Lord, bless Muhammad, Your slave and messenger, his family and descendants, and companions and salute him with a (becoming) salutation.

And our last supplication is: All praise is due to Allah.

January, 2000: Terror versus Security

By Salman Rushdie

Salman Rushdie's 1988 The Satanic Verses *is a complicated and experimental novel in which characters in the contemporary world dream about a desert city and a prophet. Obviously an allegory for the origins of Islam, many took offense to the work. On February 14, 1989, Ayatollah Khomeini, Iran's religious leader, issued a fatwa calling for Rushdie's death. Mass demonstrations spread through Muslim communities around the world and the author had to go into hiding for fear of his life. Around there were attacks on and murders of people associated with the novel's publication and translation. The Rushdie Affair became a cause célèbre for a variety of political forces, including advocates of free speech, defenders of religious freedom, anti-immigrant racists, and Islamic fundamentalists. In this piece, at the close of the 20th century, Rushdie reflects on the fragile balance between safety and freedom. This January, 2000 essay brilliantly predicts the dilemmas of the world after September 11, 2001.*

Now that the big Y2K party's over, think for a moment about the covert, worldwide battle that took place on and around Millennium Night. Behind the images of a world lit up by pyrotechnics, united for one evanescent instant by gaiety and goodwill, the new dialectic of history was taking shape. We already knew that capitalism versus communism was no longer the name of the game. Now we saw, as clearly as the fireworks in the sky, that the defining struggle of the new age would be between Terrorism and Security.

I was one of the ten thousand gathered in London's Millennium Dome, that same dome off which James Bond bounces while fighting the forces of terror in the latest 007 film. The audience knew—after hours of waiting to be frisked on a cold railway platform, how could it not?—that a mammoth security operation had been launched

Salman Rushdie, "January 2000: Terror versus Security," *Step Across This Line: Collected Nonfiction 1992–2002*, pp. 288–290. Copyright © 2002 by Random House Inc. Reprinted with permission.

to safeguard the showpiece event. What few of us knew was that a bomb threat had been made, using an IRA code word, and that the dome came within an inch of being evacuated.

For days, the world had been hearing about nothing but terrorism. The United States had spoken the current bogeyman's name—Osama bin Laden—to frighten us children. There were arrests: a man with bomb-making equipment found at the U.S.–Canada border, a group in Jordan. Seattle canceled its celebrations. One of the leaders of the Aum Shinrikyo cult was released, and Japan feared a terrorist atrocity. President Chandrika Kumaratunga of Sri Lanka made history by surviving a suicide bomber's attack. There were bomb hoaxes at a British racetrack and at a soccer stadium. The FBI feared the worst from apocalyptic groups and lunatic-fringers. But in the end—apart from poor George Harrison, wounded by one such lunatic—we got off relatively lightly.

Almost all of us, that is, because there was also the Indian Airlines hijack. The events at Kandahar airport have left no fewer than four governments looking pretty bad. Nepal, proving that Kathmandu deserves its terrorist-friendly reputation, allowed men with guns and grenades to board a plane. The Indian government's capitulation to the terrorists was the first such surrender to hijackers in years; what will they do when the next aircraft is seized? And, finally, terrorists trained in Taliban camps and holding Pakistani passports disappeared from Afghanistan into, very probably, Pakistan. Thus was a largely defunct form of terrorism given a new lease on life.

Some knees jerked predictably. An Islamist journalist, writing in a liberal British paper of the sort that would be banned in Islamist countries, complained that the "terrorist" tag demonizes members of freedom movements struggling against violent, oppressive regimes. But terrorism isn't justice-seeking in disguise. In Sri Lanka it's the voices of peace and conciliation who are getting murdered. And the brutal Indian Airlines hijackers do not speak for the people of peaceable, vandalized Kashmir.

The security establishment rightly regards the non-explosive Millennium as a triumph. Security is, after all, the art of making sure certain things don't happen: a thankless task, because when they don't happen, there will always be someone to say the security was excessive and unnecessary. In London on New Year's Eve the security operation was on a scale that would have made citizens of many less fortunate nations convinced that a coup was in progress. But none of us thought so for an instant. This was security in the service of merrymaking, and that is something we can be impressed by and grateful for. And yet there is cause for concern. If the ideology of terrorism is that terror works, then the ideology of security is based on assuming the truth of the "worst-case scenario." The trouble is that worst-case scenarism, if I may call it that, plays right into the hands of the fear creators. The worst-case scenario of crossing the road, after all, is that you'll be hit by a truck and killed. Yet we all do cross roads every day, and could hardly function if we did not. To live by the worst-case scenario is to grant the terrorists their victory, without a shot having been fired.

It is also alarming to think that the real battles of the new century may be fought in secret, between adversaries accountable to few of us, the one claiming to act on our behalf, the other hoping to scare us into submission. Democracy requires openness and light. Must we really surrender our future into the hands of the shadow warriors? That most of the Millennial threats turned out to be hoaxes only underlines the problem; nobody wants to run from imaginary enemies. But how, in the absence of information, are we, the public, to evaluate such threats? How can we prevent terrorists and their antagonists from setting the boundaries within which we live?

Security saved President Kumaratunga, but many others died. The security at George Harrison's fortress-home didn't stop the would-be assassin's knife; it was his wife's well-swung table lamp that saved him. In the past, security didn't save President Reagan, or the pope. Luck did that. So we need to understand that even maximum security guarantees nobody's safety. The point is to decide—as the Queen decided on New Year's Eve—not to let fear rule our lives. To tell those bullies who would terrorize us that we aren't scared of them. And to thank our secret protectors, but to remind them, too, that in a choice between security and liberty it is liberty that must always come out on top.